ONCE BITTEN

An Unofficial Guide
to the World of Angel

ONCE BITTEN

An Unofficial Guide
to the World of Angel

NIKKI STAFFORD

ECW PRESS

For Sydney

Published by ECW PRESS
2120 Queen Street East, Suite 200, Toronto, Ontario, Canada M4E 1E2

LIBRARY AND ARCHIVES CANADA CATALOGUING IN PUBLICATION

Stafford, Nikki, 1973–
Once bitten : an unofficial guide to the world of Angel / Nikki Stafford.

ISBN 1-55022-654-1

1. Angel (Television program : 1999–) I. Title.

PN1992.77.A53S82 2004   791.45 72   C2004-902553-8

Cover and Text Design: Tania Craan
Typesetting: Gail Nina
Cover photos: Challenge Roddie/Corbis Outline/Magma (David Boreanaz); James Milchin/Corbis Outline/Magma (James Marsters); Catherine Karnow/Corbis/Magma (L.A. skyline)
Color section, in order: Jill Greenberg/Corbis Outline/Magma; Mark Robert Halper; Challenge Roddie/Corbis Outline/Magma; Christina Radish; Christina Radish; Mark Robert Halper; Mark Robert Halper; Albert L. Ortega; Albert L. Ortega; Christina Radish; Albert L. Ortega; Christina Radish; Albert L. Ortega; Mark Robert Halper; Mark Robert Halper; Mark Robert Halper
All book covers from pages 39 to 53 are used with permission of the publishers.

Printing: Tri-Graphic

The publication of *Once Bitten: An Unofficial Guide to the World of Angel* has been generously supported by the Government of Canada through the Book Publishing Industry Development Program. Canadä

DISTRIBUTION

CANADA: Jaguar Book Group, 100 Armstrong Avenue, Georgetown, ON, L7G 5S4
UNITED STATES: Independent Publishers Group, 814 North Franklin Street, Chicago, Illinois 60610

PRINTED AND BOUND IN CANADA

ECW PRESS
ecwpress.com

Contents

Acknowledgments

A big thank you to Jack David and ECW Press for continuing to believe in me and encourage me as I write. A special thanks to Tracey Millen, for her proofreading skills and Michael Holmes, for passing on his expertise on Mexican masked wrestling. And thank-you to Jodi Lewchuk for her excellent editing of the manuscript.

Many people thought I was crazy for writing two books at once, but I managed to do it with the encouragement of a lot of family and friends. Thanks to Suzanne Kingshott for cheering me on as I wrote the book, for reading a version of the manuscript, and for spending a weekend with me during an *Angel* viewing marathon. Thanks to Robyn Burnett, Fionna Boyle, Jonathan Hale, and many other friends and family for encouraging me throughout the writing of this book.

I had a lot of help from people to complete certain sections of the book. A huge thank-you to the many people involved in *Buffy* and *Angel* who took the time out of their busy schedules to talk to me about their experiences on the shows: Amy Acker, Alexis Denisof, David Denman, Jane Espenson, David Fury, Christian Kane, Mark Lutz, J. August Richards, Stephanie Romanov, and Keith Szarabajka. I owe a big thanks to Rana at Rising Stars for helping me contact the people involved, and the agents, publicists, and managers who made the interviews happen.

For the posting board party chapter I'd like to thank Karri Phillips and Bryan Bonner for giving me insight into how the parties are put together. I'd like to thank Kristy Bratton, Virginia Obeius, and Lilian Holden for answering my many questions about their excellent Web site, CityofAngel.com. Thanks to Rhonda Wilcox, David Lavery, Michael Adams, Jana Riess, Roz Kaveney, James B. South, Glenn Yeffeth, Lisa LoCicero, Sue Turnbull, Angela Ndalianis, and Sophie Levy for spending so much time answering questions for the chapter on the *Buffy* and *Angel* academic community.

Thank you to Leslie Remencus for being so generous with her time and helping me with the music for a lot of the episode guide. Thanks also to James Reaney, who sends me wire stories on the latest *Angel* and *Buffy* happenings. And to Jennifer Kaplan, who provided me with the shooting schedules from her many visits to the sets of both shows. Thanks to Sandy Conners for offering a comment on Rising Stars, and to Lisa Rowe for helping me get the photo of the SavingAngel truck.

I have to acknowledge the amazing people in OBAVA, not only for being entertaining online, but for their companionship, support, and encouragement in person. They helped me out with the Spuffies vs. Bangels sidebar and are just a great group of people. Thanks for everything guys, you're the best.

Finally, a big thanks to Robert for putting up with me for many months as I worked on two books at once. I commandeered the television and was holed up in my office every evening and weekend for many months, and he never complained (for good reason — it allowed him to play golf guilt-free). Thank you to Piquette and Sebastian, who kept me company and have always been my muses. And, as always, my most heartfelt thanks go to Jennifer Hale. Over the years we've become inseparable, and this book couldn't have been written without your thoughtfulness and perseverance.

A Note to Readers

When my previous Whedonverse book, *Bite Me! An Unofficial Guide to the World of* Buffy the Vampire Slayer, was published in 2002, *Buffy* was finishing its sixth season, and *Angel* was finishing its third. In that book I included long, detailed episode outlines for *Buffy* and capsule reviews for *Angel*; the idea was to cover the latter but keep the focus on *Buffy*. The book also included bios of the cast of *Buffy* and *Angel* to give equal weight to both shows, and it covered the posting-board parties from 1998 to 2002.

Since its release, several readers have asked if I was planning on releasing an updated version of *Bite Me!* that would include season 7 of *Buffy* and the last two seasons of *Angel*, but I didn't think it would be fair to make people buy the entire book again just to get those. So I came up with the idea to do an *Angel*-focused book that would be not only a companion to that show but a sequel to *Bite Me!*, tying up the loose ends that were left open in that book.

I have tried my best not to repeat material that is in *Bite Me!* This book does not contain actor bios, because those were in the other book. The *Angel* episode summaries here are fleshed out and more complete, like the *Buffy* episode outlines were in *Bite Me!* I have also included season 7 of *Buffy* to finish off that episode guide. The show history that opens this book begins in 1999, when *Angel* began, so that I wouldn't just repeat what I'd written about *Buffy* in the other book. I have written only on *Angel* until the section covering the 2002–3 season, where I have included material about the end of *Buffy* (since it was not covered in *Bite Me!*). This book also contains a summary of the 2003 posting-board party, which was the final party with fans and cast members.

You do not need to have a copy of *Bite Me!* to enjoy this book — I believe *Once Bitten* stands alone for *Angel* fans. Here are a few things about the book to note: the rundown of the 2003 PBP is centered on *Angel* cast members, as there were more of them in attendance than *Buffy* ones; I've included an extensively researched chapter on how the academic world has embraced *Buffy* and *Angel;* there is a chapter on how CityofAngel.com came to be; and the *Angel* episode guide features tidbits from some of the cast members themselves talking about the episodes.

I hope I have found just the right balance with *Once Bitten*, and that readers who own *Bite Me!* will see it as complementary, without any overlap, while readers who don't have that book will find it complete on its own. One last note: People have already begun asking me why Spike is on the cover given he's such a recent addition to the *Angel* cast. He's there because he represents a constant between the two shows — he was one of the focal points in season 7 of *Buffy*, and he has always been a major part of Angel's life. He's there to show that this book will cover both shows in those capacities. And besides, it's Spike — who wouldn't want the guy on their book cover?

Nikki Stafford, August 2004
nikki_stafford@yahoo.com

Never Fading Away:
The Story of Angel

In 1753 he was turned into a vampire by Darla, a noblewoman who found him carousing in a bar and recognized his devilish potential. For 150 years they cut a swath through Europe, killing thousands of innocent people. In 1898 he killed the wrong girl, and her Gypsy father laid a curse that re-ensouled him, forcing him to relive his crimes and endure his guilt for eternity. For 100 years he existed in a cave of his own grief and solitude, until he met Buffy.

And then, in 1999, he got his own television show. Welcome to the world of *Angel*.

Angel is one of the most original characters on television. His backstory was first explored in the *Buffy the Vampire Slayer* first-season episode "Angel," where Buffy discovered the man she was falling in love with was actually a 244-year-old vampire who had tortured, raped, and murdered countless victims. But this was no ordinary vampire — he had a soul, and they were fighting on the same side. Throughout his three years on *Buffy*, Angel encountered even more heartache. He fell in love with Buffy only to experience one true moment of happiness and have his soul ripped from him once again, turning him into the evil monster he once was. As Angelus, he showed Buffy the thing he had been for 150 years, and after he stalked her friends, killed Willow's goldfish, murdered Giles's lover, and tortured Giles to within an inch of his life, not only did

Buffy have to put her feelings aside and make the decision to kill him, but she had to suffer the guilt of not having done it sooner.

And then he came back. Returned from the hell dimension he had disappeared to after Buffy ran a sword through him at the end of season 2, he had to endure the slow process of losing the beast within him and once again becoming a man. Buffy fell in love with him all over again, much to the chagrin of her friends, who believed she was putting Angel's needs before theirs. Angel knew that Buffy was the only woman he had loved in 250 years, but he also saw what that love was doing to her and told her he was leaving. In a quiet and touching moment at the end of season 3, silhouetted against the streetlights and fire trucks of Sunnydale, Angel disappeared into the shadows. He was leaving for L.A. to try to make sense of his purpose in life — and to have his own television show.

Joss Whedon got the idea to create a spinoff show for Angel when the cast and crew were filming "Becoming, Part Two," the second-season *Buffy* episode that revealed Angel's entire backstory, from becoming a vampire to having his soul returned to eating rats in alleyways to seeing Buffy for the first time. The original idea was to have Angel move to L.A., where he would meet up with Whistler, his mentor, played by Max Perlich in the "Becoming" episodes, and have several flashbacks to show how Angel had come to be. However, as season 3 of *Buffy* unfolded, Whedon decided to bring in a new mentor, Doyle, whom Angel hadn't met before.

The show was meant to be a darker, more adult show than *Buffy,* set in Los Angeles, where Buffy had discovered the seedy side of the big city in the third-season *Buffy* opener, "Anne." And the producers thought they should take at least one other character from *Buffy* to ensure viewers would watch both series. At the end of season 3, we discovered that Cordelia's father had been charged with tax fraud and the family was pretty much penniless, so it made sense to transplant that character to L.A. as well, to have her running away from her fashionable past in Sunnydale. Charisma Carpenter was a little worried about moving from such a successful show to an unknown one, but after reassurances from Joss that should *Angel* be canceled her role on *Buffy* would be secure, she went ahead and made the leap. To round out the cast, Glenn Quinn of *Roseanne* fame was brought in to play Doyle.

Joss Whedon knew that David Boreanaz had the leading man quality it would take to star in his own series.

The day-to-day duties on *Angel* were handed over to David Greenwalt, while Whedon would be an executive producer with him and oversee the scripts. Greenwalt had written "Angel," thereby creating the vampire's background, and "Nightmares," the first episode of *Buffy* to deal with the characters' darker psychological issues. He seemed like the perfect fit. Greenwalt explained where the creators were planning to take the new series: "A lot of *Angel* deals with how Angel relates to this dark, dangerous, and sometimes glamorous world of Los Angeles. This is the city of law firms, and talent agencies, and gangsters, all very real, and at times extremely unsettling. . . . Just think for a moment about L.A. There's the quest for eternal youth and beauty in this town, people who will do anything to stay young forever. Then there's the incredible divide between haves and have-nots. The rich definitely live among the poor. You add demonology to that, and you've automatically got these great issues. And right in the middle of it all is Angel, a vampire with a soul, perhaps more of a soul than most of the people in the city."

Angel would not only look at L.A. and the darker elements of life, but it would take us deeper into Angel's psyche. We had seen Angelus, the worst that Angel could be, but this series would explore the gray area of how Angel was struggling with his inner demons on a daily basis. Not that it wouldn't be without its laughs. "In addition to the morose, tormented Angel," said Greenwalt, "this time we also have an Angel with a sense of humor. In fact, all our characters, and all our situations, have a dosage of dark, unexpected humor. *Angel* is almost like a film noir with a few giggles thrown in."

The show was an immediate success, although the ratings did dip midseason, as some *Buffy* viewers decided it was too different from *Buffy*. The series was intended to be a week-by-week show with no seasonal arc (more like the *Law and Order* series), but because the writers were from *Buffy* and were accustomed to more serialized content, the format soon changed. Fans wanted the complexity of *Buffy the Vampire Slayer*. "It just didn't pop," Greenwalt said. "It didn't have resonance. Frankly, it wasn't the kind of thing we do well." The writers believed one of the problems was Doyle, one of only three regular cast members, and in the ninth episode they took a surprising risk by killing him off. Fans were shocked, and "Save Doyle" campaigns popped up everywhere. Joss supported the decision, saying it was in keeping with the spirit of the show. "[Doyle] was an interesting character, but I just wanted to shake things up by getting rid of Angel's mentor," he said. "We were setting up someone who [the viewers] thought would be there the whole time and then killed him really surprisingly. We wanted to keep the audience on their toes, keep them frightened . . . and not let them feel safe in the world they are watching."

Alexis Denisof was brought in as the newest cast member, and while some fans stopped watching (many to return in later seasons when word got out that the show was great), others thought Denisof gave the show more of a *Buffy* feeling, which helped to steer it in the right direction. The first season relied on a lot of *Buffy* crossovers to bring in new viewers (Seth Green, James Marsters, Eliza Dushku, and Sarah Michelle Gellar all had guest appearances) and its premise of a private detective fighting against a system of police officers that doesn't believe in monsters was slightly clichéd. But by the end of the season, a new, streetwise character named Charles Gunn had entered into the mix; Wesley had begun translating a prophecy involving Angel that would become integral to the series; Cordelia had found new maturity through her painful encounters with her visions; and Angel had realized that he really did need friends to help him with his mission, and he didn't have to be such a loner. By the beginning of season 2, the characters on *Angel* bore little resemblance to who they were on *Buffy,* and the series was able to overcome its origins and become its own show.

In the show's second year, there was more of a focus on Wolfram & Hart, the law firm that was using legal means to dog Angel and make his life hell. The show took on an even darker tone with Cordelia losing some of her shallow humor, Wesley becoming less of a bumbler and more of a key player, and Angel being haunted by Darla and turning from his friends. One critic praised the show for its bleakness, saying, "*Angel* makes Chris Carter's *Millennium* look like *Laugh-In.*" Because *Angel* was finding its own way, it started picking up new viewers who had never watched *Buffy* but realized they could watch one show without the other and not feel like they were missing anything.

The show also managed to retain its offbeat sense of humor. Andy Hallett was brought in to play the Host, a creature who ran a karaoke

J. August Richards, Alexis Denisof, Amy Acker, and Andy Hallett all brought their own styles to the series, and in the second season, *Angel* finally found its legs.

bar and could read a person's aura if that person sang to him. On paper the premise sounds ridiculous, but on-screen it was television gold. The Host, in his loud Liberace-influenced suits, Rat Pack–styled banter, and pop culture–infused sense of humor, added a much-needed levity to the show and quickly became a fan favorite. When Angel became so dark that he shunned his friends, went on a self-destructive rampage, and seemed dangerously close to turning into Angelus, it was the Host who confronted him about how stupid he was being. Meanwhile, Gunn became a full-fledged member of the team, Wesley became the leader, and Cordelia's visions made her more of an authority figure in the group rather than the flighty former cheerleader type she'd been in season 1. By the end of the season, after the gang had reunited through a rather harrowing experience in another dimension, David Greenwalt expressed his pleasure with how his show was going. "I think we did accomplish what we wanted to this year, which is to deepen the show and understand the history and background of our characters, particularly Angel, more than we had before, to bring him slowly, step by step, into the world of humans," he said.

Angel was overshadowed in the media that year by stories that the WB was canceling *Buffy*. *Buffy the Vampire Slayer* was having one of its best years creatively, with the appearance of Buffy's little sister, the death of Buffy's mother (and Angel made a quick crossover to the show to comfort Buffy at her mother's grave), and Buffy's own death at the end of the season (which resonated on *Angel* when he ended up leaving L.A. for the summer to deal with his grief). Unfortunately, as far as the WB was concerned, that creativity wasn't translating into revenue, and Twentieth Century Fox had increased its asking price from the WB for each episode. Jamie Kellner, CEO of the WB, made some remarks in the press about *Buffy* not having the following of a show like *ER* and how no other network had wanted the show to begin with, but UPN stepped up and offered to take the show for Fox's asking price. Joss Whedon and the cast of *Buffy* were thrilled. "It's always been great at the WB," said Whedon. "But at the highest levels, they made a corporate decision that I found unfathomable. They decided not only to not step up financially, but to sort of diss the show in the press, and to me that was unforgivable. It really hurt. But the people I dealt with, the promotional people and the creative execs, they were great. I have no beef with them. But yeah, it's nice to see a network come up and say, 'We think you're an extraordinary asset and we're going to prove that by writing this large check.'"

With *Buffy* safe from cancellation, Joss could not only concentrate on *Angel* more than he had been, but also focus on developing a new series for Fox that would be called *Firefly*. In order to lighten his load, he brought in Marti Noxon to help oversee the day-to-day operations on *Buffy* and added a second executive producer to *Angel*, Tim Minear (who had been writing some of the best *Angel* scripts to that point). "Tim is the heir apparent," Whedon told *Variety*. "If there was no Tim Minear, there would be no *Angel*. He's the unsung and unbelievably necessary hero of the show."

In its third season, *Angel* shone brighter than it had before; *Buffy's* leaving the WB was the best thing that could have happened to *Angel*. The networks refused to allow any crossover episodes between the two shows that year, and *Angel* was forced to stand on its own two feet, which it did valiantly. Severed from the *Buffy* mythology, it rivaled *Buffy* in quality. The cast and crew were excited about *Angel*'s prospects as the season got started. "When the shows separated, it kind of sucked, because it was cool to have that block of time for the two shows that were related to each other, that had stories told across both shows and [that] complement each other and contrast each other," said actor J. August Richards at the time. "So we'll be missing out on that. On the other hand, it's okay, because we get to stand on our own and be our own show and not necessarily have the *Buffy* lead-in. We have to be our own man, as they say."

The critics were also eager to see what would happen. A reporter for *TV Guide* wrote, "Since its 1999 premiere, *Angel* has solidified into an hour of quality television that rivals — and this past season arguably even outshone — its sire. In fact, if the final WB episode of *Buffy* (before its fall transfer to UPN) is an 'instant classic' — and, frankly, it is — then the four-episode fairy tale with which *Angel* rounded out the year is at least a mini-masterpiece."

Introducing Amy Acker as the new addition to the gang — and the potential love interest of two of its members — was a compelling development in the third season, as was the relationship between Cordelia and Angel (who would have seen *that* coming in season 2 of *Buffy*?!), the tensions between Wesley and the gang, and Angel's past and future catching up to him at once. Keith Szarabajka played Daniel Holtz, the vampire hunter we'd only heard about in flashback episodes, and he was the ultimate nemesis for Angel — someone who wasn't actually a villain but whom Angel had wronged terribly and who now sought revenge. A plot in which Angel finds out he's going to be a father imitated real life, as David Boreanaz got married on November 24, 2001, and announced a week later that his wife, Jaime Bergman, was pregnant and due in May 2002.

Season 3 was the strongest season yet, and critics and fans were ecstatic. By November, *Angel* boasted the best ratings in its time slot for the WB since 1998. It began appearing on year-end critics' polls as a favorite show. Zap2it.com praised the lead characters and the show's balance of darkness and humor: "The show has completely shed its spin-off tag and grown into a compelling, character-driven drama. David

Boreanaz and Charisma Carpenter have done great work, making their blooming respect-friendship-maybe-even-love relationship seem entirely natural. The supporting characters have depth as well, and the show's humor is a great counterbalance to the heavier stuff."

By the end of the year, all the characters had moved far from where they'd started. Cordelia had ascended to a heavenly plane. Wesley was abandoned by the gang and Angel had vowed to kill him. Gunn and Fred were a romantic item. Lorne left to follow his singing career in Las Vegas. And Angel was sitting in a watery tomb far beneath the ocean's surface, put there by his son, who mistakenly blamed him for a loved one's death. The critics applauded loudly. The *Chicago Tribune* wrote, "The *Buffy* spinoff could arguably be the season's most improved series, given the strengthening of the supporting cast and the Angel-is-a-daddy storyline infusing the series with a potent new punch and much-needed direction." Scott D. Pierce of *Deseret News*, long a fan of *Buffy* and *Angel*, raved, "Led by executive producer/co-creator David Greenwalt, *Angel* has delivered its best season yet." When asked about the huge changes that Wesley had to undergo, Denisof said, "I must say I loved it: it was a great opportunity to explore some of the darker layers of the characters and that's always exciting as an actor, to get the chance to find some new colors and go in a surprising direction. I've been very grateful to the writers for this angle."

Surprisingly, at the end of this phenomenal season, David Greenwalt announced his departure to helm a spring 2003 show on ABC called *Miracles*. David Simkins (*Freakylinks*) was announced as his successor, to become the show's day-to-day executive producer. However, by the first week of August, Simkins left over creative differences, although there didn't seem to be any hard feelings. "He was thrown into the deep end of the pool without any lifeguards, and so, because we didn't have the time to really get in there and break him in, just everybody decided that it wasn't going to work," said Tim Minear. Minear and Whedon decided to stay on as executive producers while also overseeing *Firefly*, while writer Jeffrey Bell was brought in to take over Simkins's position for *Angel*'s upcoming fourth season.

Earlier, on May 15, Fox had announced it would pick up *Firefly*, which would begin airing Friday nights in fall 2002. Set 500 years in the future, the show focused on Captain Malcolm "Mal" Reynolds (Nathan Fillion), a veteran who had fought in a war to unite the planets but was on the side that lost. He is left to travel around the universe on his rickety ship, the *Serenity*. Joining Mal on the voyages were Zoe, Mal's second-in-command; Wash, Zoe's husband and the ship's pilot; Jayne, the crew's muscle; Kaylee, the ship's engineer; Book, a priest; Inara, a personal companion; Simon, a doctor; and River, Simon's mentally unbalanced sister. Joss described the show as a "science-fiction Western," but with only human characters, unlike *Star Trek*. "I love spaceships," Whedon said. "I love sci-fi. I love hard-science sci-fi. I wanted to do a show without latex. I wanted to come back down to Earth and do a western. I wanted to make *Stagecoach* really bad and that was the impetus. [I don't think] there will be aliens three or four hundred years from now [when *Firefly* is set]. There would just be people, and that's the point. They're not smarter, they're not better. War hasn't been abolished. Some of them are decent, some of them aren't. Some are just trying to scrape by after being trodden on by history. . . . It's a very low-tech show. It's a sort of immigrant story, taking from all the cultures we already have and imagining them spread out over a galaxy."

When Joss turned in the original pilot to Fox, the company was unhappy with it (despite having spent a fortune on it) and made him go back to the drawing board. He tried again, and Fox was much happier with the second result, announcing late in May that it would pick up the first 13 episodes. The network gave him a budget of $1.3 million per episode. Joss decided to use the same team of writers that created *Buffy* and *Angel* each week.

In fall 2002, all three of Whedon's series got off to strong starts. Whedon's biggest concern was for his fledgling show, and the critics' reactions were mixed. *USA Today* gave it three and a half stars out of four and wrote, "If you're a fan of Whedon's work on *Buffy the Vampire Slayer* and *Angel*, I don't think you'll be disappointed: *Firefly* offers the same well-balanced blend of humor, action, sharply drawn characters and unexpected twists on genre conventions. And if you have so far resisted the vamp-call of *Buffy*, this more mainstream sci-fi adventure may be your ticket into Whedon's TV universe."

But other critics weren't so happy and said that Whedon had gone

ALBERT L. ORTEGA

ALBERT L. ORTEGA

Because of its original, groundbreaking quality, *Firefly* couldn't find the audience Fox wanted it to, and it was cancelled after only a handful of episodes. *Top:* Ben Edlund, Joss Whedon, and Tim Minear celebrate the release of the series on DVD; *bottom:* Cast members Ron Glass, Nathan Fillion, Morena Baccarin, Gina Torres, and Adam Baldwin.

too far with his Western space drama. Because Fox had shelved the two-hour premiere, airing the second episode instead, viewers were left scratching their heads and trying to figure out what was going on. Carina Chocano of Salon.com wrote that *Firefly* wasn't a cowboy Western like *Star Trek* or *Buck Rogers* had been, but instead was "the kind of western in which people shoot revolvers and ride horses and hang around back-lot sets that look as though they might have been used on *Little House on the Prairie.*" Like many critics, she reviewed the series by comparing it unfavorably with *Buffy the Vampire Slayer,* saying that after a show as deep and meaningful as *Buffy,* with characters whose emotions felt as realistic as our own, the women of *Firefly* were disappointing.

By October, there were already rumors swirling that *Firefly* was in danger of being canceled. The ratings were low (the 8 p.m. Friday night time slot didn't help), and the show that followed it, *John Doe,* had more viewers, meaning people were turning their sets away from Fox and only turning back when *Firefly* was over. Fox ordered three more episodes beyond the original 13, but on November 26, 2002, Fox President of Entertainment Gail Berman announced that *Firefly* would be taking a "hiatus." "What we know is happening with the show is the great creative growth that it's experiencing. That's why we ordered additional episodes," said Berman. "We think that Joss is finding his creative voice with this show and we need to see how that's going to work for us in December." The announcement came on the heels of the excellent episode "Out of Gas," which explained a lot of the backstory presented in the series premiere that Fox hadn't aired. Whedon said, "There's a lot of confusion, because they didn't air the pilot, which explains everything. We tried to do that as best we could in an hour show."

The "Save *Firefly*" campaign was fast and furious. Fans took out a full-page ad in *Variety* on December 9, making a promise to the network: "You keep flying. We'll keep watching." But the campaign was too late, as it appeared that Fox had already made its decision. In an ironic move, the network aired "Serenity," the two-hour pilot, as the series' swan song, and *Firefly* was officially canceled in mid-December. Almost a year later, in September 2003, Whedon announced that he had gotten a green light on a feature-film version of the television show, and it would be released in summer 2005 with the title *Serenity* (fans chuckled at the idea of using the title of the very episode that Fox had pulled in the first place). Strangely enough, Joss's first project was a failed movie that he turned into a successful television show. Now he had a failed television show that he was trying to turn into a successful movie. Joss's stubbornness has translated to triumph before, and fans excitedly await the result of his latest act of perseverance.

On *Buffy*, the season was all about the characters overcoming both the separation they had felt in season 6 and the biggest demon yet — the First Evil, the one from whom all evil in the universe originated. Willow was dealing with the death of Tara as well as the reality that she had killed a human being at the end of season 6, no matter how slimy that person was. Xander and Anya were no longer together; Anya was a vengeance demon again. Dawn felt more integrated into her sister's life but had accepted that she would never be as powerful as her sister. Giles returned to the group but was becoming the Watcher of many Slayers. Spike now had a soul but had to accept that it wouldn't change Buffy's feelings. And Andrew was back, whether or not the Scoobies wanted him to be. The Watcher's Council was obliterated, Slayers were dying, and Buffy was moving into a role of Slayer and Watcher while finally discovering her primal origins. Whedon was saying in interviews that the seventh season would be about going back to the beginning, and fans were thrilled to see glimpses of past villains, echoes of quotes or plot lines from the early seasons, and the return of the high school as one of the main settings.

On *Angel*, which had been moved to Sunday nights at the beginning of the season and then Wednesdays in January, fans had been left with the cliffhanger ending of season 3 that needed to be resolved. Wesley was no longer part of the gang, but as the season continued he would slowly return to the fold. Cordelia had become a "higher power," but when she returned she was acting strangely, and the mystery wouldn't be solved until near the end of the season. Connor had betrayed Angel and everyone else who trusted him, and he was shunned by everyone but Cordelia. Gunn and Fred faced problems of trust in their relationship, and they slowly moved apart as the season continued. Angel tried to make friends with Wesley, regain some semblance of a relationship with

Connor, and understand why Cordy was acting strangely, but another side of him appeared near the end of the season. The season was one very complex arc, and events from the previous three years came together to form a surprising ending to this season. The Angel Investigations team lost one of its members indefinitely, while the rest of the gang joined the ranks of a former enemy in a way that didn't seem possible. The season had its ups and downs, but generally was a little disconcerting for viewers in a way that *Buffy*'s fourth season had been.

Though *Angel* had an interesting storyline, it was overshadowed all year by rumors that *Buffy*'s seventh season would be its last. It was well publicized that way back in season 1, all the actors had signed seven-year contracts, and it was unlikely that Sarah Michelle Gellar — who had been saying for some time that she wanted to focus on her film career — would sign on for more. Nicholas Brendon had said in the summer before season 7 that he was convinced it would be the last, but the writers wouldn't confirm or deny the rumor. In June, Marti Noxon insisted there would be an eighth season, with or without Gellar, which raised some eyebrows. The rumors began circulating that one of the characters would spin off (most people suggested Dawn or Faith) or that the series would continue without Buffy. How a show called *Buffy the Vampire Slayer* could continue without the character Buffy the Vampire Slayer was anyone's guess, but the cast and crew were certainly keeping the fans guessing. By the end of February 2003, Eliza Dushku announced she would be starring in a new pilot for Fox, crushing the hopes of many fans who were counting on the Faith spinoff. And for anyone still clinging to the hope that Gellar might change her mind, the rumors were put to bed officially at the beginning of March.

In an article called "The Goodbye Girl" in *Entertainment Weekly*, Sarah announced once and for all that she was officially leaving the show at the end of the season, and that "*Buffy*, in this incarnation, is over." She explained how difficult the decision was for her: "I love this job, I love the fans. I love telling the stories we tell. This isn't about leaving for a career in movies, or in theater — it's more of a personal decision. I need a rest." She said that she hoped the show would be remembered fondly: "It was drama, comedy, action, horror, all of those things combined. And I just want people to remember it as a fabulous run, a fabulous seven years." She said that when she and Joss realized that season 7 was going to be a strong year, they knew it should also be its last so the show could go out on top. Co-executive producer and writer David Fury said the decision to make the announcement had been left up to Sarah, but everyone knew the show was ending: "Everybody knew it, we just weren't announcing it. And quite frankly we knew it when UPN did the two-year pickup, we knew we were working toward a two-year arc."

While the cast and crew were making the decision to end *Buffy* on a high note, there was some speculation that *Angel* might be canceled. As had happened at the end of season 5 of *Buffy*, Fox was suddenly demanding more money from the WB network to keep the show on its own network. Jordan Levin, the new CEO of the WB, finally decided that the company would pony up the extra cash and the show would no longer make a profit for the network, despite having come close to a break-even point. Of course, the WB didn't officially make the announcement until after *Angel*'s season finale on May 7, and executives on *Angel* just had their fingers crossed that it wouldn't get canceled because they hadn't exactly resolved all the plot lines and had left things open for a new direction in season 5. The announcement that *Angel* would be kept on was made just before *Buffy*'s series finale, and it contained what many fans considered to be a spoiler for *Buffy*'s finale: the news that James Marsters had agreed to continue his role as Spike over on *Angel* for the 2003–4 season. Whedon wasn't happy, especially considering the ending he had planned for *Buffy*, and the WB apologized for undercutting the profundity of Spike's "death" on the series finale.

As the final episode of *Buffy* loomed, critics offered up their final words about what the show meant to them. The *New York Times* called it "the coolest television coming-of-age horror-fantasy-love story ever told." Joss Whedon listed his 10 favorite episodes for *USA Today*, which were "Innocence"; "Once More, with Feeling"; "Hush"; "The Body"; "Doppelgängland"; "The Wish"; "Becoming, Part Two"; "Restless"; "Conversations with Dead People"; and "Prophecy Girl." Robert Bianco of the same paper, who had always been a vocal proponent of the show, wrote, "Simply put, for seven seasons, *Buffy* has been one of the

ALBERT L. ORTEGA

Saying goodbye to *Buffy* after seven incredible seasons. L-R: Danny Strong, Tom Lenk, Emma Caulfield, Alexis Denisof, Alyson Hannigan, Anthony Stewart Head, Joss Whedon, Michelle Trachtenberg, James Marsters, and Nathan Fillion.

smartest, scariest, sexiest, and wittiest shows on television. Too often dismissed as a teen show or a genre show, *Buffy* was a well-acted and often brilliantly written comedy/drama that, under its fantasy guise, treated the pains and joys of life with admirable and sometimes shocking realism."

The *Star Tribune* in Minneapolis pointed out how much the world had changed since *Buffy the Vampire Slayer* first aired, and why the loss of the show was so devastating as a result: "The irony is this: While *Buffy* sprung out of an anxious time in the late '90s, the real world today seems to have become much more dangerous than anything the Hellmouth can produce. *Buffy* provided much joy, tears, and comfort in those intervening years. But the Vampire Slayer is now going away, and we still need her. And that really bites." England's *Independent* shared its sorrows, calling *Buffy* "the most original, witty, and provocative television show of the past two decades" and saying, "The tight collegiate team who wrote and produced the show couldn't touch on a personality or plot without marinating it in their own tart mixture of mischief and paradox. With astonishing bravura, *Buffy the Vampire Slayer* has succeeded in blending the conventions of teenage soap opera with smart, dialogue-driven comedy, a phantasmagoria of supernatural motifs, and even knotty theological debate."

The finale aired on May 20, 2003; some fans loved it and some didn't, but in one way or another, it saddened all fans. The night after it aired, Joss Whedon made a visit to the Bronze posting board, and while his tone was light, it was clear he was also dismayed at having to say good-bye to his Slayer:

> Okay, so that was a thing. Thank you for hanging in with me, guys. Now at last, I can tell you guys what happens next Tuesday without lying.
> 1) I will probably have a beer.
> 2) Earth, more or less turning, pretty certain.
> 3) I might read.
> Cool! Now I get why everyone loves spoilers! I totally RUINED my beer-having for people who like surprises! I see now that I was shackled by *Buffy,* and now I'm free.
> Which, oddly enough, is not how I feel.
> Hope you liked.

By the end of May, Sci Fi Wire was reporting that Charisma Carpenter would no longer be part of the cast of *Angel* by the beginning of season 5. "The Angel/Cordelia [love story] had gone pretty much as far as we wanted to take it," said Joss Whedon. "Their romance was definitely not a popular move on our part, I think, with most fans. . . . It just seemed like a good time for certain people to move on. Not completely, obviously. I'm hoping that we'll get Charisma to do some episodes as Cordelia sometime during the year. She's a new mother, so, like Sarah [Michelle Gellar], I'm waiting to hear what her schedule is like." In August, Charisma gave an interview to the *Boston Herald* and expressed her disappointment in no longer being a part of the series. She had returned to work in season 4 only 10 days after the birth of her son, Donovan, and she thought her character would awake from her coma by season 5. "I was not prepared," she said. "I don't think you're ever prepared for that kind of situation. Seven years — that's a long time. I started that show. To not be finishing it is a pretty big deal for me. They went back to work on July 24. . . . On that day I thought, 'Oh, today is officially my first day of unemployment.'" She was still optimistic about her future and had already filmed a movie, *See Jane Date,* and would appear on a new NBC series in the fall, called *Miss Match.*

Whereas the fourth season of *Angel* had featured a complex storyline that continued from one week to the next, making it almost impossible for new viewers to tune in and understand what was going on, the fifth season would feature a more episodic feel. "The WB hoped for a show that would be a little more stand-alone-y," Whedon said. "When a show is in its fifth year, they don't expect it to get any sudden heat. They were hoping to pump the audience a little bit . . . with episodes people could jump into without being confused." The season got off to a bit of a slow start, with fans perplexed by the sudden week-to-week feeling and each episode focusing on a different character. The new setting of Wolfram & Hart was also a little baffling, and while it made the show feel fresh after three years at the Hyperion, the implications of the gang working for the enemy they had been fighting against for four years wasn't immediately clear. But once the show moved into the Shanshu territory, creating tension between Spike and Angel about which one would actually "become a real boy," and suddenly and surprisingly reintroduced old characters, it became exciting again.

By the beginning of 2004, critics were lauding *Angel*'s fifth season as its best yet. Maybe it was because *Buffy* was no longer on the air to overshadow *Angel* (even though *Angel* had been just as strong creatively as its predecessor). Maybe it was because Joss Whedon was now more focused on *Angel,* whereas previously his attention had been divided between *Angel, Buffy,* and *Firefly.* Or maybe it was because the writing and acting were stronger than ever. Whatever it was, it was working. "I do feel like there's a new energy this year," Whedon told the *Plain Dealer.* "You know, obviously, bringing James in and shaking up the cast a little bit and just having the mission statement of making the show accessible to people who haven't seen it before sort of really kept us on our toes."

On December 4, 2003, the cast and crew had a much-publicized party for the show's 100th episode (which featured Charisma Carpenter) and

The cast of *Angel* celebrates the show's 100th episode; they were shocked when news of the show's cancellation came days after the episode aired. L-R: Charisma Carpenter, James Marsters, Amy Acker, Alexis Denisof, Joss Whedon, David Boreanaz, Andy Hallett, and J. August Richards.

Joss recognized the link between the show's theme and how the show had fared over the years: "The idea of the show was redemption, and what it takes to win back a life when you've misused yours terribly." Jordan Levin attended the party and said to the media present, "It's really an honor to be here, an honor to do a show that is not only such a critical hit but one that fans everywhere support. When you can have a marriage like this it's really wonderful." When the episode aired on February 3, 2004, it was deemed an instant classic, and fans and critics alike praised the acting, the writing, and the blending of the new cast with Charisma, who brought back a sense of what the show had been like in the early years. For the first time ever, *Angel* beat out *The West Wing, King of Queens,* and *Becker* in its time slot for the show's main demographic, persons aged 12 to 34. It seemed the show could do no wrong, and it was enjoying enormous success on all fronts: with fans, critics, and demographics.

And then, on February 13, the cast and crew were told it was all over. The WB issued a press release to the public on Valentine's Day that called *Angel* and *Buffy* the "cornerstones" of the network, but said it was canceling the show. The release explained that the WB had given Joss the news when it did because it wanted to give him the chance to wrap up the series the way he wanted, rather than be left with plot lines hanging if he continued on with a sixth season in mind. The release also suggested there might be "special movie events" the following year, in which the show's saga could continue, and added, "David Boreanaz continues to be one of the finest, classiest, and friendliest actors we have had the pleasure to work with and we hope that the relationship furthers from here. The same can be said for all the actors and producers on the show."

The fans were stunned, as were the cast and crew. "We were really surprised, actually," Amy Acker told me by phone. "I think last year we expected it to happen a lot more, but this year we felt like the show was doing really well and everyone was liking it a lot, and it seemed like they were excited. We'd just had the one hundredth episode, et cetera, and it was a really big surprise. All these people liking it and tuning in and we thought, *Why now?*" How could the WB kill a show that's having its best year? Critics speculated that the WB wanted to take the network in a new direction, and that meant getting rid of the old shows that had been around for years. Others suggested it was just too expensive to continue licensing *Angel* from Fox. Joss Whedon was heartbroken, and he posted on the Bronze Beta on February 14 to express his sadness:

> Some of you may have heard the hilarious news. I thought this would be a good time to weigh in, to answer some obvious questions: No, we had no idea this was coming. Yes, we will finish out the season. No, I don't think the WB is doing the right thing. Yes, I'm grateful they did it early enough for my people to find other jobs.
>
> Yes, my heart is breaking.
>
> When *Buffy* ended, I was tapped out and ready to send it off. When *Firefly* got the axe, I went into a state of denial so huge it may very well cause a movie. But *Angel* . . . we really were starting to feel like we were on top, hitting our stride — and then we strode right into the Pit of Snakes 'n' Lava. I'm so into these characters, these actors, the situations we're building . . . you wanna know how I feel? Watch the first act of "The Body."

As far as TV movies or whatever, I'm not thinking that far ahead. I actually hope my actors and writers are all too busy. We always planned this season finale to be a great capper to the season and the show in general. (And a great platform for a new season, of course.) We'll proceed ahead as planned.

I've never made mainstream TV very well. I like surprises, and TV isn't about surprises, unless the surprise is who gets voted off of something. I've been lucky to sneak this strange, strange show over the airwaves for as long as I have. I don't FEEL lucky, but I understand that I am.

Thanks all for your support, your community, and your perfectly sane devotion. It's meant a lot. I regret nothing (except the string of grisley [sic] murders in the '80s — what was THAT all about?). Remember the words of the poet:

"Two roads diverged in a wood, and I took the road less traveled by and they CANCELLED MY FRIKKIN' SHOW. I totally shoulda took the road that had all those people on it. Damn."

See you soon.

Levin explained that the choice to cancel *Angel* was purely a business decision. "This isn't about the WB bailing out on one of its top shows," he said. "The show had a loyal core following, but it didn't have a tremendous amount of new audience upside." He added, "It was a very bittersweet parting and an end of an era for us. I have the ultimate respect for Joss as someone who created two landmark series and stood behind them the whole time." The WB, Joss, and everyone involved with *Angel* were about to find out more about the show's "loyal core following."

Within hours of hearing the news, *Angel* fans everywhere began putting their heads together to find a way to save the show. Two Web sites suddenly popped up: SaveAngel.org and SavingAngel.com. While the two organizations worked separately, they both had the same goal: to save their favorite show. Fans could visit the sites to find the mailing addresses of "targets" such as Jordan Levin and Garth Ancier of the WB, to whom fans could send postcards explaining why they loved the show and why it should stay on the air. Hundreds of bouquets of flowers were sent to Levin, and Ancier received over 500 beanie babies. The fans handled their ire calmly, not pointing fingers or being insulting, but being

When faced with the cancellation of *Angel*, the fans fought back by raising money for billboard ads like this one, that drove around L.A. and stopped in front of major studios.

kind to the executives and trying to convince them that if they kept the show on the air, they would be rewarded with a loyal viewership.

Within days the campaign raised over US$17,000 to be used to get the attention of the media (the campaign eventually collected more than US$30,000). The fans associated with this campaign took out ads in the *Hollywood Reporter* and *Daily Variety* that read, "Angel has been saving the world for years and now he needs your help," asking readers to tune in and show the WB that more viewers were out there. The money also provided for a truck-mounted moving billboard of a silhouette of Angel and the campaign's slogan: "We'll follow Angel to hell . . . or another network." The truck drove around L.A., making stops at the other studios with the hope that another network might pick up the show if the WB persisted in canceling it. Throughout March and April the two groups sponsored protests, rallies, the continued write-in campaigns, a blood drive (an ingenious tie-in to the series), and collections for food banks. They also arranged for flowers and letters of appreciation to be sent to the cast and crew of the show every week.

On Friday, April 2, Whedon was a radio guest on L.A.'s morning *Kevin and Bean Show* and joked, "There's just no place for an old codger like Angel. He's, like, two hundred and fifty, and that's not their demographic." He acknowledged his gratitude for the Save *Angel* campaigns and urged fans to keep it up: "You know, I think all the noise that's been made by the fans does help. Because we're talking about different venues for not just *Angel* but the Buffyverse in general." On May 5, at the Saturn Awards (where *Angel* tied with csi for Best Network Television Show; David Boreanaz won Best Actor on Television; James Marsters won Best Supporting Actor on Television; Amy Acker won Best Supporting Actress on Television; and *Firefly* won Best DVD Television Release), the media liaison for SavingAngel.com presented Joss Whedon with a check for US$13,000, to be given to the International Committee of the Red Cross on behalf of *Angel* fans and the two Save *Angel* campaigns. Amy Acker was touched by the organized efforts: "We were all so disappointed so the fan campaigns really helped us. We realized we weren't the only ones upset about the end."

But the fans' lobbying wasn't enough. On May 19, 2003 (exactly 365 days after the *Buffy* finale), devotees said goodbye to *Angel,* and with it, the entire Buffyverse. J. August Richards told me, "As a television insider who watches the industry, I'm pretty sure that they would not save the show as a series, just looking at other shows that were saved under similar circumstances. Based on history, I was fairly certain that the show would not be saved, but I was extremely touched and flattered that the fans would go to such lengths to keep the show around; I think it was amazing and it really showed the industry that this show meant something to a lot of people. As far as us doing DVD movies in the future, I would jump at the chance to play this character again and work with the people I work with again."

David Boreanaz told CNN Headline News that he was actually relieved at the show's end. While some fans took his words as a stake through the heart, one can't blame him. He'd played the character of Angel for eight years by 2004, and he had carried the eponymous show. While other actors were on the set for four of the eight shooting days per episode, Boreanaz had to be there for seven or eight of those days, 14 hours a day, for months on end. He expressed his gratitude for the fans' efforts, but regarding the television movies or miniseries possibilities he said, "I think whenever they want to revisit that character and bring it to a higher plateau, I would only be interested if the bar was [raised] a lot higher."

In the week leading up to the series finale, Joss Whedon conducted a press conference with entertainment reporters, and it seemed the cancellation was still like a stake through his heart. But he also revealed he would be putting that hurt into the finale: "The pain of loss when they cancelled the show? I'm going to share." He declared his appreciation to the fans for all the work they did in trying to save the show. "I was obviously enormously touched. I was really heartbroken when it got cancelled. I was really shocked. And for the fans to react that strongly for something that has been perceived sometimes as the bastard child of the *Buffy* franchise was really important," he said. "We were staring at a brick wall, which is the financial model the WB operates by. This is a really bad time for television and for television drama. . . . I just felt we didn't have a shot, or I would have been outside the WB with a placard and bullhorn myself." He added, "Ultimately the [vampire] shows were cult shows; we didn't make *Friends,* so nobody is going to use us as a financial model. And the financial models are what changed television. If I had created reality television I would have had a much greater influence, but then I would have had to KILL MYSELF."

He addressed the show's finale, which some rumors were suggesting would end on a cliffhanger. "I do not think of it as a cliffhanger at all. It is not the end of all things. It is not a final grace note after a symphony, the way *Buffy* was. We are definitely still in the thick of it, but it is, and was meant to be, a final statement about *Angel.* . . . The point of the show is, you're never done. Whoever survives the show, to get that point, will embody it, but no matter who goes on, the fight goes on. Did I make it so that it could lead into an exciting sixth season? Yes I did. But it still is a final statement, if that is what it needs to be."

The finale aired on May 19, 2004, and it was amazing. The plot device of the Circle of the Black Thorn — introduced only the week before — was actually wrapped up nicely (it was originally going to be a major part of the show's sixth season), but the episode focused on the war that the Angel team had been fighting and the ultimate effect that war had had on each member. The critics and fans loved it — an incredible 5.3 million viewers tuned in to watch (where were they when we needed them?) — and the episode's title, "Not Fade Away," was an appropriate one. The *Toronto Star* marveled, "It's difficult to imagine something as smart, uncompromising and meaningful — and let's not forget funny — as Whedon's shows would be allowed a chance to find an audience in the current television climate, where cheap, easy, and stupid make network executives pant."

It's astonishing, and almost unbelievable, that both shows

ALBERT L. ORTEGA

Joss Whedon's wife, Kai, hugs him at the *Buffy* wrap party for his many extraordinary accomplishments.

have ended. The characters of *Angel* had transformed so much by the end of season 5 that they were barely recognizable as the same characters who had begun the series. Wesley had been comic relief in the beginning, and then a source of our tears and sorrow in the finale. Cordelia had been a flighty cheerleader, but actually became a higher being because of her selflessness. (*Cordelia.* Imagine that possibility back in season 1 of *Buffy.*) Angel had come full circle. In season 1 he had been a vampire with a soul who was broody, isolated, and trying to help the helpless out of guilt, but by season 2 he was surrounded by friends and had a prophecy telling him he would be forgiven for his sins if he continued along the right path. He was granted the gift of a son, something that was previously deemed impossible, and he lost that son only to get him back again (as a hostile teenager hell-bent on revenge) and again (as a loving son who knew what his father had sacrificed for him). But in the end, the prophecy — the one thing that had kept Angel fighting the good fight above all else — didn't matter, and he realized he was going to fight evil because it was the right thing to do, not because he himself might benefit from it.

Angel and *Buffy* changed the face of television irrevocably. The series were also compelling enough that multiple viewings don't diminish the episodes but in fact illuminate things that we might have missed the first time. Consequently, fans will no doubt be turning to their DVD players and continuing to discuss the shows with like-minded aficionados for years to come. While we will mourn the loss of both series, we can also anticipate the next project that Joss Whedon might be working on and hope that someday soon we'll discover a new set of characters that will simultaneously transport us to another world of imagination and help us discover something about ourselves.

There may still be hope for spinoffs for projects involving the characters from *Buffy* and *Angel*. Rumors are still circulating about a Giles-based *Ripper* series, or a Spike television movie, or an animated series. If Joss Whedon decides to explore his universe further, the fans will be there. And even he agrees that the stories haven't all been told. "I don't think the Buffyverse is dead," he says. "I don't think anyone saw enough of muppet Angel."

Posting Board Party 2003:

The Monster's Ball — Last Dance

Beginning in 1998, fans who posted at the Bronze posting board (originally on the official WB *Buffy* site, it moved to UPN and eventually took up a home somewhere else as the Bronze Beta) gathered once a year somewhere in L.A. to meet the people they had been chatting with online. Over the years, *Buffy* and *Angel* regulars like Joss Whedon, David Boreanaz, Nicholas Brendon, Alyson Hannigan, and dozens of others attended as surprise guests, making the evenings even more special for the fans who had flown in from all over the world. On February 15, 2003, the Bronzers held their final posting-board party at the American Legion Hall in Hollywood and said farewell to the show that had brought them all together in the first place.

VIP Attendees

Actors: James Marsters, J. August Richards, Andy Hallett, Alexis Denisof, Danny Strong, Tom Lenk, Adam Busch, Eliza Dushku, Julie Benz, Mark Lutz, Ron Glass, Summer Glau, Vladimir Kulich, Alexa Davalos, James C. Leary, Camden Toy, Sarah Hagan, Iyari Limon, George Hertzberg, Jeff Ricketts, David Denman, Jonathan M. Woodward

Crew: Joss Whedon, David Fury, Mere Smith, Drew Goddard, Jane Espenson, Douglas Petrie, Tim Minear, Stephen S. DeKnight, Drew Z. Greenberg, Rob Kral (composer), Dayne Johnson (makeup), Elisabeth James, Dan Kerns (gaffer), Heidi Strickler (Amy Acker's stand-in), Joel Heyman (David Boreanaz's stand-in), Rob Hall (makeup)

Other VIPS: Maryelizabeth Hart, Jeff Mariotte, Erika Amato, and Jeff Stacy (Velvet Chain)

Music: Darling Violetta, Common Rotation, Four Star Mary, Andy Hallett

Money raised: $30,000 for the Make-A-Wish Foundation

As many people assumed season 7 was going to be *Buffy the Vampire Slayer*'s last, it had already been announced that The Monster's Ball would be the final posting-board party for fans. The evening got underway around 6 p.m. on Saturday, although several pre-parties had been thrown the night before and get-togethers had gone on all day. Dayne Johnson, the makeup artist for *Angel*, had been working steadily all afternoon with his crew to re-create some of the most memorable monsters from *Buffy* and *Angel*, including the Beast, the Übervamp, Skip, and several vampires. Throughout the evening, the musical entertainment was constant, VIPs arrived at a steady rate, and the fans had a fabulous time gathering in person and getting a chance to meet the stars personally, up close.

The planning for this party, like the others, started far in advance. Over the years, several people who were involved in planning the original PBP formed a committee so they could plan each event properly and make sure every detail was in place in time for the big night. Karri Phillips, a.k.a. Phoenix; Bryan Bonner, a.k.a. Blade; and Peter Hueser, a.k.a. Morbius, made up the central committee. According to Karri, the planning for the evening began in August, and sign-ups for the party began in November. With only 300 tickets available for the event, Bronzers had to respond quickly, as tickets were distributed on a first-come, first-served basis. "Controlling the insanity is one reason tickets

Clockwise from top left: Joss Whedon signs a copy of *Bite Me!* (a very fine book indeed); Alexis Denisof was all smiles, but explained that his fiancée, Alyson Hannigan, was filming *American Wedding* and couldn't attend; Eliza Dushku was a fan favorite, despite battling a cold; Julie Benz sidles up to The Beast.

are limited," says Bryan. "The other is logistical. Each venue has a maximum number of occupants that can't be exceeded. Therefore, in calculating the number of attendees we also have to account for VIPs plus guests, bands plus guests, security, and media. Not to mention that the PBPs have always been about the fans from the posting board, so controlling ticket numbers was a method to help ensure posting-board members got priority. Few people know that the third PBP came very close to shutting down on the day of the event because the fire marshal paid us a surprise visit at the venue site. Luckily, we were mostly in compliance and were able to address any concerns. As a result, the party went off without a hitch."

The next step was trying to get the word out to the VIPs — that is, the cast members and crew of both shows. Each year the committee made up invitations and sent them to the studios and to the actors' representatives, hoping for the best. In many cases, word of mouth from cast members who attended in previous years would lure the newer cast members out to the parties to see what they were all about. "I remember one year," says Karri, "Joss took most of the actors out to dinner after that day's filming and then kind of just brought them all to the party since they were all in the same car." Joss Whedon was always a huge supporter of the PBPs, and he attended every one. The committee never asked for RSVPs from the VIPs, and even if they did receive a tentative confirmation, they didn't reveal the names of the guests who would be in attendance to the other Bronzers just in case the guest couldn't show up, which would have left people disappointed. So who would actually be there from the shows always remained a mystery to the fans.

Before the second PBP in 1999, the committee came up with the idea of donating money to the Make-A-Wish Foundation. Every year the amount collected grew higher and higher, and money was raised through auctions at the party and beforehand and any extra donations Bronzers offered leading up to the event. "The idea to turn the PBP into a charity event came from our CEO, Morbius, who also was the force behind incorporating the committee as a not-for-profit corporation," says Bryan. "Morbius's idea was simple: Use our loyalty to the shows to benefit others. Not only did this have the direct effect of benefiting the Make-A-Wish Foundation, but it also helped generate significant VIP

Top: Bryan Bonner (Blade), Karri Phillips (Phoenix), and Peter Hueser (Morbius) pose with some creepy-looking friends; *bottom*: The casts of *Buffy* and *Angel* hold up the check for $30,000 that fans helped raise for the Make-A-Wish Foundation.

attendance because the events were for a worthy cause." In 1999 the Bronzers raised $6,000; then $11,000 in 2000; $12,000 in 2001; and $20,000 in 2002. For the final party, they managed to raise a whopping $30,000. The cast and crew of both shows were touched by the impact the show had had.

The Monster's Ball was a great evening for fans of both shows, and in the end, there were actually more A-list actors from *Angel* than *Buffy* who came along. James Marsters was one of the first to arrive. He hung around the VIP area for a while, and when he eventually made it upstairs to the throng of Bronzers, he was immediately swarmed by fans and remained surrounded for the rest of the evening. If you looked over in his direction periodically, all you could see was a peroxide-blond head in the midst of a sea of fans. Alexis Denisof arrived soon after and explained to fans that his wife-to-be, Alyson Hannigan, was in New York filming the third *American Pie* movie and couldn't make it. J. August Richards arrived with Alexa Davalos (Gwen Raiden), and as it was her first PBP, she looked a little taken aback by the scene. The Troika showed up separately, with Adam Busch taking the stage with his band, Common Rotation. Tom Lenk and Danny Strong moved easily among the crowd, hamming it up with the fans. Joss Whedon visited with the Bronzers he'd gotten to know over the years and was showing off pictures of his and wife Kai's new baby. Ron Glass, from *Firefly*, wandered into the room unnoticed for a few brief seconds before he was quickly swarmed by fans of that show. Sarah Hagan (Amanda on *Buffy*) was also attending her first PBP, and she looked completely overwhelmed for much of the evening. Eliza Dushku made a surprise visit, but she was losing her voice and couldn't say much to the fans. Vladimir Kulich (the Beast) arrived and towered over everyone there, and his deep, resonant voice sent chills down everyone's spines.

Andy Hallett arrived and charmed the fans before taking the stage to sing for the attendees. During his set, the "monsters" that Dayne Johnson's crew had assembled took the stage to dance, which was a surreal sight. David Denman (Skip) remembers that moment as one of the highlights of the party: "It was so much fun because they called it The Monster's Ball and they had all these guys dressed up in costume. What was so funny was when they all went out on stage to introduce the monsters, they were, like, 'We have this guy,' and everyone's, like, 'Yay,' and then this guy, and everyone's yelling. And then they said, 'And here comes Skip' and everyone just went nuts and were screaming and my wife looked at me and went, 'Are you kidding me?' That was the best thing to see — the character you're playing being a walking action figure and everyone just going crazy." The Skip demon ended up forming a congo line in the audience during Andy Hallett's next song.

One fan who traveled from Canada, Suzanne Kingshott, was thrilled by the evening. "Having always heard about these types of events but never having attended one, I was quite excited and curious to see how they really played out," she said. "I wanted to know if they could be as great as they sounded, and I found that this PBP was even more than I could have imagined. Being able to walk up to some of your favorite actors and have a conversation with them was fantastic. To see them in person took some getting used to. I remember thinking, *Do these guys really care about who we are?* and realized when Alexis Denisof made the point of addressing me, in his oh-so-charming way, by my first name (read from my name tag) that they do care. To me, there's nothing better than that kind of confirmation — that even though you only see these actors on a television in your living room in Canada, you can actually meet them in person at an event like this and have all of your expectations met and then some. It's a wonderful feeling to know that these actors so genuinely care about their fans and are so modest about their unbelievable talent (in particular Julie Benz, who was absolutely charming and stunning in person — although to even center out one cast or crew member is unfair, as they were all brilliant and incredibly accommodating). To have James Marsters pull you in closer to him for that photo you crave is like no other feeling! Seriously, though, an event like this makes you appreciate the show, actors, and crew even more — the 2003 PBP is definitely an event that I will never forget."

The VIPs seemed to enjoy themselves at the posting-board parties as much as the fans did, even if occasionally the passion of the fans could be a little surprising. "I went in 2002 and 2003, and the first time I went it was really overwhelming," says Denman. "I had no idea that people were such fans of the character and to see people so into the show, at first it's a little alarming, and then you get over it, and you go, 'Well,

Top: James Marsters goofs around with some fans and volunteers; *bottom*: Eliza Dushku and Joss Whedon, who had both been to previous posting board parties, enjoyed themselves throughout the evening.

ALBERT L. ORTEGA

ALBERT L. ORTEGA

Top: The makeup coordinators of *Buffy* and *Angel* pose with that evening's creations. Can you name all the demons? *Bottom:* Robert Hall puts the finishing touches on Skip.

look, these are the people that keep us on the air. Thank god they're here and they care this much and they're this excited.' It makes it a little less odd. One of the people who put the party together, they didn't call me the second time because they thought I was so freaked out that I wouldn't come back. I happened to be doing a show that week and everyone on the show was, like, 'You're coming to the party, right?' and I was, like, 'Uh yeah, I guess I will,' and one of the organizers said to me when I showed up, 'I can't believe you're here! I never thought you'd come back!' and I was, like, 'No, it's a lot of fun!'"

For the fans, these were nights to remember. I was there in 2003, and what struck me was how the cast and crew never acted like they were more important than anyone else there, and there didn't seem to be any of the huge rock-star egos you might have expected to find. James Marsters was funny and sweet and talked excitedly about the episodes with the fans, showing that he was as into the shows as the fans were. Alexis Denisof was a real gentleman, taking an interest in everyone he talked to. Julie Benz was as beautiful up close as she is on-screen, and she seemed to be enjoying herself very much.

The posting-board parties created memories for the fans that they'll have for a lifetime. Says Bryan Bonner, "Some of my favorite memories include being the MC for the evening and announcing the donation with the VIPs and Make-A-Wish representatives; chatting with Julie Benz and Joss Whedon; seeing non-cast like David Fury, Ben Edlund, Tim Minear, Mere Smith, Marti Noxon, and others treated like rock stars; and relaxing in the VIP area. One of my best memories is the personal phone message I got from James Marsters the day of the party asking if one of his bandmates from Ghost of the Robot could attend the party. In order to convince me he was legitimate he said, 'I'll do the voice for you' and left the rest of the message as Spike. It was great! I played it for all of my friends." Karri's favorite memories involve spending time with her fellow Bronzers. "Meeting all of the guys I worked with and getting to do something I would have never thought myself capable of was my favorite aspect of the party," she says. "When we started these things I was barely out of college — I had no experience with anything of that magnitude. Because of this party I got to meet people I would have never gotten to meet, including people from

Andy Hallett keeps the crowd entertained by belting out some great musical numbers.

my favorite shows (one of whom I have developed a great friendship with), and I got to go places I would have never thought to go."

It's a sentiment many fans felt just by watching *Buffy* and *Angel* throughout the years. But these lucky fans, they got a little something extra.

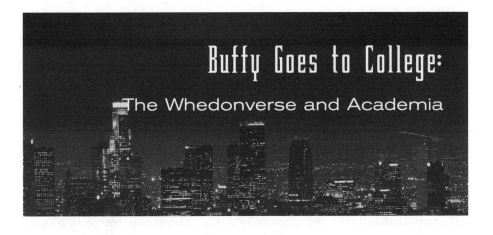

Buffy Goes to College:

The Whedonverse and Academia

Every *Buffy the Vampire Slayer* fan has had it happen. You mention that you watch a show called *Buffy the Vampire Slayer* to someone who has never seen it and you'll get one of several responses, ranging from a vacuous stare to a raised eyebrow to outright laughter. "The look" is usually followed by, "That show with the little girl running around in a short skirt?" or "Oh my *god*, isn't that a kids' show?" You smile, that thought roaming through your head — "Ah, you silly, silly person, you have no idea" — but it's hard to come across as actually sounding superior when arguing the merits of a show called *Buffy the Vampire Slayer*. You can try *The Simpsons* tactic — "Hey, saying *Buffy* is a silly kids' show is like saying *The Simpsons* is a mindless Saturday morning cartoon" — and watch their laughter turn to earnestness as they argue that *The Simpsons* is a *very serious and intelligent show*, but they probably won't be turned to your side.

Discussing *Angel* isn't any better. More often than not you'll get the confused look of someone who's never heard of it and you'll try to explain the premise: "It is a spinoff of *Buffy*, and it's about this vampire with a soul who's 250 years old and he, uh, runs a detective agency that tries to . . . stop evil and there's . . . um . . . wacky sidekicks?" But you won't get anywhere.

Now imagine being a distinguished scholar, teaching at a university, and trying to convince your colleagues that *Buffy* and *Angel* are series worth discussing in the classroom. Or writing serious scholarly papers on Spike as a Christ figure. Or devoting an entire three-day symposium to an exploration of these two series. Now *those* are the devoted and downtrodden *Buffy* fans.

Convincing scholars that *Buffy* is a serious show for academic study might not be as difficult as it sounds, however. *Buffy* viewers are intelligent people, and many fans can be found in university departments around the world. Consider the two-day symposium at the University of East Anglia in Norwich, England. From October 19 to 20, 2002, scholarly fans convened at the university for a conference entitled "Blood, Text, and Fears: Reading Around *Buffy the Vampire Slayer*." Topics such as sex and violence, language, science, and music co-existed with themes of cultural identity, vampire ecologies, and queering *Buffy* and *Angel*. Attendees were treated to such thought-provoking essays as R. Roberts's "From *Metropolis* to *Melrose Place*: Morphic Resonance in *BtVS*"; E. Rambo's "Yeats's Entropic Gyre and Season Six of *BtVS*"; M. Mills's "Meaning and Myth: Leitmotivic Procedures in the Musical Underscore to *Angel,* Season One"; and D. Amy Chinn's "Queering the Bitch: Spike, Transgression, and Erotic Empowerment."

Sophie Levy is an academic at the University of Toronto who believes *Buffy* provides endless topics and themes for intellectual discourse. "What fascinates me about *Buffy,*" she says, "is the show's fierce interest in knowledge as empowerment, which is combined with an equally fierce disdain for institutions that guard knowledge and their 'hoops . . . jumps . . . [and] interruptions.'

"*Buffy* is an extremely knowing show," she adds. "It reflects a great deal of contemporary critical theory and is able to make passing reference to cult horror films and avant-garde art movements on equal footing. This endless referentiality is a pleasure to engage with since it invites a knowing laugh from academics but also suggests that the show's creators are aware of their audience's intelligence (rare in American TV)."

Levy presented a paper at the "Blood, Text, and Fears" conference on why academics, especially feminists, are fascinated with *Buffy*: "I suggested that Buffy's own path to knowledge, through the Gothic institution of the Watcher's Council and the Hellmouth, mirrored feminist theory's understanding of its own institutional history — and that, as women in academia, we have all at one time or another felt like 'a sick girl in an institution.' *Buffy* represents this sensation of abjection as a source of strength in episode after episode, even as the show also explores our relationship with these demonic texts/grand narratives that haunt and attract us, and how/why we need to come to an understanding of this as feminist critics of pop culture and members of academia."

At the conference, Levy was impressed by the knowledge of the other scholars present and how the topic of *Buffy* kept her interested from paper to paper. "There were three lecture rooms side-by-side with connecting doors along a corridor at their rears — people would pass from room to room between papers, and it was possible to sustain a focused interest even as one moved around." Because the show has so many facets, Levy has seen it discussed in just about every subject. "I've heard people talking about the show intellectually in English, cinema studies, media studies, cultural studies, women's studies, sexual diversity studies, philosophy, theology, and even physics (although strangely, not history)."

A month after the East Anglia conference, a second *Buffy* symposium was held in Melbourne, Australia, at Melbourne University. The university's head of cinema studies, Angela Ndalianis, was the brains behind the event. She had been watching *Buffy* since it first aired. "I loved the humor," she says, "and from an academic perspective I was especially drawn to the way Whedon experimented with genre mixing (horror, soap, comedy, et cetera) and genre conventions — often thwarting our generic expectations in the process." Within 24 hours of announcing the symposium, Ndalianis received over 250 e-mails asking for details about the event, and within a week she collected over 50 submissions for papers.

The response to the event was huge, and completely unexpected by Ndalianis. "Over 500 people showed up and we had to turn people away because the venue only seated about 380 people," she explains. "Some people were crying because they couldn't get in; others were on their knees begging to get in. We also had set up a television in the foyer so that people could listen to the talks."

These days *Buffy* and *Angel* are discussed among scholars with the kind of fervor usually reserved for a heady book of literature, but for fans of either show, the seriousness with which these series have been deconstructed doesn't seem ridiculous. *Buffy* and *Angel* have long been shows that focus on complex characters and emotions, surprising plot twists, dark symbolism, and sophisticated language tropes. Their epic storytelling style has made the writers' names as common as the stars' to avid viewers, and Joss Whedon is seen as an auteur whose work is worthy of praise and study. The mythologies of both shows reached epic proportions by their respective finales, and with 254 episodes combined, there is a lot more material in these two series to analyze than one would find in any book.

Since the first episode of *Buffy* aired in March 1997, there has been serious discussion and dissection of the show's main themes and plots online. As the seasons went on, more people discovered the show, more critics wrote about its intelligence, and more scholars recognized its achievements and saw the sophisticated discussions that were taking place on the Internet.

One of those scholars was David Lavery. An English professor at Middle Tennessee State University, he was teaching a course on film history when a student approached him and asked if he'd be watching the premiere of *Buffy*'s fourth season. He responded that he didn't watch the show (he had hated the movie), but his student was so insistent that he sat down that evening and watched "The Freshman" and was pleasantly surprised by what he found.

"I think it was the very smart, very intertextual humor that first grabbed me," he says. "On all levels — the writing, the characters, the narrative, the semiotics — it seemed to me a natural for intensive study." Soon after he discovered *Buffy*, he came up with the idea of doing a book of academic essays written by various scholars, and he approached Rhonda Wilcox, a professor of English at Gordon College in Barnesville, Georgia. She had first watched *Buffy* on a whim and, like Lavery, was pleased with what she saw: "The name intrigued me. I figured that the show would be either really stupid or that *Buffy the Vampire Slayer* was the anti-stupid. Fortunately, it was the latter."

David knew Rhonda through the Popular Culture Association in the South and an essay she had written for a book on the *The X-Files* he had edited. Wilcox suggested putting out a call for papers on an academic listserv, and they suddenly got a deluge of submissions. They chose 20 to be included in their book *Fighting the Forces: What's at Stake in Buffy the Vampire Slayer* (Rowman & Littlefield, 2002), an excellent overview of the series that covers a broad range of themes, from language to mother-daughter relationships to fan relationships to the show's characters. Wilcox says it's the diversity of the show's topics that allows so many themes to be explored academically: "One of the great things is that the richness of *Buffy* means that different

scholars can see their different interests reflected, whether it's language, or references to the classics, or visual cinematic allusions, or feminist beliefs, et cetera." Lavery agrees that "whatever discipline a scholar/fan may be from, he or she seems to find *Buffy* fertile ground."

However, there was still the matter of the other essays that Wilcox and Lavery couldn't fit in the book but wanted to publish. So they came up with the idea of an online journal. *Slayage: The Online International Journal of Buffy Studies* is a quarterly online collection of academic essays relating to all things *Buffy,* and it can be found at www.slayage.tv. The idea was Lavery's, and the continuing support of the community keeps it going. "We started out with articles from people who had been (for one reason or another) taken from the book," says Wilcox. "Since then, we have received a continuing stream of submissions, which are read by board members. We often get an upsurge of submissions after an academic *Buffy* conference." Professor of Philosophy James B. South agrees that "*Slayage* . . . is the prime mover, I think, for ensuring that scholarship on *BtVS* is up to high academic standards."

The book was well received among fans and scholars. Writer Jane Espenson said she enjoyed it and even Joss Whedon's former professor at Wesleyan College told the editors that Whedon had spoken highly of the book. When asked why it is that English departments tend to gravitate to pop-culture subjects, Lavery offers, "Some people in English (though by no means all) are open-minded and ready for the challenge of a new text that challenges them. And I think some in English are just plain bored with the old subjects."

British writer Roz Kaveney found out about *Fighting the Forces* too late to get a submission in, so she decided to do her own book. Upon first discovering *Buffy*, she liked everything about it, "the wit, the romantic despair, the music, the inventiveness." Kaveney was an Oxford grad in English literature who had edited several sci-fi anthologies and contributed to the *Cambridge Companion to Women Writing in English*, as well as co-edited the *Fantasy Encyclopedia*. "I was fascinated with liminality and liminal beings, with pariah elites, with wainscot societies, with the thing bought at too dear a cost and so on. [*Buffy*] is a show that knowledgeably inhabits all these tropes — how could I not love it?"

Kaveney approached one publisher, who was interested until its youth adviser told her *Buffy* was "old hat," but the next publisher she contacted showed more interest. She rounded up some professional contacts she'd worked with in the past, then word got out she was working on the book and she received more submissions. The resulting book was *Reading the Vampire Slayer*, which is now in its second edition (Tauris Park Paperbacks, 2001 and 2004). The book is another general look at motifs of the show, from an extensive overview of the show's themes, written by Kaveney, to essays on topics ranging from feminism to identity to heterosexuality.

The book's original edition was met with favorable reviews in the press and was even reviewed in the *Times Literary Supplement.* Jane Espenson and fellow writer Steven S. DeKnight liked it and were interviewed for the second edition. The fans liked its format, its overview of the show's themes, and how it acted as a fine complement to *Fighting the Forces.*

Now that there were two general scholarly books on the market about *Buffy,* it was inevitable that the genre would branch out into specific areas. The first of these topical volumes was *Buffy the Vampire Slayer and Philosophy: Fear and Trembling in Sunnydale,* by James B. South (Open Court, 2003). The book was part of Open Court Publishing's line of popular culture and philosophy titles, and South had begun putting the manuscript together in 2001. South had first been attracted to *Buffy*'s "witty dialogue, its appealing characters, and its campy subversion of the horror genre," he says. "The first inkling I had that the show might hold more promise was watching the first-season finale. I found that episode particularly thought-provoking as I watched Buffy come to initial terms with her identity as slayer." By the second season, "the clever continuity and the deepening of the moral complexity of the Buffyverse convinced me that this show would repay continued and repeated watchings."

South is a professor of philosophy at Marquette University in Wisconsin. When South first discovered *Buffy,* he knew it was "the best example of a show that could be thoughtfully explored from a philosophical angle. And I think that popular culture more generally needs such an

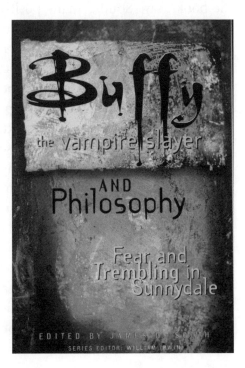

exploration, and that philosophy itself needs to remember that popular culture exists: from a purely pragmatic stand, it's the single most dominant force shaping cultural attitudes, and any philosopher who wants to do more than teach philosophy in the classroom needs to reflect deeply on their culture, including its popular elements."

Buffy the Vampire Slayer and Philosophy is a fascinating book for both scholars of philosophy and fans who want to dig much deeper into the psyches and analyses of the characters. The book is divided into five sections: Buffy, Faith, and Feminism; Knowledge, Rationality, and Science in the Buffyverse; Buffy and Ethics; Religion and Politics in the Buffyverse; and Watching Buffy. The various scholars use theories from such philosophers as Plato, Aristotle, Kant, and Nietzsche to explore these various topics, and a layreader who might not be familiar with the philosophers might come to better understand them through the Buffyverse examples used in the text.

The book was featured in *Entertainment Weekly*'s review section, and fans appreciated this more focused addition to the scholarly oeuvre of *Buffy* publications. "I've received lots of e-mails from fans who've read the book," says South, "many positive, some not so much, and a few hostile. And the sales figures for the book have been very gratifying. Having given several talks on *BtVS*, I've been struck by just how much (and how deeply) this show has affected its viewers."

For South, the philosophical aspect of the show that interests him most is the show's darkness. "For a popular TV show to routinely be as dark as *BtVS* often struck me as extraordinary," he says. "However, it also is a show that regularly discussed strategies for dealing with that darkness without pretending that any of the answers were easy or easily universalized. That is, while there are lots of interesting philosophical issues touched on by the show, the ones I'm most attracted to have to do with the way the show articulated a variety of (not always consistent) approaches to dealing with life's 'big moments.' So, while none of us may face a trio of nerds with world domination on their minds, we all face seasons of loneliness, despair, and alienation — times in which nothing seems 'real' or 'right' — and Buffy's struggle to deal with those issues is potentially illuminative for our own struggles to overcome those 'forces of darkness.'"

Soon after James B. South's book was released, another specific academic book came out: *Slayer Slang: A Buffy the Vampire Slayer Lexicon,* by Michael Adams (Oxford University Press, 2003). Adams is an English professor at Albright College in Reading, Pennsylvania, specializing in medieval and Renaissance literature and the history of English. He was an assistant on the *Middle English Dictionary* as well as a contributor to the *American Heritage Dictionary of the English Language,* Fourth Edition (2000). He has written extensively on language and lexicography and told me that

"writing about *Buffy* is part of an ongoing interest in mapping current speech and connecting it to the history of English. From my perspective, studying *Buffy* isn't self-sufficient, though certainly it could be for someone with different interests. As a consequence, I haven't taught a *Buffy* course, but I refer to slayer slang in nearly every class I teach — when language history, variation, change, innovation, or the social impetus for any of these comes up, as it invariably does, *Buffy* and its language find their way into the conversation."

Slayer Slang was the first *Buffy* academic book that was written by one person rather than being a collection of essays. Adams used his knowledge of English to explore the intriguing use of language on *Buffy* and to create an exhaustive lexicon of that language. It's perhaps the most focused of the *Buffy* academic books, and by the description it might seem that some knowledge of semiotics might be needed to understand it. However, it's actually an absorbing look at an aspect of *Buffy the Vampire Slayer* that many critics target as the single most interesting thing about the show. In the opening section, Adams uses linguistic examples from the episodes to explain how the series explores language and how he created the lexicon. The show's focus on language offered a perfect way for Adams to explain some of the more difficult concepts of semiotics in an easy-to-understand way. "*Buffy* introduced new words, and played with the processes by which words are formed, at an astonishing rate," he says, "and it also was rhetorically clever, the verbally sharpest show on television. I enjoyed both features, but chose to write about the former — *Buffy*'s rhetoric is a huge subject and would be very difficult to handle well, but lexical treatment was a reasonable project and it was, after all, words used unexpectedly that drew me to the show in the first place. I'm willing to claim, in spite of recent linguistic interest in *Seinfeld* and *Friends,* that *Buffy* is the most linguistically innovative show ever — no other show even remotely compares, for reasons articulated in *Slayer Slang*."

The book itself came about in an interesting way. While watching episodes, Adams began collecting some of the slang from the series as a hobby, but when he realized how variable and interesting the language usages were, he began looking at it from an academic position of study. In January 1999 he attended a meeting of the American Dialect Society. "At that meeting, I presented a paper titled 'Slayer Slang,'" he recalls. "As I prepared the paper, my sole ambition was to inform other language scholars about the show, its language and linguistic practices, and its relationship to mainstream English. But an astonishing number of people attended the session in which I gave the paper — they were all *Buffy* fans, drawn from the concurrent meeting of the Linguistic Society of America by the mere mention of *Buffy.* I'm only guessing, but 'Slayer Slang' may have been the first academic paper to deal with the show, so it was more of an 'event' than I had realized. At the meeting, Erin McKean, editor of *Verbatim: The Language Quarterly,* asked if she could publish an expanded version of the paper. I agreed, filled in some gaps, and it appeared in two parts in *Verbatim* later that year."

The paper created considerable discussion, and two years later, when McKean became an editor at Oxford University Press, she suggested Adams expand his findings into a full-length book, which he was fully prepared to do, having continued to collect examples of slang from the show. When the book was released in June 2003, it was reviewed in the

U.S., Canada, and England with a mostly positive reception. Scholars were amazed by Adams's research, and when I interviewed David Lavery, he referred to *Slayer Slang* as "an extraordinary piece of scholarship."

Unfortunately, several reviews said that the book's introductory chapters (which provide an overview of the show's linguistic importance as a prelude to the actual glossary) were "beyond" the fans, who wouldn't get the material. However, Adams was convinced the fans *would* understand these sections because *Buffy* aficionados are generally considered more intellectual than fans of other shows. Sure enough, the critics were proved wrong. "I wrote the book with confidence that fans would find the introductory material interesting, and reviews on Amazon, comments in blogs, et cetera, confirmed my sense that many *Buffy* fans were intellectually interested and more than capable of deciphering an academic treatment of slayer slang," Adams says. "If one takes *Buffy* as a work of literature, as a 'text' on its own terms, the rhetoric is probably *more* important than the lexicon. But, from a linguistic point of view, the stuff I write about and illustrate so amply in the glossary is more important — the rhetoric isn't affecting American speech; the lexicon and the practices by which the lexicon is formed are."

Adams recounts an amusing encounter he had with one unhappy consumer when he found a "disheartening" review of the book in a chat room. "One participant recounted that she had bought the book but was disappointed, because it didn't include her favorite items of slayer slang, such as 'Hello, salty goodness!' She didn't find the book's approach interesting or valuable, so she returned it. I clicked on her e-mail link, apologized for not writing the book she had hoped for, and explained that while I had written about words, she was interested in rhetoric, and that I hadn't set out to write the book she wanted. She wrote a friendly message in return, in the course of which she formed several new words with *-age* and *-y*. This sort of suffixation had become second nature to her, which was exactly the point of the book — speech in *Buffy* had affected mainstream speech. When she read about it in the book, she didn't view such finicky issues of word formation significant, but her e-mail confirmed their significance and proved my point, which gave me a big happy!"

As Michael Adams was moving his study of *Buffy* into a very focused

Seven Seasons of

Buffy

Science Fiction and Fantasy Writers
Discuss Their Favorite Television Show

Introduction by Drew Goddard, co-writer
"Conversations With Dead People"

Edited by Glenn Yeffeth

aspect of academia, Glenn Yeffeth was trying something a little different. A self-described "ex-corporate guy who fell in love with *Buffy* and with publishing, at roughly the same time," Yeffeth is the publisher of Benbella Books, a publishing house that creates books on various aspects of sci-fi television and movies. One of Benbella's first books was *Joss Whedon: The Genius Behind Buffy,* a book that Joss Whedon supported, even supplying the blurb, "Possibly the finest book of the century; it's exactly like *A Tale of Two Cities,* but with 30% more me." Yeffeth had read *Fighting the Forces* and *Reading the Vampire Slayer* and thought both were very good books, but he wanted to create an anthology that wasn't academic, that instead discussed *Buffy* on a level that wasn't so highbrow but was still aimed at the fans. When he was at Worldcon, an annual sci-fi convention, he found a lot of sci-fi writers who were *Buffy* fans, and he came up with the idea of a nonacademic book of essays, which was eventually titled *Seven Seasons of Buffy: Science Fiction and Fantasy Writers Discuss Their Favorite Television Show.* "*Seven Seasons* is written entirely by fanatical Buffy fans," he explains, "most of whom are professional writers, not academic. And it deals with the issues fans talk about, like who's the perfect match for Buffy, instead of issues like the Marxist dialectic in Sunnydale or some such."

Yeffeth set about finding the writers who would be perfect for his book. "We know a lot of folks in the SF community already," he says, "and we approached others. Word spread, even to the romance community, and I got an e-mail from a well-known romance writer threatening my life if she weren't allowed to contribute. Naturally, she's in the

FIVE SEASONS
OF ANGEL

Science Fiction and Fantasy Writers
Discuss Their Favorite Vampire

EDITED BY GLENN YEFFETH

anthology (and did a fantastic job)." When the book came out it was enormously popular, and fans enjoyed the fresh approach to an anthology, with writers creating smart and thoughtful essays without being academic or too lofty.

The book performed beyond Yeffeth's expectations and was such a hit that he decided doing one on *Angel* would be a no-brainer. At the time of writing, *Five Seasons of Angel: Science Fiction and Fantasy Writers Discuss Their Favorite Vampire* is scheduled for publication in fall 2004, and Yeffeth says it's at least as strong as its predecessor. It follows the same approach as *Seven Seasons of Buffy* — talking about *Angel* from the perspective of fans and insiders, with essays ranging from one on Angelus as a metaphor for the high-school bully to Dan Kerns's very funny look at what it's like being the head lighting director on the set of *Angel*.

Following Yeffeth's example, Jana Riess wrote a book on the spirituality of *Buffy* without the lofty academic speak. Its publication has started opening some eyes to an important theme in the series. When it comes to *Buffy* and *Angel*, you can always count on one thing: somewhere there's a member of a parents' organization or religious group watching the episodes, madly taking notes to prove that these two shows represent everything that is wrong with television. As I point out on page 303 of *Bite Me!* the Parents Television Council has had both shows on its hit list for years, and it probably will continue to target them long after they have gone into syndication. Of course, most groups that deride the show have no idea what it's actually about, don't watch it regularly, and have tuned in to one episode and assume they can speak about the shows authoritatively. They often point out that Joss Whedon has declared himself an atheist, taking that as proof the show has no morality. They object to its depictions of violence or sex, arguing that it celebrates darkness in the world and in humanity.

The problem is, they're missing the bigger picture. They're not noticing that it's the symbols of Christianity that actually stop the vampires from hurting people, that the main theme of *Angel* is redemption, and that *Buffy* is about finding oneself and helping to vanquish evil. Willow might be a Wiccan, but she's also Jewish. Xander is an Episcopalian. Riley attended church faithfully. Drusilla (before she went mad) was going to become a nun. Angel has a "thing" for convents. *Buffy* and *Angel* are actually very religious programs, when watched on a certain level, where good triumphs over evil and everyone must learn to fight the evil within. There are several hell dimensions and at least one heaven (where Buffy existed for a short time between seasons 5 and 6). The shows boast several clergypersons as fans.

Jana Riess had noticed all these things and more. "At first the humor and the clever writing drew me in," she says, "and then I became involved with the characters. Only then was I ready to consider some of the weighty ethical issues that are dissected in the show. I think this suggests something important about good fiction: it must succeed first as story before it can undertake a point of view. On *Buffy,* serious issues are handled thoughtfully and provocatively, but I never feel bludgeoned by The Message." Riess has two master's degrees and a doctorate in religion but left the academic world to become the full-time religion book review editor at *Publisher's Weekly.*

"I had an epiphany one day when I realized that some of the most interesting conversations that I had with friends and colleagues about ethics and spirituality began as conversations about *Buffy* episodes," she says. The idea for a book on the element of spirituality in *Buffy* began to take shape in her mind, and she found a publisher. The resulting book was *What Would Buffy Do?: The Vampire Slayer as Spiritual Guide* (Jossey-Bass, 2004), a lighthearted and fascinating book on Buffy as a "savior in a micro-mini." Riess explores personal spirituality through self-sacrifice, change, death, anger, and humor; companionship through friendship, mentors, and forgiveness; and saving the world and its consequences, conquering darkness within ourselves, and personal redemption. "I am fascinated by the theme of self-sacrifice in both shows," she explains, "and in the concept of a heroism that emerges from self-denial . . . I see relationship and accountability at the heart of the series. Many of the spiritual themes of the series are grounded in relationship: forgiveness, change, mentoring, and the power of friendship.

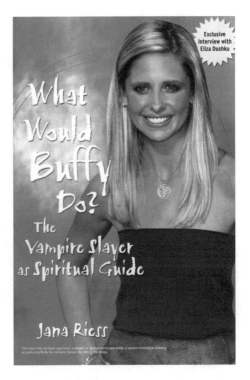

"I'm also very interested in redemption. Obviously, several of the characters on these shows have committed atrocities that most of us will never have to think about. Spike and Angel in particular struggle constantly with the need for redemption. The shows adopt an almost karmic sensibility, where evil can be blotted out only by the good that is performed to erase it. In one scene Angel essentially tells Faith that her good acts may never balance out her evil ones in the cosmic scale, but that she has to try. No matter what, he says, she will still be haunted. I find this a realistic accounting of the road to redemption, despite my personal Christian faith."

Although Riess is an academic, she had to change the tone of her book so it would fit her publisher's Religion in Practice series. "I had to work hard at writing for a popular audience and not an academic one. It helped when we started framing it in terms of Xander's question: 'What would Buffy do?' That helped me articulate some of the other questions I wanted to explore: What can we learn from the knowledge that we are going to die? How can we possibly forgive the unforgivable? Why is humor so necessary?"

The book had only been out for a couple of weeks when I interviewed Riess, but she was already getting reaction from readers.

Aforementioned academics David Lavery, Rhonda Wilcox, Michael Adams, and James B. South provided praise for the back cover of her book, as had Nancy Holder, the author of the *Watcher's Guide* books. Riess interviewed Eliza Dushku, who had read two of the sample chapters and said she enjoyed them and passed them on to Douglas Petrie, who had been the co-executive producer of *Buffy* and was working as a writer on *Tru Calling* at the time. Most rewarding for Riess has been the response of people whose views have been altered by reading her tome: "Religious people who might have dismissed *Buffy* have told me they are taking a second look and wondering what they might have missed about it. And *Buffy* fans have been writing to tell me that the book pointed out some elements and connections that they had not noticed before. This is what I hoped would happen." When I spoke to David Lavery, he referred to *What Would Buffy Do?* as "beautifully written and incredibly smart" and had put it on his course syllabus.

Heady discussions of these shows isn't reserved for academics, however. What fans and scholars love so much about *Buffy* and *Angel* (and what ultimately causes most of the arguments and divisiveness among fans) is that so little of the show is black and white. The shows' gray areas are what keep fans discussing the multiple layers and engaging in lively debates on what the characters are about or what the scenes represent. But it's this ambiguity that makes the show so interesting. Some fans believe Buffy belongs with Angel; others say with absolute certainty that she loves Spike. Some believe that Connor is an impetuous child; others believe he's been deeply wronged and has every right to be as angry as he is. Some believe Spike tried to rape Buffy; others say he never would have gone any further than he did. Some say that Tara's death was necessary for Willow's story arc to play out; some say it was completely unnecessary and Tara never should have died.

For most fans of the show, these discussions/arguments can be carried out in person with friends or online with other devotees. Both shows are known for their active online communities, and for those who can't make it to an academic symposium on *Buffy*, they can have deliberations that are just as stimulating in the comfort of their own homes. "My guess is that *Buffy* happened to be the show that was current at the point when Internet discussion became a viable option," says Roz Kaveney. "I don't think this is more than synchronicity, but that synchronicity is certainly a fact of interest in itself." Michael Adams praises the online communities: "The posting board discussions of *Buffy*, especially at the Bronze and Bronze Beta, but elsewhere as well, were often very intelligent and informed. Sure, there was plenty of drivel and plenty of chat that supported board culture and indulged fandom; but much of the serious, sustained commentary on the show was really valuable.

"In short, if so many people are talking so intelligently on the Internet about a television show or anything else, whatever it is warrants academic attention."

Among the academics, the same disagreements and different viewpoints prevail. Depending on the particular area of study, one scholar will view, or "read," the shows differently and will have different sympathies for characters than other scholars. One of the most telling questions I asked each of the academics was which of the characters provides the most discourse among scholars and which is most important for academic study. As Kaveney points out, "Almost any major character in the shows repays study — if some have been more discussed than others, it is because they are closer to the mindset of people who do the discussing. Thus, there is possibly more discussion of Willow than of Cordelia, and certainly not enough discussion of the show's evil women." Sophie Levy agrees, saying, "I think scholars with different subject positions find themselves identifying with, or against, different characters (most academics endured Willow- or Xander-like experiences at school, and now we're all Giles. Or Jenny, if we're cool)."

Each of the academics chose their favorite characters based on how much they've been able to study them within their area of research or how much they identified with the character. David Lavery and Rhonda Wilcox, who have studied various aspects of both shows, took a generalized view of the characters.

"Buffy herself has, of course, provoked great interest, as has Angel," says Lavery. "Willow is getting more and more attention. Spike, of course, has inspired the most attention. We need much more consideration of many characters: Giles, Xander, Cordelia, Wesley, Anya,

Andrew, Faith." Wilcox supports Lavery's assessment: "Can you spell S-P-I-K-E? And Willow, and always Buffy herself. . . . Many other characters could use further study. Well, of course, we're certainly not done with those three yet by a long shot either. I found my way in emotionally through Willow, but I came to really relate to Buffy, too. She just works so darn hard, keeps having to deal with so much — and that I think a lot of us can identify with."

James B. South, who looks at the characters from a philosophical perspective, has a different viewpoint: "The characters I've always found most compelling are the title characters: Buffy and Angel (not in the Buffy *and* Angel sense) simply because they are the characters around whom all the stories revolve and because their stories (Buffy's growth, Angel's recognition that nothing he does is ever enough) are the ones I find resonant with the perennial philosophical issues that most interest me." Michael Adams chose the character who has the best way with language: "Buffy is the leader when it comes to deep study, without a doubt. She's the most interesting character, the character who carries the most bona fide conflict, and she is the most complex character, I think, by far. . . . She is the best with language, among other things. She sets the standard and defines the terms, over and over again. She's incredibly normal and incredibly not. She is a character of great humor and great pathos, and both are evidently in her all of the time, as they are in anyone who lives fully. Buffy defends herself with flippancy and cleverness — she is fundamentally earnest, not an easy thing to be in life, let alone on television. She's the only character on television that I have ever admired."

Jana Riess, whose study focuses on spirituality and religion, chose the characters who have probably sacrificed the most: "On *Angel*, I most identify with Wesley, and I wish I'd been able to do more with him in my book. On *Buffy*, the character that fascinates me most is Buffy herself. I wish I could be more like her."

The academic books, symposia, and online discussions are only the tip of the scholarly iceberg. *Buffy*-related discourse has found its way into university classrooms, and even elementary and secondary schoolteachers are using *Buffy* as a teaching tool. David Lavery offered a summer English course specifically on *Buffy* at Middle Tennessee State University from

May 17 to June 4, 2004. In the first week, each day was devoted to a different season of *Buffy.* Next, the students attended the "Slayage" conference in Nashville, Tennessee, and the final week was used to look at *Buffy*-related topics, such as intertextuality, religion, the Watcher's Council, lesbianism on television, dreams, Buffyspeak, and many others. The two texts for the course were *Fighting the Forces* and *What Would Buffy Do?* (see sidebar for the detailed course agenda). Lavery points to similar *Buffy* courses at the University of Arizona, Birmingham Southern, Ursinus, UNC Chapel Hill, and many others around the world.

Agenda for Dr. Lavery's *Buffy* course

Meeting 1 Monday, 5/17: The Buffyverse; Clips from *Buffy the Vampire Slayer*: The Movie; *Screening of* A&E Biography: Buffy the Vampire Slayer; *"Previously on* Buffy the Vampire Slayer*" (from the 100th episode); "Designing* Buffy*"; "A* Buffy *Beastiary"; "Special Effects"*

Meeting 2 Tuesday, 5/18: *BtVS,* Season One; Read all of Riess, Appendix B: Who's Who in *Buffy;* Season One in Riess, Appendix A: A Guide to *Buffy*'s Seven Seasons; Interview with Joss Whedon on "Welcome to the Hellmouth" and "The Harvest"; Season One DVD Trailer; Clips from the Unreleased Pilot, "Welcome to the Hellmouth," "Never Kill a Boy on the First Date," "Angel," "Nightmares"; Screening of "Prophecy Girl"

Meeting 3 Wednesday, 5/19: *BtVS,* Season Two; Season Two in Riess, Appendix A: A Guide to *Buffy*'s Seven Seasons; Clips from "School Hard," "Halloween," "Lie to Me," "Surprise," "Innocence," "Passion"; Screening of "Becoming" (Parts One and Two)

Meeting 4 Thursday, 5/20: *BtVS,* Season Three; Season Three in Riess, Appendix A: A Guide to *Buffy*'s Seven Seasons; Clips from "Faith, Hope, and Trick," "Band Candy," "Lovers Walk," "The Zeppo," "Earshot," "The Prom," "Graduation Day" (Parts One and Two); Screening of "The Wish"

Meeting 5 Friday, 5/21: *BtVS,* Season Four; Season Four in Riess, Appendix A: A Guide to *Buffy*'s Seven Seasons; Clips from "The Freshman," "Pangs," "Hush," "Superstar," "The Yoko Factor," "Primeval"; Screening of "Restless"

Meeting 6 Monday, 5/24: *BtVS,* Season Five; Season Five in Riess, Appendix A: A Guide to *Buffy*'s Seven Seasons; Clips from "Buffy vs.

Dracula," "Fool for Love," "Family," "Checkpoint," "Spiral," "The Gift";
Screening of "The Body"; Final Exam Available

Meeting 7 Tuesday, 5/25: *BtVS,* Season Six; Season Six in Riess,
Appendix A: A Guide to *Buffy*'s Seven Seasons; Clips from "Smashed,"
"Wrecked," "Tabula Rasa," "Normal Again," "Seeing Red," "Villains," "Two to
Go," "Grave"; Screening of "Once More, with Feeling"

Meeting 8 Wednesday, 5/26: *BtVS*, Season Seven; Season Seven in
Riess, Appendix A: A Guide to *Buffy*'s Seven Seasons; Clips from
"Lessons," "Conversations with Dead People," "Bring On the Night,"
"Show Time," "Get It Done," "Storyteller," "Lies My Parents Told Me," "Dirty
Girls," "Empty Places," "End of Days"; Screening of "Chosen"

Meeting 9 Friday, 5/28: No Class; The *Slayage* Conference on *Buffy the
Vampire Slayer*

Meeting 10 Saturday, 5/29: No Class; The *Slayage* Conference on *Buffy
the Vampire Slayer*

Meeting 11 Tuesday, 6/1: Forces of Society and Culture: Gender,
Generations, Violence, Class, Race, and Religion; Critical Essay Due

Meeting 12 Wednesday, 6/2: Forces of Art and Imagination (Past):
Vampires, Magic, and Monsters; Journal Due

Meeting 13 Thursday, 6/3: Forces of Art and Imagination (Present): Fan
Relationships, Metaphoric and Real

Meeting 14 Friday, 6/4: The Future of the Buffyverse; Final Exam Due

Course Requirements

Critical Essay: A critical/interpretative essay of at least 1,500 words on
some aspect of *BtVS;* Due: 6/1; 25% of Grade

A Journal: An informal account of your attendance at the *Slayage*
Conference. I will expect at least 100 words on each of 10 different
papers you heard at the conference. Due: 6/3; 25% of Grade

Final Exam: A take-home exam consisting of a menu of essay topics, from
which you will select two, responding with essay answers. These topics will
all be "leading questions," intended to inspire your own comprehensive syn-
thesis of course ideas, questions, problems. You will have almost two weeks
to complete this assignment. Distributed: 5/24; Due: 6/4; 25% of Grade

Class Participation: Active engagement in daily discussion and attendance at the conference; 25% of Grade

A teacher doesn't have to create an entire course about *Buffy* to use the show in the classroom, however. Lisa LoCicero, a Spanish teacher at Greenhills School in Ann Arbor, Michigan, uses *Buffy* to help her students learn Spanish and gives presentations to other teachers about how they can integrate *Buffy* studies into the classroom to teach their students. One of her students introduced her to *Buffy* when the show was in its second season, saying, "The writing is *so* good, señora!" She respected her student's opinion, and the next night she tuned in to watch "Innocence." It grabbed her immediately: "I knew it was different and pedagogically useful from the get-go and started referencing it immediately in my classroom. . . . I spent part of each class the following Wednesday on the subject as I determined who did and didn't watch the show regularly, and what they had to say about it. This is valuable from a pedagogical standpoint because all discussion is in Spanish, and the exercise also serves as a review of both past tense and historical present narration, as well as providing an [opportunity] to acquire useful, interesting, and sometimes eccentric ancillary vocabulary."

Bringing a show like *Buffy* into the classroom — a show that appeals to younger people while still providing the opportunity for deeper analysis — allows the teacher the opportunity to explain difficult and abstract concepts by using events on *Buffy* as examples. LoCicero mentions another educator at Greenhills, chemistry teacher Cathy Renaud, who uses *Buffy* to teach the concept of a double-replacement reaction, in which parts of the compounds switch to create two new compounds (Fred would be so pleased!). "As she explains it, the characters each represent a chemical compound," says LoCicero. "As it should be, Buffy is together with Spike, and Cordelia is with Angel. However, once they get together and have a chemical reaction, presto-chango! The compounds have switched around and have changed both their partners and forms. Now, Buffy and Angel are together, and Spike and Cordelia."

For language teachers, just discussing the shows in a second language is a useful teaching device. One exercise LoCicero uses is to show an episode of *Buffy* and have her students create the dialogue that would go with the episode (not a translation of the English, but a rewriting of it). Another is to show them dream sequences from "Restless" and have them write in Spanish "how what they see reflects their understanding of our collective definition of what constitutes oneiricism [similar to surrealism]."

Sue Turnbull is a media professor at La Trobe University in Australia who has actually published a guide to teaching *Buffy* in the secondary-school classroom. Co-written with Vyvyan Stranieri, the guide is called *Bite Me: Narrative Structures and Buffy the Vampire Slayer,* and it is published by the Australian Centre for the Moving Image (copies can be purchased at www.acmi.net.au). The book was written specifically for a media studies course in Victoria, Australia, but could be applied to any course that studies *Buffy* or *Angel* as narrative texts. "Vyv and I both loved the show from the start — and thought it might be perfect classroom study material in terms of its stylistic and narrative complexity," says Turnbull.

James B. South has used *Buffy* in his university philosophy classes. "I haven't taught a course on *Buffy* (though I am going to do so in fall 2004), but I have used episodes in class to illustrate various philosophical issues," he says. "'The Wish' is a good discussion starter for exploring the idea of multiple natures within us; 'Anne,' with its evocation of an old-time proletarian hero, is great for talking about exploitation and alienation in work (as is 'Doublemeat Palace'); and 'Selfless' is nice for illustrating how difficult it is to forge an identity." Sophie Levy agrees that *Buffy* is useful in the university classroom: "As a politically engaged teacher, I am interested in students' pop-culture experience/knowledge of pedagogy and education — *Buffy* is a prime site for studying this, because it is so diverse in its representations of teaching and learning, and particularly strong in endorsing education and knowledge as empowering for women if/when they pursue it on their own terms."

Levy points to *Buffy* itself as containing examples of unorthodox learning: "Buffy's relationship with Giles is a pedagogical paradigm — even when she comes to him in 'Buffy vs. Dracula' and asks him to teach her about her history, that decision is made and pursued as an 'independent study,' as it were, with Dawn as a case study whose differences allow Buffy to explore her own powers. *Buffy* encourages postmodern learning (watching TV for credit, for example; or defending your thesis on Rasputin's alternate history; or learning witchcraft!), and it presents intellectual ability in a positive light — not least through its amazing range of linguistic registers, and its verging-on-radical gender and sexual politics."

With shows such as *Buffy* being used in the classroom, students not only find an alternate way in to a subject but learn to watch television shows actively rather than passively. They learn to read what they see on television as an actual text, which helps their analytical skills at an earlier age. As LoCicero puts it, "I love my job, I love my kids, I love my subject, and I love intelligent television. It took me a little while to figure out that I really could bring them all together."

Now that *Buffy* and *Angel* have ended, a question remains: Will the scholarship continue, or will it die out as new shows garner interest? Before, scholars could only speculate about what would be the ultimate fate of the characters, but now they have closed texts for both shows, and to some that means the scholarship can now truly begin. "It definitely makes a difference to scholarship that the show is now a complete work," says Adams. "Naturally, I think of the language first. I can study the show now as a 'closed corpus,' which allows me to argue differently, because, for any linguistic feature, I can consider every relevant example. One area I haven't gone into much yet is what linguists call 'stylistics,' the role of language in a particular literary text, and I couldn't really until the show was finished, because conclusions about how a character speaks (or how one character's speech influences that of the others), for instance, will differ depending on how much of the show one considers. And I think the same would be true of much inquiry into the show. What *Buffy* has to say about death, life, love, purpose, will, responsibility — you name it — can't really be estimated without considering the whole series. I guess you could say that all topics worth pursuing are 'bigger' in the context of the whole show."

South agrees: "I do think that with the end of the shows certain types of scholars will be in a position to see the themes more clearly and completely (those who work from a literary and philosophical perspective, for example). At the same time, I suspect that scholars of the sociology of fandom will be working on an ongoing series of projects as *BtVS/Angel* fandom evolves without new canon stories. Of course, fan fiction, fan videos, and the like will continue to be made and will be worth discussing, but perhaps not by philosophers. I also expect a bit of a backlash, since much of the scholarship to date has been on the mostly laudatory side, but the shows were hardly perfect and it will be interesting to see just how they hold up under continued scrutiny."

On May 28 and 29, 2004, the largest *Buffy* academic conference yet converged in Nashville, Tennessee. Presented and organized by David Lavery and Rhonda Wilcox, the conference boasted over 200 presenters and attracted over 350 scholars from around the world. David Lavery called it a resounding success, and Rhonda Wilcox says it was a joy: "Being able to discuss our thoughts on this artwork we love without having to explain the basics — we all loved that. I heard repeatedly that there was a very high proportion of excellent papers in comparison with the standard academic conference. People also repeatedly said that the discussions afterward were as wonderful and productive as the papers." Lisa LoCicero laughs while admitting that she lived on fruit and Slim-Fast bars so she wouldn't miss anything: "The keynotes I attended were phenomenal — the presenters all extremely approachable. I had great conversations with scholars from all sorts of different academic fields. I talked *Buffy* in the whirlpool with a musicologist and a religion scholar. . . . And not since graduate school have I been around so many Ph.D.s. Really, it was a fantastic experience."

For Michael Adams, the most important aspect of the conference was that the scholars were all discussing something they loved, and they weren't ashamed to hide it. "David Lavery's paper at the conference included a quotation from J. Hillis Miller about how we naturally study best what we love," he says. "Thus, while mindless, fannish response to the show is out, there's no reason for those studying *Buffy* not to love the show — indeed, there's every reason for genuine appreciation to guide critical and scholarly response to the show, as much as it does one's reading of Shakespeare, Dickens, or anything else simultaneously worth loving and writing about." *Slayer Slang* was awarded the Mr. Pointy Award for the Best Book in *Buffy* studies. "The statuette is obscene," Adams laughs.

Jana Riess launched *What Would Buffy Do?* at the conference, and the response was so overwhelming that her publisher had to rush more copies to the hotel the following day. She was thrilled with the conference. "The level of discourse was very high, but there was no posturing or pretense," she says. "It was obvious that the scholars who came (some at great expense or from a great distance) were there because they love the show, but they did not suspend their critical faculties just because they were also fans. I was particularly impressed by the amazing number of disciplines represented. There were the expected ones, like English literature, film studies, folklore, and religion, but also many other disciplines, like musicology, technology, linguistics, and psychology. I think that the participants learned a great deal from each other, as everyone brought their particular expertise to bear on the Buffyverse. I hope we can do it again."

It's clear that *Buffy* and *Angel* fandom, and particularly Buffyverse scholarship, shows no signs of waning. There are already more academic books in the works (Wilcox is working on a volume of her own, which will show readers that *Buffy* is indeed art and should be studied as such). Some day both series may be seen as pioneers, in that serious academic work was produced from seemingly mainstream pieces of pop culture. "One of the exciting things about *Buffy* is that it invites conversation among many different kinds of viewers, from ivory tower to armchair experts," says Adams. "Each can offer something valuable and each can learn a lot from listening to the others."

When I talked to David Fury a year ago, just as *Buffy* was coming to an end, he marveled at the impact the show had had on the academic community. "I couldn't speak for Joss, but we think it's amazing and cool and it's kind of neat to find a book on a bookshelf and find the stuff you wrote quoted in there. It's amazing. Nobody sets out to be a cultural phenomenon; I can't imagine that Joss ever imagined that it would be that, but he's enormously gratified that it has, that what he set out to do has been recognized by the intelligentsia, and it's very rewarding for us. It feels really good to know we're respected like that."

I asked Jane Espenson, who has always been a big supporter of the scholarly research on *Buffy*, if she would comment on what it has meant to her and why she thinks the phenomenon happened in the first place. "I'm floored and thrilled that something I was involved in has received this kind of attention from the academic world," she responded. "I think it's a huge tribute to the deep emotional and societal forces that Joss tapped into when he created this world and the amazing characters who people it. He never allowed the writers to tell a story because it was simply interesting to us; he required that it be *about something.* Anything else he dismissed as being 'just moves.' Every story had to have meaning and emotional resonance or he wasn't interested. It's this integrity of purpose that makes the show worthy of study, I believe. Most works executed by large groups of people don't have a singular enough point of view to allow meaningful study. Joss Whedon gave us that point of view. Thank goodness he actually had something to say."

CityofAngel.com:
The Ultimate *Angel* Site

In the world of Web sites devoted to television shows, two words help fans sift through the volume of online material: *official* and *unofficial*. The official sites usually contain very few bells and whistles, are more informative than fun, contain official messages or interviews with the celebrities, and are sanctioned by the people or the networks they represent. The unofficial sites, or fan sites, have more pages and downloads, feature more detailed and specific analyses of the show, and usually are more up-to-date, but the fans who run them have little to no access to the people on the show.

In the case of *Angel,* one site has been able to break down the barrier. While the WB owned the page that could be considered the official *Angel* site, it was inadequate for diehard fans of the show — it had interviews that were taken down once new ones went up and was only a link off the main WB network home page. There is another site that fans consider the "official unofficial" *Angel* site: CityofAngel.com.

The site was created by Midwest-based Virginia Obeius when the Web designer, who was a big fan of *Buffy the Vampire Slayer,* wanted to create a Web site that would emulate the darker side of the show and be different than the sites she had been designing for her clients. Unfortunately, there was a plethora of *Buffy* sites out there, and by the show's fourth season it would have been difficult to step in and contribute something new and unique to the online *Buffy* community. But then *Angel* came along, and after Obeius saw the episode "Rm w/ a Vu," she was convinced that it was going to be a great show. "I originally tried to get Fox to let me design the 'official' site," she explains. "But since that turned out to be a dead end, I decided to make a site that was 'better' than usual official sites — one that was driven by people with a true passion for the show and not limited to 'design by committee' and red tape. That said, we determined early on to always endeavor to show respect to the rules set forth by Fox and the desires of Joss and Company."

Virginia wanted to design the site but not write it, so for those duties she recruited fellow Bronzer Kristy Bratton. Along with a few other Bronzer volunteers, Virginia and Kristy were able to prepare enough material to get the site off the ground. CityofAngel.com began with character and episode guides, an image gallery, and a Flash intro, and these features are still the key elements of the site. The staff decided to revamp (no pun intended) the site's design every year for the first three years, refining the style and format. As time went on and the site began getting more visitors, new elements were added, making the site the delightful maze it is today.

Kristy Bratton, who lives in New York, explains that early on, the staff wanted to provide a behind-the-scenes glimpse of the show that other sites hadn't been able to. "Being a fledgling Web site with no knowledge of what we could or could not do — other than copyright infringements — we believed, 'Just ask until we were told no.' So, the most important thing to me was giving the fans something they'd never gotten before: a true, ongoing 'behind-the-scenes' look at the creators of the *Angel* series. We all see the actors, and most fans know the names of the writers and of course Joss Whedon, but there are so many more people behind the helm. Our very first feature interview was with *Buffy* novelist (and *Angel* comic-book writer) Christopher Golden; he was so kind and supportive and really opened the door for us. We owe him a lot! Then we approached the *Angel* comics that Dark Horse was doing at the time and interviewed artist Christian Zanier, followed by special effects makeup artist John Vulich of Optic Nerve and the special visual effects of Loni Peristere at Digital Magic (now Radium). No one told us 'No.'" Since then, the CoA staff has interviewed people such as Joss

Whedon, Elisabeth Röhm, J. August Richards, David Greenwalt, Julie Benz, Tim Minear, Amy Acker, and many more.

The question is, why didn't the WB shut them down? In the early days, Virginia approached the people at Fox and the WB with press material and asked for "official" status, but the networks refused to give it, saying they weren't interested in doing official sites after the *Buffy* one had taken so much time and money to keep up. Undeterred, she continued to send them materials to keep them updated on what CoA was up to, and perhaps it was this honesty that made the WB leave the site alone. As Kristy puts it, "They were shutting *Buffy* fan sites down right and left then and we figured they'd get around to us, but they never did. On a positive note, and not to sound boastful, but the quality in which we presented the site and maintained it without crossing too many of those boundaries was a PR opportunity dream for them. We did all the work, offered a great site to the fans, and it didn't cost them a thing."

Virginia agrees and adds, "It's a mutually beneficial relationship. There have even been a couple occasions where VIPs have told us that they found our site invaluable in finding out more about the show. How cool is that? Plus, they'll send us things to post or give away on the site every once in a while. Our visitors love it and it makes us feel that much more validated for all the hard work we put in. Of course, it makes us all wish we didn't have a 'no staff' rule on the contest entries!"

The volunteers involved in CoA first realized they were considered legitimate when they were acknowledged by none other than Joss Whedon himself. Virginia posted a message on the Bronze posting board one night when Joss was on, asking him if he was aware of CityofAngel.com, and he replied that he had seen the site and thought it was good. She and the others involved in the site were ecstatic. "Everyone on the series has been a huge support to CoA," says Kristy. "Every interview, whether it be Amy Acker (Fred) or Ian Woolf (assistant director), every request, from demon makeup applications for the Posting Board Parties by Robert Hall (Almost Human, a movie makeup company) and Dayne Johnson (*Angel* makeup artist) to auction item requests of the production assistants — all have been gracious, generous, and accommodating above and beyond for the site! I think some of the biggest support has come from David Greenwalt, who gave us use of his original songs written for *Angel,* and Rob Kral (*Angel* musical composer), who gave us a few of his original scores as well to use on our CoA media player. Dayne provided us with unique continuity photos of the demons, which helped us create the Beastiary."

Kristy adds that the writers and production crew have been especially supportive of the site: "They've told us on many an occasion that if it were up to them, we'd be the official site. That's a very nice compliment."

Virginia and Kristy traveled to DragonCon in August 2000 and interviewed Jane Espenson and Tim Minear, who gave them their first promos. Today, the promos, or "greetings," that welcome visitors to CoA are a favorite among visitors to the site. When you log on, you'll be welcomed to the site by an *Angel* VIP. The idea came to Kristy when she was on her way to DragonCon, but she says, "we never thought we could pull it off and we certainly never thought it would become this huge." There are about 50 different greetings on the site, and you never know which one will pop up when you arrive (keep clicking on the VIP link to listen to more). Each VIP will state his or her name, welcome you to the site, and then add a tagline about *Angel.* Kristy explains how the tagline idea happened: "That was the genius of Tim Minear. He did our very first promo and actually rewrote it, having that writer's prerogative I assume! It actually began, 'Hello, I'm . . .' but he insisted that 'Hi' was an easier lead-in to the name, whereas 'Hello' made you pause. Who was I to argue? And then he completely ad-libbed his tagline: 'Angel, he's Angelicious!' Jane Espenson followed his lead and the competition began! Each VIP tried to outwit the other, although not everyone could come up with a clever tagline on the spot." Some of the best ones include Julie Benz saying, "Angel: Hmm, bite me!"; Clare Kramer (Glory on *Buffy*), saying, "Angel? I've already sucked his brains!"; and Joss Whedon's "Angel: seventy percent more interesting than soap."

I asked Kristy if she could provide a mini "walking" tour of the site for readers who haven't yet checked it out, and she did, in a lighthearted style that is typical of the writing you'll find on the site.

"Let's take a stroll, shall we? We begin on the home page, which offers a quick overview as to what's new in the City. But this is also a fun page not to be so quickly passed through; the header image changes with some memorable moments of the series, and if you pass your cursor between Angel and Spike, the images fade in and out. If you listen closely you'll hear water droplets in the tunnel and Angel's footfall. Then, of course, the mystery VIP greetings! In the behind-the-scenes column, we regularly change the photo, typically showing Joss in action on set.

"News Page: Here's where you'll first find recent news about the series on the Web, followed by our own exclusive features and any upcoming events around the world where cast and crew may be appearing. Plus, there is an invaluable link on the sidebar to the article archive of every interview feature we've done at CoA.

"Episodes: We have a complete guide to all five seasons that includes a main-page twenty-two-episode listing to each season; each episode links to a complete episode summary (broken down into acts and scenes) and an editorial review complete with a rating and rounded off by the episode's quotation highlights.

"Characters: Although this has just a character heading, it's a pretty meaty section of the site. It contains bios for all the main characters (including their actor counterparts), seasonal breakdown of featured supporting characters, a Wolfram & Hart section, the Beastiary, and an interactive pre-*Angel* timeline. We have to stop a minute here because the Beastiary is incredible and the timeline is pretty unique. First, the Beastiary is the ultimate demon database; Wesley would have killed for this. You can select a demon by species or name, from a Drokken demon to an Archduke Sebassis, or click on the icon image. You'll then be privy to a bio and a graphic composition that kicks ass thanks to Virginia and Dayne Johnson! Currently there are eighty-one demons logged.

"The timeline is probably the only remaining element of the original site. A moving timeline takes you through all the events of Angel's life in Sunnydale leading to Los Angeles. The top of the bar scrolls you across the seasons (*Buffy* 1–3 and *Angel* 1) while the bottom plots each episode. Click on an episode and a 'key moment' of that episode appears along with a quote, sound bite, and photo image. It's a pretty cool graphic accomplishment and one Virginia is still proud of.

"Gallery: It's just that — a huge gallery of recent photos of the cast, crew, and featured events for fans to look at. Each event CoA has covered or been a part of (for example, the Buffy Posting Board Party) has dozens of great shots of all the VIPs who attended.

"Forums: Certainly the most popular section for the fans, CoA boasts three separate forums for fans to gather, meet, and talk about *Angel* (and *Buffy*); a help desk (where the CoA staff can answer questions); an *Angel*-specific forum; and the Insane Asylum, where anything can and does happen.

"The Underground: This is the newest addition to the site, the only element we added this season. It's just a little place for the fans to go and play that is less formal than the rest of the site. It also houses the CoA media player — where fans can listen to exclusive music tracks like David Greenwalt's 'L.A.,' sung by Christian Kane in the episode 'Dead End' — e-cards, banners, and backgrounds. There are polls and the staff's own episode stakes-ratings board.

"Store: This started out as a place to review tie-in merchandise such as the *Angel* comics and novels, but it quickly evolved into a full-blown merchandise listing. We don't sell anything here; we just provide product information and links for fans. Though we do have a line of CoA T-shirts and other items, just in case fans like us, too.

"Credits: Probably the most important and least viewed [section] of the site, but you have to give credit where it is due. Here you'll find bios on both Joss Whedon and David Greenwalt, a comprehensive crew listing, and, finally, a list of the CoA staff with responsibilities and e-mail addresses.

"And that concludes our tour! Thank you for visiting and please remember to stop by our gift shop and purchase a little demon plushy for your spawn. (Just kidding — we don't have plushies.)"

CityofAngel.com has grown to a staff of 15 unpaid volunteers (Virginia, Kristy, Lilian Holden, Jeff Ritchie, Tara DiLullo, Susan Smith, Julie Reynolds, Hollie Edmond, Sue Grimshaw, Nicola Jones, Sarah Wallis, Devon Weller, Chad Olson, Michael Conrad, and Krista DeRoo) and over 100,000 registered members. There are staff members in every time zone of the U.S. and also in the U.K. and Belgium. They've never actually all been in one room at the same time, but they're hoping to be able to one day. *Angel* viewers have been very supportive of the site, and one of the best aspects of working at CoA is the feedback the staff gets from the fans. "I'm always surprised and pleased when someone (at a convention) recognizes my staff badge or T-shirt and tells me how much they enjoy the site," says Virginia. "It just makes you feel good knowing that you've helped people from countries all over the world come together to share their common interest." Maintaining CityofAngel.com takes a lot of time, and the staff pays for its upkeep out of their own pockets and has no sponsorships or advertising, so it's the fan support that keeps them going. "CoA is a huge undertaking and many a time we've all wanted to hang it up, it's just too much work," says Kristy. "But then we'd get this amazing e-mail from one of the fans on how much they appreciate all the effort we put into the site and we're like, 'Oh hell, what's the new feature about?' so they've been a great inspiration."

Working for the site has also given several staff members a chance to hone their skills and find work in similar areas. Staff writer Tara DiLullo now writes for the official *Buffy* and *Angel* magazines. Another staff writer, Jeff Ritchie, moved to L.A. in pursuit of a screenwriting career. CoA's public relations representative, Lilian Holden, is an actress in New York City with several independent film credits under her belt. Virginia Obeius continues to use CoA as a learning ground for her professional Web design. Sarah Wallis is studying theatrical makeup application in London.

Being a staff member has some other perks as well. Lilian Holden recounts one of her experiences of being invited to the set of *Angel*: "I first visited the *Angel* set in March 2003 while delivering a gift to Dayne Johnson from CoA, thanking him for making up monsters for the 2003 PBP party. Dayne was sweet enough to offer a tour of the set, at which point my huge smile almost cracked my face in two.

"It started with a visit to the makeup trailer, where Dayne was putting the finishing touches on Lorne's hands. They have very advanced, high-tech airbrushes to 'paint' on the special effects. Andy Hallett, being ever the gentleman, welcomed me. A bit later we joined him, David Boreanaz, and Amy Acker on set and watched while they shot a scene from 'The Magic Bullet.' Andy was being shoved into the wall by David and his jacket got smeared with wax from a candle. Andy had a great sense of humor about it, lamenting how he could not show his back for the rest of the takes. A little while later Charisma made her way there behind set walls and boxes, her progress slow, as her pregnancy was close to its due date. After the scenes were shot, Amy was kind enough to chat with Dayne and me for a couple of minutes. Eventually, CoA featured Amy in an in-depth spotlight article.

"As my incredible good luck would have it, there was a second unit being directed that day by Steven DeKnight. (As a side note here, Steven DeKnight is one of the best people to populate the earth. I met him at the 2001 PBP when I was just beginning my involvement with CoA and he spent a good fifteen minutes encouraging me to follow my dreams, just because that's the kind of person he is.) Dayne led me to the lobby of the Hyperion Hotel, where Alexis was shooting a pickup scene for 'Inside Out.' I was able to say hello to Steven briefly, wishing that I could stay on the lot forever instead of having to leave soon. Everyone from the set was so courteous and made me feel very welcomed. Speaking to Andy Hallett was a great highlight because of his high spirits and great sense of humor."

The second time the gang was on the set, Kristy got the amazing opportunity to be turned into a vampire by Dayne Johnson. "After five years covering this show, I finally had to step up to the plate when the Wolfram & Hart Review party came along," she says. "I knew we'd want another group of demons in makeup to mingle with the fans and this would be my last chance. I offered myself up to Dayne Johnson and became Drusilla for a night! Sitting in the makeup chair and watching Dayne 'turn' me was quite amazing: he went full throttle — fangs to feral lenses."

Kristy has conducted most of the interviews with the cast and crew and has a lot of favorite memories of those. "As a writer myself, my personal favorite has to be Marti Noxon," she says. "I've always loved Marti's writing and she's a gifted talent and a strong role model for women in this industry. Plus she's one of the nicest people you'll meet. She, Jane Espenson, and Mere Smith are quite a female powerhouse. Julie Benz was just a blast! I've never laughed so much in an interview. We did the interview in London and it was a big girl-fest. She has so many great stories (many of which did *not* make it into the feature, by the way!). Karen Sheperd (Eliza Dushku's stunt double) was impressive. Karen is an incredible woman and quite the breakthrough in female martial arts — she really awed me. Joss and David Greenwalt were certainly highlights. But I really loved the tech features — you never see that stuff and it was remarkable."

In return for the cast and crew's continuing support of the site, the staff of CoA has always been generous in giving back to the show. On the occasion of *Angel*'s 100th episode, they took out an ad in the *Hollywood Reporter*, which was doing a special tribute issue to the show, to let the cast and crew know how much the fans and the CoA staff appreciated everything they did. Lilian says that the CityofAngel staff always tries to provide as much publicity as possible for the show and the various projects that the actors have been working on outside of *Angel*, such as Christian Kane's album. She adds, "Additionally, our focus has been to provide insightful and informative features about the people behind the scenes, the usually unsung heroes who create the essence of *Angel* but who never get to step in front of the camera. Of course, nothing would have been possible without the willingness of *Angel*'s crew and cast to share with the fans. And that speaks to the generous spirit of Joss Whedon, David Greenwalt, and everyone else involved. The importance they have placed in connecting with the audience in a real and meaningful way is written in every episode, in every storyline, and, fortunately for us, in every interview they have generously granted to CityofAngel.com."

Now that the series has come to an end, CityofAngel.com plans to keep up its work for the countries who will be getting the episodes much later than the United States, and for the readers who will want updates on what the cast and crew are continuing to work on. It's the fans that make the site what it is, and the staff of CoA recognize that contribution and hope the support continues. Says Kristy, "There are so many memories, so many great times, it really can't be properly expressed in words, but we hope that we have provided the fans, Joss, and his talented assemblage an honorable reflection of the fun, excitement, joy, laughter, and tears that they have given us."

Angel and Buffy on the Web

While CityofAngel.com is the best of the *Angel* sites on the Web, there are plenty of other sites that are devoted to specific aspects of Joss Whedon's shows. The following is a list of my personal favorites, although there are literally thousands out there to be seen.

GENERAL SITES

Buffyworld
www.buffyworld.com

One of the most comprehensive *Buffy* sites available, this one is constantly updated and includes transcripts, screen captures, and trailers for all episodes of all five seasons of *Angel* and all seven of *Buffy*.

The Sanctuary Devoted to David Boreanaz and Angel
www.trinityofiniquity.com

An excellent site with insightful commentary, explanations of all the popular-culture references on the show, and reviews by regular posters. The Screening Room contains the complete episode guide, the Gallery hosts screen captures, and the Library features fan fiction.

Whedonesque: Joss Whedon Weblog
whedonesque.com

An excellent resource for all things Joss, this is a forum where people can post links to stories they've seen and information they've found and then discuss them. The site is entirely powered by its visitors, so check it out and see if you have something to contribute. Be warned: you could end up there for hours.

The Buffy Dialogue Database
vrya.net/bdb/index.php

Ever tried to remember in which episode Wesley called Illyria a Smurf? This excellent site has dialogue archives from both series, searchable by keyword so you can find that exact quotation you've been looking for. It also features a character breakdown that lets you discover their best lines.

Sonya Marie's Buffy the Vampire Slayer and Angel Series Links
www.bitterwisdom.com/btvsurls/search

Once you scroll past the copious ads at the top, this is an excellent search engine for all things *Buffy* and *Angel*. The sites are organized into various categories that make searching easy for even the newbies on the Net.

Angel/Buffy Miscellaneous Links
links.metalthorn.com/abmisc.html

For anyone who is entering the world of *Buffy* and *Angel* fan fiction, this is a great place to start. With links to dictionaries, how-to guides, and advice on how to write certain characters, this page is a one-stop resource for any new fan-fiction writer.

Rising Stars — Your Fan Relation Connection
www.risingstarsblvd.com

Rising Stars possesses one of the nicest groups of people working for the Buffyverse. The organization hosts official Web sites for actors, but it goes far beyond the call of duty. Fans call and e-mail the company all the time asking for news about the stars, and while the fan mail can sometimes be overwhelming, the company tries to help anyone looking for information.

One fan wrote to me to say, "I think they are different from other Web site companies because they take their time to stop what they are doing and answer our calls and help us out. They have helped me and many others on many occasions getting fan-mail addresses for people they don't even represent. Rana, the owner, has come out of meetings to help a fan in need, no matter how small or big a situation it is. She makes sure we stay happy when other companies or webmasters don't give you the time of day. Jen, the head Webmistress, always answers an e-mail within hours.... I wish more companies and Web sites would take an appreciation for the fans like Rising Stars does." Currently Rising Stars hosts official sites for J. August Richards and Jarrod Crawford from *Angel* and runs several charity contests for the chosen charities of other actors on the shows.

Remember Angel
www.rememberangel.com

A great site dedicated to the memory of *Angel*, "Remember Angel" has an episode guide to the show, a guide to the characters, role-playing games, a posting board, and constantly updated contests for *Angel* fans. Check in regularly because the site is always changing, with new items available to be won.

NEWS SITES

Angel and Buffy News
www.buffy.nu

The best news site for the latest on *Buffy* and *Angel*, this site boasts dozens of new articles every day. The disadvantage of the site is that there doesn't appear to be a complete archive, but if you check it every day (or subscribe to the newsletter for updates) that's not a problem. There's also a search engine that allows you to search for a specific topic or article.

Buffy Online – Trek Archives Network
www.slayerverse.de/tanet/net_buffy_us/index.php

A beautifully designed news site that is updated daily with photos, links, and articles. The articles are searchable by topic, and viewers can post their thoughts on each piece.

Buffy News – Slayage
www.slayage.com

A listing of the latest *Buffy/Angel* news on the Web, this site is archived back to November 2000, but it doesn't have as many articles as the buffy.nu site. However, it's worth checking out for Daniel Erenberg's thoughtful opinion pieces and for Ron's entertaining reviews of *Buffy* and *Angel* episodes.

ACADEMIC SITES

Slayage: The Online International Journal of Buffy Studies
slayage.tv

The mother of all academic sites, this site is run by Rhonda Wilcox and David Lavery, authors of *Fighting the Forces* (see the "Buffy Goes to College" chapter in this book). The issues of *Slayage: The Online International Journal of Buffy Studies* are archived here and are readable as PDF files. This is also the best site for finding out if any *Buffy* academic conferences are coming up and seeing the latest dissertations on *Buffy* and *Angel* from scholars around the world. One of the most interesting *Buffy* sites around.

All Things Philosophical on BtVS and AtS
www.atpobtvs.com

Long one of my favorite sites, ATPOBTVS is still going strong, with discussions on everything from Kierkegaard to Machiavelli to Illyria's political philosophy. Some knowledge of philosophy is probably helpful, but for the majority of the site, the arguments are written in clear language that isn't difficult to understand. If you've ever questioned something someone did on either show was right, this is the site for you.

Above the Law
www.abovethelaw.net

Have you ever wondered if vampires should have fewer rights than other citizens? Or if Buffy really has the right to slay demons? And how do vampires have sexual intercourse if they have no blood flow? You'll find lots of various discussion groups at this site, which boasts forums on "mythos, metaphysics, and morality on *Buffy the Vampire Slayer.*"

THE WEIRD AND THE WONDERFUL

Once More, with Hobbits
www.omwh.com

One of the funniest *Buffy* sites around. If you liked "Once More, with Feeling" and are a *Lord of the Rings* fan, you will love this site. A group of very talented *Buffy* fans has taken the soundtrack to "Once More, with Feeling" and substituted words sung by Frodo, Samwise Gamgee, and others. Not only do the words fit the music, but the feelings expressed by the *Buffy* characters are similar to those of the *LoTR* characters. MP3s are available for a few of the songs. Highly recommended.

Sasha's Custom Made Figures
www.btinternet.com/~msbigpileofdust

This site is a lot of fun to browse. A sculptor who lives in the U.K. has devoted much of her time to creating original action figures based on those from *Buffy*, *Angel*, *Firefly*, and *Fray*. She takes existing figures and changes them by sculpting over them and repainting them. The results are unbelievably accurate representations of characters from specific episodes. For Sasha it's a hobby, not a business, and she always gives due credit to the manufacturers of the original figures. Her work is available for purchase through the site, but if a particular character has already sold, it's too late — she only makes one copy of each character in a specific outfit.

ACTOR SITES

The following are the best sites for the actors of *Angel* and *Buffy*. Many are official and sell autographs and other merchandise pertaining to the actors. The unofficial sites are excellent resources for information about the cast of the shows.

www.david-boreanaz.com
www.charisma-carpenter.com

www.james-marsters.com

www.andyhallett.com

www.jaugustrichards.com

www.amy-acker.com

www.betsyda.com/denisof/denisof.html (Alexis Denisof)

network23.com/hub/ahas (Alyson Hannigan Appreciation Society)

www.smgfan.com/index1.htm (Sarah Michelle Gellar)

www.nickbrendon.com

www.michelle-trachtenberg.com

www.ashead.com (Anthony Stewart Head)

www.anya.org.uk (Emma Caulfield)

www.tomlenk.com

MAILING LISTS

To join a mailing list on the Internet, one of the best starting resources is Yahoo Groups (groups.yahoo.com), where you'll find several of the best mailing lists around. My personal favorites are JossBTVS (a general *Buffy/Angel* list), OBAVA (a list of Canadian *Buffy* fans, although it has members from around the world), and spoiler-crypt (which is no longer a spoiler mailing list since the show is now over). You can find lists for specific actors, characters, fan-fiction writing — pretty much anything you'd like to talk about with other fans. At the time of writing there were approximately 4,000 *Buffy/Angel* mailing lists available through Yahoo.

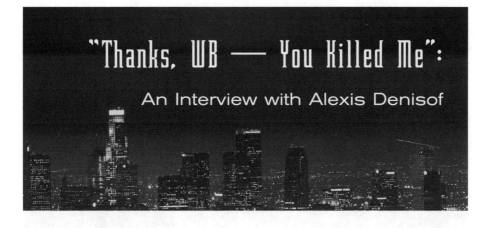

"Thanks, WB — You Killed Me":

An Interview with Alexis Denisof

I conducted several interviews for this book (see Episode Guides), but when I spoke to Alexis Denisof, he gave me such thorough answers that I didn't want to break up the interview. Wesley is one of the most complicated characters on television, and the best way to explore the character is to start at the beginning and interpret the entire series through his eyes. Denisof has done just that in this interview, so I decided to run it in its entirety to give readers a sense of one actor's interpretation of his character. Warning: This interview contains spoilers, so if you don't want any surprises ruined, do not read it unless you've seen every *Angel* episode.

When you were called back to reprise the character, did they give you a reason why they thought Wesley was a better fit on *Angel* than on *Buffy*?

I met with Joss to discuss the possibility of Wesley joining the show and at that time he explained that they wanted to bring in a lighter quality to the show, and they thought Wesley would be ideal for it. He was a very different person at the time, and he offered a little more of the comedy in a more obvious and overt way that they were looking for, and it gave a chance for the darker stuff to be carried by Angel and then Cordelia could go either way. I

Alexis Denisof's character, Wesley Wyndam-Pryce, has come a long way from his bumbling beginnings on *Buffy*.

think they felt it expanded the colors available to them in the show, by bringing Wesley into the fold.

So when you were brought in you had no idea they would make him as serious as they did?

Well, we certainly also discussed that to make Wesley a regular feature character meant a certain amount of overhauling because he'd be insufferable week in and week out if he had maintained the disposition that he had on *Buffy*. So they sent him off on the back of a motorcycle chasing demons between the two shows so he could arrive with a bit of a tougher persona, but still being the goofball that he was. In that way it left him open to continue that journey towards manhood, as it were. Certainly we acknowledged at that time that we would really take our time discovering and tinkering and evolving the character. Did I know that we would end up where we were in seasons four and five with Wesley? No, I had no idea. To be honest, I don't know that any of the writers or even Joss realized the possibilities of the character at that point. When we were just discussing bringing him into the show, it was really just a case of how can we get the guy to fit, what can we do to make him fit, and what will be the potential after we've done that. And it turned out that there was a deep potential, but we didn't realize the extent of that potential until much later on.

By season 2 we were getting little hints that Wesley's upbringing wasn't exactly a positive experience for him, but we only received intimations of it and no real backstory until the father showed up in season 5. Did you create a history of Wesley in your head, and if so, how did you picture his upbringing?

Yeah, I had a fairly detailed idea of who he was and where I thought he'd come from, some of which was useful to share with the writers and some of which wasn't. They had their ideas, and I had mine. There's kind of a strange process that goes on between actors and writers when you're evolving a character like that, so although there's a sort of overall plan, each step of the way is a discovery for all of us. Certainly we all set off heading in the same direction and knowing that we were going to take our time. We wanted it to be a very organic process so that he wouldn't just come to the show as a completely revised being; it was the events and interactions in the course of the series that caused the change in the character and the potential in the character to be realized.

I had a kind of silly script in my mind of what his past had been like, but nothing like what a good writer would come up with. [Laughs] But it's part of my process as an actor to flesh in the history of the person, just because that's my preference. It gives a safe ground to stand as a character, and then when things come up it creates levels of complication and gives the character a chance to respond in an interesting way to what's going on. So sometimes the result of that work that you do in preparing the character creates an idea in the writers' minds because they see the character responding in a certain way to the situation around him, and sometimes they just make an arbitrary decision to make this be a key element to the character's history and we'll just explore that now and it comes as a complete surprise to you. After many years of thinking one way about him you discover that no, he didn't have abusive parents; he was an orphan! But we were all pretty much on the same page. The ideas that I had about him were more or less the same ideas that came to fruition as we went on to explore the character.

We've seen Wesley go from a slapstick comic character to a serious one in season 2 when Angel abandoned the group, to a grief-stricken one in season 3 when Fred chose Gunn, to a very dark character in season 4 when everyone abandoned him. Which aspect of this character was the most fun to play?

I have an unsatisfactory answer to that, which is there isn't really one aspect of the character that I treasure as being preferred to all the others because what I love *is* the complexity of him and the journey. So for me the enjoyment has been the transformation from buffoon to slightly useful member of the group to more useful member of the group to having real friends and people that you care about and onwards and onwards, through all of the layers and levels that the years of the show provided. It makes me very grateful as an actor to have the chance to do that because it is very rare on TV that you're permitted to evolve in that way. Generally, once the parameters are set for where you're going to be with the persona of the character that's pretty much it, and you have to bring that in every week because it's a very structured environment where the events can change but the people aren't permitted to. But part of the thrill for all of the people working with Joss is that absolutely all of the characters change as much as the events, so in fact that's what he is interested in, and that's part of why I love working with him because it's what I'm interested in. Events are exciting but they're only interesting to me because of how they affect the people involved in the events. So that's the story of both shows, really: How have these people changed as a result of the events and the relationships they are in, so that's what we explore over the years. Out of that comes a show with great fights and special effects and poignant romances and oddball comedy and all of that are part and parcel of the journey the characters are making in their evolution. But I guess we look back on it now after five years it seems like this sensible, methodical journey from A to Z that Wesley and Willow and all the other characters have made, but it really doesn't feel that way. We sit down before season one and talk about the possibilities and then set off on this exploration.

The experience is much more like a multitude of doors and corridors and they're available to the characters at all times. We consider which doorway to go through, choose one and go through it, and there's a corridor you go along for a while which is a result of that doorway and you come to another series of doorways and you pick another one . . . and hopefully by the end the reason it's interesting is because you've just explored an awful lot of rooms within that character and that's why I love doing it. If Wesley were a home, we really saw everything from the attic to the cellar. [Laughs] What more could you ask for?

You've been on both shows, so was the feeling on the sets different from one to the other or was it actually pretty similar?

Things were executed similarly because the demands of the shows were similar inasmuch as they attempt a very unusual and ambitious mix of action, genre, special effects, makeup, intimate dialogue – there's just a little of everything, which is why they're both exciting shows to watch, so in that respect it was a similar experience. But it was also different because the people involved were very different. It's two separate crews and two separate casts even though there's a certain amount of overlap in both, but by and large it's like two schools studying the same thing but they're different schools. *Angel* had a different feel from *Buffy;* the material was darker, it's more mature, so in that sense there was a different atmosphere, but otherwise there were similarities but also differences.

We were on a big lot and we shot at Paramount, so that always felt different – being three or four stages out of the thirty available at Paramount as opposed to the three or four stages available that are that lot. So the whole world was *Buffy* when you drove onto the lot where *Buffy* shot, whereas Paramount was an enormous going concern with many other films and TV shows going on, so it sort of has practical differences in the way in which you go to work on both shows. But the set life was huge fun on both shows – great personalities, a lot of fun, a lot of laughter, and people there to support you through the long, cold nights. [Laughs] And make you go on when you wanted to quit.

CHRISTINA RADISH

Joss Whedon and Alexis goof around while Joss models his new hat.

Was Joss really involved in *Angel* throughout or only near the end when he didn't have to have *Buffy* on his plate as well?

He was always involved but at different distances, sometimes close up and sometimes from afar, depending on the demands of his other work. When he was overseeing all three shows – *Angel, Buffy,* and *Firefly* – and had other projects on the go, it was hard to see as much of him physically as you would like, but he's still watching every episode and he's still breaking the stories and he's still connected to what's going on, but at other times he's been much more directly involved. I've always been a bit of a pain in his ass because I was always nagging him to direct and write for us because I feel the show was really built on his back and we need him to come in and redefine it every so often, right in close with us. It's very special when he's directly involved.

If you don't know what the storyline will be ahead of time, what was the biggest surprise for you when you opened up a script and saw what the writers had planned for Wesley?

They had told me that he was going to get shot in "The Thin Dead Line," but they didn't tell me anything else, so I opened up the script and thought, *Uh oh . . .* [puts on British accent] *I think we may be losing our Wes.* [Laughs] I think that's the one that was a pretty big surprise, but they're so smart and clever and they come up with these amazing ideas and you think, *Oh, of course, that's the only thing that could happen!* I don't know how they do it.

What has been your favorite storyline or moment on the show?

Oh boy, that's tough after five years. I have highlights from each season; pretty much every time Wesley fell over in season one I loved. [Laughs] I just loved the physical humor of that first season. I loved at the end of that first episode with him – he's trying to leave and doesn't want to leave and he's looking wistfully at their breakfast on the table and they finally ask him to stay. I love "Guise Will Be Guise" when he pretends to be Angel; that offered a lot of fun for the character. Certainly Fred coming along added a great emotional, personal potential for the character. I liked the stuff with Gunn where we went from being friends to being rivals. I love "Spin the Bottle"; it was just great fun to do because we'd been going along pretty dark for a while and the character was getting tougher and tougher and it was great fun to regress back to the silly Wesley of the past – uptight, slightly confused teenager that he was. Certainly this season the death of Fred and the birth of Illyria was a very powerful day on the set. That will be the one day that I will always remember, when we shot all the scenes of Fred dying. There are a lot of days to treasure.

Just the fun of goofing off with Amy and Andy and David and J. August and later on with James — they're just a great group to be around. There was something terrific about nearly every day, and there was often something that was a drag about every day, but that would be different for each person, I would think.

When you found out that Wesley would be responsible for Angel losing his son, were you happy about how that was going to be to play or did you think, *Uh oh . . .* ?

I was worried because our shows are taken a little more personally by the fans than your average crime procedural drama, where if the character gets into a morally complicated area then no one is too worried about it. With our shows people get very involved in the characters and kind of live through the ups and downs of the characters on the show, so I was very aware that we were getting into a complicated area. People were beginning to have faith in Wesley, which was something that I wanted, and it was a huge challenge when you consider that would have been a huge thing to imagine when he was on *Buffy,* when he was pretty much universally loathed (in a hopefully amused and loving way). But still, it wasn't a character the audience would put their trust in, and certainly wouldn't want other beloved characters putting their trust in. So we worked at making that possible and I was concerned that that was in jeopardy with the turn that was happening in the character.

But I trust Joss ultimately, and I always think that if you're worried about something, then that's where you should go. If you're afraid that it's dangerous for the character, then that's exactly the direction you need to go in, because that's where you find out who the character is. So for all of my telling you that I knew who he was, you don't really know who the character is until you test the character, and that was a huge test for the character and it's in those moments that you find out what's in there. It's the same for the writers: they'll have ideas but until they challenge the characters and stretch them and put them in demanding situations or compromise them horrendously — either physically or morally or emotionally — then they can't find out what they're working with and part of why Wesley was enjoyable for me was every time we threw him into the lion's mouth he came out bloodied but somehow a little bit more glorious.

Did Wesley love Lilah?

Love is a term that, when people say it, they know exactly what they mean and the other person has an idea of what that person means – and do the two people mean the same thing? So you and I could interpret this forever because you probably have a concept of what you mean by *love* and then I interpret it in my way and then it gets interpreted by both Wesley and Lilah and we don't really know where we are with that question. But what was the nature of their relationship? I think that it's everything you see on the screen, which is two people highly charged by the danger of their interaction and fascinated by the possibility of having a future with somebody they can't have a future with. So it's sort of like Icarus – the closer Icarus gets to the sun, the wings made of wax melt and he falls to Earth. And that's sort of how I feel about [Wesley and Lilah]. The closer they get, the heat is too intense and they burn each other. They desperately want to trust each other and they don't know how and they desperately want the intimacy and they don't know how and they're really interesting together as a result. They definitely have chemistry, those two characters. I can't sum it up as *Yes, he loves her* or *No, he doesn't;* it's really more a question of the possibility of love rather than the actuality of love.

Wesley has failed in so many things, whether it's as a Watcher or as the leader of Angel Investigations, and these failures have driven a lot of his actions. Do you think when Faith came back to deal with Angelus that Wesley finally succeeded as her Watcher?

Maybe from the viewer's perspective that might be the case, but what I love about Wesley is he's moved so far beyond even needing that. It's really immaterial to him whether he succeeds or fails as a Watcher at that point. What's more important is achieving the next step in the fight, and whatever is required, whatever has to be done, he will do his utmost to get it done. So he'll take everything he knows about being a Watcher and everything he knows about Faith and put that to good use. Does it mean he succeeds in being a Watcher? I don't know; if he were to do that in some conscious way it would be to go back and relive his life and that isn't him. For him, he's all about the collection of failures. He's so utterly human because all of these failures are what make him who he is. It's what makes him useful, it's how he solves problems, it's how he evolves, because he encompasses failure.

You see a lot of champions who are extremely narrow human beings because they can only exist in the realms of victory, and so this is what Wesley really brings to the show: a human, just a little man, who sometimes succeeds and a lot of the time fails and tries his hardest not to fail again and keeps getting up and going right back in to try again, having failed. I didn't really know he had that in him when we started, and that was something that Joss kept building in the character. It just kind of breaks your heart to watch him be broken time and time again and still pick himself up and walk back into the fight and figure out what needs to be done. So that's why I say when the Faith arc comes around for the second time, the story is so much bigger than whether he's a good Watcher or a bad Watcher, because he's so far beyond being a good or bad Watcher at that point that I love that he can succeed as a Watcher and not have it be important to him at all.

In "Orpheus" the writers brought over Alyson from *Buffy;* was it strange doing scenes with her now that you had a relationship with her off-screen?

It was fun, I loved it. It was a little bit distracting because she is insanely cute and I would find myself drifting off and forgetting that I'm supposed to be performing. [Laughs] I was just kind of staring, gaping at my beloved. When I managed to concentrate it was a lot of fun doing scenes with her. I think we enjoyed that we found we still had fun because we hadn't done that for a while, not since *Buffy* and then the ill-fated movie we did together right after *Buffy* [*Beyond City Limits*], so we hadn't really worked together in a scene and I was really glad they gave us a chance to. I think it's a nice little scene. I wish they'd had her on more often.

In season 5, the characters have lost all memories of Connor and Connor's existence. But Connor was so much a part of the events that had

Alyson Hannigan and Alexis Denisof walk down the aisle after being married on October 11, 2003.

informed the previous two seasons, one wonders how the gang could remember much of anything that had happened in the previous two years, and most of all, how they came to be at Wolfram & Hart. Did you have any thoughts about that when you were playing Wesley this season?

Well, this was a complicated area for all of us. I certainly quizzed Joss a few times on "Well, how does this work?" and the writers as well, and we were all trying to figure it out, what were the dynamics of this. It's not as clear-cut as the memory has been wiped, we're now starting over again, because you wouldn't know how to feed yourself and you'd be starting over as an infant, and that would be pre-posterous. I don't know that I could sum it up as accurately as the writers could, but my sense of it was that key events were eliminated and filled in with vague events, and the gap was knitted together with the before and after of that event. The person of Connor was eliminated from the memory, but the journey that happened was not. I said to Joss, "If all of this stuff is gone then should I regress the character to pre–season four and start there?" and we all felt that wasn't very interesting, to re-tread stuff that had been gained by the characters. It's more a case of selective memory and a sense of events that have taken place, but no specific memory of taking Connor and Angel suffocating me or me having my throat slit, but having a memory of there being a battle, where I was injured in the neck. So that's kind of how I filled that stuff in and kept the character where he was in terms of the progress he made through the course of that year.

It was worth it to do it that way because once the memories are restored it means Wesley can respond to them from a current standpoint rather than having to get too weird about jumping back and forth between them. Joss had said the mind-wipe wasn't going to be permanent so I knew at some point in the season we were going to go through the process of reliving it and the interesting aspect of it was having that stuff come up and having to deal with it a second time, but not being the person you were when you had to deal with it the first time. So that's what made it a worthwhile narrative choice on the writers' part to do that. We got to explore what it was to have these events relived, but have the people be different because they're a year older and things have changed and the ground shifted. But we couldn't do it right away because there was a lot of practical stuff to be dealt with, with integrating into Wolfram & Hart and having Spike integrate into the team, so it wouldn't have been appropriate to have gotten into the memory stuff too early in the season.

Did the group dynamic change drastically after they brought in James Marsters?

Yes, it was definitely different, as it would be with the addition of any character, and it was different with all of the characters who were introduced over the years. I mean different in lots of different ways. He brought a nice humor and a kind of rebelliousness to the group and challenged Angel in a new way, which is always good for characters to be challenged, especially your leads. On paper you think, *Wow, two vampires, two black leather coats, both have souls, is this gonna work?* [Laughs] You worry a little, but they did such a great job with the idea and James is such an outstanding performer that I think it worked great. I'm sorry we didn't get more time to let that go because we were just getting to the point where Spike was integrating, so season six would have been fantastic as far as the group was concerned. We were just getting used to him being part of the gang.

How difficult was it keeping a straight face while filming "Smile Time"?

Impossible. We just giggled all through it, and I think some of it is on-screen. [Laughs] Very difficult; it was just hilarious. Did they nail Angel or what? It was *so* funny. The stuff the puppeteers did off-camera was even funnier than what got on-screen. It was just riotous. You've got to love a show that goes from that to the death of one of the main characters in one week.

Right before the end, Wesley had just recovered his memories of what had happened with Connor, and he seemed to be hanging by a thread emotionally because of Illyria. Was Wesley on the verge of a nervous breakdown, do you think?

I think he sort of has it. I think if you followed Wesley and veered away from everything else going on I think you'd see a man going through a slow, protracted nervous breakdown. At times it's acute and at other times it's at bay. I do think he kind of comes through it, but it's difficult. It's a very difficult second half of the season for him, definitely, and the trauma of the robo-dad and the trauma of the death of Fred. The way I looked at that was that Wesley was a guy that fought all his life for the possibility that the world was worth saving. And in Fred, he discovered *why* the world was worth saving. So when he loses that, it becomes very tenuous for him, it's very difficult for him to go back to saving the world in a specific way because as the seasons go on the world becomes worth saving because Fred is in it. And so he comes unstitched a little when she's not in the world anymore. It's not in his nature to give up and it's not in his nature to let that defeat him utterly, but he is a human being.

I hate that I keep going back to it, but I think he's important to the show because he's the only one who isn't enhanced in some way. There aren't any other simple human beings on the show — even Gunn has a demon upgrade — and once Fred goes he's alone in a way. And it isn't that he hasn't been alone in his life before, because I think he's had a very long life of being alone until he met Angel and company. And that's why they're so important: . . . they gave him the first real community in his life, clearly much more so than his family. When Fred dies, I think he feels very alone, and so I don't think he gives up, but I think he reacts to it. And that's why the stories are told, to see what happens to people when things go wrong and when things go right. Obviously we would have loved much more time to have explored that whole journey. It got compressed a little because of the WB canceling the show, because really, all that stuff was going to spread much deeper into the sixth season.

The finale. Our hearts were certainly ripped out when Wesley died, and it was beautifully done with Fred by his side the way he'd been by hers. Were you satisfied with the way they ended your character's arc?

Oh, very. It was sad; Joss called and said, "How do you feel about this?" and I was like, "Oh . . . ouch!" [Laughs] But I couldn't think of anything more fitting, and I have learned over the years that if Joss has a feeling you definitely go with it, and I liked that it was a little death in the arms of a vision, because the temptation would be a blaze of glory for a character that one has become fond of. There's a part of you that wants him on the back of a horse charging into ten thousand demons and saving the world, and he doesn't do any of those things; he fails in his battle with the enemy and dies a very human death. So to me it was the perfect human death of a human life.

It's hard to talk about because there are just some things and some moments that are left to what they are. I feel the scenes say so much more than what I could really say about them, and by talking about them I feel I make it a little bit less than what it was for me to do, and I don't want to make it less for the people it's important to. It's beautifully dubious in the way that all of the tender moments are with a Joss show, because of course it isn't really Fred talking to him, and we've already heard in previous episodes that Fred's soul has been disintegrated. So you have to leave it up to the viewer to decide whether Wesley is resting in peace or resting in the agony he was enduring in life, and I'd prefer not to share my thoughts on that because I feel it's up to each person to invest what they see fit in his passing.

Was the death scene the last scene you filmed?

Yes. Just by chance, it was my last night on the show. So it was a very profound sense of closure, more than you could even encompass in words or in thoughts. It's a long journey we've all had to take. I'm glad that was my last day.

Did you know anything about what was going to happen to your character in season 6? Had they begun discussing it before the news of the show's cancellation came in?

Had there been a season six, it had not been intended that Wesley would die. That was something that became possible

With both *Buffy* and *Angel* over, Alyson Hannigan and Alexis Denisof have time to contemplate their futures. With their talents, who knows how far they can go . . .

with the event of the end of the show. But he might have chosen to have done that anyway and gone ahead and done season six without Wesley, but I don't think that was Joss's intention because we had discussed some really cool stuff with Illyria and the possibility of how Illyria channels Fred, and some very complicated stuff along those lines. We didn't get to do very much of that but we certainly touched on that with the one episode with her parents. When the cancellation orders came in, Joss started thinking about the possibilities for the finale and he had already conceived broadly about how we go out of season five, and this other possibility arose in his mind about what characters would survive and what characters wouldn't. So a lot of things didn't change, but one thing that did change was the life of Wesley. So, thanks, WB – you killed me. [Laughs]

Are You a Senior Partner or a Mailroom Assistant?

The *Angel* (and *Buffy* Season-Seven) Trivia Quiz

So you've watched all the episodes, you feel like you know the characters as well as members of your own family, and you're mourning the loss of *Angel* and *Buffy* now that both are over. But have you been paying close attention to the details? The following are 100 questions ranging from fairly easy to difficult, but all are questions about things that have been said only once in an episode (in other words, I won't be asking for the name of the female liaison to the Senior Partners in season 5 of *Angel*). For *Buffy* fans, there are also questions about the seventh season of that series. Write down your answers as you go (if you constantly check the back of the book, you're sure to accidentally see an upcoming answer) and then rank yourself out of 100 (or, if you don't watch *Buffy*, rank yourself out of 85). Answers are on page 417. Good luck!

Angel, Season One

1. How many wars has Angel seen?
2. Which year did Phantom Dennis die?
3. What is Doyle's full name?
4. How old was Doyle when his demon side first showed?
5. What was his profession when he got married?
6. What is the name of the boat on which Doyle dies in "Hero"?
7. What is Cordelia doing when she receives her first vision?

8. Which kind of motorcycle does Wesley ride?

9. What is the name of the convention hall that holds the demon auction where Cordelia almost gets her eyes extracted?

10. Which kind of demon impregnates Cordelia in "Expecting"?

11. In "I've Got You Under My Skin," which three cities had the Andersons lived in before moving to L.A.?

12. When Angel was turned into a vampire, who was the first person he killed?

13. When is Cordelia's birthday?

14. What was the name of Cordelia's palomino when she was younger?

15. How much does Wolfram & Hart offer to pay Faith to kill Angel?

16. According to Faith, what are the five torture groups?

17. What did Angel's father do for a living?

18. Where did Lindsey go to law school?

19. What is the name of the hospital Cordelia was taken to at the end of season 1?

Angel, Season Two

20. When did the Hyperion officially close as a hotel?

21. When was the Hyperion hotel built?

22. How many rooms are in the Hyperion?

23. Which kind of software did David Nabbitt produce that made him a billionaire?

24. How old is Virginia when Wesley meets her?

25. In "The Shroud of Rahmon," Wesley and Cordelia go to a party. Which celebrity do they meet?

26. What was Darla dying from in 1609?

27. What was Holland Manners's wine cellar originally built to be?

28. What is the name of Anne's inner-city kids' shelter?

29. After Angel fires his staff, they all go to Caritas to drown their sorrows and consider singing for the Host. Cordelia contemplates singing something by Shania Twain or Madonna; what does Wesley consider singing?

30. What was the name of the fundraiser that Wolfram & Hart organized for Anne's shelter?

31. Which color does the Host say Angel's aura is?

32. What is the name of the health-care facility that takes care of Wolfram & Hart employees?

33. On which date did Fred go missing from the library?

34. What is the full name of the library from where she went missing?
35. From where is the Groosalugg summoned to come to Cordelia?

Angel, Season Three

36. What is Cordelia's title at Angel Investigations according to her business card?
37. What does Fred say is the one nice word she remembers from Pylea?
38. Which kind of demons does Sahjhan hire to be Holtz's minions?
39. Shortly after Connor is born, how many Web sites are offering a reward for his death?
40. What was Justine Cooper's sister's name?
41. What was Holtz's baby son's name?
42. Which college does Angel want to send Connor to?
43. When Angel buys the tickets to the ballet, which band did Gunn want to go see instead?
44. When Angel buys the little hockey shirt for baby Connor, which number is on the shirt?
45. How many cabinets are required at Wolfram & Hart to contain Angel's file?
46. What is the full name that Holtz gives to Connor?
47. Where does Holtz intend to go with Connor and Justine in "Sleep Tight"?
48. At the beginning of "Double or Nothing," Fred and Gunn are helping an elderly demon couple. How long has the couple been together?
49. What was the Groosalugg's mother's name?
50. Which book does Lilah give Wesley the first time she shows up at his apartment?
51. When Connor returns from Quor-toth, what is the first thing we see him eat?
52. As Angel readies to take Connor in as his son, he asks Cordelia what a fair allowance would be. What amount does he suggest to her?

Angel, Season Four

53. What is the name of the Senior Partner who helps out Lilah in "Deep Down"?
54. In "Ground State," how many times does Gwen Raiden say she has been struck by lightning?
55. How much is the Axis of Pythia worth on the black market?
56. When Angel is possessed in "The House Always Wins" and Cordelia manipulates the slot machine he's playing, what does he win?

57. Wesley is forced to give Lilah a one-dollar bill because he says a certain forbidden word when talking about the two of them. What is the word?

58. What is the location of the Watcher's Academy that Wesley attended?

59. In "Calvary," Wesley finds Lilah in the sewers and she's holding a book with an extra section that's missing in his copy. What's the name of the book?

60. What was Faith charged with and what sentence was she given?

61. What prison did Faith go to after being charged?

62. In "Players," what does LISA stand for?

63. When Cordelia sneaks up on Lorne in "Players" and he has a Magic 8 Ball, what does it say when he turns it over?

64. What is Gunn's grandmother's name?

65. When Fred asks the guy who works in the Magic Bullet bookstore for a book on mind control, what is the title of the book he holds up?

Angel, Season Five

66. Who chose Harmony out of the steno pool to become Angel's assistant?

67. How many days is Spike's essence trapped in the amulet before he re-emerges in "Conviction"?

68. What is the name of Nina's niece?

69. When Angel calls Fred into his office to complain about the lab's budget, how much over their quarterly budget projection does Eve say Fred has gone?

70. Which university did Eve attend?

71. According to Sirk, where is the Cup of Perpetual Torment located?

72. Which brand of perfume does Harmony wear?

73. How old was Dana when her family was murdered in her home?

74. Which video game is Spike playing when Lindsey comes to visit him in "You're Welcome"?

75. When Angel arrives at the Smile Time studio and heads toward the nest egg (before he's turned into a puppet) what does the sign say on the door?

76. What is the name of Fred's stuffed rabbit?

77. Where in England is the Deeper Well located?

78. What are Fred's final words?

79. How old was Knox when he first discovered Illyria?

80. What is the name of Illyria's temple?

81. In the hell dimension where Lindsey goes, what is the name of his son?

82. Which school does Connor attend as part of his new life?

83. When Lorne is tailing Illyria in "Time Bomb," what is the code name he gives her when he talks to Angel on the walkie-talkie?

84. After Spike's leather duster is destroyed in "The Girl in Question," how many new coats does Ilona send to Wolfram & Hart in L.A.?

85. After Spike is applauded for his poem in "Not Fade Away," what does he say his next poem is called?

Buffy, Season Seven

86. When Dawn is standing in front of her new classmates and introducing herself in "Lessons," what is the first thing she says she likes to do?

87. What are Buffy's office hours when she's working at Sunnydale High?

88. What was the name of the village where Anya and Olaf lived?

89. In what year did Anya become a vengeance demon?

90. According to Tara's grave, on which day was she born?

91. To cover up what she really did for R.J., what does Anya admit to doing to get his attention at the end of "Him"?

92. Which subject did Holden Webster study in school?

93. What does Aimee Mann say when she leaves the stage at the Bronze in "Sleeper"?

94. When is the Sunnydale High library scheduled to have its grand opening?

95. Which genre of film does Principal Wood say he likes?

96. Which childhood character did Chloe like?

97. When the gang retrieves the knife with which Andrew stabbed Jonathan, there's something written on it. Which language is the inscription?

98. Caleb tells the First about a choir girl he once killed. What town was she from?

99. Who is the Mayor's favorite character in *Little Women*?

100. Which character has the final line of dialogue on the series?

Angel Episode Guide

The following episode summaries may contain spoilers (plot points about the shows), so I advise readers to watch the episodes first and then read the commentaries to avoid any surprises being ruined. The opinions expressed here are mine only, so feel free to disagree. The guide is written so that it seems I'm sitting on the couch discussing an episode with you after watching it — I hope it feels the same to you. The nitpicks and bloopers mentioned are not meant as criticisms of the show but just fun things I found while watching.

At the end of each episode entry, you'll find special notes of interest. **Highlight** features something that happened in the show that was particularly funny or poignant. **Interesting Facts** gives some outside information about the episode, either telling a behind-the-scenes story or explaining a reference made in the episode. For some episodes I have quotations from people involved with those shows; these quotes follow the "Interesting Facts" section. The interviews I conducted for these sections were with J. August Richards (Gunn), Amy Acker (Fred), Christian Kane (Lindsey), Stephanie Romanov (Lilah), Keith Szarabajka (Holtz), David Denman (Skip), Mark Lutz (the Groosalugg), Jane Espenson (co-executive producer and writer on *Buffy*), and David Fury (co-executive producer and writer on *Buffy* and supervising producer and writer on *Angel*; his interview was conducted in April 2003, so it was a year earlier than the others). **Did You Notice?** points out little things the viewer might have missed, details that either foreshadow another episode or are just something small of interest. **Nitpicks** are things that seemed to be inconsistent but might be explained by another viewer. **Oops** contains bloopers and continuity errors I spotted in the episode. The *Buffy* **Connection** explains *Buffy* references for the readers who watch *Angel* only and not *Buffy*, but it also draws parallels between the two shows for the readers who watch both. **The Boy Ain't Right** appears in seasons 3 and 4 and catalogs all the ways Connor isn't like a regular boy. **Wolfram & Hart** keeps track of the strange customs of the evil law firm while also tracing the development of Angel's antagonism with it. **Music/Bands** lists the music heard in the episode, and I must thank Leslie Remencus for this information. She is the former Webmaster of the *Buffy/Angel* music pages at Buffymusic.net, but she had to take the Web site down. She graciously sent me a CD-ROM with all the music information so I could use it for this section. Many episodes don't feature any music other than the show's score, which is composed by Robert J. Kral, with Christophe Beck contributing some music in the show's first season. For each season I have listed recurring characters, and they do not appear in the individual episode cast lists.

Starring:

David Boreanaz as Angel

Charisma Carpenter as Cordelia Chase

Glenn Quinn as Francis Doyle

Alexis Denisof as Wesley Wyndam-Pryce

J. August Richards as Charles Gunn (Season Two)

Amy Acker as Winifred "Fred" Burkle (Season Three)

Vincent Kartheiser as Connor (Season Four)

Andy Hallett as Lorne "The Host" (Season Four)

James Marsters as Spike (Season Five)

Mercedes McNab as Harmony (Season Five)

Season One

October 1999 • May 2000

Recurring characters in season 1: Elizabeth Röhm (Kate Lockley), Christian Kane (Lindsey McDonald), Stephanie Romanov (Lilah Morgan)

1.1 City Of

Original air date: October 5, 1999
Written by: Joss Whedon and David Greenwalt
Directed by: Joss Whedon
Guest cast: Tracy Middendorf (Tina), Vyto Ruginis (Russell Winters), Jon Ingrassia (Stacy), Renee Ridgeley (Margo), Sam Pancake (Manager), Josh Holloway (Good Looking Guy), Gina McClain (Janice)

Angel moves to L.A., where he meets up with Doyle and Cordelia.

"Look, high school's over, bud. You gotta make with the grown-up talk now," says Doyle when he first meets Angel. Within the first five minutes of this episode, the audience already knows this is a much darker and different program than *Buffy*. Gone are the high-school teachers and adolescent romances. Los Angeles is the real, gritty world, where people go either to find a way to stand out from the rest and become famous, or to blend into the walls and be forgotten. The voice-over at the beginning is reminiscent of old detective movies, immediately suggesting that this series will have noir elements. It's strange to see Angel as his own person and not as one of the Scoobies, helping out or standing silent and brooding while Buffy gets upset. This is his show, and we'll have to get used to it. It will take place mostly at night (for obvious reasons), focusing on the seamy underbelly of L.A. However, in the beginning, *Angel* will have to rely on the mythology and background established on *Buffy* to create its foundation, and it'll take until season 2 before it's able to stand fully on its own.

Glenn Quinn was an excellent choice to play Doyle. Previously seen on *Roseanne* as Becky's dopey husband, Mark (and hiding his Irish accent), Quinn is someone viewers may recognize, but he isn't so linked to that character that he's typecast. Doyle is charming but silly, a personality that audiences immediately latched on to, and he's reminiscent of Whistler, the other mentor that Angel had in "Becoming, Part One" on *Buffy*. Rumor has it that Angel's sidekick was originally supposed to be Whistler, but the creators couldn't secure Max Perlich for the job. Doyle is an appropriate sidekick and conscience for Angel not only because he is half demon and knows how it feels to be caught between two worlds, but because he's Irish, like Angel.

After the void she left behind in "The Freshman" on *Buffy*, it is a relief to see Charisma Carpenter on this show (though Angel wasn't particularly relieved to see Cordelia). Cordelia is still her endearing, thoughtless, crass self, and we love her for it, though we discover there's a sad side to her: her fabulous condo in Malibu is actually a dingy apartment. She continues to be the damsel in distress, but not for long. Over the course of this series we'll see Cordelia develop from the silly dingbat she was on *Buffy* into a mature warrior woman.

David Boreanaz proves he can carry his own show with the coolness of a movie star, and there's an element of humor in this episode that will remain throughout the series. Boreanaz is able to try out acting techniques that are closer to what he did with Angelus than what he's done with Angel, and now, with the focus being on him rather than his effect on Buffy, the writers can explore this truly fascinating character. In Sunnydale Angel could remain the loner, only associating with Buffy and the Scooby gang, but here in L.A. he's forced to try to connect with other people, and the result is often painful to watch. Angel sputters and comes off as a creep and can't figure out how to introduce himself to others (he can't exactly tell them that his friend had a "vision" involving them without it sounding like a pickup line). Angel also faces problems fighting crime because he's a vampire and can't chase villains into the daylight. Watching Angel develop into a more confident person and capable champion will be an interesting arc as the series continues.

"City Of" is an excellent pilot (with an amazing opening theme song), and the series will pick up where *BtVS*'s "Anne" left off. With its quick cuts between scenes and its more adult humor ("she's a stiffener, all right") and scenarios, *Angel* has a lot of potential to become its own show. In this episode, Russell is a great villain who represents all that Hollywood is about: allure and destruction. We're also introduced to Wolfram & Hart, which will be a major force in episodes to come, and Angel's good-guy detective agency is established. Angel is the brooding vampire with a past he has to atone for, Doyle is the "sensitive" half-demon, and Cordy is, well, Cordy. Together, they form a very promising team.

Highlight: Angel jumping into the wrong mysterious black convertible.
Interesting Facts: When Joss appeared on the Bronze posting board shortly after this series began, he addressed the oft-asked question of how he could head up two shows simultaneously: "Somebody asked how me and Greenie can do both shows and stay sane — well, something's gotta fall by the wayside there, and we naturally decided we could do without all that sanity. No problem with that so far, except I keep pitching the Angel-debates-socioeconomics-with-a-sturgeon season arc and Greenwalt thinks his lungs are plotting against him. But expect the same

quality television you've always gotten, except without the quality, and possibly a little less television."

Christian Kane Says: "I actually auditioned for the role of Riley. Marc went in and read with Sarah and then I went in and read with Sarah and came out and I felt really good about it, but the problem was, I was too dark a character. They wanted someone more clean-cut and all-American, so they went with Blucas. I never auditioned for Lindsey; I went in to audition for Riley and then *Angel* came up and they said, 'Do you want to play a lawyer on *Angel*?' One of the reasons I did it was because of David Boreanaz. He and I were buddies, and I knew it was his pilot, so I definitely wanted to work with David. I figured it was a one-episode thing — quick, get in there, say your lines, grab a little money, and then get out — and look what happened."

Did You Notice?: According to the Wolfram & Hart business card, the firm has offices in New York, Los Angeles, Paris, London, and Cairo. (Interestingly, they don't list the office in Rome that we see in "The Girl in Question").

Nitpicks: One thing that will become annoying in weeks to come is the constant repetition of Angel's backstory. Doyle confronts Angel and tells the long, sad story of the vampire with a soul, and what happened when he was Angelus. It's something that will be repeated over and over again, as if to fill in the non-*Buffy* viewers on what had come before *Angel*. The problem is, the vast majority of viewers are *Buffy* fans and are all too aware of Angel's history. Not only that, but it didn't make much sense dramatically to have Angel sit and listen to his own story as if he'd never heard it before. Also, why would a woman who is being stalked not only tell Angel, a complete stranger, where she's from but also accept a ride from him? And wouldn't a high-rise building have thicker glass in its windows? Finally, why don't Lindsey's business cards actually have his name on them? You'd think a huge law firm like Wolfram & Hart could afford individualized business cards for its employees.

Oops: In the early episodes you can clearly make out the difference between David Boreanaz and his stunt double in the fight scenes. Also, Angel goes to the L.A. Public Library in the middle of the night, but none of the branches in L.A. are open 24 hours, and most close at 8 p.m.

The *Buffy* Connection: In the *Buffy* season-four premiere that ran the same night as the *Angel* premiere, Buffy's mother's phone rings and Buffy picks it up, but no one answers. She hangs up and doesn't think anything of it, but viewers who tuned in to *Angel* afterward realized who it was on the other end when we saw Angel's half of the scene played out.

Wolfram & Hart: In this episode we first hear of the evil law firm that will become Angel's nemesis. The lawyers who work there refer to themselves as a "full-service law firm" and fabricate elaborate stories in order to cover up things their clients may have done. They make sure their clients (who are mostly demons) are never accused of or charged with any crimes.

Music/Bands: Wellwater Conspiracy's "Right of Left Field" (*Brotherhood of Electric: Operational Directives*) plays at the pool hall; we hear "Maybe I Belong" by Howie Beck (*Hollow*) when Angel talks to Tina at the coffee shop; and "Ladyshave" and "Teenage Sensation" by Gus Gus (*This Is Normal*) play at Margo's party.

1.2   Lonely Hearts

Original air date: October 12, 1999
Written by: David Fury
Directed by: James A. Contner
Guest cast: Lillian Birdsell (Sharon Richler), Obi Ndefo (Bartender), Derek Hughes (Neil), Johnny Messner (Kevin), Jennifer Tung (Neil Pick-Up Girl), Tracey Stone (Pretty Girl), David Nisic (Slick Guy), Ken Rush (Guy), Connor Kelly (Regular)

Angel has to find a demon that is preying on lonely people at bars and eviscerating them.

It's difficult to find someone in L.A. if the only description you have to go on is that they're lonely; after all, this is the town where *everyone* is lonely. Just as *Buffy* bases its main plots on metaphors for larger issues, so too will the writers on *Angel* use parallels — in this case, the basic premise is that hanging out on the L.A. bar scene will suck the life out of you. Literally.

We're introduced to Kate, the angry, bitter, and sad police officer who trusts no one. While Kate is an interesting foil for Angel, the writers seem to be turning *Angel* into a full-blown detective show. Angel's supposed to be the gumshoe and Kate's the hard-boiled cop who stands in his way, but that's been done so many times it's tired. Thankfully, Kate will soon develop into a more interesting character. Here, she embodies the cliché of the person who will always make the mistake of believing one thing stubbornly: she refuses to listen to Angel, believing he is the creature that is killing people. Later we'll see her more vulnerable side, which is hinted at in this episode. Kate is lonely, and being a tough cop isn't exactly making her a magnet for men. She opens up to Angel about how difficult it is living in L.A., just as Doyle, Cordelia, and Angel discuss how much easier dating was when they were younger. Interestingly, we also see the flip side when the "Screech" says the opposite — having been a nerd and an outcast in high school, he finds dating a lot easier now.

Cordelia is hilarious in this episode, always with the quick retorts to everything Angel or Doyle says, and watching these early episodes when the series is in its fifth season, you become a little nostalgic for her oblivious chatter. Doyle has developed the hots for Cordy, and watching him clumsily try to endear himself to her while hiding his demony half will be fun for the next few episodes.

"Lonely Hearts" is a strong episode, but it's clear that *Angel* will be trying to find its way for a while.

Highlight: Cordelia's reaction when Angel tells her the demon is a burrower: "It's a donkey?"

Interesting Facts: On *Buffy* we've always heard that you have to invite vampires in or they can't enter your home. In this episode Doyle adds the stipulation that "as long as you're alive" they can't enter, but apparently vampires can enter the abodes of dead people. That's a new one (and it explains how Angel entered Russell's home in the previous episode), but it will be used throughout the series.

Did You Notice?: Cordelia's prophetic statement about Doyle's visions: "If that was my gift, I'd return it." Also, when Kate and Angel go into the bar the second time, notice how the guy sitting near Kate describes himself to sound like one of the *Buffy* Troika of season 6.

Nitpicks: We're two for two with Cordelia mentioning Angel having lost his soul with a perfect moment of happiness thing.

Oops: When Cordelia and Doyle are standing at the bar and are threatened by the thugs, Doyle's arm is behind Cordelia when we see them from behind and at his side when the camera angle is in front. When Kate catches Angel in Sharon's apartment, she slaps a handcuff on one of his wrists, but it disappears immediately afterward. Finally, Angel walks down a rather bright street, which was a mistake in filming; the scene was supposed to be filmed before dawn, but the crew couldn't get things ready in time and instead it appears that Angel is enjoying a lovely morning stroll. Joss addressed the problem on the Bronze posting board: "Re: Angel. Sunlight. Yeah, that's been a problem. It's just hard for the [director of photography] to light the show and avoid it entirely. And then tonight there was a shot that was colortimed so that what was supposed to be pre-dawn came out like post-dawn. Bear with us, we know it's not all there yet."

The *Buffy* Connection: When Kate tells Angel to go to hell, he says, "Been there, done that," a reference to Buffy having put a sword through him in "Becoming, Part Two," which sent him to hell for years (see "Deep Down").

Music/Bands: "Deadside" by Ian Fletcher (no album) plays during Doyle's vision; Ultra-Electronic's "Dissonance" (*Gotham Recordings: The Soundtrack*) plays at the dance club when Kevin introduces himself to Sharon; when Cordy, Doyle, and Angel arrive at the club, we hear "Girlflesh" by THC (*Adagio*); Kathy Soce's "Do You Want Me" (*Gotham Recordings: The Soundtrack*) plays when Angel talks to Kate at the bar; Sapien's "Neo-Climatic" (*Penn Music Group*) is heard right after the bar fight breaks up; we hear "Ballad of Amave" by Chucho Merchan (*Extreme Music Library — Jazz*) as Cordy, Doyle, and Angel discuss socializing; "Lazy Daze" by Mark Cherrie and Ian McKenzie (*Big Beat Generator*) plays when Angel talks to Kate outside the bar; Chainsuck's "Emily Says" (*Angelscore*) plays when Kevin's friend talks to the bartender and Angel listens in; "Touched" by Vast (*Visual Audio Sensory Theater*) plays when Kate searches Angel's apartment; Adam Hamilton's "For You" (Techno CD by MasterSource) plays when Kate waits for Angel at the club; and "Quango" by Helix (*Extreme Music Library — Techno*) plays when the bartender tries to pick up women.

1.3   In the Dark

Original air date: October 19, 1999
Written by: Douglas Petrie
Directed by: Bruce Seth Green
Guest cast: Seth Green (Oz), James Marsters (Spike), Kevin West (Marcus), Malia Mathis (Rachel), Michael Yavnieli (Lenny), Ric Sarabia (Sunglass Vendor), Tom Rosales (Manny the Pig), Gil Combs (Bouncer), Buck McDancer (Dealer), Jenni Blong (Young Woman)

When Oz takes the Gem of Amarra to Angel in L.A., Spike follows to try to get it back.

This is an excellent episode and the first crossover of characters from *Buffy* to *Angel*. It also has great examples of the painful decisions Angel will have to make now that he's fighting evil full time. He's been handed the one thing that he needs to fight evil all the time, something that makes him even better than human — a ring that makes him impervious to all harm. He would be able to walk around during the day and no stake could pierce his heart and kill him. Yet when he first sees it, he cringes as if someone had just shown him a wooden cross.

Spike is the perfect foil for Angel in this episode, and at the time there was some talk that he might come over as a series regular (it would take four more years for that to happen). When David Boreanaz has to play opposite James Marsters, a different side of him comes out, like he's trying to match Marsters move for move. It happened in season 2 of *Buffy*, and it'll happen again in season 5 of *Angel*. Oz, too, seems to fit right in with the L.A. world, and his mystery machine is one tough crime-fightin' vehicle.

One thing the *Angel* series will emphasize is that Angel will always be forced to make difficult choices. On *BtVS* he walked away from Buffy despite knowing she was the only woman he'd loved in 250 years because he knew it would be best for her. On *Angel* he'll make even tougher decisions, often hurting himself in the process. His decision at the end of this episode is for all the people who are terrorized by the demons that come out at night — whether those demons are horned and scaly or are drug dealers and pimps. Angel believes he needs not only to atone for his sins but also

Spike (James Marsters) shows up in L.A. for some mischief . . . and a bit of torture.

to be punished severely (why else would the guy drive a *convertible*?). Even though he tells his torturer in this episode that he wants forgiveness above all else, would he accept it if it were offered to him?

Highlight: The opening scene of Spike mocking Angel from afar: "Say no more. Evil's still afoot! And I'm almost out of that Nancy-boy hair gel that I like so much. Quickly, to the Angel-mobile, away!"

Interesting Facts: For the above scene the writers borrowed the premise of comedian Lenny Bruce's stand-up routine "Thank You, Masked Man," where he wonders why the Lone Ranger never stuck around for thank-yous. Notice how the menacing guy in the opening scene is actually named Lenny.

Nitpicks: What's that, Spike? Angel has a *curse*? You don't say! I'm glad someone pointed that out, because it isn't enough that Doyle and Cordelia have done it already! Also, Spike refers to Angel as his sire again, but we'll find out next season that Drusilla actually sired him. Joss Whedon tried to get around this inconsistency by saying that a sire could be anyone in the line (and since Angel sired Drusilla, it's fair game to say he is Spike's sire), but in "What's My Line? Part Two," the season-2 *Buffy* episode, Giles explains that a sire is indeed the one who makes an individual a vampire, a definition that will continue to be used throughout both series. And at one point, Marcus says vampires are like people who live and breathe, but vampires don't breathe. Finally, vampires have highly attuned senses, so why does Marcus wear glasses?

Oops: Vampires don't need to breathe, so there's no way Spike would have been able to strangle Angel, which he almost does.

The *Buffy* Connection: The *Buffy* episode that immediately preceded this one was "The Harsh Light of Day," in which the Scoobies find out that Harmony is a vampire, Spike and Harmony are a couple, and Spike is searching for the Gem of Amarra. This jewel is described by Giles as the "holy grail of vampires," as it renders the wearer impervious to all harm. Spike finds it, but Buffy gets it back and gives it to Oz, sending him to L.A. to deliver it to Angel. Also, Cordelia mentions a demon raised by Drusilla and Spike that burned people from the inside, a reference to the raising of the Judge in "Surprise."

Music/Bands: Marcus plays Mozart's Symphony no. 41 while he tortures Angel.

1.4   I Fall to Pieces

Original air date: October 26, 1999
Teleplay by: David Greenwalt
Story by: Joss Whedon and David Greenwalt
Directed by: Vern Gillum

Guest cast: Tushka Bergen (Melissa Burns), Andy Umberger (Dr. Ronald Meltzer), Carlos Carrasco (Dr. Vinpur Narpudun), Brent Sexton (Beat Cop), Garikayi Mutambirwa (Intern), Kent Davis (John), Jan Bartlett (Penny), Patricia Gillum (Woman Patient), Christopher Hart (Hands Performance)

Angel must stop a neurosurgeon who is stalking a woman, but things get complicated when he realizes that the man has learned to detach parts of his body.

"I Fall to Pieces" continues the theme of messed-up dating in L.A., and it is the scariest episode yet. Again, as in the first episode, a woman is being stalked, although this stalker, Dr. Meltzer, represents every woman's fear that she is being watched by someone. It is eerie enough that he can detach his eyes so that they float around and watch her every move, but when he detaches his hands and they run around like Thing in her apartment, the creep factor soars.

This episode establishes a routine for the series as well. Doyle will get the visions, Cordy will complain about money, Angel will visit with Kate, Wolfram & Hart will be involved in the events somehow, and eventually the gang will get to the bottom of the case. However, we will also see Doyle begin to hit on Cordelia and show that he has feelings for her. Meanwhile, Cordy will start to see the downside of living in L.A., and being exposed to other people's pain all the time will begin to get to her. Of course, her new empathy doesn't stop her from thinking that Angel Investigations should charge people in need if the team can help solve their problems. Angel, on the other hand, believes he's on a mission and can't take money from people who need his help. It's this continuity and character development that saves the show from getting tired. Early on the writers rely on monster-of-the-week episodes to move the story along and let us get to know the characters (much like season 1 of *Buffy*), but once the characters begin working together harmoniously, the show really takes off.

Highlight: Doyle admitting he might be slightly attracted to Angel.
Interesting Facts: For the *Buffy* fans, Andy Umberger has appeared on *Buffy* as D'Hoffryn, the demon who is responsible for Anya's being a vengeance demon.
Did You Notice?: Melissa's building is the Los Altos Apartments, which is used in seasons 2 through 4 as the exterior of the Hyperion Hotel, the future site of Angel Investigations. In this episode, when the police officer enters Melissa's building, you can see what the real lobby of the apartment building looks like; the one used in later seasons is a set.
Nitpicks: Cordelia says she recognizes the yogi from the doctor's book because she'd seen him on public television. When would she have watched public television? And how could Ronald have changed Melissa's PIN on her bank card? You need to do that

with the bank card, in person, at a bank, and he couldn't have done it without her being there. Also, Angel hates the coffee at Angel Investigations, but vampires have deadened taste buds, and he probably wouldn't have noticed just how bad it is. And if Ronald's eyes follow Melissa everywhere, why didn't he ever see her meeting with Angel? Finally, the doctor injects Angel with a paralytic tranquilizer that will stop his heart, but because Angel's heart doesn't beat and his blood doesn't circulate, there's no reason it should have affected him at all.

Oops: At the office party, Melissa has a cake that says "Benji," and she scrapes off the *j* and the bottom part of the *B* to make it a *P* (it's supposed to be "Penny"). But when she turns the cake around, the name clearly has a *y* at the end, as if it had been spelled "Benjy," meaning it was accidentally spelled differently on two prop cakes. Also, Ronald types in Melissa's PIN at the ATM but doesn't specify an amount. Yet, money comes out.

The *Buffy* Connection: In "Prophecy Girl," Xander goes home to listen to country music, "the music of pain," and he puts on Patsy Cline's "I Fall to Pieces."

Wolfram & Hart: Ronald Meltzer is represented by Wolfram & Hart, and when Kate checks a previous complaint that Melissa made against him, she notices that W&H ended up getting him cleared. Kate refers to W&H as the law firm "Johnny Cochran is too ethical to join."

1.5 Rm w/ a Vu

Original air date: November 2, 1999
Teleplay by: Jane Espenson
Story by: David Greenwalt and Jane Espenson
Directed by: Scott McGinnis
Guest cast: Beth Grant (Maude Pearson), B.J. Porter (Dennis), Marcus Redmond (Griff), Denney Pierce (Vic), Greg Collins (Keith), Corey Klemow (Young Man), Lara McGrath (Manager)

Cordy's new apartment is haunted by a ghost that seems intent on killing her, but she refuses to seek help because her place is rent-controlled.

While *Angel* is a series about what the title character has done in the past and how he must atone for it, it's also a show about how the other characters are dealing with the demons of their own pasts. Doyle has made a lot of bad choices in his life, and now he's paying the price with bookies and thugs showing up at his apartment and threatening his life over money owed. He refuses to give Angel his background story, although he promises he will some day, and just accepts that his life will be a difficult one because of the path he chose to take. But he's not the only one whose choices have led him to where he is today.

This exceptional episode focuses mainly on Cordy, and how her high school snobbery and bitchiness aren't necessarily a thing of the past. As head of the popular girls at Sunnydale High, she made Willow's life hell, taunted Jonathan and Xander, and seemed completely oblivious to the pain she was causing the nerds and unpopular kids around her. Until now.

Cordelia finally moves out of her roach-infested dive and into a new, fabulous apartment, one that represents everything she used to be: rich, stylish — and powerful. When she encounters a mean-spirited and dangerous poltergeist, Cordelia comes to terms with who she was in the past and seems to feel guilt about it for the first time. Despite hating the things she said in high school and knowing how she made the lives of others miserable, it's hard not to feel sorry for her as she sits paralyzed with guilt over what she has done. Just as Angel makes decisions that will punish himself, so too does Cordelia become complicit in her own punishment. But this is Cordelia Chase, and she's not an easy one to destroy. When she eventually realizes that the way out of this situation is to embrace the bitch within, she's able to uncover what is really going on in her apartment.

"Rm w/ a Vu" is an excellent look at how what we've done in the past can haunt us in the present, and how even our worst qualities can be turned into good ones.

Highlight: The "community" apartment Cordelia checks out, complete with public urination, group meetings, and chanting at 4 a.m.

Interesting Facts: The main difference between poltergeists and ghosts is their activity and ability to affect our concrete world. Ghosts are visible specters that carry the essence of the people they once were. Poltergeists can move objects and make noise, and they are often angrier versions of the ghost. It is believed that poltergeists can pick up on the emotional fragility of their victims, which is what happens in this episode when Maude detects Cordelia's soft spot and goes right for it. Technically, Dennis is also a poltergeist because he can move objects, but because of what Cordelia does for him he remains a friendly presence. Also, Jane Espenson came on the Bronze posting board to talk about choosing to have Angel answer the door in nothing but a towel: "Okay — Angel dripping wet in a towel . . . actually, first I wrote the scene with him reading a book, fully clothed. Then I thought, hey . . . not [a] particularly cinematic choice . . . what might work better? Dripping wet and naked just suggested itself . . . and what do you know . . . I think it's a little better than the whole book thing. But America didn't get to hear all the funny lines I wrote about *Wuthering Heights*. Oh well."

Did You Notice?: Does the name "Phantom Dennis" sound familiar? The writers have joked that it is a play on the Star Wars film title *The Phantom Menace*.

Oops: The noose that pulls Cordelia up to the chandelier keeps disappearing during the big battle. Also, after the Kailiff demon shoots out the tile in the fireplace, it magically reappears after Cordelia tells the ghost to get out of her house.

The *Buffy* Connection: Cordelia tells Doyle that her high-school graduation was "a rough ceremony," something that will be brought up again in the season-4 episode "Slouching Toward Bethlehem." She's referring to the events of "Graduation Day, Part Two," where the keynote speaker, the Mayor, turned into a giant snake, attacked the students, killed the principal, and disappeared into the high school, which Buffy and the gang blew up to destroy him.

Music/Bands: "You Always Hurt the One You Love" by The Mills Brothers (*Stardust: The Classic Decca Hits & Standards Collection*) plays on Cordy's radio as the ghost tries to scare her; and Angel listens to Beethoven's Symphony no. 9 as he's toweling off.

1.6   Sense and Sensitivity

Original air date: November 9, 1999
Written by: Tim Minear
Directed by: James A. Contner
Guest cast: John Capodice (Little Tony Papazian), John Mahon (Trevor Lockley), Ron Marasco (Allen Lloyd), Alex Skuby (Harlan), Kevin Will (Heath), Thomas Burr (Lee Mercer), Ken Abraham (Spivey), Jimmy Shubert (Johnny Red), Ken Grantham (Lieutenant), Adam Donshik (Uniform Cop #1), Kevin E. West (Uniform Cop #2), Wilson Bell (Uniform Cop #3), Colin Patrick Lynch (Beat Cop), Steve Schirripa (Henchman), Christopher Paul Hart (Traffic Cop)

The police officers in Kate's precinct become simpering, overly sensitive basket cases after a sensitivity training course.

"Sense and Sensitivity" is the *Angel* debut of future executive producer Tim Minear. The episode seems to draw a line between sensitivity and oversensitivity, showing that people don't seem to possess enough of the former and society pushes people toward the latter. Throughout the hour we see a lack of sensitivity between father and daughter, between friends, and between boss and employees. Angel could stand to notice how hard Cordelia and Doyle work and stop giving them the awful cleanup jobs, and it wouldn't hurt Trevor Lockley to show some kindness to his daughter every once in a while. Unfortunately, when a lack of sensitivity gets out of hand, the Dr. Lauras of the world step forward, offering huggy-bear solutions and hollow advice. Kate stands up to her father ineffectually and publicly, driving a further wedge between them rather than patching things up. Angel becomes the New Agey boss who worries about everyone's feelings but becomes ineffectual as a fighter.

This episode gives some background on Kate's character, and we discover why she acts like such a hardass all the time: she's trying to prove to her father that she can be like him and to her fellow officers that she's not an "emotional" woman. We find out that Trevor forced Kate to suppress her grief when her mother died, and that he suppressed his own. It's this grief that needs to be let out every once in a while in order to stay sane.

Though the script is strong, this episode has its problems. The actors pretend they're drunk in order to come off as overly sensitive (think of the scene with Kate at Angel Investigations), and it doesn't work. Also, everyone says they're acting with "sensitivity" when they should be saying "oversensitivity," since having sensitivity isn't a bad thing. Kate's confession to the room of police officers is so heartfelt, and her father is so nasty about it, we can't help but think that if he'd been more sensitive to her feelings, she'd be a healthier person today (Elisabeth Röhm is excellent in this scene). Oversensitivity can be detrimental, and not having any sensitivity upsets others, so everyone needs to find a middle ground. By the end of the episode, everyone crawls back inside themselves and pretends nothing has happened, which can be just as hurtful as the crazy pop therapy that charlatans try to sell people.

Highlight: Angel saying, "You could be a rainbow and not a painbow."
Interesting Facts: The guy who plays Tony Papazian's henchman now stars on *The Sopranos* as Bobby Baccalieri, the right-hand man to Corrado "Junior" Soprano.
Did You Notice?: Allen Lloyd must be a demon of some kind, because Angel enters his house with no invitation. Also, the address Angel gives Kate so she can find Tony Papazian is 8843 Hyperion Way, "Hyperion" being a name we'll hear more of next season.
Nitpicks: Where did Angel get the really loud outfit to use at the pier? He reaches into the back of his car like he just happens to have crazy Hawaiian shirts back there all the time.
Oops: In the very beginning, when Kate is chasing Spivey, he throws a bag that lands on top of a car, but when Kate kicks him, it's gone. Also, Allen Lloyd's name tag says "Lloyd" on it rather than his first name.
Wolfram & Hart: W&H represents Tony Papazian and the lawyers know about his arrest before he calls them. They use some supernatural mojo to get Kate and the other officers out of the way. This is the second time we hear mention of the "Senior Partners" who make the big decisions, and we find out that if a client commits a crime publicly, W&H reserves the right to drop that individual as a client. W&H catches Angel on tape and realizes he's becoming a more serious problem, worthy of attention.
Music/Bands: In this episode, we hear Solomon Burke's "Everybody Needs Somebody to Love" and "Baby (I Wanna Be Loved)" (*Home in Your Heart: The Best of Solomon Burke*).

1.7 The Bachelor Party

Original air date: November 16, 1999
Written by: Tracy Stern
Directed by: David Straiton
Guest cast: Kristin Dattilo (Harry), Carlos Jacott (Richard Howard Straley), Ted Kairys (Ben), Chris Tallman (Nick), Brad Blaisdell (Uncle John), Robert Hillis (Pierce), Lauri Johnson (Aunt Martha), Kristen Lowman (Mother Rachel), David Polcyn (Russ)

Doyle's ex-wife shows up with a new fiancé who wants Doyle to come to his bachelor party, but Doyle doesn't realize what's in store.

Doyle becomes more than two-dimensional comic relief in this episode, where we finally find out something about his past, who he is, and how he feels. After pining for Cordelia for several episodes, his crush is almost reciprocated when she realizes he's braver than most men she's dated, but just as she's about to tell him that, his ex-wife walks in the door with a new fiancé. Through Harry, Doyle's ex, we learn what Doyle was like before and what happened to him when he realized he was a demon. We also learn that the drinking and gambling he's involved in now are more a means of self-punishment than they are pleasurable vices.

The most interesting part of this episode is when we find out Doyle was a sweet-natured, loving man who taught grade school and volunteered in community organizations. When he discovered he was a demon, it was too much for him to handle and he began to drink and show hostility toward his wife and those around him. No matter what Harry told him about accepting his difference, he refused to listen and eventually drove her away. He allowed his belief about his nature — if he's a demon, he must be demonic — to get in the way of the caring man that he was, and he destroyed himself. The demon in Doyle was harmless; it was the man that was the problem.

Whereas Angel and Spike both have demons in them that have at one time clawed their way to the surface to take over their bodies, Doyle has always had control over his demons — he just didn't know it. When he fights, he refuses to let his demon face show because he's scared it'll make him more of a demon. Angel questions him about it, which is strange considering Angel also suppresses the demon within himself, although he shows its face when it suits him in a fight. Doyle changes by the end of the episode, but when Cordelia enters the room he immediately hides his demon side once again, as if seeing it will make her change her mind about him. Soon Doyle and everyone else will realize that it's not what you are, but who you are, that counts.

Highlight: Angel and Doyle acting like two big brothers when Cordelia's date walks in.
Interesting Facts: Carlos Jacott, who plays Richard, has appeared in all three of Joss

Whedon's television series. He played Ken, the devious teen counselor, in "Anne," the season-3 premiere of *Buffy*, and he also appeared as Lawrence Dobson in the *Firefly* episode, "Serenity."

Nitpicks: They say that the bachelor-party ritual of eating the first husband's brains is from an ancient prophecy, yet divorce wouldn't have been very common in ancient times if demon history is anything like human history. Also, when Doyle is put into the box, his head is sticking out through a very large hole. Why didn't he just pull his head into the box like a turtle?

Oops: When Richard first turns into a demon, you can see that only Carlos Jacott's hands have been painted red when, at one point, his coat sleeve moves up slightly and his white arm is visible.

The *Buffy* Connection: Cordelia says that after Xander she didn't want another fixer-upper, referring to her year-and-a-half relationship with Xander — a bit of a nerd — on *Buffy*. The vision Doyle has at the end of the episode will send Angel back to Sunnydale for the *Buffy* episode "Pangs." The conclusion of that episode will be *Angel*'s "I Will Remember You."

1.8   I Will Remember You

Original air date: November 23, 1999
Written by: David Greenwalt, Jeannine Renshaw
Directed by: David Grossman
Guest cast: Carey Cannon (Female Oracle), Randall Slavin (Male Oracle), Sarah Michelle Gellar (Buffy), David Wald (Mohra Demon #1), Chris Durand (Mohra Demon #2)

When Angel touches the blood of a demon and becomes human again, he and Buffy finally have a shot at a normal relationship.

"I Will Remember You" is a heartrending episode, giving fans of the Buffy-Angel relationship (B-A shippers, or Bangels, as they're called online) exactly what they've been waiting for. In one hour, we see a day in the life of "normal" Buffy and human Angel, complete with everything they were previously unable to do. The problem is, we also see what's wrong with that relationship. Angel is rendered as powerless as Buffy was in "Helpless," and Buffy now has to fight to save his life as well as the lives of everyone else. (Not only that, but typically, the writers of *Angel* ensure nothing happens on the show that would alter what happens on *BtVS*, so one can watch *Buffy* in syndication without missing anything. In other words, this relationship is doomed.)

While being immortal might seem like a pretty cool gift, we realize in this episode that it's not all roses. Angel can't taste food (it's why he doesn't eat), he can't walk in the

Back in season one of *Buffy*, Angel and Buffy seemed meant for each other, but as they got older, their relationship became too complicated.

sun, he can't enjoy the simple pleasures in life. Oddly, his vampire senses can smell a demon or a person a mile away, yet he begins to gag when he smells a corpse for the first time as a human, showing us that even odors are different for him. Also, being a mortal, the theme of time becomes important. Because he'll no longer live forever, time is something that is limited for him, and the theme figures throughout the episode: Angel winds his clock at the beginning of the episode; he gives his watch as a gift to the Oracles; there's a time warp while he's talking to the Oracles; Buffy says there's not enough time left for them; and, finally, Angel smashes his clock over the Mohra demon.

This episode features the Oracles for the first time, and we're warned of an impending doom that the players on *Angel* will soon have to fight. But the *Angel* plot points are secondary to the Buffy-Angel relationship. In the end, inevitably, the relationship is not to be, and the steps Angel takes to save Buffy from emotional harm just deepen the complexities of his character. As if he didn't have enough pain to carry around, he now bears the knowledge of something Buffy will never know. The final moments of their relationship are the most painful for any fan to watch, and it's interesting that Sarah Michelle Gellar has her finest acting moment of the season — on *Angel*. She is absolutely brilliant, in no small part because of her chemistry with David Boreanaz. Scenes like this prove just how drab the Riley-Buffy relationship, which is just blossoming on *Buffy*, is in comparison.

Highlight: Doyle saying he wants to go out and make his mark on the world and Cordelia replying, "We had a cat that used to do that."

Interesting Facts: When Angel begins gorging himself and Doyle says, "Orson, we're in a situation here!" he's probably referring to Mork of *Mork & Mindy*, who would contact his superior, Orson, to tell him about the situation in every episode. Mork also often made fun of Orson's weight, which would apply here.

Did You Notice?: The Mohra demon tells Angel that the "end of days" is near and that a great darkness is coming, a brilliant foreshadowing of season 4.

Nitpicks: Not to be rude, but it seems unlikely that Buffy eats "cookie dough fudge mint chip" ice cream on a regular basis. By this season, she looks like she indulges in only the occasional carrot. Also, if Mohra blood has regenerative properties, it probably has a lot of healing power. Why didn't Angel and Buffy preserve some?

The *Buffy* Connection: On "Pangs," the *Buffy* episode that preceded this one, Angel goes to Sunnydale after hearing about Doyle's vision because he believes Buffy is in trouble. The gang's Thanksgiving feast is attacked by a tribe of Chumash Indians who want revenge for having been wiped out centuries before. Angel remains outside Giles's house while the others fight the demons inside. Angel makes his presence known to Giles, Willow, Xander, and Anya but remains hidden from Buffy until the

Native Americans are stopped, and Xander accidentally lets slip at the dinner that they'd all seen Angel. Strangely, the Chumash Indians weren't half the threat that other demons are in this season and subsequent ones, so it's not clear why Doyle had a vision about this particular danger. However, it's clear the writers were looking to pull *Buffy* fans over to *Angel* early on, and this was the perfect way to do it. Also, Buffy refers to their talk at the beginning of "I Will Remember You" as another heartfelt sewer talk, the first having taken place in "The Prom" when Angel broke up with her. Finally, the song that plays when Angel walks into the sun and kisses her is the Buffy-Angel theme that always played on *Buffy* when they were together (brilliantly, it changes to a major key from the sadder minor one it had been on *Buffy*).

1.9   Hero

Original air date: November 30, 1999
Written by: Howard Gordon and Tim Minear
Directed by: Tucker Gates
Guest cast: Tony Denman (Rieff), Anthony Cistaro (Scourge Commander), Michelle Horn (Rayna), Lee Arenberg (Tiernan), Sean Gunn (Lucas), James Henrikson (Elder Lister Demon), David Bickford (Cargo Inspector), Christopher Comes (Storm Trooper #2), Paul O'Brien (Captain), Ashley Taylor (First Mate)

L.A. is besieged by an army of the apocalypse, and a prophecy states that only a sacrifice of the Promised One can stop it.

Two tearjerkers in as many weeks — this is what the Buffyverse is all about. This episode is about sacrifice and what makes a hero, and there's no doubt that Doyle was as heroic as any character on *Angel* or *Buffy*. The show was also written in the spirit of Joss Whedon's "Don't get too comfortable as a regular on my show" motto (as characters Jenny Calendar and Principal Flutie, among others, discovered on *Buffy*). Whedon and his writing staff take daring chances that few other shows would take, and eliminating a major character only nine episodes into a series (when there are only three leads!) is a huge one.

The episode seems to have been inspired by the Nazi Holocaust. The Scourge, who are some of the creepiest demons ever to appear on *Angel*, are all dressed as SS officers, marching around and declaring that half-breeds will be killed, leaving only pure-bloods in the world. Similarly, the Nazis declared all Jews tainted and believed that one day there would be a pure Aryan race if they could rid the world of Jews. Rieff, a Lister demon pursued by the Scourge, accuses Doyle of "passing," which many Jews did by dyeing their hair blond and hiding in attics and other secret places to avoid detection by the Nazis. Rieff's own family and other demons hide in small compartments under the floorboards. When Angel attends a rally of the Scourge where the leader declares that all non-purebloods will be annihilated, it is similar to one of Hitler's rallies. Like Hitler, the leader is small but a dynamic public speaker.

Just as Doyle finds out the sacrifice that Angel made in the previous episode and declares him the "real deal" as far as heroes go, Cordelia discovers the secret that Doyle has been hiding and realizes that he, too, is a hero. In "The Bachelor Party" we learned that Doyle covered up his inner demon by becoming a worse human being, but here he finally uses his demon side to save people. The demon in him makes him the hero, which is the concluding, bitter irony of his life. And in his final moment, what he passes on to Cordelia will make her a hero as well.

CHRISTINA RADISH

In the end, Doyle died a hero. The actor who played him, Glenn Quinn, died suddenly in December 2002. He will be missed.

Highlight: The repetition of Doyle's advertisement for Angel Investigations at the end of the episode: "When the chips are down, and you're at the end of your rope, you need someone that you can count on. And that's what you'll find here — someone who will go all the way, who will protect you no matter what. So don't lose hope. Come on over to our offices and you'll see that there are still heroes in this world. [Pause] Is that it? Am I done?"

Interesting Facts: Some fans were so outraged by the surprise ending of this episode that they launched a "Save Doyle" campaign to bring his character back, but he never returned. Sadly, Glenn Quinn did receive one further credit on *Angel* in season 4 (see "Long Day's Journey") and Doyle's ad for Angel Investigations was played one last time in the season-5 episode "You're Welcome."

Did You Notice?: Doyle calls Cordelia "princess," a foreshadowing of the Pylea episodes in season 2.

Nitpicks: On *Buffy*, in "Graduation Day, Part One," Anya tells everyone that all demons walking the earth are only half-demons, that all of them are "tainted" with a human side. She says there are no pure demons, and only through an Ascension, which the Mayor is trying to organize, can a demon become pure. In other words, the Scourge are as tainted as those they are hunting, which is either a continuity error or a comment on the discrepancy between Hitler's pursuit of a pure, blond-haired, blue-eyed race and his own dark hair and dark eyes. Also, if there are no pure demons, then Angel should have been incinerated when the Scourge commander turned on the beacon, since his human side is still within him.

Oops: Doyle tells Cordelia to go to Pier 12, but when the scene cuts to Angel we see a flash of a sign that says "Pier 39," the same image used in "Sense and Sensitivity." Also, if the Lister demons are hiding under the floor, the only way they could pull the rug over the trapdoor is if they had a string attached to the end closest to the door's opening that they could pull from inside the shelter (as seen in *Schindler's List*). However, when the Scourge throw open the trapdoor, there's no string attached to the rug, so there's no way the demons could have pulled it over themselves like they did. Finally, the take of Doyle's ad shown at the end of the episode is not the same one we saw in the beginning.

The *Buffy* Connection: In "Surprise," the Judge said that Spike reeked of humanity, the very thing Angel says about Doyle in this episode.

1.10　Parting Gifts

Original air date: December 14, 1999
Written by: David Fury and Jeannine Renshaw
Directed by: James A. Contner
Guest cast: Maury Sterling (Barney), Carey Cannon (Female Oracle), Randall Slavin (Male Oracle), Jayson Creek (Producer #1), Sean Smith (Producer #2), Sara Devlin (Producer #3), Jason Kim (Soon), Brett Gilbert (Reptilian Demon), Henry Kingi (Kungai Demon), Lawrence Turner (Hank), Cheyenne Wilber (Concierge), Dominique Jennings (Mac), Kotoko Kawamura (Ancient Korean Woman)

Cordelia discovers that Doyle left her a "parting gift," and when a new "rogue demon hunter" comes to L.A., the Angel Investigations duo is reunited with an old acquaintance.

With "Parting Gifts," the arc of the series really gets started. Cordelia has inherited Doyle's visions and immediately discovers the physical pain they cause and how dangerous such a "gift" can be when the wrong people find out about it. The scene of the demon auction is eerie and frightening, but luckily, a rogue demon hunter comes to the rescue.

Yes, folks, Wesley Wyndam-Pryce is back in all his bumbling, stuttering goodness. Although he only lasted nine episodes on *Buffy* before being clotheslined in the first seconds of the graduation-day battle, Wesley left an impression on the fans — and the writers — and he has been given a second life on *Angel*. Like Cordelia, Wesley was a comic foil on *Buffy*, but on *Buffy*'s more serious spinoff, both Wesley and Cordelia have a chance to shine in a way they never could on their parent show. Wesley is a comic character for most of this season, although he will eventually become one of the series' darkest and most complex characters. We get a glimpse of who he will become when he talks about himself as a failure in this episode, mentioning how he lost two Slayers and now can't do his new job adequately. Adding Alexis Denisof to the show is a stroke of genius, and he's able to inject new life into *Angel* just as fans were wondering where the writers were taking it.

Of course, both Cordy and the fans are still in mourning for Doyle and aren't quite ready to accept Wesley as his replacement just yet. The producers cleverly kept Glenn Quinn in the opening credits and didn't yet add Denisof permanently so as to maintain the suspense that they might bring back Quinn after all. But Angel's discussion with the Oracles in the opening scene puts an end to any hope that this might happen, and with "Parting Gifts," it's time to move on, without Doyle, to the next arc of the series.

Highlight: Cordelia's disastrous audition.

Interesting Facts: Cordelia keeps saying "the PTB," which is a shout-out to the online fans who write "TPTB" when referring to "the powers that be."

Did You Notice?: Barney is an Empath demon, as is the Host, who will appear in season 2, but either there are different kinds of Empath demons or the writers just hadn't figured them out yet, because Barney doesn't look like Lorne (he's not green, he has extra horns, and he has floppy ears) and he can sense what a person feels just by being near them, whereas Lorne's powers are different. Also, the auction itself, in which Barney says Cordy could be used as a slave and Cordy begins mouthing off about what she's worth, parallels a scene in the upcoming season-2 episode "Over the Rainbow."

Nitpicks: The female Oracle takes offense to Angel's asking them to reverse Doyle's death, and she tells him that if they do it'll leave Doyle's atonement unfulfilled. What did Doyle have to atone for? His gambling debts? Also, a demon jumps out a second-storey window and Angel doesn't follow him? It is nighttime; why doesn't Angel chase him? And Barney reads Cordelia's mind and figures out she's "twentysomething," but that would make her at least a year older than Buffy, which isn't right (Buffy will turn 19 in January 2000). Did she fail a grade in school? Finally, why would Cordelia's eyes be worth anything if extracted? The visions come into her head, not her eyes.

The *Buffy* Connection: During season 3 on *Buffy*, the Watcher's Council deemed Giles too close to Buffy personally to continue as her Watcher, so it replaced him with

Wesley Wyndam-Pryce, the stuffy, jittery British Watcher. Wesley developed a crush on Cordelia that culminated in the two of them kissing each other in the season finale only to realize they felt absolutely nothing and were better off apart.

Wolfram & Hart: A w&h lawyer attends the demon auction and outbids the other demons for Cordelia — apparently this is one of the firm's ways to obtain priceless demon parts. In this episode, the lawyer acknowledges that Angel has become an enemy to w&h and often stands in the way of the firm's progress by thwarting their efforts.

1.11   Somnambulist

Original air date: January 18, 2000
Written by: Tim Minear
Directed by: Winrich Kolbe
Guest cast: Jeremy Renner (Penn), Nick McCallum (Skateboard Kid), Kimberleigh Aarn (Precinct Clerk), Paul Webster (Uniform #1), Brien DiRito (Task Force Member #1)

Angel fears he may have unknowingly returned to his evil ways when he dreams of murdering people and those very people are found dead the next day.

This episode is an excellent hour of flashbacks, revelations, and a reminder that Angelus will always be inside Angel, waiting to re-emerge. Some of the best *Buffy* episodes are ones that show viewers snippets of the pasts of the centuries-old demons on the show, and the flashbacks on *Angel* are no exception. Angel is such a fascinating character, with such a rich, terrifying history, that these glimpses into his past, which show us what a horrible creature he once was, remind us again and again that the Angel of today has a lot to atone for. He might be able to save a person every night, but can that make up for the hundreds, if not thousands, he murdered in cold blood for 150 years?

In "Somnambulist," Angel is haunted by his past crimes in his sleep, and we discover that he's actually receiving visions of Penn, a protégé of his from the 17th century who is back in L.A. and re-enacting some of the murders he and Angel committed centuries ago. Penn is cold, calculating, and ruthless, and Angel taught him everything he knows. Like Angel (and almost every other character on both shows), Penn despises his father and everything he does is a kind of warped revenge for his father's Puritan ways. Also like Angel, Penn's first murders were of his own family members, and he enjoyed killing them. Now he's back, and Angel feels the glee of Penn's murders in his own dreams and worries that he'll never be able to escape the Angelus within. When Angel says that Los Angeles is very much like where he grew up, he realizes the city reminds him of who he once was (Los Angeles = Lost Angelus).

Meanwhile, Kate finds out the awful truth about what Angel is and what actually lurks in the L.A. darkness. The earlier scene of her detailing Penn's modus operandi is excellent, as she describes Angel perfectly without knowing it. It's strange that she has been a police officer for as long as she has without realizing her city is crawling with demons, but like so many others, Kate has turned a blind eye to what is around her. At first Kate is the Scully to Angel's Mulder, but when she does some research of her own, her reaction is swift and judgmental, and it puts a rift between her and Angel that may never be closed. However, he doesn't hate her for feeling the way she does; in fact, he agrees with her, knowing that he deserves all her venom. After all, he's been dishing it out to himself for 100 years.

Highlight: Cordelia adamantly standing up to Wesley's suggestion that Angel might have gone bad again, and then her complete 180. Cordy: "He is my friend and nothing you or anyone else can say will make me turn on a friend." Angel: "Cordelia, he's right." Cordy: "You stake him and I'll cut off his head."

Did You Notice?: When Cordy and Wes are looking at an old newspaper article dated October 26, 1929, about recent murders in L.A., the column on the right boasts the headline "Wall Street Confident as Stocks Surge."

Nitpicks: Penn tells Angel that he lost track of him and waited for him to return "until the nineteenth century," and Angel replies that he got held up in Romania. But Angel's fateful visit to Romania happened on the eve of the 20th century (1898), not the 19th. And why is it that when a demon runs out of the room, no one *ever* chases it? Penn races out of Angel Investigations with a coat over his head to avoid the sunlight, and Cordelia and Wesley just stand there rather than run after him. And how did Kate get her information about Angel? Giles had a hard time tracking down information about Angel in season 1 of *Buffy* and was only able to find tidbits in the Watcher Diaries (which Kate would have no access to), and it's not like mystical books about the demonic underworld are just hanging out in her local library. Finally, Kate hands out pictures of Angel, yet not one officer recognizes him from her father's retirement party.

Oops: Wesley is reading a newspaper at one point, and while it's folded in half you can read part of the headline about people fleeing apartments. But when he hands the cutout article to Cordelia the headline reads, "Third Body Found in Alley," and he says it had been the front-page headline. Also, after Penn and Angel fight the final time, Angel falls directly into a patch of sunlight without getting the least bit smoky.

The *Buffy* Connection: Over on *Buffy*, commando boy Riley has just found out that Buffy is a Slayer and doesn't quite believe in her "fairy tale" stories of the supernatural. The Kate and Angel arc is very similar, and it seems to be happening at the same time.

Music/Bands: In this episode we hear Lunatic Calm's "Leave You Far Behind" (*Metropol*).

1.12 Expecting

Original air date: January 25, 2000
Written by: Howard Gordon
Directed by: David Semel
Guest cast: Daphnee Duplaix (Serena), Ken Marino (Wilson Christopher), Josh Randall (Bartender), Doug Tompos (Dr. Wasserman), Louisette Geiss (Emily), Julie Quinn (Pregnant Woman), Maggie Connelly (Nurse), Steven Roy (Jason)

Cordelia gets more than she bargained for when she goes on a date and ends up nine months pregnant the next morning.

With a gestation period shorter than Gabrielle's on *Xena*, Cordelia wakes up out-to-there the morning after what seemed like the perfect date. Like in "Rm w/ a Vu," Cordelia believes she's in this predicament because she's being punished (she's quickly becoming a poster child for why you shouldn't bully other kids in school).

The incident is a metaphor for dating in the big city, where guys take women out on one-night stands and leave them pregnant with their children. The fetus seems to grow so quickly, the mother can barely put her life in order. Cordelia becomes moody, eats disgusting things, and snaps at Wesley for not possibly knowing what she's going through, but despite being cranky, she becomes attached to the baby and will do anything to protect it, developing a fierce mama-bear complex. (And for anyone who's been pregnant, the scene of her snapping at the stranger for touching her stomach is priceless.) In this case, her pregnancy also seems to stand for surrogate motherhood and the pain surrogate mothers endure when they give their children away. The end scene, with the women wearing white robes and sitting in a tank of filthy water, could also be a metaphor for people coming to L.A. and being roped into religious cults, where they're baptized as new people.

This episode is important mostly for how the relationship among the triumvirate strengthens as a result of what happens. In the beginning, Wesley is hanging around, wondering if he might be of some use to Angel and Cordelia, and Angel is wondering why Cordelia never tells him what's going on in her life (consider the source). We discover that Cordelia has cut herself off completely from her family when Serena tells Angel that the guys were attracted to the fact that Cordy had no family to turn to. Again, Cordelia believes that what is happening to her is a punishment for the way she behaved in the past. But Wesley and Angel come through for her, first by showing up at her apartment, concerned because they hadn't heard from her post-date, and then by doing everything they can to save her life. Cordelia's parents might not be in touch with her, but she has a new family with Wesley and Angel, and by the end of the episode she realizes she can trust them with her life.

Highlight: Angel and Wesley going to the wrong house at the beginning of the episode.

Did You Notice?: This is the first time we see Wesley shoot a gun (with amazing accuracy as well), which will become a staple weapon of his in later seasons.

Oops: When Cordelia drinks the blood it runs down the sides of her mouth, yet not a drop ends up on her protruding belly when she turns toward the camera.

Music/Bands: When Cordelia is talking to the guy at the bar, we hear Splashdown's "Games You Play" (*Blueshift*).

1.13   She

Original air date: February 8, 2000
Written by: David Greenwalt and Marti Noxon
Directed by: David Greenwalt
Guest cast: Bai Ling (Jhiera), Colby French (Tae), Heather Stephens (Demon Girl), Sean Gunn (Mars), Tracy Costello (Laura), Andre Roberson (Diego), P.J. Marino (Peter Wilkers), Honor Bliss (Girl), Chris Durand (Demon Henchman #1), Alison Simpson (Demon Girl #1), Lucas Dudley (Security Guard)

Angel tries to help a society of women hoping to avoid painful and life-altering procedures at the hands of men when they come of age.

"She" is an entertaining and very funny episode, but the metaphor gets a little muddled. On the one hand, Princess Jhiera, who has arrived from another dimension, is fighting to save the women of her culture from being mutilated by the men. She explains to Angel that when the women come of age, the ridges on their backs are removed, which renders them unable to make decisions on their own, and they become slaves to the men of their culture. The act is clearly pointing to female genital mutilation, a barbaric practice that still occurs in some Third World countries, where the clitoris is removed from young girls so that they won't be sexually promiscuous. The problem is, in this episode Jhiera says that the ridges are the source of a woman's free will, passion, personality, and sexual and physical strength, which, if the metaphor is followed all the way through, would suggest that a woman's personality is in her genitalia.

The ridges on the backs of the women burn a bright red when they become aroused, and by merely touching them, Wesley and Angel also become aroused, suggesting that it's the men who can't control themselves, not the women. However, because the metaphor of genital mutilation is so obvious, it borders on being misogynistic in that it suggests these women are dangerous to others and to themselves because of their overwhelming passions. They're kept on ice in a spa because, as the spa owner says, they need to cool down and "mellow" before they can deal with the world.

That said, the hour is redeemed by its funny moments, including Wesley and

Angel dancing at Cordelia's party; Angel's inability to use a cell phone (a motif that will come up again and again); Angel giving a spontaneous lecture on Manet's "La Musique" and subtly suggesting he might have been the subject of Baudelaire's "Le

Angel and Cell Phones

From the beginning of the series, it's been a running joke that Angel and technology don't go together very well. One of his biggest hang-ups is cell phones, which is a source of constant grief for Cordelia. Here are some of the moments when he's been unable to use his phone:

★ Angel can't figure out how to talk on it, fumbles with the cord when he's trying to recharge it and drive at the same time, and eventually says it's been made by a bored warlock. Later, Wesley tries to call him and Angel's turned it off. ("She")

★ Angel bangs away at the door of a meat locker after being locked in rather than calling Cordy and Wesley for help. When they point out his folly, he says the phone probably wouldn't have worked anyway. He adds that he's the boss and will say when and where they use the cell phones. ("War Zone")

★ Cordelia's cell phone cuts out when she and Angel are in the sewer, and he rolls his eyes in a way that suggests he never trusted the gadget in the first place. ("Heartthrob")

★ When Angel's cell phone goes off in the sewer, he jumps into the air out of fright, like he's not used to hearing it. ("Fredless")

★ Cordelia explains to Fred that it's not worth it to leave Angel a message on his cell phone, because he has no idea how to check his voice mail. ("Offspring")

★ Angel turns on his phone and hears a beeping noise. When he tries to answer the cell, another guy tells him it's actually his voice mail indicating he has a message waiting, not a call coming in. ("Provider")

★ Fred says she can't reach Angel on his cell phone, and Cordelia says that that doesn't mean anything considering he still doesn't know how to use one. ("Benediction")

★ Angel pulls out a cell phone to call Cordelia and it slips over the edge of a cliff, causing him to mutter, "I hate those things!" ("Tomorrow")

Vampire"; and Wesley finally being welcomed into the fold as a full-fledged member of Angel Investigations. The scene at Cordelia's party shows the dichotomy between Angel and Wesley. Angel is so uncomfortable in social situations that he retreats to a dark room for fear he'll embarrass himself in public. He tells Wesley that with people he does one of two things: bites them or avoids them. Wesley, on the other hand, has a total lack of self-consciousness, is socially inept, and never worries about making an ass of himself. With Cordelia's help, the two of them will find a middle ground where they both develop a healthy sense of self-consciousness mixed with self-confidence.

Highlight: The single funniest moment in season 1, when David Boreanaz shows off Angel's Elaine Benes–type dance moves at Cordy's party. Hilarious.

Interesting Facts: Princess Jhiera is played by Bai Ling (a.k.a. Ling Bai), a film star in her native China who is known for her outspoken protests against her country's injustices. Bai Ling is best known for playing the attorney who defends Richard Gere in *Red Corner*, a movie in which the Chinese judicial system is seriously called into question. The movie was banned in China and Hong Kong, and Bai Ling suffered ostracism as a result. She was scheduled to appear in two films by Chinese directors and they both backed out on her; her passport was revoked and she has been banned from her native country. By the time the film came out, Bai Ling was already a U.S. citizen and had been studying acting in New York since 1992 (she left China three years earlier after having been involved in the Tiananmen Square riots of 1989). She has since appeared in *Anna and the King* and has had guest roles in other films, including *Nixon* and *The Crow*. She will appear as Senator Bana Breemu in the upcoming third installment of the Star Wars prequel trilogy.

Did You Notice?: This episode features the second time Cordy mentions "Steve Paymer, David Paymer's brother." David Paymer is a recognizable character actor who played Norman Litkey on *The Larry Sanders Show*, and he was nominated for an Academy Award for Best Supporting Actor in 1993 for his role in *Mr. Saturday Night*. His brother, Steve Paymer (who actually attends Cordy's party), has had a few small roles on television and was a writer for the sitcom *Mad About You*. This is also the first time "portals" between demon dimensions are mentioned, something that will become crucial in later episodes.

Nitpicks: If a vampire doesn't have a body temperature (people often remark that Angel feels cold to the touch), then why did Angel have to take a cold shower? Also, why is there only one person on duty in that massive spa? And finally, Jhiera goes to great lengths to get the girls away safely and then leaves them alone to come back and "glow" with Angel?

Oops: Angel hooks his cell phone up to its recharger in the car, but when he calls Cordelia on it moments later the cord is no longer attached to it.

The *Buffy* Connection: Wesley insists that he's very rarely taken hostage, which is an inside joke regarding his first appearance on *Buffy*, in which he was promptly taken hostage.

Music/Bands: At Cordy's party we hear "Strangelove Addiction" by the Supreme Beings of Leisure, from their self-titled CD; "In Time" by Morphic Field, from their self-titled CD; and "Light Years On" by 60 Channels (*Tuned In . . . Tuned On*).

1.14 I've Got You Under My Skin

Original air date: February 15, 2000
Story by: David Greenwalt and Jeannine Renshaw
Teleplay by: Jeannine Renshaw
Directed by: R.D. Price
Guest cast: Will Kempe (Seth Anderson), Katy Boyer (Paige Anderson), Anthony Cistaro (Ethros Demon), Jesse James (Ryan Anderson), Ashley Edner (Stephanie Anderson), Patience Cleveland (Nun), Jerry Lambert (Rick the Clerk)

Angel and Wesley try to exorcise a demon that possesses a little boy only to be met with a horrible discovery.

"I've Got You Under My Skin" is an outstanding episode with lots of surprises. Through the story of Ryan, a child possessed by a demon that is making his parents' lives a living hell, we learn more about the other characters on the show. Wesley was apparently abused and tortured by his father and has often tried to make his father proud, to no avail. The demon in Ryan taunts Wesley for his inability to get past what happened to him as a child (and his Harry Potter–like sleeping accommodations). Even Wesley slips near the beginning of the episode when he says that a father doesn't have to be possessed to terrorize his children. Although the abuse is hinted at throughout the series, we'll never find out exactly what happened to Wesley, only that it's made him a broken man in adulthood. Suddenly his clumsiness becomes sad rather than funny, and his dark turn in seasons 3 and 4 seem inevitable in retrospect.

Angel is dealing with the guilt that he didn't save Doyle when he had the chance. He accidentally calls Wesley "Doyle" in the middle of an argument between Wes and Cordy, and Cordelia asks Angel why he never says Doyle's name. As was suggested in "Sense and Sensitivity," Angel isn't exactly someone who shares his feelings, so, as usual, he's kept his emotions about Doyle bottled up. It has to be difficult for Angel to keep asking everyone to kill him if the need arises, though — no wonder his self-esteem is so low. Cordelia's visions are starting to become more painful for her, which will become a more important plot point in season 3.

This episode is a great homage to *The Exorcist*, with a possessed child appealing to its mother's sympathies while being ministered to by both a superior and an inferior priest (Angel believes Wesley isn't strong enough mentally for the exorcism, and Wesley knows Angel can't physically do it). However, it has more twists and turns than the film and will keep you guessing throughout.

Highlight: Wesley smelling Cordelia's brownies and telling Angel he thought he'd tracked something in on his shoe.

Interesting Facts: Wesley insinuates that Lizzie Borden had an Ethros demon inside her. Lizzie Borden was accused of killing her parents with an ax in August 1892 in Massachusetts. The crime prompted the first national murder investigation in American history, and she was charged, strangely, with three counts of murder (killing her stepmother, killing her father, and killing both). After a two-week trial the following summer, during which no physical evidence was presented, Borden was acquitted. To this day, several theories abound. Most believe she actually did commit the crimes (she was seen burning her dress shortly after the murders; she showed very little emotion upon discovering her parents dead; she had allegedly tried to buy poison from a pharmacy shortly before the murders and was refused; and she continually corrected the officers on the scene that Abby Borden was her stepmother, not her mother) and was let off because she was a churchgoer who taught Sunday School, and the public probably couldn't fathom that kind of woman doing such a thing.

Did You Notice?: The store where Cordelia goes to buy the box needed to contain the demon is called Rick's Magick 'n' Stuff (it's a hilarious scene, with an owner who acts more like a used car salesman than a serious magick shop proprietor).

Nitpicks: Paige says that they have burglar bars on their windows, yet at the end of the episode Angel smashes through Stephanie's window without having to pull any bars off. Were the bars only over Ryan's windows? Also, it's very rare for a bedroom door to open out into the hallway as Ryan's parents' does, especially when the doors of the other two bedrooms open inward.

Oops: After Cordelia finishes pouring the binding powder on the floor, she stands up and the jar looks as full as it was when she began. Also, when Angel runs down the stairs to pull Paige off Ryan, David Boreanaz looks like he can't stop laughing, and soon after, as Wesley holds the cross to Ryan and is speaking Latin, you can see Boreanaz start to laugh again and drop his head.

1.15   The Prodigal

Original air date: February 22, 2000
Written by: Tim Minear
Directed by: Bruce Seth Green
Guest cast: Julie Benz (Darla), John Mahon (Trevor Lockley), J. Kenneth Campbell (Angel's Father), Henri Lubatti (Vampire), Frank Potter (Uniformed Delivery), Eliza Szonert (Chamber Maid), Bob Fimiani (Grounds Keeper), Christina Hendricks (Bar Maid), John Maynard (Uniformed Worker), Glenda Morgan Brown (Angel's Mother), Mark Ginther (Head Demon Guy), John Patrick Clerkin (Black Robed Priest), Mike Vendrell (Suit #2)

Past and present come together when Kate faces her feelings about her father and we learn about Angel's relationship with his father.

For those who loved the *Buffy* season-2 finale, "Becoming," and were clamoring for more backstory on how Angel was turned into a vampire, this episode has it. Angel was a drunken layabout named Liam who spent his free time in bars and strange women's beds. His father condemned his behavior, and when Liam becomes Angelus we see (once again) just how brutal he was. He kills his family, one by one, relishing the death of his father. It's interesting that David Boreanaz has made Angel such a charismatic character that we can watch scenes like these and still like the guy.

Meanwhile, Kate's father is involved in some dirty dealings and is killed by vampires, and she blames Angel and "his kind" for what happened. In an interesting juxtaposition, we see Angel's tombstone in 1753, which says "Beloved Son" (ironic wording considering he had been sent away by his father, who hated him), and Kate's father's tombstone in the present day, with the eerily similar wording "Beloved Father" (in fact, she never saw eye-to-eye with him, and he was a hard and often cruel man). Earlier, Lockley calls Angel "son" and we see a shadow pass over Angel's face. He tells Angel that he can't possibly know why a father would do the things he does for his children and that sometimes sacrifices have to be made, a prophetic moment in light of the later events of seasons 3 and 4.

The parallels don't end there, however. Angel sees his father as someone who was never proud of him, but what he fails to realize is that he never gave his father a reason to take pride in him. Liam was a drunken lout who deserved to be banished from his father's home: he fondled the female servant, got into bar fights, and was an all-around loser. Yet through Angel's eyes we're supposed to see the father as an unfair Puritan who treated his son badly. Similarly, Kate believes that her father has never been proud of anything she's done, but he secretly is proud of her and worries about her well-being. What he does in this episode is for her ultimate benefit — or so he believes — but because he refuses to tell her what he really thinks, she'll never know just how proud of her he really was.

Fathers have never been the "good guys" in the Whedonverse, and when Darla tells Angelus that he'll never get his father's approval now that he's killed him, we know he'll be searching for it for the rest of his life, just like Kate and Wesley.

Highlight: The office alarm going off during the demon fight.

Interesting Facts: The episode gets its title from the biblical story of the prodigal son (Luke 15:11–32), about a man who has two sons. The youngest asks for his half of the property and wastes it on prostitutes and a good time. After becoming impoverished and almost starving to death, he realizes he must go to his father, apologize to him, and ask to work in his fields.

Angel discovers in "The Prodigal" that sometimes, you can't go home again. In which case, you just slaughter your family instead.

When he returns home his father welcomes him with open arms and has a huge celebration in his honor, because he'd thought his son was dead. The other son, who had always worked in the fields and had been faithful to his father, asks why his wastrel of a brother is getting such treatment. The father replies that all of his remaining property belongs to the good son, but the party is to give thanks for the return of the son he thought he had lost. Interestingly, there's no real ending to the story or any moral to be taken from it other than the message that you can always go home (a message that Angelus twists in a grotesque way).

Did You Notice?: We find out that Angel's real name is Liam and that he became "Angel" when his sister saw him in the doorway after he was dead and said he must be an angel. Angelus is the Latinate form of Angel, so Darla probably called him that thinking she was adding a bit of flair to his name.

Nitpicks: There is a lot of sunlight coming into that police station; how was Angel walking down the hallways when they're so bright?

Oops: Wesley refers to the Kwaini demon's vivisection, but that's when you cut something open while it's still alive, and Angel had already killed it. Wesley should have said "autopsy."

The *Buffy* Connection: When we see Liam turned into a vampire, the scene is interspersed with scenes from the season-2 *Buffy* episode "Becoming, Part One."

1.16   The Ring

Original air date: February 29, 2000
Written by: Howard Gordon
Directed by: Nick Marck
Guest cast: Markus Redmond (Tom Cribb), Douglas Roberts (Darin McNamara), Scott William Winters (Jack McNamara), Anthony Guidera (Ernie Nellins), Chris Flanders (Mr. Winslow), Marc Rose (Mellish), David Kallaway (Doorman), Juan A. Riojas (Val Trepkos), Michael Philip (Announcer), Mark Ginther (Lasovic)

Angel is kidnapped and made part of a demon gladiator team that has to fight and kill 21 demons before the members will be set free.

When this episode first aired, many people compared it with *Fight Club*, a hit movie at the time, but it's closer to *Gladiator*, which was released in May 2000, after "The Ring" aired. In *Fight Club*, the fighters actually choose to be part of the club. The demons in "The Ring," like the slaves in *Gladiator*, have no choice but to fight their way to freedom.

The tables are turned in this episode, as Cordy and Wes have to try to save Angel from certain death. Without Angel around, Wesley is forced to be the brawn, and viewers finally get a glimpse of what Wesley has learned in his time away from Sunnydale. He manages to take four goons on his own and shows an impressive skill (again) at firing a weapon and hitting a tiny target. Cordelia and Wesley are usually seen fighting with each other, so it's great to see them working together, using Wes's patience and Cordy's ingenuity to come up with a solution.

Angel once again shows that he's not willing to lower himself to play the demon games, and when he should be fighting for his life he instead "pulls a Gandhi" and stands back peacefully, allowing himself to be pummeled. However, when he's been physically hurt with a knife, the demon in him takes over and he suddenly fights back. Angel has a lot of willpower, but certain things will let the demon within him loose, which intensifies his worry that he'll never be free of Angelus.

Highlight: Wesley and Cordelia's argument about Wesley's fuddy-duddy ways versus Cordelia's obsession with clothing.

Interesting Facts: When Cordelia is looking through the online demon database, Wesley asks her if it has an entry for the Vigories of Oden Tal. When she replies that it doesn't, he says there's still a place for traditional research. The Vigories of Oden Tal were the women from "She," which insinuates he's continuing to do research on them, as if they were coming back. At the time "She" aired, there was a lot of promo tied to the episode that suggested Bai Ling would return to the show, but the writers eventually scrapped the idea and "She" became a one-off episode. Also, "Trepkos" seems to be a favorite name for writer Howard Gordon. He was also a writer on *The X-Files*, and one episode featured a character named Daniel Trepkos. Finally, Scott William Winters played a boxer on the HBO series *Oz*.

Stephanie Romanov Says: "Right before getting the call to audition, the person I was dating at the time said *Angel* was his favorite show and he was, like, 'You have to watch this show,' and so I watched the show and the very next day I got a call for an audition for it. Isn't that wild? The audition was for a guest spot. There was no mention of it possibly being recurring. I said to my manager, 'I want to play this in a way that they'll want to bring me back.' So it worked out well, I think."

Nitpicks: It seems strange that Wolfram & Hart would have gone to all the trouble to get Darin to procure Angel so they could proposition him, only to let him walk away after asking him politely to come work with them.

Oops: During the first fight, Angel's game face shows up after he's been slashed by the demon, but as the demon lunges toward him, you can see that the stunt double is already wearing the game face moments earlier. Also, during the final scene, Angel's bullet wound keeps switching shoulders, and after he throws down the stake rather than killing Trepkos, the blood on the bottom of his shirt momentarily disappears.

The *Buffy* Connection: The argument Cordy and Wesley have about computers versus books is similar to the one Giles and Jenny Calendar had in the season-1 episode "I Robot, You Jane" on *Buffy*.

Wolfram & Hart: Representatives from W&H are present at the demon fights (the firm's probably bankrolling it), and while these lawyers are considered a major force in the demon world, they've managed to keep themselves off the online demon database that Cordelia uses as a search tool. We meet Lilah Morgan for the first time, and she offers to get Angel out of his situation if he'll come and work with her (it looks like she has a bit of a crush on him).

Music/Bands: When we first see Lilah in a bar, the song playing in the background is "Consciousness (Aware of You)" by Morphic Fields, from their self-titled CD.

1.17 Eternity

Original air date: April 4, 2000
Written by: Tracy Stern
Directed by: Regis Kimble
Guest cast: Tamara Gorski (Rebecca Lowell), Michael Mantell (Oliver Simon), Robin Meyers (Masseuse)

Angel and the gang meet famous actress Rebecca Lowell, who wants Angel to turn her into a vampire so she can stay young and beautiful (and remain on a hit sitcom) forever.

Being a television or movie actor can be a painful thing. Hollywood has strict rules on what an actress can or, more important, can't eat (just look at the actresses on *Buffy*), and many child stars have turned to crime, depression, or suicide when they continue to get older but their on-screen personas stay the same age. In this great episode, writer Tracy Stern draws a parallel between the immortality of vampires and actors who remain the same age on television forever. And, finally, we get a glimpse of Angelus.

Like Cordelia, who has seen the seedy side of acting in L.A., Rebecca Lowell, a former soap actress, finds out the hard way that even when you make it in Hollywood, your dreams can quickly become a nightmare thanks to the people you thought were your friends. People who are close to her use her fame for their own ends, and people who work for her are always plotting to get her into the pages of the tabloids (not a place any actor wants to be). When she meets Angel and realizes what he is, she suddenly sees a way to remain young forever. The plot is particularly apt to this series, as Boreanaz is playing an immortal yet can't stay young-looking forever (just compare Angel in season 5 with Angel in season 1 of *Buffy* to see a huge contrast).

When Rebecca tricks Angel with her happy pill, the result is a terrifying reminder of what lurks beneath the smoldering exterior of our favorite vampire. Although I'm always thrilled to see Angelus rear his ugly head, this scene was particularly frightening because of the danger Rebecca was in. The Angelus of *BtVS*'s season 2 was back, scaring Rebecca, mocking Cordelia, and taunting Wesley. Just as he did with Willow in "Innocence," he shuts the lights out in the house so that his prey is at a distinct disadvantage. Angelus loves his mind games, and as always, he preys on the one thing his victim's can't guard — their deepest insecurities.

In the end, there is a sobering of the relationship among the trio, but also a strengthening, because now each knows where he or she stands. For all of Cordy's superficiality, she realizes that truth can help her go further in her acting career than a bunch of hangers-on telling her how great she is. And Wesley, while hurt by what Angelus says to him, forgives Angel and knows that it's not him talking. Wesley's mature response to what must have been a painful experience for him (Angelus probably said many of the same things that Wesley's father had said to him when Wes was a young boy) shows how he's already beginning to change on the show, but some day he'll find that the same forgiveness from others might not be so forthcoming.

Highlight: The opening scene of Angel and Wesley trapped in a theater with Cordelia onstage: "We might try shouting 'Fire!' — it's not technically a *crowded* theater."

Interesting Facts: Angel says the only movie vampire he ever believed was Frank Langella, who played the legendary dark one in the 1979 film *Dracula* opposite Sir Laurence Olivier and Kate Nelligan. Also, the play Cordelia is in at the beginning of the episode is Henrik Ibsen's *A Doll's House*, but the scene she is doing is in act 1, which is why Wesley's comment that there's only one hour left seems a little strange.

Did You Notice?: Cordelia refers to the "donkey demons," which are the burrowers from "Lonely Hearts."

Nitpicks: How did Angel get into Rebecca Lowell's house without being invited in?

1.18   Five by Five (Part One)

Original air date: April 25, 2000
Written by: Jim Kouf
Directed by: James A. Contner
Guest cast: Julie Benz (Darla), Thomas Burr (Lee Mercer), Tyler Christopher (Wolfram & Hart Lawyer), Eliza Dushku (Faith), Rainbow Borden (Gangbanger), Francis Fallon (Dick), Adrienne Janic (Attractive Girl), Rodrick Fox (Assistant DA), Thor Edgell (Romanian Man), Jennifer Slimko (Romanian Woman)

Faith arrives in L.A. and is immediately hired by Wolfram & Hart to kill Angel.

At the beginning of this episode, Angel, trying to convince someone to testify against a drug dealer, tells him that we all have to face our demons at some point. "Five by Five" is about coming face-to-face with one's demons, and while Angel compared himself with Faith in the *Buffy* episode "Consequences," here we get a more direct parallel.

We're taken back to 1898, when Angel first had the curse inflicted upon him (and we think of Faith and her first kill). Darla shuns Angel and tells him he's dirty. He walks the streets haunted by his past deeds, but he is forced out of necessity to continue to attack people (just as Faith was shunned by the Scoobies and became a serial killer). Faith now arrives in L.A. and begins attacking people in a bar (to the sounds of Rob Zombie's apt "Living Dead Girl") before being recruited by Wolfram & Hart and receiving her mission from Lindsey and Lilah, which she accepts without question when she realizes who she's being sent to kill. Interestingly, while Faith and Angel are

Angel discovers that he and Faith (Eliza Dushku) have a lot more in common than he thought.

struggling with coming to terms with their past misdeeds, Angel, of all people, reminds Wesley of his own. As Wesley tries to argue with Angel about dealing with Faith, Angel spits back that Wesley is responsible for how she is, alluding to the fact that Wesley had captured Faith just when Angel was about to make progress with her last season on *Buffy*. It's a harsh moment, but maybe, as Cordelia suggested in the previous episode, Angel is trying to be more honest with people.

The scene where Faith captures and tortures Wesley also paints her as analogous to Angelus, who tortured a Watcher in "Becoming, Part Two" on *Buffy*. Like Angelus, Faith has become a monster, only she still has a soul and is haunted by her crimes *while* she is committing them. The fight scene between her and Angel is incredible; ultimately, as she did in the *Buffy* episode "Who Are You?" (see "The *Buffy* Connection" below), she sees herself as an evil monster who must be destroyed. The final scene, where she begs Angel to kill her while the rain falls, is gorgeous. In a sense, Faith is baptized at this moment, and it signals a new beginning for her.

Highlight: Angel making small-talk with the shallow Wolfram & Hart lawyer.

Did You Notice?: Faith never actually uses her catchphrase, "five by five," even though it's the title of the episode. The title is an ironic one, because her phrase means "everything's okay," when in this episode, it's not.

Nitpicks: Angel calls Giles, who tells him that Faith left Sunnydale a week prior, but the shows are supposed to be running concurrently. Faith left Sunnydale in the *Buffy* episode that aired February 29 and appeared on *Angel* on April 25, so it's closer to two months. Also, if Phantom Dennis can move things, why doesn't he fight back when Faith begins attacking Cordelia? And when Angel stumbles away from his victim in the 1898 flashback, he mutters to himself in Romanian. Wouldn't he be speaking English to himself, since that's his first language?

Oops: Cordelia's apartment door originally opened onto an outdoor corridor, but this time the corridor seems to have closed-in hallways. Her apartment number was previously 212, and in this episode it's 6, which makes no sense because it's a second-floor place (it'll go back to 212 in future episodes). And when Faith is sitting on the windowsill after torturing Wesley with a piece of glass, the shape of the piece she's holding in her hand is different from the one she actually drops in the next cut. When Faith grabs the butane lighter near the stove, the knives in the canister behind her are arranged evenly. When the camera cuts away and back, the knives have been moved to one side and there's suddenly a blue pot sitting near the canister. Also, Angel shouldn't have been able to enter the loft where Faith was torturing Wesley. The owner of the place is still alive and in the hospital, and Angel was never invited in by that person, so there's no way he could have entered the private residence.

The *Buffy* Connection: Faith is one of the best characters ever on *Buffy*. When a Slayer dies, another Slayer is called forth. Buffy died momentarily in season 1, bringing forth Kendra, who became the new active Slayer. When Kendra died, Faith was called, making her the active Slayer (only her death can bring forth another one). Faith was tougher, less sensitive, and had a lot more emotional baggage than Buffy, and one night she accidentally killed a man. She turned rogue, refused to listen to Wesley (who was acting as her Watcher as well as Buffy's), and aligned herself with the Mayor, the Big Bad of season 3, who treated her like a daughter. Angel tried to talk to her, but at the last minute Wesley came in with his goons, chained her up, and said he was taking her back to England to answer to the Watcher's Council. Faith escaped, and at the end of the season Buffy stabbed her and put her in a coma, where she's been ever since. Earlier in season 4 on *Buffy*, Faith woke up and immediately vowed revenge ("This Year's Girl"). She performed a body switch with Buffy and encouraged the gang to kill Faith, who was actually Buffy trapped in Faith's body. Buffy convinced the others that she wasn't Faith and managed to switch the bodies back, but only after Faith had a minor breakdown, showing all of us that she hates herself more than anyone else ("Who Are You?"). Faith left Sunnydale and headed for L.A.

Wolfram & Hart: This episode and "Sanctuary" show us more about Wolfram & Hart than we've been privy to up to now. w&h knows how to make witnesses "disappear" if they will hurt the firm's case. w&h also has a security system that detects when vampires enter the building. The company seems to have eyes and ears everywhere, and in this episode Angel humiliates Lindsey and Lilah finds out Faith is in town and recruits her to kill Angel and get him out of w&h's way.

Music/Bands: Faith dances to Rob Zombie's "Living Dead Girl (Subliminal Seduction Mix)" (*American Made Music to Strip By*).

1.19   Sanctuary (Part Two)

Original air date: May 2, 2000
Written by: Tim Minear and Joss Whedon
Directed by: Michael Lange
Guest cast: Thomas Burr (Lee Mercer), Alastair Duncan (Collins), Eliza Dushku (Faith), Sarah Michelle Gellar (Buffy), Jeff Ricketts (Weatherby), Kevin Owers (Smith), Adam Vernier (Detective Kendrick)

Angel tries to help Faith admit her mistakes and regain her soul, but Buffy suddenly appears in L.A., wanting nothing but revenge.

This is a fantastic *Angel* episode, filled with betrayal, complex relationship issues, and more analogies of how Faith's predicament is like Angel's. Angel shows Faith the sympathy and understanding that was denied him when he got his soul. The evil arm of the Watcher's Council shows up in L.A., having followed Faith from Sunnydale, and the members try to lure Wesley into helping them capture her again. It's interesting that when they corner Giles in "Who Are You?," he complies, whereas Wesley, the "weaker" former Watcher, is reluctant. Kate continues her quest to bring down Angel and prove he's evil, while Faith tries to come to terms with the things she's done. Just as all the murders Angel had committed a century earlier came flooding back to him when he got his soul, Faith begins to remember everything she did — and can't possibly apologize for.

Cordelia and Wesley, understandably, are hurt and confused when Angel gives Faith sanctuary after what she did to them. We see a more serious side of Wesley in this episode, but as mentioned above, he also comes through in the end and makes major strides toward becoming a hero.

And then Buffy shows up. Angel has discovered that Riley is in the picture, so perhaps that knowledge contributes to his lack of sympathy for her, but Buffy, in her own way, is self-centered, refusing to see the other side. Granted, she has just walked into Angel's apartment and caught him embracing Faith, the woman who tried to kill her along with her friends and family. But Buffy accuses Angel of being in a murderers' club with Faith, eventually mentions her new boyfriend, and tells him she could never trust him. All this, of course, after she's punched him in the face. Buffy explains that Faith has come after her and tortured her family, and she just wants to destroy the rogue Slayer. Later, Buffy tells Faith that no one else has ever made her a victim. Hmm. . . . She seems to have forgotten a certain vampire who tortured her Watcher, killed Giles's lover, threatened her friends, and tried to kill her mother. Funny how she forgave him and chastised others for not forgiving him as well. Yet interestingly, just as Buffy was oblivious to the suffering of her friends, Angel refuses to consider why Cordelia, Buffy, and Wesley are so upset that he's helping Faith after she has tortured each one of them.

At the end of the episode is one of the most intriguing Angel-Buffy moments we've seen, where he tells her to get out of "his" city once and for all (an echo of Buffy's reference to Sunnydale as "my town" in "I Will Remember You"), and she purposely tries to hurt him once again. This encounter signals an end to *Angel*'s being in *BtVS*'s shadow — he tells her to leave him alone, and it's a subtle way of announcing that Buffy will no longer be coming over to *Angel*, which will allow it to become its own show with its own mythology, no longer relying on crossovers with *Buffy* to bring in new viewers. (See "The *Buffy* Connection" below for the conclusion of the episode.)

Highlight: Buffy yelling at Angel for hitting her, and him replying, "Not to go all schoolyard on you, but you hit me first."
Interesting Facts: When Wesley hits Weatherby at the end of the episode he whispers,

"One hundred and eighty." This is a perfect score in the game of darts, when all three darts are in the triple 20 section on the dartboard, scoring 180 points.

Did You Notice?: We see Wesley playing darts in a pub, and later he shoots a dart into someone's neck. Is that where he learned his amazing aim at small targets?

Nitpicks: Lilah says that "apparently" Angel used to date a vampire Slayer. Wouldn't Buffy feature rather prominently in Wolfram & Hart's files? We discover in season 3's "Dad" that W&H has 35 cabinets devoted to Angel's history; did the firm only just start compiling them? Also, Wolfram & Hart, the Watcher's Council, and the police department all have the same photo of Faith. Does she have a press kit with headshots in it or something? And speaking of which, why did the Watcher's Council slide a photo of Faith across the table to Wesley, when he already knows what she looks like?

Oops: In the bar where the evil Watchers corner Wesley, the camera zooms in on a sign above the table that says "Please, No Smoking." But when the camera pulls back, the sign reads "Thank You for Not Smoking."

The *Buffy* Connection: This episode concluded on *Buffy* the following week in "The Yoko Factor." Angel follows Buffy back to Sunnydale, where he has a run-in with Riley, her boyfriend (who's been told by Xander about the trigger that causes Angel to lose his soul). They get into a huge fight, beat each other up, and then Angel visits Buffy at her dormitory, followed closely by Riley. When Buffy realizes what's happened she's infuriated and speaks to Angel. He tells her he only wanted to apologize, which he then does, and she says he was right to say what he said in Los Angeles, that they really do live separate lives now and it's best to keep it that way. Before leaving, Angel tells her he doesn't like Riley, echoing the sentiment of *many* fans.

Wolfram & Hart: Lilah and Lindsey commission a demon to be the cleanup person on the Faith situation; since she hasn't come through with her side of the deal, they put a price on her head. Kate knows what kind of business W&H conducts, but it's not clear the other officers do.

1.20 War Zone

Original air date: May 9, 2000
Written by: Garry Campbell
Directed by: David Straiton
Guest cast: Michele Kelly (Alonna), Maurice Compte (Chain), Mick Murray (Knox), Joe Basile (Lenny Edwards), David Herman (David Nabbitt), Sean Parhm (Bobby), Sven Holmberg (Ty), Rebecca Kingler (Madam Dorion), Kimberly James (Lina)

While Angel Investigations is doing a job for dot-com billionaire David Nabbitt, the team encounters a vampire-slaying gang led by Charles Gunn.

Angel has proven that he's a big, broody hero who is trying to atone for his countless crimes of the past. But in "War Zone" we're introduced to a group of angry vampire hunters who fight for vengeance and to save the lives of innocent people on the streets. Charles Gunn, who will become a regular character, is just as broody as Angel, with a stubbornness that rivals Cordelia's. In one episode he goes from a vigilante trying to rid the streets of a vampire menace to a pained brother wreaking vengeance for his sister's death. Like Angel, Gunn doesn't work alone, and while his team, truck, and weaponry are very cool, they lack the strength and quick reflexes to fight properly, and the gang suffers many casualties. Gunn is also like Angel in that he carries the weight of the world on his shoulders. He blames himself for Alonna's death and will punish himself for the rest of his life for it, but that's what Gunn is all about. He refuses to forgive himself anything — even Alonna tells him that he's full of guilt — and that's who he is. Rather than give up that guilt, he moves on with it, making it an essential part of his character. J. August Richards is a great actor, and the agony on his face as Alonna speaks to him during their final meeting is painful to watch.

This episode also introduces David Nabbitt (who returns in "To Shanshu in L.A." and "First Impressions"), the dot-com billionaire who is looking for some help and companionship and carries a hefty check that will help get Angel Investigations off the ground. He provides the much-needed humor in what is an otherwise dark episode, and he and his lifestyle contrast with the impoverished, hand-to-mouth, struggling-to-survive existence of Gunn and his soldiers.

Meeting Gunn brings back some buried feelings for Angel (not that he ever buries his guilt very deep), and he sees what the loss of Gunn's sister has done to the young gang leader. We can tell Angel is wondering how many families he destroyed in this way, and later he refers to himself as Angelus in front of Gunn, as if no matter what he does right, the evil will always be percolating right under the surface. Seeing Gunn's determination, Angel realizes what his own quest should be.

Highlight: Nabbitt asking Angel if he's familiar with *Dungeons & Dragons*, and Angel saying he's seen a few.

Interesting Facts: David Nabbitt was originally meant to be a recurring character, but David Herman's schedule couldn't accommodate the reappearances and eventually he disappears. Herman has starred in movies such as *Office Space* and *Dude, Where's My Car?* He has also appeared in *24* and done regular voice work on *King of the Hill* and *Futurama*.

J. August Richards Says: "It wasn't difficult coming into an already established cast. I didn't have to work with anyone except for David, so it made it a lot easier because I got to create something that was solely my own and not feel like I had to catch up with anybody else. I was doing my own thing; all of my other scenes were with other guest stars, so it really wasn't a matter of fitting in until the second season. Everybody was so cool right away that it really wasn't an issue for me. At that point in the business there was this new phenomenon where every audition became 'Guest star, possible recurring character,' but you knew it usually meant nothing. So I went into this assuming it was a one-time gig and then Diane Acrey, the hair lady, told me, 'You're in the next script!' and I was, like, 'Really?' So we did the next episode and then in that one she said, 'You're in the next script again!' So after my last night on season one, David Greenwalt pulled me aside and said, 'Well, kid, everyone around here really likes you so it looks like a go for next year.' So that was a really cool moment."

Did You Notice?: The lead vampire fighting Gunn's gang is named Knox, which will be the name of a recurring character in season 5. Also, in the demon brothel you can see one of the Vigories of Oden Tal. And Lina (the demon in the brothel who speaks to Angel), or one of her kind, is seen briefly in an alley at the very beginning of "City Of" during the voice-over narration.

Nitpicks: Angel has said on a number of occasions that a vampire doesn't need to breathe, yet after Gunn's gang chases him down an alleyway, he's panting against the wall. This is one of those Buffyverse inconsistencies: the writers originally said vampires *couldn't* breathe (in "Prophecy Girl" Buffy stops breathing and Angel is unable to resuscitate her) and later changed it so that they have breath but don't need to use it. Even so, as evidenced in the scene with Gunn, this detail remains inconsistent. Also, in this episode the members of Gunn's gang are mostly white, but when they reappear in "The Thin Dead Line" they're mostly African-American. Finally, Angel asks to be invited into Gunn and his crew's quarters, but they're squatting in an abandoned warehouse, so Angel doesn't require an invitation.

Oops: When Angel is fighting Gunn's gang, he takes an arrow through his hand. Yet when Cordelia is patching him up his hand appears to be perfectly healthy.

Music/Bands: A Friend from Rio's "Para Lennon and McCartney" (*Hi-Fidelity Lounge, Vol. 1*) plays at Nabbitt's party.

1.21 Blind Date

Original air date: May 16, 2000
Written by: Jeannine Renshaw
Directed by: Thomas J. Wright
Guest cast: Thomas Burr (Lee Mercer), Sam Anderson (Holland Manners), Jennifer Badger Martin (Vanessa Brewer; incorrectly listed as Vanessa Weeks in the credits), Keilana Smith (Mind Reader #1), Dawn Suggs (Mind Reader #2), Charles Constant

(Security Center Guard), Scott Berman (Vendor), Derek Anthony (Dying Black Man), Rishi Kumar (Blind Child #1), Karen Lu (Blind Child #2), Alex Buek (Blind Child #3)

Angel tries to find a blind assassin whom Wolfram & Hart is protecting before she kills three children.

"Blind Date," while ostensibly about a blind woman who appears to be able to see in a way that only becomes apparent at the end of the episode, is actually more focused on Wolfram & Hart and what it does to people. We've seen Lindsey in other episodes, but now he becomes a three-dimensional character. Many of the lawyers at Wolfram & Hart are human, and while most can suppress the guilt they feel about what they're doing to innocent people and the legal system in general because they're earning a lot of money, some realize that what W&H does is detrimental. Lindsey cannot live with himself any longer knowing the kind of people he's been getting acquitted, and he turns to Angel. It's interesting that while Angel took Faith under his wing and promised to help her atone, he's sarcastic and dismissive when it comes to Lindsey's apparent remorse. The difference is that Angel could sense Faith was genuinely sorry and ready to change, whereas something about Lindsey tells Angel he might still be swayed to the side of darkness. Despite Lindsey's admittedly sad story of his difficult and impoverished childhood, Angel refuses to show him any sympathy, and it's probably for good reason. Someone with such an unfortunate past is likely to be more easily swayed by money (Holland seems to sense the same weakness in Lindsey). Much like the seer, Lindsey acts with his heart in this episode, but eventually he'll act upon his desire. In season 2, Lindsey's purpose will change.

Angel finally becomes frustrated with Wolfram & Hart. All season, no matter what he does, W&H continues to do business, continues to get its demonic clients off the hook, and stands in the way of his doing good. The firm is so powerful that it can do things outside the law and cover them up, and it always stays one step ahead of Angel, foiling him every time. Angel has been thwarting W&H's efforts of late as well, but his actions haven't been enough. Angel rarely shows his frustration, so the scene where he blows up in front of Wesley and Cordelia and tells them they should just give up because people like the ones at Wolfram & Hart can't be stopped is a rare one. It's also a prophetic one.

The storyline involving Vanessa Brewer is interesting, even if it gets overshadowed by the Lindsey storyline, which is clearly more important. She is a "seer" who doesn't use her eyes to see, and the fight between her and Angel is great, showing how quickly he can size up his foes and uncover their fighting styles. Her condition parallels her with Angel, who can also feel certain things and knows them to be right or wrong. Just as he knows not to trust Lindsey fully when Lindsey walks in the door at Angel Investigations, so too does he feel something coming off a metal tube in the Wolfram & Hart vault

Lindsey (Christian Kane) returns and begins to question the actions of Wolfram & Hart.

when he's there. Anyone else would have ignored the feeling, but Angel is connected to what is in that tube in such a way that he feels compelled to grab it. What he brings back to Wesley will become pivotal to the entire series and will spark Angel's motivation to do good from this point on.

Highlight: Gunn helping to distract the w&h guards: "Evil white folks really *do* have a mecca!"

Interesting Facts: Holland Manners is played by veteran Sam Anderson, best known from television's *Perfect Strangers*, *Growing Pains*, *Boston Common*, and character roles in movies such as *Forrest Gump*.

Christian Kane Says: "I got the call and they said, 'We want you to come back and reprise this role,' and I thought, *Well, now I'm gonna have to watch it again and remember who this guy is.* The first scene coming back was a trial, and it was so weird because they kept saying after that, 'Well, they want another one, they want another one.' Then I came close to being booked for *Band of Brothers*. I read with Tom Hanks, and it got very close, and they were talking about planes and flying out, but something happened — I'm not sure exactly what, but whatever it was it did not go through, so I was available for more *Angel*, which was great for me. That's where 'Blind Date' came in. I was able to do that episode, and that's the episode that really made people stand up and really start loving this character and wonder what he was all about."

Did You Notice?: When Cordelia is looking up Vanessa Brewer in the police files, she says that the woman was arrested the first time for fleeing the scene of a homicide. If you freeze-frame the screen, you can read that Vanessa was actually fleeing the scene in a car and was charged with driving without a license. The charges were dropped when the police realized she was totally blind. The second arrest mentions Brewer's case couldn't be taken seriously because giggling could be heard in the courtroom over the absurdity of the accusations.

Nitpicks: When Cordelia asks what the Nanjin are, Wesley stands up and says they are cave-dwelling monks who believe enlightenment is seeing with the heart, not with the mind. He says it like he's known it all along, but if you look closely at the computer monitor in the shot, you'll see he's simply quoting the definition on the screen word for word. Also, why does Wolfram & Hart have shamans that sense vampires and vampire detectors at all entrances of the building when many of its clients and freelancers are demons? Finally, the records room is a dingy room in a sublevel of Wolfram & Hart, but in season 3's "Dad" we'll see it's actually a large room that houses a woman who keeps all the files and records cataloged in her head.

Oops: Lindsey tells Angel that the files he's looking for will be on sublevel two in Wolfram & Hart, but when he arrives you hear the elevator say, "Entering sublevel three." And when Wesley is reading out loud off the computer screen he says the three seer children are being brought together for the first time, but it doesn't actually say that anywhere on the monitor.

The *Buffy* Connection: Cordelia calls Willow for help in decrypting the Wolfram & Hart disks, and Willow tells her she's been decrypting disks all day, too. She's referring to some disks that Spike stole from Adam to gain access to the Initiative, and Willow spends time during "The Yoko Factor" and more in "Primeval" decoding them.

Wolfram & Hart: The company employs mind readers to keep out bad seeds, and when it says it "terminates" an employee, it makes sure that person won't be working elsewhere. W&H's vault is guarded by a demon.

1.22   To Shanshu in L.A.

Original air date: May 23, 2000
Written and directed by: David Greenwalt
Guest cast: Sam Anderson (Holland Manners), Todd Stashwick (Vocah), Carey Cannon (Female Oracle), Randall Slavin (Male Oracle), David Herman (David Nabbitt), Julie Benz (Darla), Louise Claps (Homeless Woman), Daren Rice (Uniform #1), Jon Ecklund (Uniform #2), Lia Johnson (Vendor), Robyn Cohen (Nurse), Susan Savage (Doctor), John Eddins (Monk #1), Gerard O'Donnell (Monk #2), Brahman Turner (Young Tough Guy)

Angel's fate has been predetermined, but only if he is able to rise to the occasion and fulfill his destiny.

The best episode of season 1, "To Shanshu in L.A." is fast paced, suspenseful, and contains all the elements we'll need to fully appreciate season 2. Wesley continues to work on the ancient prophecy that Angel discovered in the previous episode, while he and Cordelia discuss how Angel might always be in the world but never a part of it. Meanwhile, Angel finally "grows a pair," as Angelus would put it, and snaps at Kate, telling her he refuses to be blamed for every petty grievance she has about her life. She's now the joke of the police force and must endure the taunts of the other officers for actually seeing what's out there, but it's about time Angel stopped her from sniping at him every time she sees him.

Wesley finally makes a breakthrough in the translation of the prophecies of Aberjian — reading that the vampire with a soul will "shanshu," or die — but Angel is completely unfazed. When Cordy is paralyzed by a barrage of visions filled with pain and heartbreak and Wesley is rushed to the hospital with severe burns, Angel becomes far more concerned about his friends than his own future foretold. The pain on Angel's face as he moves between hospital rooms shows just how mature David Boreanaz has become as an actor: his eyes speak volumes. Angel has realized that Wolfram & Hart can come at him through his friends (something it'll do again and again), which is one of the reasons he withdraws from those he's close to in season 2.

Charisma Carpenter is also a standout, and this episode signals a shift in Cordelia's character from a self-centered princess to a mature woman who is aware of the perils around her and wants to help people. She has seen the pain of the world around her and realizes her mission with the gang is more important than the latest style of Prada shoes. Angel also has an important revelation when he realizes Cordelia and Wesley aren't hangers-on that argue a lot in the kitchen and cause him grief, but are close friends and associates that he needs and cannot lose.

Gunn is recruited to help once again, showing that Angel really trusts him and setting him up as a major part of the show. He understands, appreciates, and respects Angel's loyalty to his friends, which is one of the things that will draw Gunn to the team next season. Meanwhile, Wolfram & Hart resurrects an enemy from Angel's past that will jump-start his season-2 downward spiral, and Angel and Lindsey are involved in a disturbing confrontation that will spark storylines in seasons 2 and 5. At the end of this suspenseful episode, Wesley realizes his translation might have been a little off, and we find out the true — and exciting — place Angel has in the larger scheme of things. If you recognize the allusion made in the title (think William Friedkin movie), then you can guess the prophecy.

Highlight: Angel's great spin on an old saying: "Don't believe everything you're foretold."
Interesting Facts: Lilah reminds Lindsey of a time the W&H Senior Partners made one of the lawyers, Robert Price, eat his own liver. Robert "R.D." Price was David Greenwalt's assistant on *Buffy* and became the associate producer of *Angel* in its first season as well as the director of two episodes.
Christian Kane Says: "I was offered *Summer Catch* and spent a summer filming that with Marc Blucas. We were out there at the same time, and we finished with baseball

practice, filmed a little bit, and then went back home just at the time that *Buffy* was coming on. So Marc and I watched *Buffy*, and then we watched 'Blind Date,' and Marc goes, 'You want to see something f---in' hilarious, just awesome?' And I said, 'Yeah.' So we got into his car and went up to the production office, and we logged on to the computer because we were on Southport Island so we didn't have any computers really. So he says, 'Watch this' and he logged onto [the Bronze posting board] as me and him. From what I've heard the thing crashed. [Laughs] It was unbelievable. I'd been working for a while and I'd had people out there who were fans of shows of mine, but this was unbelievable. It was crazy to realize the fanbase these two shows had that I had no idea I was getting into."

Did You Notice?: The prophecy mentions the "coming darkness," a reference to what happens in season 4. Also, this is the last we'll see of the original Angel Investigations offices.

Nitpicks: How could the immortal Oracles be killed by mortal means? Also, the doctor tells Angel that they've given Cordelia a CAT scan, but they can't seem to sedate her. She couldn't have had a CAT scan if she was moving like that; the body needs to be completely still for the machine to get a proper reading.

Oops: When Cordelia is leaving the art stall at the outdoor market, the bracelets on her left wrist shift to her right wrist in one shot, and then back to her left.

The *Buffy* Connection: While we've seen Darla in several *Angel* flashbacks, she was one of the Master's cronies in season 1 of *Buffy*. In "Angel," the episode where Buffy first discovers that Angel is in fact a vampire, Darla comes after Buffy with two guns and Angel stakes her, killing the woman who had sired him and had been his lover for 150 years.

Wolfram & Hart: The firm hires demons to perform a complex ceremony that would appear to do the impossible and bring back someone who might help to destroy Angel.

Music/Bands: When Cordelia goes to the market, the busker playing guitar is Grant Langston, and he's performing "Time of Day" (*All This and Pecan Pie*).

Season Two
September 2000 • May 2001

Recurring characters in season 2: Andy Hallett (The Host), Stephanie Romanov (Lilah), Christian Kane (Lindsey), Julie Benz (Darla), Sam Anderson (Holland Manners)

2.1   Judgement
Original air date: September 26, 2000
Teleplay by: David Greenwalt

Story by: Joss Whedon and David Greenwalt
Directed by: Michael Lange
Guest cast: Justina Machado (Jo), Eliza Dushku (Faith), Rob Boltin (Johnny Fontaine), Iris Fields (Acting Teacher), Keith Campbell (Club Manager), Jason Frasca (White Guy), Andy Kreiss (Lizard Demon), Matthew James (Merl Demon), Glenn David Calloway (Judge), EJ Gage (Mordar)

When Angel accidentally kills a woman's champion, he must come up with a way to save her life before a tribunal kills her.

"Judgement" is a great beginning to season 2. From the Host singing "I Will Survive" (which could be the theme song of the series), to Cordelia putting her duty to Angel Investigations above all else, to Wesley being a suave guy in a pub (with just a little bit of the buffoon left in him), to the Angel Investigations triumvirate striding into the gym, we realize that this team is *very* different from the team of season 1. They work together, they believe in their mission, and they get the job done. Cordelia has actually become a good actress, as if the barrage of visions she received in "To Shanshu in L.A." gave her the maturity she needed to emote more realistically. Wesley is more self-assured, and all three have clearly defined their respective jobs within the company and work together perfectly. They are still wondering what Wolfram & Hart was trying to raise at the end of last season, but recently they've been rather busy, with many cases on the go. The major elements of the season are all packed into this episode: the Host and Caritas (each of which is a brilliant concept); the Hyperion Hotel; Angel's Pinocchio-like quest to become human; the teamwork of Angel Investigations; Merl the parasite demon; Gunn as a strength Angel can rely on; Wolfram & Hart as Angel's continuing nemesis; and the, um, staggering talent of Angel's singing voice. Ahem.

Although the plot of the woman being chased by the tribunal is a little skewed (we're never told why they're after her baby or what she's on trial for), it shows how determined Angel is to fulfill the prophecy, and when he suffers a setback it hits him personally. Angel's attitude seems to be a little brighter now that he realizes all his efforts to save people are not just a means to atone for his past — they're leading him toward a personal reward: the opportunity to become a human being and live a normal life.

The final scene of the episode, where Angel goes to see an old friend, is a pleasant surprise, bringing us full circle to his quest. We see how so many people on both *Buffy* and *Angel* are on personal quests for redemption. A great beginning to what will be a stunning second season.

Highlight: Angel singing for the first time, and his choice of music.

Andy Hallett joins the series this season as The Host, the inimitable owner of a demon karaoke bar.

Interesting Facts: The Host accuses Angel of being curt, then says, "Who's a little curt Jurgens from *The Enemy Below*?" *The Enemy Below* is a 1957 film starring Curt Jurgens and Robert Mitchum about the battle between a U.S. commander of a submarine and a German commander of a U-boat. (It might have been the inspiration for the season-5 episode "Why We Fight.") Justina Machado, who plays Jo, is best known now as Federico Diaz's wife, Vanessa, on *Six Feet Under*. Finally, this is the episode where we discover Angel's affinity for the Barry Manilow ballad "Mandy," which was first released in 1975. What is so brilliant about his choice is that the Manilow song "Could It Be Magic," which was released right after "Mandy" but wasn't a hit, is one of the few Manilow pieces to be written in a minor key and is based on Frédéric Chopin's Prelude in C Minor. Darla states in this episode that this prelude is one of her favorite melodies, so Angel probably associates the two songs (and if he'd sung "Could It Be Magic" at Caritas, audiences wouldn't have recognized it as readily as "Mandy").

Christian Kane Says: "I thought after 'Blind Date' they might make me a series regular, but instead they picked up my boy J. He was one of my really good friends — we hit it off that season and he's still to this day one of my closest friends. I was happy for him, and then they started bringing me back, and I thought, *Okay, I'm okay.* But I really wanted to be a series regular."

Did You Notice?: This is the first time we hear David Boreanaz say, "Thank you, thank you very much" during the end credits. Also, the plot of a pregnant woman who just wants to have her baby but is being hunted parallels a major storyline coming up in season 3.

Nitpicks: Unfortunately, this episode is the first time the word *champion* is used to describe Angel over and over again, and we'll have to suffer through it for another four years. Also, when Angel comes after Kamal, why doesn't Jo yell out that he's her protector rather than just standing there and letting Angel kill him? The way Angel keeps reassuring her that everything is okay makes it seem like he is onside, so why does she not explain to him that he is fighting the wrong person before it is too late? And finally, why would Kamal leave dozens of candles burning in his apartment with all that wooden furniture in the place?

Wolfram & Hart: W&H has been keeping Darla under wraps all summer, apparently prepping her over a long period of time before revealing her to Angel.

2.2   Are You Now or Have You Ever Been?

Original air date: October 3, 2000
Written by: Tim Minear
Directed by: David Semel

Guest cast: Melissa Marsala (Judy Kovacs), John Kapelos (Roland Meeks), Tommy Hinkley (Private Investigator), Brett Rickaby (Denver), Scott Thompson Baker (Actor), J.P. Manoux (Bellhop), David Kagen (Salesman), Terrence Beasor (Older Man), Julie Araskog (Over the Hill Whore), Tom Beyer (Blacklisted Writer), Eve Sigall (Old Judy)

We flash back to 1952; Angel is staying at a hotel inhabited by a Paranoia demon that is feeding on the souls of the patrons.

This is one of my favorite *Angel* episodes. Finally — a flashback that doesn't take place in the 19th century. In 1952 Angel is more broody than ever, and he's cooped up in a hotel where he talks to no one and keeps completely to himself. He dresses like James Dean, drinks his blood from a glass bottle, and has brief heroic moments followed by shows of complete apathy toward human beings. He meets Judy, a light-skinned African-American woman who is passing as white. "Passing" was a common phenomenon in the first half of the 20th century, and there have been several books and poems written about it. One of the best is *Autobiography of an Ex-Colored Man* by James Weldon Johnson, a novel about how an African-American man passes as a white man and gives up his heritage in order to be accepted into white society. (The term was first mentioned on *Angel* in "Hero" when Rieff accused Doyle of passing.) Just as Judy is passing for white, Angel is passing for human, and as we'll see again and again, Angel takes on the cases of those people with whom he can identify (like Faith). In this instance, Angel realizes that like himself, Judy is trapped between two worlds and is being persecuted by both. "Are You Now or Have You Ever Been?" flashes between the present, where Angel has asked Cordelia and Wesley to research the Hyperion Hotel, the place he stayed in 1952, and the past, where the viewer sees what really happened at the hotel as opposed to what the newspapers reported.

Even though Angel has a soul in 1952, you wouldn't know it from his actions, and we discover yet one more grisly act of revenge he committed back then. He has cut himself off from everyone and, surprisingly, is drinking human blood — albeit not directly from humans. We'll see several more of his transgressions in upcoming episodes, showing that having a soul was a rocky path for Angel to tread (which is why he had to stop drinking human blood). In the 1950s Angel is bitter about the things that have happened to him, but he doesn't go off the deep end completely until the 1970s (see season 4's "Orpheus"). It's interesting that many fans have commented on Spike's continuing to do nasty things when he first gets his soul, but we've seen Angel committing crimes 50, 60, and 70 years after getting his. It's a long road to redemption, but part of Angel's problem is that he was surrounded by people who didn't deserve help or sympathy. While the 1950s is generally celebrated as a time that represents good old

American values, it was also the time of McCarthyism, when homosexuals had to hide their orientation and African-Americans could be shunned because of the color of their skin (the episode's title alludes to this reality of the McCarthy era). Paranoia ruled the day, but the paranoia that began then has multiplied over the years into its present form. The bomb drills that children in the 1950s had to perform (crawling under their desks when they heard a siren, which would apparently save them from a nuclear attack) have evolved into CNN's present terror alerts.

Angel sees the hypocrisy around him and is disgusted by it, which causes him to remove himself from society and become even more introspective than usual. It's interesting that he chooses this place — the scene of his darkest crime since getting a soul — to carry out his duties at Angel Investigations.

Highlight: Wesley's paranoia about being called paranoid.

Interesting Facts: The hotel is aptly named. Hyperion, the father of the sun god, was blinded by his enemies at night but could see during the day. Similarly, the occupants of the hotel become more paranoid in the evenings, committing horrible deeds, and act with more reason during the day. Also, Tony Amendola, who plays Master Bra'tac in *Stargate SG-1*, plays the Thesulac demon, but he's uncredited.

Did You Notice?: Although Wesley and Gunn met in the previous episode, this is the first time they work together, and they're arguing already. Also, the scene where Judy speaks to Angel at the planetarium is a clear homage to the film *Rebel Without a Cause* (which was released in 1955, three years after the events of this episode; perhaps James Dean stole Angel's look?). They're at a planetarium; Judy looks like Natalie Wood; Angel is dressed in the red jacket, white shirt, and jeans that James Dean wears at the end of the movie; and he's smoking, something we never see him do except in "Redefinition."

Nitpicks: Maybe the writers thought referring to Julie Araskog's character as "Over the Hill Whore" was funny, but I think it's tasteless. Also, the article that Wesley reads about Judy says she's been on the run for several years, but how is that possible when she's so young? And she's just been carrying the money around all this time? And the bank *still* has a private investigator tailing her when she's not exactly the sharpest knife in the drawer?

Oops: Judy tells Angel that she worked for the City Trust Bank of Kansas, but when Wesley is looking through the newspaper clippings, the one about her states she worked for the Union National Bank. Also, if you freeze the screen on the article, you'll see the last two paragraphs are the same. Finally, when Angel goes to see Denver at his bookstore in 1952, you can see two stars on the Hollywood Walk of Fame outside, but the first stars on the Walk of Fame were unveiled on February 9, 1960.

Music/Bands: Angel hears "Hoop-de-Doo" by Perry Como with the Fontane Sisters

(*All Time Greatest Hits, Vol. 1*) coming from the neighboring hotel room in one of the flashback scenes.

2.3   First Impressions

Original air date: October 10, 2000
Written by: Shawn Ryan
Directed by: James A. Contner
Guest cast: David Herman (David Nabbit), Chris Babers (Henry), Cedrick Terrell (Jameel), Edwin Hodge (Keenan), Lucas Babin (Joey), Alan Shaw (Deevak), Angel Parker (Veronica), Ray Campbell (Desmond), Sarah Brooke (Nurse), Janet Song (Dr. Thomas), Kelli Kirkland (Young Black Woman)

As Angel begins to have dreams of Darla, Cordelia declares herself Gunn's protector and races off in an effort to save him from the danger she sees in a vision.

Cue the beginning of the downward spiral that will mark most of season 2. As part of the overall plan Wolfram & Hart has for Angel, Darla now inhabits his dreams in passionate ways. He can't seem to get to sleep fast enough and refuses to tell the others what is happening to him. The last time Angel saw Darla he killed her, and now he's dreaming about being with her in intimate situations. Angel's at his most vulnerable in his dreams, as we all are, and Darla makes him want to protect her while convincing him his friends don't care about him.

While Darla begins to take Angel out of the picture, the others are forced to fend for themselves. Cordelia gets a vision that involves Gunn and shows how brave she's become when, unable to reach Wesley or Angel, she grabs some mace and an ax and heads out on her own. The ensuing scenes of dialogue between Cordy and Gunn are brilliant and show a lot of chemistry between them that the writers never really explored. She deems herself his protector, something that he sees as more of an insult than a gift, but "vision girl" sticks to his side like glue and shows an incredible amount of courage against a very large foe. She also shows how much she's gotten used to her new life when she remains calm and composed when Veronica gets hurt.

Wesley and Gunn seem to have gotten off on the wrong foot (their mutual animosity will return in seasons 3 and 4), and Angel and Wes become the bumbling duo that doesn't do much to help Cordelia or Gunn in the situation. Gunn becomes more of a three-dimensional character and seems to come closer to becoming part of the A.I. crew. When Vanessa gets hurt at the party, Gunn blames himself for her wound, just as he still blames himself for the death of his sister Alonna. Angel is a big, broody, brawny guy who tries to help the helpless, and Gunn is so much like him it's scary. Cordelia eventually tells him that he's his own worst enemy, eerily foreshadowing what we'll be thinking about Angel by midseason and what will happen to Gunn in the fifth season. By the end of the episode, Gunn has accepted Cordelia's quirky behavior, Cordy is feeling good about herself for helping vanquish the demon, and Angel heads right back into bed to dream about Darla. Wolfram & Hart has him exactly where it wants him.

Highlight: Angel's flashy pink motorcycle helmet that makes him look like the Pink Ranger.

J. August Richards Says: "At first I was given some general direction to take the character in, and certain parts of it worked and certain parts of it didn't. Each season I decided to work on something on my own, something that I wanted to add to the character, and nothing I ever shared with anyone, but there were different aspects of the character I wanted to highlight or work on or improve at, and that's how the character sort of developed into the person he is now."

Did You Notice?: Angel choking Wesley is foreshadowing a less funny but similar incident that will happen next season (and again in season 4's "Deep Down").

Oops: When Darla takes off Angel's sweater, his tattoo is nowhere to be seen. He hasn't had it removed surgically, however, because it shows up again in the next episode.

Wolfram & Hart: Wolfram & Hart is able to infiltrate Angel's dreams and affect his behavior when he's awake.

Music/Bands: At Desmond's party, we hear Kurupt's "Who Ride Wit Us" (*The Streetz Iz a Mutha*).

2.4   Untouched

Original air date: October 17, 2000
Written by: Mere Smith
Directed by: Joss Whedon
Guest cast: Daisy McCrackin (Bethany Chaulk), Gareth Williams (Mr. Chaulk), David J. Miller (Man #1), Drew Wicks (Uniform Officer), Michael Harte (Detective), Madison Eginton (Young Bethany)

As Angel's racy Darla dreams continue, a woman with telekinetic powers who is recruited by Lilah needs him to help her.

Telekinesis, the ability to make objects move by using the mind, has featured in several movies — most notably Stephen King's *Carrie*, directed by Brian De Palma — and there is still much debate about whether it is possible. Those in the know agree that you cannot make an object move by wishing it to; rather, the ability has to do with the subconscious. In "Untouched," Bethany is a telekinetic who can't control her powers, and things move and shake whenever she gets upset. There's an insinuation that her father has molested her; abuse is a common scenario in fictional representations of telekinetic power. In *Carrie*, for example, the title character has a cruel mother who makes her feel dirty for being a pubescent woman. Wesley infuriates Bethany by mentioning her father, and when Wolfram & Hart sends her father over in the flesh to coax her into returning home, all hell breaks loose.

The episode introduces a lot of character development. Wesley tries radical measures for cracking the case and gets himself (and the others) hurt because of it. His methods work, but they infuriate Angel, who doesn't like Wesley's "means to an end" way of thinking. Cordelia can be understanding to a point, but if she sees the possibility of her friends being threatened, she'll step in. She tells Bethany to back off from Angel; while she feels

Darla (Julie Benz), once the woman of Angel's dreams, is back . . . in his dreams.

sorry for Bethany's predicament, she worries that Bethany's lack of control could spell serious danger for Angel or herself. Gunn helps out again, and Cordy convinces Angel to pay him on a case-by-case basis, an arrangement Gunn gladly accepts.

Wolfram & Hart gets in the way again, but this time Lindsey and Lilah seem to be playing dueling demons. Lindsey is orchestrating the whole Darla scenario, while Lilah has recruited an unsuspecting Bethany. The two clash when Bethany wanders into Angel's room one night and offers to have sex with him: Lilah is ordered to keep her "special project" away from Lindsey's. This story's tie-in to the ongoing drama is that just as Bethany has no control over her power because of her sexual frustration, Darla has complete control over Angel by satiating his.

Highlight: Lilah telling Bethany she's special, "in the old, nonretarded sense of the word."
Interesting Facts: This episode was the first one written by Mere Smith. She was

originally a fan of *Buffy* who posted often on the Bronze posting board and was a well-known adorer of Joss Whedon. Eventually she sent him a script, and he hired her as one of the writers on *Angel*. She's written some of the best episodes on the series. Also, the levitation of the father is an homage to another Brian De Palma film, *The Fury*, where a telekinetic boy floats in the air above his father.

Christian Kane Says: "I loved working with Stephanie Romanov. We ended up coming up with this whole Boris and Natasha thing we'd always say on set. We would hold hands and walk down the yellow brick road but when we get to the end we're going to fight over who gets the number one spot. In real life everyone else was a series regular, and everyone else was kicking the shit out of us for two years, so there was a lot of love between us in real life. I still talk to her every once in a while and we're still really great friends. It really felt like with everybody else as a series regular, everybody else had superpowers and we were kind of written in there as the raw meat put out to attract the animals. It was like me and Stephanie against the world, and we put a lot of that into our characters, so it was Lindsey and Lilah against the world but we knew if we won, we were going to come to blows between me and her and one of us was going out. I wish they'd have brought her back in the final season because it would have been great to have seen the dynamic in that as well."

Nitpicks: Cordelia says she keeps an extra outfit at the Hyperion to change into, and is wearing it, yet when Bethany shows up she gives her another outfit. Where did she keep that one?

The *Buffy* Connection: Angel tells Cordelia that she doesn't know what it's like to have a rebar through her torso, and she retorts that, actually, she does. In "Lover's Walk," she caught her then-boyfriend, Xander, in an embrace with Willow, and in shock she ran away, but the stairs under her collapsed and she went through them, impaling herself on a rebar.

Wolfram & Hart: Apparently the lawyers give talks at schools, trying to suss out which students might be ripe for recruitment, as either lawyers, freelancers, or clients.

2.5   Dear Boy

Original air date: October 24, 2000
Written and directed by: David Greenwalt
Guest cast: Juliet Landau (Drusilla), Stewart Skelton (Harold Jeakins), Sal Rendino (Man), Cheryl White (Claire), Matt North (Stephen), Derek Anthony (Hotel Security Guy), Darren Kennedy (Cop #1), Rich Hutchman (Detective Carlson)

Angel finally realizes that Darla is alive, but no one will believe him, especially not Kate.
    "Dear Boy" is a heart-pounding episode in which Darla rises to new heights of

sadism. Not satisfied with haunting Angel only during his dreams, she moves to his waking hours, allowing him glimpses of her. This is enough to convince him that she's alive, but his friends find it hard to believe, especially when they see her walk into the sunlight. Darla reports to her bosses that Angel is starting to crack, and good ol' Kate comes back into the picture, desperate to get the goods on Angel and put him behind bars, where she thinks he belongs. She also reveals a racist side to herself; when Kate meets Gunn for the first time, she immediately asks for his ID and gets a fellow officer to run a check on him. We never saw her pull something like that with Wes or Cordelia.

In a flashback scene of Angel and Darla in their glory days, we see how they turned Drusilla into a vampire. The return of Juliet Landau is an absolute thrill, even if it is only for a few episodes — she's as amazing as she ever was on *Buffy*. She's able to move from a tortured good girl on the verge of a nervous breakdown to a batty bad girl on the verge of a nervous breakdown in one line. Up to this point we've only heard about how Angel drove her mad — now we actually see it.

Back in the present, Darla finally corners Angel in a convent, where we discover she only *appears* to be working for Wolfram & Hart; instead she sees Angel as her possible salvation, and vice versa. She tells him Angelus is always under the surface and he should let him out (too bad she missed season 2 of *Buffy*). Julie Benz and David Boreanaz are powerful in this scene, seeming to dance with one another back and forth, one minute looking like they're in love, the next hating one another. The on-screen chemistry is evident, and the viewer believes they've shared a long and shadowed past. The episode ends with a warning that things will only get uglier, and we fans can't wait to see how.

Highlight: Angel trying to convince Wesley and Cordelia that he's not crazy and that he really did see Darla — between the clowns and the big talking hot dog.

Did You Notice?: The vampire transformations are far more sophisticated than last season.

Nitpicks: Kate asks, "Who's Darla?" How could she not know who Darla is? In season 1 she was able to tell Angel who he was, when he was turned into a vampire, and when he got his soul. There's no way she could have researched any history of Angelus and not come across a mention of Darla.

Oops: Cordelia tells Angel that Darla is at 1409 Galloway in Studio City, but Galloway Street is actually in Pacific Palisades, just off Sunset Boulevard. Also, when Angel transforms into his game face, that squeaky noise that sounds like skin rubbing across a leather seat is missing. Finally, the picture of the hotel the officer gives Kate shows a big Hyperion Hotel sign that isn't actually in any of the street shots we later see.

The *Buffy* Connection: We've been told on *Buffy* that Angel drove Drusilla mad and that madness has continued in her as a vampire (we know that all vampires are versions of their human selves, and Dru is no exception). Eventually, Drusilla hooked up with Spike and the two of them became the Syd and Nancy of the vampire world.

Wolfram & Hart: Lindsey is starting to fall for Darla, and his feelings will lead to his ultimate hatred of Angel.

Music/Bands: When Angel sees Darla outside, we hear "Stinky Stinky Ashtray" by Damn! (*Bossa Brava! Vol. 3*).

2.6   Guise Will Be Guise

Original air date: November 7, 2000
Written by: Jane Espenson
Directed by: Krishna Rao
Guest cast: Art LaFleur (T'ish Magev), Brigid Brannagh (Virginia Bryce), Patrick Kilpatrick (Paul Lanier), Todd Susman (Magnus Bryce), Danica Sheridan (Yeska), Saul Stein (Benny), Frankie Jay Allison (Thug #1), Michael Yama (Japanese Man #1), Eiji Inoue (Japanese Man #2), Ed Trotta (Man)

When Angel goes off to visit a swami at the Host's request, Wesley pretends he's Angel to help protect the daughter of a powerful man.

The always brilliant, always entertaining *Buffy* writer Jane Espenson penned this very funny episode about two fakes trying to be other people. Angel visits someone who asks him how he thinks others see him, and through Wesley, we see the answer. "Guise Will Be Guise" allows Alexis Denisof to show the hilarious and broody sides of his character. Posing as Angel, Denisof's Wesley pulls off some absolutely brilliant slapstick moments: freaking out when a mirror is in the room and insisting it be covered; being forced to drink blood and pouring it into a nearby plant; pretending to be burned by a cross. It is amazing to think this is the same Wesley as the one we'll see in season 4.

Meanwhile, the Host gets Angel into yet another pickle when he sends him to a swami, a man who looks less like a spiritual advisor than someone from Tony Soprano's gang. Yet despite being a little shady, he seems to hit Angel's problems on the head when he says that Angel is his own worst enemy; that he piles up problems around himself; and that he needs to exorcise himself of Darla, which he could do by finding a pretty blond thing, bedding her, and going all medieval on her before leaving her (you can tell a *Buffy* writer is at the helm of this episode). He probes the meaning of many of Angel's quirks and makes yet another comment about Angel's hair gel, something that Spike loves to razz him about ("Don't get me wrong; you're out there fighting the ultimate evil, you're gonna want something with hold").

David Boreanaz also gets a chance to show his comic side, not just in scenes with the swami, but when Angel returns to the city and the gang tries to rescue Virginia. Angel becomes obsessed about Wesley wearing his coat, about being called a eunuch, and he's clearly a little annoyed that Wesley was able to step into his shoes so convincingly. As the swami pointed out, Angel has set himself apart as a dark hero, wearing black and driving his gas-guzzling convertible, and bumbling Wesley somehow steps into that role and convinces a bunch of people that *he* is the dark, brooding vampire. That's gotta hurt.

This is an excellent episode that provides some much-needed comic relief before the dark episodes that will follow.

Highlight: Wesley pretending to be Angel and wandering into Bryce's house only to lurch backward when he realizes he hasn't yet been invited in is one of the funniest moments on this series — *ever*.

Jane Espenson Says: "I loved writing for *Angel*. It simply became less practical as the worlds of the shows became more divergent and as the *Angel* staff became more settled into their own rhythm of story-breaking and writing."

Did You Notice?: Bryce named his daughter "Virginia" for a reason that becomes obvious when we see how he's going to use her on his birthday.

2.7 Darla

Original air date: November 14, 2000
Written and directed by: Tim Minear
Guest cast: Mark Metcalf (The Master), Juliet Landau (Drusilla), James Marsters (Spike), Zitto Kazann (Gypsy Man), Bart Petty (Security Guard)

Through flashbacks we see how Darla became a vampire, what life was like when she was with Angelus, and how her past is impacting her present.

A beautiful, beautiful conclusion to the *Buffy* episode "Fool for Love," "Darla" uses flashbacks to give us insight into who these vampires were before the timeline of the series and to reflect the actions of the present day. We find out that Darla was a prostitute dying of syphilis in the Virginia Colony when the Master "saved" her from her condition (it's great to see Mark Metcalf again, and he's just as brilliant as he was in season 1 of *Buffy*). Similarly, in the present, Angel wants to "save" Darla from the clutches of Wolfram & Hart, which he believes will destroy her. We see Angel meet the Master for the first time (a metaphor for a boyfriend being introduced to his girlfriend's father) and taunt him about "living in the sewers" and not having any human contact. In the present, however, Angel lives exactly like the Master: with only a few people by his side

In "Darla," we flash back to the 19th century, where Spike (James Marsters) and Drusilla (Juliet Landau) joined Angelus and Darla.

and forced to move about in the sewers. The only difference is that they have very different mission statements. In 1880, Drusilla complains that she's all alone and, seeing how Darla and Angelus have each other, says she, too, wants someone to spend eternity with. In the present, Darla has made it clear to Angel that she wants to live forever again, and she wants to be with him. Previously, we saw Darla kick Angel out of their house when she discovered he had a soul, telling him he was disgusting. Now we see that his predicament actually cut her much deeper and she returned to the gypsy camp to order the father to retract the curse and take Angel's soul away again. In the present, she's living with her own agony of having a soul, and just as Angel warned her, the guilt for what she's done in her life is starting to haunt her.

But the most important flashback is to 1900. Angel, having lived with his guilt-ridden conscience for two years, returns to Darla and begs her to take him back. He can't live with the knowledge of what he's done to people, but he doesn't want to be away from her. In the present, Darla is realizing the same guilt: she has smashed her mirrors so she doesn't have to look at herself, and she now begs Angel to make her a vampire. When he refuses and she tells him that he should return the favor she'd given to him, it's a chilling moment. It was Darla who thrust Angel into a life of murder and torture, and since he got his soul back in 1898, he's been living with the horrible knowledge of what they did together. She cast him out when he wanted reprieve, and now she's asking him to make her a murderer again. The cold words he uses in response — "You damned me" — sum up his life for the last 250 years and show that while he might still be weak to her charms, he hasn't forgotten what she really is.

The scenery of this episode is beautiful, and Tim Minear is quickly becoming the best writer on *Angel*. "Darla," easily one of the best episodes of *Angel*, shows how a crossover is possible without one show being dependent on the other; *Buffy* fans were able to watch "Fool for Love" and not "Darla" and still enjoy a great episode, and vice versa. But taken together, these two episodes are phenomenal.

Highlight: The Master's disgusted response to his minions after he meets Angelus for the first time: "He won't last. I give it a century, tops."

Did You Notice?: In 1880, Drusilla says to Darla, "I could be your mummy," foreshadowing what happens later this season.

Nitpicks: Why did it take Darla seven years to introduce Angel to the Master?

Oops: Darla couldn't have been in the Virginia Colony (known as Jamestown) in 1609. The first colonists to Jamestown were 104 men, who arrived from England in 1607. Two other "supplies" of settlers arrived in 1608, but of the newcomers, only two were women: Mrs. Thomas Forrest and her servant, Anne Burras. Burras was married in November 1608, and no further settlers arrived the following year. So there were no single women in the colony in 1609.

The *Buffy* Connection: "Darla" immediately followed the *Buffy* episode "Fool for Love," in which Buffy asks Spike to tell her how he killed the two Slayers. We get flashbacks about who he was before he was turned into Spike, how Drusilla sired him, how the two joined Darla and Angelus to become a rampaging foursome, and how he killed the Chinese Slayer in 1900 and the New York Slayer in 1977. It's a beautifully written episode, and the scenes with Drusilla, Angel, and Darla overlap with scenes in this *Angel* episode. Also, the Master mentions the "Order of Aurelius," an order he first describes in season 1 of *Buffy*, and the order Spike ends in season 2.

Wolfram & Hart: Lindsey's feelings for Darla deepen, and Holland tells him she will be terminated soon. Holland sets up Lindsey for a fall when the firm realizes Lindsey's too personally involved in his case.

2.8   The Shroud of Rahmon

Original air date: November 21, 2000
Written by: Jim Kouf
Directed by: David Grossman
Guest cast: W. Earl Brown (Menlo), Dwayne L. Barnes (Lester), R. Emery Bright (Detective Turlock), Tom Kiesche (Detective Broomfield), Robert Dolan (Bob), Michael Hagy (Jay-Don), Jim Hanna (Surveillance Cop #1), Danny Ricardo (First Cop), Tony Todd (Vyasa)

Angel poses as a flashy vampire from Las Vegas when he discovers that a bunch of demons will try to steal the Shroud of Rahmon, a deadly shroud that can drive people crazy.

This episode opens with a distraught and weary-looking Wesley talking about how everything went wrong. The flashback plot device — where we see the ending first and then go back in time and lead up to it, discovering the why and how — hasn't been used on *Angel* before, even though it's a staple in detective shows (and shows like *The West Wing* and *Alias*). In this case, it's a little overdone, as Alexis Denisof seems to be almost over-playing his part, although we could chalk it up to the effect the shroud has had on him.

We're led to believe that Angel has killed Kate, who is particularly annoying in this episode. When she meets Angel at his apartment, she taunts him by referring to "blindingly sunny courtrooms" and makes other vampirist remarks. He threatens her, which is just what she wanted him to do, and it gives credence to what happens later. The character of Kate has overstayed its welcome; it worked in season 1, when Kate initially asked questions and then became a convert, finally believing that there was indeed another underworld out there. But by season 2, when the show is more mythological and focused on a larger arc, she doesn't serve much of a purpose, and it seems the writers don't know what to do with her.

Although this episode is a bit of a filler installment, all the characters are involved, and David Boreanaz gets to show us another side of his acting chops as the flashy, smooth-talking vampire from Nevada. Jay-Don is a little like Angelus, with his wit and lack of tolerance for other people's mistakes, and he talks a lot like John Travolta. However, the episode ends on an unnecessarily foreboding note, when Wesley worries that Angel's bloodlust might have been awakened. The more telling moment occurs earlier, when Angel is almost overcome by the shroud. In his eyes we see his human half fighting his demon half, refusing to let it out. But perhaps some of that demon half made it to the surface, because from this point on he's pretty far gone.

Highlight: Cordelia's classic comment: "I'm not big on shrouds. They're an after-you-die outfit."

Interesting Facts: The most famous shroud is the Shroud of Turin, a linen cloth that bears the image of a crucified man. Many people believe it is the shroud of Jesus Christ, while others believe it is a hoax. It is the property of the Catholic Church and has been kept in Turin, Italy, since 1578.

Nitpicks: Wesley says that Angel hasn't tasted human blood in a "*very* long time" and is concerned that the encounter with Kate might have awakened Angel's bloodlust. It hasn't been *that* long, actually; he fed on Buffy in that series' season-3 ender, "Graduation Day, Part Two," which was less than two years earlier. And what is with Cordelia's horrid Monica Lewinsky hair? Also, why does Angel carry a lighter when we know he doesn't smoke? Finally, if the shroud makes people crazy, why doesn't it seem to affect Kate or the other police officers?

Oops: The nitroglycerine the demons are using to blow up the vault is yellow, but it should be clear or a very, very light yellow (otherwise it's probably contaminated). And if the shroud was inside a box made of consecrated wood, Angel wouldn't have been able to carry it — it would have burned his hands.

2.9   The Trial

Original air date: November 28, 2000
Teleplay by: Douglas Petrie and Tim Minear
Story by: David Greenwalt
Directed by: Bruce Seth Green
Guest cast: Jim Piddock (Overseer), Juliet Landau (Drusilla), Evan Arnold (Geek Vampire)

Lindsey reveals to Darla that she's got two months to live, and she becomes desperate for immortality once again.

Another spectacular episode of *Angel* — season 2's continuity definitely makes it very different from season 1. Again flashing back and forth between the past and the present, this episode reveals that when Wolfram & Hart made Darla human again, she was reinflicted with the disease that almost killed her human self in the first place. We jump to a time when Darla and Angelus were being chased by a vampire hunter named Holtz (which will take on more importance in season 3) and she betrayed Angelus to save her own skin. Is she betraying him once again? Can he believe everything she says? And how can he be her salvation? Angel believes that if he can save this one tormented soul, which has been damaged and bruised almost beyond redemption, then maybe he'll be on his own path to salvation, even if it means his corporeal death. In Darla, Angel sees his own future as a human.

The episode title comes from a series of harrowing trials that Angel must endure while trying to save Darla, and only in watching just how much he will risk for her life does she realize that maybe she's okay the way she is. Interestingly, Angel's willing to die to save Darla, whereas he wasn't willing to become human to be with Buffy. In "I Will Remember You" Angel believed the world needed him as a champion, but in "The Trial" he believes his life is worth giving up to save Darla's.

Meanwhile, Lindsey has become an important character. It's now clear that he loves Darla, and it's killing him to realize that she's dying. Even he doesn't trust Wolfram & Hart's medical report, so he commissions several himself. Once again he betrays the people who sign his checks (presumably in blood) for love. The scene where Angel visits Lindsey's apartment is interesting, because Angel actually comes off as the petulant one. When he realizes Lindsey loves Darla, Angel mocks him and says that he himself was with her for 150 years, like it's a contest of some sort. When

Lindsey points out that Angel didn't love her, Angel counters that like himself, Lindsey has no soul and is incapable of loving Darla. The problem is, Angel's logic is skewed: Lindsey might work for a soulless corporation and appear to be heartless, but he does have a soul — he is human and is as capable of caring for Darla as Angel was capable of loving Buffy.

This episode is important for the resonance it will have in later seasons. Not only is Holtz mentioned, but by the end of the trial Angel has earned a life — and it's not given to Darla. We'll see what that life will be in season 3 and what impact all this will have in season 4.

As anyone would expect with such heavyweights as Minear, Greenwalt, Petrie, and Bruce Seth Green at the helm, this episode is a stunner.

Highlight: The magnificent slow-motion ending in the motel room, one of my favorite conclusions to any *Angel* episode.

Nitpicks: So far we've found out that vampires can enter a room if it's a public place, if it's inhabited by a demon, and if the inhabitant has died. Now Angel says that he can enter a motel room because it's a public accommodation? Tell that to the police if you've just sauntered into a room someone else has paid for. A motel room is not a public accommodation as long as it's been paid for and is inhabited. Also, during the second trial, why didn't Angel try tiptoeing over the floor in the spots between the crosses or doing some backflips to minimize the damage to himself? We know he's capable of such feats. And, as much as I love the ending, it seems strange that Angel didn't sense Drusilla's presence. Dru can sense when Spike is near, Darla senses Angel, and Angel knew when Penn was in town, meaning vampires can tell when one that they've sired is at hand, yet Angel didn't know Drusilla was nearby. Finally, why do vampires get their victims to drink from their chests? It's not like having them drink from the wrist, where the blood would flow more freely.

Oops: When Angel goes to Caritas to see the Host, someone hands the Host a drink, and then in the next scene he's handed the drink again. During the first trial, the camera shoots over Angel's shoulder and the butler should be standing in front of him, but he's suddenly gone, and then back again. And when Angel is pulled into chains at the beginning of the third trial, you can see blood on his mouth from the previous trial, but in the next scene, it's suddenly gone. Also, in that same scene, the person we see from behind is clearly not David Boreanaz. While Boreanaz is in good physical shape, the person we see from behind has bulging biceps and is completely ripped; from the front, Boreanaz does not sport the same physique. Finally, when Juliet Landau runs her finger over her chest to make the cut, you can see it's already there, and her fingernail isn't actually anywhere near the cut.

The *Buffy* Connection: Just as Angel feels completely helpless with Darla and says there's nothing he can do to save her from the disease, on *Buffy*, Buffy has discovered her mother has a brain tumor and there's nothing she can do to save her.

2.10   Reunion

Original air date: December 19, 2000
Written by: Tim Minear and Shawn Ryan
Directed by: James A. Contner
Guest cast: Juliet Landau (Drusilla), Stephanie Manglaras (Landlady), Karen Tucker (Female Shopper), Erik Liberman (Erik), Katherine Ann McGregor (Catherine), Michael Rotondi (Burly Guy)

When Angel can't stop Darla from being reborn as a vampire, he decides to forget about redemption in order to spend all his time hunting her.

A pivotal episode for season 2, "Reunion" brings back Drusilla in all her craziness and Darla in all her seductive vampiness, and we even get a glimpse of the evil Angelus. A true family reunion. Juliet Landau is terrific, making Drusilla as loopy as ever, and listening to her speak and watching the way she moves her body is always a delight. She's still hilarious in every scene, and it's through her that we can tell how far gone Angel is. Throughout the episode Angel moves from feeling the sadness of losing Darla to blaming himself for letting it happen to assuming a sense of duty — if he can stake her before she rises, he'll still be able to save her from the darkness of her inevitable soulless existence. But when he arrives too late, he seems to lose hope. He blames himself because he sired Drusilla — he takes responsibility for his spawn's having sired another. He's angry and uncaring when the gang attempts to help someone who is suicidal, and Cordelia, Wesley, and Gunn all realize they're starting to lose Angel, but they don't know what to do about it.

The shock of this episode is what happens to Angel when he realizes that it's too late to save Darla, and that his mistakes have led to the return of one of the fiercest known vampires, who is only too happy to be coming back for seconds. This is a woman who, only hours earlier, Angel was willing to sacrifice his very life for, and now he begins to believe that no matter what he does, he'll continue to be punished. He also assumes that he'll be blamed for what Darla does from this point forward because he couldn't stop her evil resurrection. With that belief, something in Angel snaps, and he skips over the problem itself and goes to the source, attempting to eradicate the people who have dogged him at Wolfram & Hart. The result is a devastating loss of the humanity he's worked so hard for, and when he recognizes the dark path he's on, he shuns his friends and co-workers. At this moment, the season takes a very dark turn.

CHRISTINA RADISH

We bid a not-so-fond adieu to Holland Manners (Sam Anderson) in this episode, but sometimes things are not always as they appear.

Highlight: Angel treating Cordelia's unexpected vision like a bathroom break: "She should have done this before we left the hotel."

Christian Kane Says: "I get a lot of fan letters, which is really nice when people take the time to write. It's really hard to get back to everyone, but I try to read everything because they took the time to write it. I've gotten everything from sick, satanic stuff — I guess they think that I'm really my character — I've had little girls start crying when they meet me because they're happy and I've had them cry because they're scared to death. It's very awkward, this particular role, because the kids who watch it sometimes can't differentiate between me and the character. I always play the bad guy, never the good guy, so people are always a little shaken when they see me."

Did You Notice?: Drusilla walks into Holland's wine cellar and says, "Pretty lawyers all in a row," which is a reference to the *Buffy* novelization of Spike and Drusilla's backstory, *Pretty Maids All in a Row*.

Nitpicks: In season 2 of *Buffy*, Drusilla went through a personality change: her battiness changed to a more methodical madness and her crazy behavior became more dangerous. But on *Angel* she seems to be back to the old Dru: crazy for crazy's sake.

Oops: When Darla rises from her, uh, flowerbed, she doesn't have any toenail polish on, but by the time she gets to the clothing store soon afterward, her toes have been nicely painted red.

Wolfram & Hart: The Senior Partners, whom we don't see, pass their messages down to other lawyers, and Holland relays to Lindsey and Lilah that their efforts have been much appreciated. Lindsey tells Angel that he wants him dead and looks amused when Darla and Drusilla show up to the "tasting."

Music/Bands: In this episode, we hear "Shock" by Fear Factory (*Obsolete*).

2.11   Redefinition

Original air date: January 16, 2001
Written by: Mere Smith
Directed by: Michael Grossman
Guest cast: Brigid Brannagh (Virginia), Nicolas Surovy (Hunt Acrey), Juliet Landau (Drusilla), Matthew James (Merl), Joel Stoffer (Vampire #1), Brad Kalas (EMT), Jamie McShane (Demon), David Wolfson (Bartender)

Cordelia, Wesley, and Gunn are on their own after being fired by Angel, and Angel's out to wreak vengeance on Darla and Drusilla.

And the dark just keeps getting darker. This gloomy, graphic episode should definitely not be shown to kids. As Angel moves deeper within himself, he first gets rid of his dozens of drawings of Darla (in a prophetic way: in the fireplace) to prepare physically and mentally to wage war against Darla and Drusilla. Through a chant-like voice-over that sounds as if it has no life left in it, Angel tells us how he's readying himself, and when he sees Darla at one point, he realizes he's still too close to her emotionally to do what he must.

Meanwhile, without jobs, Gunn, Wesley, and Cordelia do what all self-respecting Los Angelites do when they have no money and no future: they get drunk and sing karaoke at Caritas. When they receive a vision from the powers that be and answer it, they realize that they might not have Angel's strength, but they have the caring urge within them to fight the good fight. So they do, and while they might have to visit the hospital a little more often than they did before, they realize it's worth it. Wesley is the one who eventually goes to Angel to inform him that Angel Investigations will continue to operate with or without its leader. Over at Wolfram & Hart, Lindsey believes he was kept alive because Darla truly loves him and is upset when he realizes she saved one other lawyer. While desperate for some reciprocation of the love he feels for her, he is starting to realize that in having made her soulless, he'll never have his feelings returned.

Angel, who finally corners Darla and Drusilla in what turns into a grisly scene, has given up fighting for noble causes and has let part of the demon within him surface so he can destroy what he believes is the true evil. As he says at the end of the episode, the other three can fight the good fight — he's here to win the war. The thing is, he's *not* fighting the war, and he's not looking at the big picture. He's so focused on Darla and the destruction she will wreak on him, not on the others, that he's lost sight of what he was supposed to be saving ultimately — himself.

This episode is pivotal in the *Angel* series because from this point on, Wesley is going to be more serious, Gunn is officially part of the gang, Cordelia is not so quick to forgive, and Angel begins to accept that his darker persona must co-exist with his lighter one.

Highlight: Cordy, Gunn, and Wesley fighting at Caritas.

Stephanie Romanov Says: "When the writers originally conceived of Lilah, the way they wanted to see the character at first was more, she's bad, she's evil. It was more black and white than the way I wanted to play her. And at the audition I played it exactly as they wanted it. And then when we started filming I changed it. [Laughs] That's what I wanted, though, and I said to them, 'True evil is ambiguous and difficult to define and identify because the really badass people stab you in the back.' So I definitely purposely played her that way, which I think made her even more evil than we would have thought."

Did You Notice?: Drusilla has visions like Cordelia, although where Cordy's help people, Drusilla's are ignored. Drusilla is a bit of a Cassandra in that no one believes her (or pays any attention to her) until it's too late. Not only does she see the future, but she can see into the heart of things, such as whether Angel is himself, Angelus, or something else entirely. Also, Angel never actually speaks a word of dialogue in this entire episode.

Nitpicks: How did Darla and Drusilla get into Wolfram & Hart? Not only did they massacre several Wolfram & Hart staff members, but, as we learned in the previous episode, Darla is an untagged vampire. Also, Angel sets Darla and Drusilla on fire, something he's done to other vampires. Darla grabs a sledgehammer, runs to a fire hydrant, and douses both their flames in the spray. Every other vampire dusts instantly. Furthermore, their hair seems to be intact after the incident, and they don't show any long-lasting scars (the latter could be chalked up to a vampire's quick healing powers).

Oops: When Angel is questioning Merl you can see Merl's tongue, something he claimed not to have in "Judgement." Also, Angel's tattoo is back in the final scene, but it's placed much higher than it was originally. It should be lower on his shoulder blade and not necessarily noticeable through a tank top.

The *Buffy* Connection: Cordelia mentions that Angel is consistent — always letting some blond drive him over the edge (Mere Smith is always great at sticking subtle *Buffy* references into her scripts).

Wolfram & Hart: When something goes wrong with a w&h plan, the Senior Partners find someone to blame and know how to pin the entire thing on that person. Lindsey and Lilah are promoted to co–vice presidents of Special Projects.

2.12   Blood Money

Original air date: January 23, 2001
Written by: Shawn Ryan and Mere Smith
Directed by: R.D. Price
Guest cast: Julia Lee (Anne Steele), Gerry Becker (Nathan Reed), Mark Rolston (Boone), Matthew James (Merl), Jeffrey Patrick Dean (Dwight), R. Martin Klein (Husband), Jason Padgett (Holden), Jennifer Rosa (Serena), Deborah Carson (Liza)

Angel begins following a woman who works at a homeless shelter when he discovers she's had dealings with Wolfram & Hart.

While "Blood Money" is an entertaining and satisfying episode, there's a brilliant character choice that might have slipped by some viewers. Anne, a worker at a homeless shelter in L.A., should look familiar to *Buffy* viewers. As Chantarelle in "Lie to Me," she was a vampire worshiper who thought all vamps were like Lestat — romantic and wonderful. She was wrong. In "Anne," she was Lilly (the same character with a name change), who had moved to L.A. and believed in Ken, a social worker who convinced homeless kids that there was a better life for them — and she ended up in a hell dimension as a result. Buffy was hiding out in L.A. at the time, using her middle name, Anne, while working as a waitress. At the end of that episode, Buffy told "Lilly" she could have the name "Anne" if she wanted, because Buffy was going back to using her first name. It looks like "Anne" took Buffy up on that offer.

Now, with that past behind her, Anne's a worker in a homeless shelter (probably to make up for all the kids Ken hurt) and she's faced with yet another dilemma: does she believe the law firm that's offering her a ton of money and helping to raise funds for the shelter, or does she believe a vampire who's been following her, stealing her wallet, and taking pictures of her? Because we know her past, we know what an excruciating decision this is for her, and we worry that she'll trust the wrong people yet again. It takes guts to introduce a character that's been partially developed on one show into another without showing any flashbacks or scenes from the original (the only hint that Anne's been on *Buffy* is when Merl says she has changed her name a few times), but knowing that there is a payoff for those who catch on makes the risk worthwhile.

Meanwhile, Gunn, Cordy, and Wesley are learning to work together, and Gunn and Wesley are actually getting along when they're fighting side by side. Cordy gets the visions, and Wes and Gunn do the fighting, the squealing, and the peeing of the pants. We get our last glimpse of the Angel Investigations business cards, with their "unique" logo ("Looks like a lobster . . . with a growth"), and the trio is prepared to move on without Angel, because they no longer need him.

Angel appears to take his eye off the prize to help Anne, but considering the prize is Wolfram & Hart, he's still playing the same game. However, two episodes ago he almost allowed a kid to commit suicide because he couldn't be bothered to save him, and in the last episode he was so dark and depressing that Darla couldn't figure out if he was Angel or Angelus. Pursuing Anne will help him with his quest to take down Wolfram & Hart (Anne later says that his plot to foil the firm was just a scam), but he's been so obsessed with Darla lately that it seems strange he could focus on another blond for an entire episode. As a result, this episode feels more like filler and not a part of the larger seasonal arc.

Highlight: Wesley's striptease on camera.

Christian Kane Says: "Doing the scenes with David was the most fun for me, because we're really good friends. I was there when he got the show, I was there when his life got a little tough with relationship problems, until he met Jaime Bergman. I was at their wedding, and David called me right after Jaden Rayne was born. We've been that close; he's like family. His mom called me to tell me what a great job I did on *Las Vegas* last week. When his parents come into town I'll go out with them and we'll do dinner. We've spent the last four New Years together just to start the year together. It's a really good camaraderie. But when the camera starts rolling we just want to kill each other. It's funny because we'll laugh and laugh and laugh and we'll be telling jokes, not even going over our lines, and they'll say, 'Action,' and it's, like, boom — we switch. The funny thing about David and me is, we've worked together so well and so long that if you notice, we don't take our eyes off each other. If one person does, the other person will stab him in the back. Then there's a break and we laugh and start telling jokes again. In the first season, if you look closely and they're filming over his shoulder to me I'm, like, 'I'm gonna kill you' and he's laughing his ass off and then they film over my shoulder back to him and he's, like, 'I don't think so' and I'm laughing, and you can totally see it."

Did You Notice?: Cordy records herself auditioning for a milk ad, which is probably an inside joke about the fact that David Boreanaz shot a Got Milk? ad around the same time.

Nitpicks: Angel met Anne and actually had an argument with her in "Lie to Me," and we find out later that he has a photographic memory. So why doesn't she look the least bit familiar to him when he can supposedly see someone after 150 years and remember them instantly? And why were Lindsey and Lilah in charge of the bogus charity fundraiser? It hardly seems like a Special Project for Wolfram & Hart. Finally, watch how Cordelia's hair will change drastically from one episode to the next. In "The Shroud of Rahmon," she gets that Monica cut, but by the next episode, the bouffant nature of the hair has lessened somewhat. Then she cuts it shorter. In "Redefinition," we can see a few highlights. In this episode, there are even more highlights, and by the end of the season, her hair will be cut just past her ears and be as blond as it is presently brown. How is Cordelia finding all the time and money to be at the hairdresser almost every day?

The *Buffy* Connection: Aside from the Chantarelle/Lilly/Anne connection, at the charity fundraiser one of the soap actresses is stopped by a wealthy woman, who asks her if the show made her character gay for the sake of ratings. It's a question that was being asked of the *Buffy* writers a lot after Willow came out in season 4, a year before this episode.

Wolfram & Hart: The firm uses charity organizations as fronts for taking most of the donations to fund its own operations.

Music/Bands: When Angel visits Anne at the shelter, we hear "Legion" by Junkie XL (*Big Sounds of the Drags*); "Let 'er Rip" by The Dixie Chicks (*Wide Open Spaces*) plays at the charity benefit.

2.13   Happy Anniversary

Original air date: February 6, 2001
Teleplay by: David Greenwalt
Story by: Joss Whedon and David Greenwalt
Directed by: Bill Norton
Guest cast: Brigid Brannagh (Virginia), Matt Champagne (Gene), Darby Stanchfield (Denise), Victoria A. Kelleher (Val), Danny LaCava (Mike), Eric Lange (Lubber Demon #1), Geremy Dingle (Student Clerk), Michael Faulkner (Guy on Stage), Norma Micheals (Aunt Helen)

The Host warns Angel that the world is coming to an end because of a scientist who is going to attempt to stop time.

A filler episode, "Happy Anniversary" shows that when Angel's not around, Wesley, Gunn, and Cordelia are able to snag clients on their own and solve crimes successfully. It also gives Angel a chance to rant to the Host (outside of Caritas for the first time) about the futility of his lot: no matter how much good he does in the world, he'll never be allowed to atone for what he's done in the past. The Host observes that Angel's heart is no longer in the game and says that he's tired of Angel's mopiness (speaking for most of the viewers at this point). He tells Angel that he *was* a champion, but these days, he is the furthest thing from it. He asks Angel what he is really thinking. The others had tried to get Angel to talk about this situation, too, but he wouldn't speak to them about it. The Host, however, is someone who might be able to offer Angel some advice — Angel isn't so close to him that friendship interferes with the sharing of opinions.

Andy Hallett and David Boreanaz yuk it up away from the set. When Angel is at his broodiest, The Host drops by to try to snap him out of it – and save the world.

The episode's main plot line involves a scientist who's unable to connect with his girlfriend, so he discovers a way to stop time just as they're making love. What he doesn't realize is that time will stop not only for them but also for everyone else. It's up to the Host and Angel to prevent him from doing so.

The problem here is that in a storyline where we're supposed to watch Angel going deeper and deeper within himself and getting darker and darker, a night out with the Host puts a comic spin on things, hurting the momentum of the season. Angel seems almost chipper by the end of the episode and admits that he's wronged his friends and should try to connect with people, which is starting to make "Redefinition" seem completely out of place where it was. But it's a momentary lapse, and in the next episode we'll be back to the brooding.

Highlight: Wesley's hilarious Sherlock Holmes routine.
Did You Notice?: The Host stops himself before saying that Wesley will be playing a huge part in something. By the end of season 3, we'll know what that is.
Nitpicks: How did Angel take out books from the library without a card?
Oops: When Gene is talking to Val while standing in front of his board, the formulas

behind him keep changing every time he goes to write something. Also, Angel tells the Host he's trying to atone for 100 years of unspeakable evil, when it's actually closer to 150. Finally, when Angel fights the Lubber demons in the street, the one he had hit with the car, who was lying on the road, disappears.

Music/Bands: At the party at the end of the episode, we hear Mocean Worker's "Hey Baby" (*Mixed Emotional Features*).

2.14 The Thin Dead Line

Original air date: February 13, 2001
Written by: Shawn Ryan and Jim Kouf
Directed by: Scott McGinnis
Guest cast: Julia Lee (Anne), Mushond Lee (Jackson), Jarrod Crawford (Rondell), Cory C. Hardrict (Ray), Kyle Davis (Kenny), Camille Mana (Les), Darin Cooper (Police Officer), Brenda Price (Callie), Darris Love (George), Matthew James (Merl), Geoff Koch (Street Cop), Jerry Giles (Desk Sergeant), Steven Barras (Captain), Suli McCullough (EMT), Marie Chambers (Mother)

A gang of zombie cops clamps down on crime in its precinct, but innocent people are dying as a result.

On the surface, this might seem to be another monster-of-the-week episode where we move away from the main plot line and watch the characters battle some demon or other. But instead, all the key players are involved in the story, even if they don't realize they're helping each other out. Gunn, Wesley, and Cordelia have a new office and are finding clients. Meanwhile, Gunn learns from his former gang members that rogue cops are beating up neighborhood people who are on the streets after dark. Enter Anne again with her homeless shelter, and the police officers attack her place specifically. Gunn's former friends snipe at him for "playing demon detective," a sort of gentle push that will become more hostile in "Belonging" and "That Old Gang of Mine." Gunn has been useful to Angel and the team because he knows the streets better than any of them, but in helping out his new friends, he's left his old ones without a leader.

Angel meets with Kate, and he visits the shelter to find out for himself if these officers are as bad as everyone says they are. The visual metaphor is interesting: while Wesley and the gang fight from the inside of the shelter, Angel remains on the outside, looking in and trying to do things his way. When Wesley, who believes the officers are good, shows up and tries to talk one of them out of threatening Gunn, he is shot and almost dies. But when Gunn and Cordelia work together to insure that doesn't happen, the threesome becomes a full-fledged team.

The episode is an interesting allegory about the problem with police, and in particular, the LAPD. Police exist to protect the people, but black citizens may feel like they need protection from the police. Gunn tells Anne that if he walks outside he'll be an immediate target for the rogue police officers because he's "walking while black." He and his friends laugh, but it's a serious problem. Of course, the end of the episode shows the grim flipside — without the police, the drug dealers rule the streets, and murderers and rapists are everywhere. In today's society, the source of the problem is a difficult choice between the scumbags on the streets and police officers who themselves force certain people to live in fear. The episode boils the issue down to crime rates versus cop brutality, and Gunn suggests it's the drug dealers and crime lords that allow a police station to justify its brutality. As the episode concludes, Kate smugly tells Angel that they just "gave back to the community" the crime rates that had been in decline. However, the crimes were there all along — they were just being carried out by the police, who were not reporting them.

Highlight: Cordelia's comment after she finds out Gunn is going to do something stupid: "Hey, Gunn graduated with a major in dumb planning from Angel University. He sat at the feet of the master and learned well how to plan dumbly."

J. August Richards Says: "The ass-kicking vampire hunter is the part of the character that I like the most. I love to play him when he's in a fight scene, when his objective is clear, ridding the world of vampires. I do a lot of the stunts. I do all of the fight stuff, but all of the throws — like, if I'm going to be catapulted across the room — I won't do that, but I do all of the hand-to-hand combat."

Did You Notice?: There's a discrepancy between reports of how many lawyers died in the Wolfram & Hart wine-tasting massacre. Gunn refers to 20 bodies, Darla says she killed 15, and Kate says only 13 bodies were at the scene.

Nitpicks: While the exterior of the shelter is the same one we saw in "Blood Money," the interior looks homier and less institutional. When Anne sees Cordelia and Wesley for the first time, she doesn't recognize them, even though they were both on the tape that played at the charity event a couple of episodes earlier. Also, although she's come to the office to find Gunn, she seems surprised that the place is called Angel Investigations. How did she find him if she didn't know that that's where he now works? And when a tough guy shows up, she simply lets him in so that there's no trouble. Does she feel the same way about rapists? What kind of shelter allows the evil inside? Finally, why didn't Anne use some of the money she received from the fundraiser to buy iron doors? The doors on the shelter are mostly glass, and while the interior wrought-iron doors might keep out intruders, someone could easily break the glass and shoot those inside through the second doors.

Wolfram & Hart: Angel harasses Merl for more information and finds out there will be an important meeting concerning a new client named Diaghilev the next night, but we never hear about this client again.

Music/Bands: At the homeless shelter, we hear OutKast's "Ms. Jackson" (*Stankonia*) and Seldom Seen's "Who's Got My Back," from their self-titled CD.

2.15   Reprise

Original air date: February 20, 2001
Written by: Tim Minear
Directed by: James Whitmore Jr.
Guest cast: Brigid Brannagh (Virginia), Thomas Kopache (Denver), Gerry Becker (Nathan Reed), David Fury (First Worshiper), Chris Horan (Second Worshiper), Jolene Hjerleid (Singing Lawyer #1), Wayne Mitchell (Singing Lawyer #2), Marie Chambers (Mother), Eric Larson (Internal Affairs Guy), Shirley Jordan (Internal Affairs Woman), Carl Sundstrom (Lieutenant), Kevin Fry (Skilosh Demon)

As Wolfram & Hart comes under its 75-year review, Angel discovers a ring that can take him to Wolfram & Hart's "home office."

This is an amazing episode that brings all the season's plots to a head, with nearly everyone seeming to give up. Angel stops trying to be nice to the gang (not that he was making great strides with that, anyway) and storms into their office, rude and uncaring, to get what he needs. Virginia, who has been dating Wesley since "Guise Will Be Guise," gives up on the relationship because she can't be with someone who is involved in such a dangerous profession (wasn't her dad a wizard?). Meanwhile, the police department, fed up with Kate's chasing demons and monsters, forces her to turn in her badge. Furious with herself for letting her father down, she stops trying to live up to his standards and begins drinking herself to death.

Only Cordelia refuses to give up. Facing an unpaid invoice for a job well done (remember that girl with the eye in her skull in the last episode?), Cordy rushes over to the client's place in the middle of the night when promised the payment, not realizing she's heading to her certain doom.

Over at Wolfram & Hart, the lawyers are up for their 75-year review, and Lindsey and Lilah are both worried. They've made a ton of errors with Angel and Darla, and now they'll have to face up to them. Until Angel unknowingly averts their doom. Angel gives up on everything, discovering a way to get to the "home office" and taking it. Jumping on an elevator to Hell with Holland, he discovers a painful, awful truth, one that will change his entire outlook on his mission and his personal quest. It's a great scene, and after the buildup of everything that's happened thus far, this episode provides the breaking point.

"Reprise" is a great climactic episode that builds up to such a height that it can't help but come crashing down. The episode ends with a familiar scene: Angel has sex with Darla and, in the middle of the night, sits bolt upright, gasping. Uh-oh.

Highlight: When the Host tells Angel that the two downsides to living in this dimension are the possibility of getting killed and the "so-called 'musicals' of Andrew Lloyd Webber."

Interesting Facts: At the beginning of the episode, the light-haired guy sacrificing the goats is *Angel* writer and producer David Fury (see "Smile Time"). Also, after the episode aired, Tim Minear posted on the Bronze: "Here's how something like this happens. We all sit around scratching our heads. Then Joss says something to the effect of 'Can Holland come back all dead and take Angel on an elevator ride to hell but end up right back where he started?' then I just try to work out the details. The bush is burning, and its name is Joss."

Christian Kane Says: "In the first season money was Lindsey's main objective. Because of his past, I believe that's why he did the things he did. If you put a price on something, that's where you really tell the measure of a man. Coming from poverty made him want the money no matter what the cost — he just wants the cash. In season two it changed, and it became for love. Because he did all this stuff for money and all of a sudden Darla shows up. He's very taken with this woman, and I think the money thing just kinda went out the window. She introduced him to his heart. I don't think it was there before. Before he just cared about moving up in the firm, but she introduced him to actual feelings again. The only two things I know that will turn a man against himself are love and money, and I think that's what happened, and that's when money really wasn't important anymore. Even though he didn't end up with her, she made him remember who he used to be."

Nitpicks: It's a shame that Drusilla has just disappeared when she and Darla were making such a great team. We see Denver again, the bookstore owner from "Are You Now or Have You Ever Been?" and he should be 80 years old in this episode because he said he was just over 30 in 1952, but he looks more like he's in his 60s. Finally, in both this episode and "Redefinition" we're reminded that the gang saved Virginia as she was about to be sacrificed to the goddess Yeska — do the writers think our memory is so short that we need a reminder every time we see her? It's not like we're going to mistake her for Cordelia.

Oops: Angel was just impaled on Darla's sword, yet when he wakes up at the end of the episode, shirtless, there's no mark on him whatsoever. He usually takes a day or two to heal from wounds like that.

Wolfram & Hart: We discover several things about the evil law firm in this episode. w&h has a 75-year review, and Lilah is trying to convince Lindsey to work with her to make sure they come out on top at the audit (this despite trying to double-cross him in "Redefinition"). A lawyer's contract with Wolfram & Hart extends beyond life, and the firm has been around since the dawn of time in the form of one evil or another, from the Khmer Rouge to people yelling at each other in the streets. w&h has an apocalypse "scheduled." We also see one of the Senior Partners, and he ain't pretty.

2.16 Epiphany

Original air date: February 27, 2001
Written by: Tim Minear
Directed by: Thomas J. Wright
Guest cast: Marie Chambers (Mother), Kevin Fry (Skilosh Demon)

Angel has a sudden moment of clarity where he realizes the error of his ways and the long road he'll have to take to get back to where he was.

Someone's been reading their James Joyce. Before the 20th century, the word *Epiphany* was used in a Christian context only, to refer to the moment when Christ revealed himself to the Magi. But Irish novelist Joyce changed that when he developed the literary epiphany, a moment of absolute knowledge that comes suddenly in a flash of recognition, usually during an otherwise normal circumstance. One of the most famous literary epiphanies occurs in Joyce's *A Portrait of the Artist as a Young Man*, when protagonist Stephen Dedalus sees a woman standing in water, holding her skirts up, and is suddenly filled with such a joy he can hardly contain himself.

Similarly, in "Epiphany," Angel sleeps with Darla, and when it doesn't bring about the "moment of true happiness" that occurred with Buffy, he realizes the demon inside him doesn't control him, he doesn't belong with

CHRISTINA RADISH

Lilah (Stephanie Romanov) and Lindsey (Christian Kane) have done everything they can to claw their way to the top – and sometimes they use those claws on each other.

ANGEL "Epiphany"
Shooting Schedule
Mon, Jan 22, 2001

Scene #43 **EXT - LINDSEY'S APT - Day** D2 1/8 Pgs.
Lindsey's ruined truck w/note

Cast Members
  7. Lindsey

Extras
    1 Utility Standin
    2 Pedestrians

Props
    Note

Makeup/Hair
    Lindsey beat up

EFX Makeup
    Demon blood/guts
    Stump for Lindsey

Costume
    Lindsey messed up

Art Dept/Set Dressing
Lindsey's truck messed up

Transportation
    1 Lindsey's damaged truck

Notes
Possible ND cars for street

RETURN TO HOUSE

Scene #16pt **INT - SHARP'S HME - Night** N1 5/8 Pgs.
Cordelia meets Skilosh demon - END ACT 1

Cast Members
  2. Cordelia
  11D. Lead Skilosh Demon

Extras
    1 Standin Cordy
    2 Utility Standins

Props
    Cordy's bag

EFX Makeup
    Demon MU

Additional Labor
Lens Tech

Grip/Electric
DfN

Scene #16pt **INT - SHARP'S HME - Night** N1 1/8 Pgs.
Cordy's vision of demon

Cast Members
  2. Cordelia
  11D. Lead Skilosh Demon

Extras
    1 Standin Cordy
    1 Utility Standin

EFX Makeup
    Demon MU

Special Equipment
Video camera

Additional Labor
Lens Tech

Grip/Electric
DfN

Notes
Shoot on Video

Scene #18 **INT - SHARP'S HME - Night** N1 1 3/8 Pgs.
Cordy talks to the lead demon

Cast Members
  2. Cordelia
  11D. Lead Skilosh Demon
  12D. Stunt Skilosh #1
  13D. Stunt Skilosh #2

Extras
    1 Standin Cordy
    3 Utility Standins

Props
    Cordy's bag

EFX Makeup
    Demon MU

Additional Labor
Lens Tech

Grip/Electric
DfN

Two pages from the "Epiphany" shooting schedule.

COURTESY JENNIFER KAPLAN

Scene #23   INT - SHARP'S HME - Night   N1   1 6/8 Pgs.
               Cordy gets pronged - END ACT 2

Cast Members   **Props**
  2. Cordelia   Cordy's bag
 11D. Lead Skilosh Demon   **Additional Labor**
 12D. Stunt Skilosh #1   **EFX Makeup**   Lens Tech
 13D. Stunt Skilosh #2   Back eye blinks
  14. Stunt Coor   Demon MU   **Grip/Electric**
                              Snakey prong thing   DfN
Extras
  1 Skilosh demon
  1 Standin Cordy
  1 Utility Standin

Scene #31   INT - SHARP'S HME - Night   N1   1/8 Pgs.
               POV of Cordy and Skilosh

Cast Members   **Props**
  2. Cordelia   Cordy's bag
  3. Wesley   **Makeup/Hair**
  4. Gunn   Cordy has third eye
 11D. Lead Skilosh Demon
 12D. Stunt Skilosh #1
 13D. Stunt Skilosh #2

Extras
  1 Skilosh demon
  1 Standin Cordy
  1 Standin Gunn
  1 Standin Wesley
  1 Utility Standin

Scene #30, 32, 35   EXT - SHARP'S HME - Night   N1   2 3/8 Pgs.
               Wesley and Gunn watch; decide not to wait

Cast Members   **Props**
  3. Wesley   Wesley's wheelchair
  4. Gunn

Extras
  1 Standin Gunn
  1 Standin Wesley

Scene #15, 16pt   EXT - SHARP'S HME - Night   N1   6/8 Pgs.
               Cordelia arrives; enters

Cast Members   **Props**
  2. Cordelia   Cordy's bag
Extras   **Transportation**
  1 Standin Cordy   1 Family car
  1 Taxi driver   1 Taxi
  1 Utility Standin

Darla, and his soul can be saved (when he crawls onto the balcony in pain while the rain whips at him it's a little much, though, and it doesn't convey the sense of radiance the term *epiphany* is meant to imply). He rushes to try to save Kate from committing suicide, the Wheelèd One from being killed, and Cordelia from being, um, implanted. The initial scene, in which Darla realizes that having sex with her hasn't brought about his legendary moment of happiness, is amusing (although you have to feel a little sorry for the gal) and a perfect parallel for a girl who worries she "wasn't that good."

Angel's moodiness has been born of his need for redemption. At the end of season 1 he discovered that someday he would be forgiven for the things that he's done, but throughout season 2, Wolfram & Hart has stood in his way so many times that he just decided to give up on the big picture. If he couldn't thwart Wolfram & Hart, he believed his redemption wouldn't be forthcoming. And if he couldn't have redemption, he didn't want anything but revenge. Now he realizes it's not the big picture that counts, it's the little things. Meanwhile, Lindsey is dealing with his own frustration after learning through Darla how to love again. Unfortunately, that love has been unrequited, and Lindsey realizes that everything he's done for her wasn't enough. He's seen the evil at the core of Wolfram & Hart, and he knows that by sticking around he'll never be happy.

The best part of this episode is that everyone gets to clear the air in his or her own way and begin to move on. Angel tells Darla that she's saved him by making him realize he can't save her. Wesley has a great scene where he tells Angel how much he's hurt all of them and how much they — especially Cordelia — have changed as a result. Gunn is angry and doesn't try to hide it, telling Angel that someday he just might have an epiphany of his own. Cordelia tells him that her feelings have been hurt (a wonderful moment). Lindsey embraces his redneck background and shows up in his Sanford and Son truck to beat the crap out of Angel, showing that he recognizes he'll never be able to escape being a hick from the wrong side of the tracks. And Kate stops blaming Angel for all her problems. Each character's "epiphany" is completely believable for who each is, showing what a handle Tim Minear has on this series.

Highlight: The Host's "pep talk" to Angel: "I think I'm speaking for everyone when I say if all you're gonna do is switch back to brood mode, we'd rather have you evil. Then, at least . . . leather pants."

Interesting Facts: When the Host realizes Angel has changed, he says, "Zuzu's petals," a reference to *It's a Wonderful Life*. In that film, the main character, George Bailey, is forced to hit rock bottom to see how good his life has been and how much he has touched others, much like Angel. When he's back to reality, he reaches into his pocket and finds the petals of a flower his daughter Zuzu had given him earlier, and he has his epiphany at that moment.

Christian Kane Says: "In the scene with the sledgehammer, the only piece of clothing that wasn't mine was the flannel shirt; everything else was mine, even the boots. They were very nice to give me that little outlet on my way out in the second season. As a character choice, I think Lindsey wanted nothing to do with w&H at that point, so that was his way of going back to his roots. Also, I wasn't about to fight David in a suit. I'm mortal, so I needed a little help and that sledgehammer happened to be in the back of the truck."

Did You Notice?: The hours of Angel Investigations are Monday to Thursday: 10–6; Friday: 10–9; Saturday: 9–9; Sunday: closed. It appears that even demon hunters acknowledge the Sabbath. Also, despite the appearance that Angel and Kate's relationship is finally going to be a pleasant one, this is actually the last time we see her, which is a good thing. As interesting as her character became in the first season, she wasn't necessary in the second and dragged the show into the "TV cop" territory that's been overdone.

Nitpicks: Okay, we get it. Angel had an epiphany. Does everyone have to keep saying the word over and over again? Also, while it's true Angel's been acting like a real bastard lately, Wesley mentions that Angel stole a book, but the books were Angel's to begin with. Wesley didn't show up in "Parting Gifts" with a bunch of ancient tomes on the back of his motorcycle — the library belongs to Angel. He employed them; they stole office supplies.

Oops: When Angel whacks Lindsey's hand with the sledgehammer, it shatters as if it were made of plastic, yet we've seen him flex it before and it appeared to have been made of rubber in earlier scenes.

2.17   Disharmony

Original air date: April 17, 2001
Written by: David Fury
Directed by: Fred Keller
Guest cast: Mercedes McNab (Harmony), Pat Healy (Doug Saunders), Alyson Hannigan (Willow), Adam Weiner (Caged Guy), Rebecca Avery (Caged Girl)

Harmony shows up in Los Angeles and immediately hooks up with her old pal Cordelia, who doesn't know that Harmony's a vampire.

"Disharmony" is a very funny, tongue-in-cheek episode that opens with one of David Boreanaz's best lines — "Man, atonement's a bitch" — and makes fun of flighty high-school friendships, misunderstandings, and motivational speakers (hey, that last one is too easy!). Angel is trying to deal with no longer being the boss of Angel Investigations, and his attempts to find his new place on the team will be largely unsuccessful.

Harmony comes back into Cordelia's life, and the leaps and bounds of progress

Cordy's made with her maturity seem to take a backseat when she meets her vacuous former buddy, who seems to be longing for a return to the way things used to be. When Harmony comes into Cordy's room and admits she's changed and can't keep herself away from Cordelia's lusciousness, the double entendres begin. The metaphors continue with Harmony later saying that trying not to bite people is like being a smoker who is trying to quit. The overall theme of the show is how much people change after high school. Cordelia revels in how much she loves her new life, despite its being at times impoverished, not including the stellar acting career she wanted, and making her a prime candidate for a lifetime of singlehood. Harmony, on the other hand, pines for the days of high school, wishing she was one of the popular girls again. The song she chooses to sing at Caritas is perfect.

When Angel and Wesley catch on, they try to stake Harmony, but Cordelia won't let them. It's interesting that after Harmony treated her so terribly in the *Buffy* episode "The Wish" — pretty much the last time they had any contact — Cordelia is so quick to forgive her, whereas with Angel she makes it clear that they're not friends and he'll have to try very hard to regain her trust. Clearly, Angel means more to her than Harmony. The motivational speaker with his pyramid scheme is very funny, telling the vampires how they can get ahead in the world by creating an army of like demons while contributing to the "food bank." At the end of the episode, we discover that Cordelia's emotions may not run as deeply as we thought. No matter how far from Sunnydale she is, she'll always have a little Harmony in her.

Highlight: Cordelia's response to Willow over the phone after realizing that Harmony is undead: "Harmony's a vampire? All this time I thought she was a great big lesbo! [Pause] Oh, yeah? Really? Well, that's great . . . good for you!"

Nitpicks: While this very funny episode isn't exactly meant to reflect the show's overall attitude to vampires, it's surprising that Gunn isn't a little angrier than he is about Cordelia cutting Harmony some slack. He had to kill his own sister to protect the innocent from her kind, yet Harmony's allowed to walk free? Also, why does Wesley ascend to the position of boss of Angel Investigations and not Cordelia?

Oops: When Wesley and Angel burst into Cordelia's apartment to "save her," Harmony throws her hands up. Watch as the camera cuts back and forth and her hands are up, then down, then up again.

The *Buffy* Connection: Harmony was Cordelia's shallow best friend in high school, but she didn't have much to do with Cordy after Cordelia began dating Xander. She was turned into a vampire at the ill-fated graduation-day ceremony and left the show, only to return in *Buffy*'s fourth season as Spike's girlfriend. The "relationship" doesn't exactly work out (it's the breakup she refers to throughout "Disharmony") and she ends up in L.A.

2.18 Dead End

Original air date: April 24, 2001
Written by: David Greenwalt
Directed by: James A. Contner
Guest cast: Gerry Becker (Nathan Reed), Michael Dempsey (Irv Kraigle), Mik Scriba (Parole Officer), Meagen Thomas (Young Lawyer #1), Ted Broden (Young Lawyer #2), Dennis Gersten (Dr. Michaels), Kavita Patil (Nurse), Pete Gardner (Joseph Kramer), Stephanie Nash (Wife), Steven DeRelian (Bradley Scott)

Lindsey is fitted with a human hand that has a mind of its own, and Cordy has a graphic vision that's tied to Lindsey's surgery.

One thing about those epiphanies: they tend to leave one with a new sense of humor. In the last episode and for the rest of the season, Angel is less broody and more giddy. He kids around with the gang, plays a prank on Lindsey, and cracks jokes about who he used to be. Although it's fun at first, after a while one almost longs for the old Angel from season 1 (don't worry, he'll be back).

"Dead End" is a very eerie episode with a grotesque conclusion, and it marks Lindsey's exit from Wolfram & Hart. Christian Kane puts in a great performance, ranting and raging all over the screen about his "evil hand issues," and his final scene in the board-room is priceless. Lindsey has always been a complex character. He's come from an impoverished background into a firm that is the epitome of evil, and during his tenure he flip-flops from bad to good, last season having been seduced by money and belongings, and this season by love. In "Epiphany" he accepted his hickness and came after Angel, which may have been a more fitting conclusion to his character arc, since it would have made more sense for him to have driven out of town after that violent incident. But instead he's leaving town angry with Angel, but angrier with Wolfram & Hart. It'll take a few seasons, but eventually we'll see the long-term effects of what w&h did to Lindsey.

Cordelia, meanwhile, is no longer recovering from her visions. Her head is pounding, she's crying uncontrollably, and the more graphic visions are causing nightmares, during which she relives the incidents over and over. Unfortunately, this is a portent of things to come. Wesley realizes the main reason Doyle was able to stomach the visions was because of his demon half. Cordelia is a human being, and the visions are beginning to take their toll on her.

Highlight: Angel complaining about Lindsey's song: "What is that? Rock? Country? Ballad? Pick a style, pal."
Interesting Facts: David Greenwalt wrote the song that Lindsey sings at Caritas, which is called "L.A."

Christian Kane Says: "I once walked into a room and Tim Minear was sitting there writing. I said, 'What are you doing?' and he said, 'I'm writing the next episode ['Epiphany'].' And I just looked at him . . . for fourteen hours I'd been wearing this hand that wouldn't move. I couldn't eat lunch because they'd cut off my right hand, I couldn't sign anything, I couldn't do anything. I never became ambidextrous but I did a lot of stuff I'd never used to with my left hand on the set. I looked over at him and I said, 'Kill me.' He said, 'Are you serious?' and I said, 'I'm sick of this suit, I'm sick of this hand, it's not fun for me anymore.' I'm not a suit guy. I'm in a world of heroes and I'm here pushing a pen. That's bullshit about the pen being mightier than the sword because it wasn't for me. Everyone started feeling I was really sick of it. The hand took forty-five minutes to put on, I couldn't move it, and by the end of the day I would have arthritis so bad because I couldn't move my fingers. It was sweaty; at the end of the day I had to drive with my hand out the window because it just stank so badly. It wasn't just a little thing I flipped on — it was a glove, a brace, another glove taped, and then paint. It took a lot to put on and by the end of the day my hand hurt . . . they started gluing the brace on my hand because it wouldn't stay there and it would crack the paint. Taking that thing off every night was taking the skin off my hand. All the way up the middle my hand was white and raw. The writers began feeling what I was feeling, and I was very fortunate when they said, 'We're going to give you your hand back and we'll take away the suits.'

"Lindsey singing was totally David Greenwalt's idea. I'd given him a CD of some of [my] music and David's a really big music fan. I came and sat down in his office and he's like, 'I wanna do a song,' and I'm like, 'All right!' I got a whole bunch of songs and played him a couple of ideas, and then I went back and started filming again, and he came up to me and said, 'I've written you one.' He's a really good songwriter so it was fun for him. My guitarist and I went into the studio; we got the song the day before, I think, learned it that night and the next morning, and went into the studio and did three or four takes of it. There was no editing done to it; it was one shot the whole way through the song he wrote, which was 'L.A.' I'd never seen him in that light before, just smiling and having the time of his life because I think that David Greenwalt loves music just as much as he loves film. As a matter of fact, I know he does, if not more."

Did You Notice?: When Lindsey hacks into Nathan Reed's computer files, the Special Projects Reevaluation screen contains the following folders: Project History, Personnel Rosters, Manners Massacre, Bethany Project, Project Darla, Drusilla (vampire), Project Angel, Vampire Detection, Lilah Morgan, Lindsey McDonald, Youth Cntr. Project, Demon Relations, Terminated Employees, and Pending Projects.

Nitpicks: Wesley tells Gunn that last year Cordelia had a bunch of visions and ended up in the hospital because of them and Gunn says, "Oh." But Gunn was at the hospital acting as security for Cordelia, and he *told* Wesley and Cordy that he had been there, so why are he and Wes acting like he doesn't know what happened? Also, Lindsey leaves town to escape Wolfram & Hart, but as we've seen with Holland Manners, w&h can find its employees after death and force them to continue working for the firm, so why can't it find Lindsey and force him to come back? Perhaps it has more power over dead people than living ones?

Oops: The files storage office isn't in the basement the way it was in "Blind Date."

Wolfram & Hart: The firm has the ability to transplant body parts for its employees, and it brings in a shaman (who costs $250,000 each time) to finish off the surgeries. Lindsey advises Angel that he can't let the people at Wolfram & Hart make him play their game; he has to make them play his.

2.19   Belonging

Original air date: May 1, 2001
Written by: Shawn Ryan
Directed by: Turi Meyer
Guest cast: Jarrod Crawford (Rondell), Darris Love (George), Brody Hutzler (Landok), Kevin Otto (Seth), Maureen Grier (Woman), Lynne Maclean (Claire)

When a beast suddenly appears in Caritas through a portal, the Host begs Angel Investigations to kill it, and tells them about his home, where the beast came from.

"Belonging" is the first of an amazing four-episode arc centering on Pylea, the Host's native world, where things are black and white, the inhabitants are either champions or slaves, and there is no art or music. The Host is a little more nervous than usual when the beast comes through the portal, and it's Cordelia's vision of a girl opening a portal in a library that forces the team to hunt down the beast.

Meanwhile, the members of the team are having doubts about who they are and the paths they've chosen. Gunn battles his former gang, which loses a member because its strength is dwindling without him, and he's torn about which team he should be fighting alongside. Wesley calls his father to tell him he's now in charge of Angel Investigations, only to be reminded of how many times he's screwed up before. Angel is having problems asking Wesley for instructions when he's so used to giving them, and as if proving Wesley's father correct, he's starting to take on some of Wesley's former bumbling characteristics (accusing an innocent woman of being an evil witch, showing up at Cordy's commercial and having her ignore him). Cordelia gets an acting gig, but the director treats her like dirt. And the Host — who we discover is actually Krevlorneswath of the Deathwok Clan (Lorne for short) — is dealing with the issues of inferiority that had forced him to leave Pylea in the first place.

All these problems eventually come together. The gang accidentally opens another portal, bringing forth Landok from Pylea (who talks like Keanu Reeves), and in order to send him back they must figure out how to open yet *another* portal. When Landok is injured and begs Lorne to perform the death ritual, the scene cuts to Gunn and his gang cremating their dead member to prevent him from turning into a vampire — a death ritual of their own, and a very nice parallel. George's death is just one more thing Gunn will blame himself for. The fang gang (minus Gunn for now) figures out how to open the other portal, but things don't go as well as they'd hoped, and they will all be forced to face their personal demons in a different land.

Highlight: The Host finally telling everyone his name is Lorne, pointing to his face to indicate why. Also, Angel's incredulousness at the fact that no one else has ever heard of *Bonanza* is hilarious.

Interesting Facts: This is Shawn Ryan's final episode of *Angel* as a writer. He went on to create the award-winning television series *The Shield*, which stars Michael Chiklis.

J. August Richards Says: "What I like about my character is that he's really really strong, he's very serious, but he's really goofy and corny. He's really corny at times, which makes me love him in some ways and he's very dedicated, extremely committed. And that's something that I lack a little bit, but he's so dedicated to his mission and I really like that about him."

Did You Notice?: The set of Cordelia's commercial is a foreshadowing of Pylea. The director calls her "princess," puts her in a skimpy bikini outfit, and Angel worries that she's actually his slave. Angel wanders onto the set and stands under the fake sunlamp, pretending he's standing in the sun, and marvels at how he's not bursting into flames.

Nitpicks: When the Drokken beast comes through the portal, he hits several patrons. Lorne says the beast didn't kill anyone, it just maimed them. Yet later we discover that the sanctuary spell makes it impossible to even hit another beast, so his explanation was inadequate. Also, when Landok comes through the portal, why doesn't he immediately refer to Cordelia and Wesley as cows and assume they're Angel's slaves? Finally, shouldn't Cordelia know better than to read *any* book in a foreign language out loud, especially one she's just seen in a vision?

The *Buffy* Connection: When Cordelia first takes her robe off for the director, you can see a faint silver scar where the rebar had impaled her on *Buffy*.

2.20   Over the Rainbow

Original air date: May 8, 2001
Written by: Mere Smith
Directed by: Fred Keller

Guest cast: Amy Acker (Fred), Susan Blommaert (Vakma), Persia White (Aggie), Daniel Dae Kim (Gavin Park), Michael Phenicie (Silas), Brian Tahash (Constable), William Newman (Old Demon Man), Drew Wicks (Blix)

Cordelia ends up in Pylea and is turned into a slave, and the others try to figure out how they can rescue her.

The title of this episode is borrowed from the 1939 film *The Wizard of Oz*, and it's appropriate — we're not in Kansas anymore (we're not in Oz, either, which Cordelia realizes when she tries clicking her heels together three times, to no avail). Cordelia is immediately captured and called a "cow," and she meets Fred, the girl in her vision who had disappeared from the library five years earlier. Cordelia's sarcasm is great in these scenes as she complains about being called a cow, only being worth one pig, and having to carry everything for her "mistress," something Cordelia is definitely not used to doing. Unfortunately, she has a vision at the wrong time and discovers just how superstitious Pyleans are about someone with "the sight."

Angel is desperate to find Cordy; after working so hard to earn her trust, he can't deal with not having her in his life now. But it's Lorne who must make it through the biggest emotional conundrum in this episode: does he return home to Pylea and face his dreadful past, or stay in L.A. and continue trying to forget where he came from? Gunn faces the opposite problem; unlike Lorne, he longs to get back to his roots and believes his new life is holding him back. Where Lorne's predicament is played for laughs, Gunn's tortured decision is a serious one, and we can see the pain of being put in this situation on his face. Gunn's crew is fighting daily battles to save lives in his neighborhood while the Angel crew is focused on the war. Is it possible to suggest that one mission is more important than the other?

The scene where all the men finally make it to Pylea is hilarious: Angel discovers the sun there is different than the earth's — "Can everyone just notice how much fire I'm not on?" — while Lorne finds out that sometimes you just can't go home, and Wesley and Gunn realize that humans aren't exactly welcome in Pylea. They try to take on the 70 or so Pyleans who threaten them — but it doesn't quite work out. In the end, they're going to be forced to face a horrible trial, and they can only imagine what creature might be waiting to decide their fate.

Highlight: Gunn's response when Lorne tells them that Pyleans are xenophobic: "I don't get it. Why are they afraid of Xena? I mean, I think she's kind of fly."
Amy Acker Says: "I had watched *Angel* a little bit before I got the part. A bunch of people in college used to have a *Buffy/Angel* night. I wasn't really a part of the group, but my boyfriend's roommate was, so we'd see it now and again. So I'd seen it before

and went to audition and it was for this librarian named Logan. Joss always wanted a boy's name and had joked that maybe they could call me George or something. When I auditioned I had no idea [Fred would] be crazy in a cave, but I liked the idea that she wasn't an ingénue — she was smart and quirky, but all the boys still liked her."

Interesting Facts: Persia White, who plays Lorne's friend Aggie, was on *Buffy* in the very first episode as Aura, the girl who finds the dead guy in her locker. At the end of "Rm w/ a Vu," Cordelia is on the phone with Aura, catching up on Sunnydale gossip.

Mark Lutz Says: "Pylea was a pre-existing set that had been up there for years and years; it's up near Magic Mountain about an hour north of Los Angeles. They actually used it on an *Angel* episode before, in 'Darla': it's the scene where they're in the Boxer Rebellion in China. It used to be a farm or ranch and it's been used in a ton of Westerns; it's booked all the time."

Did You Notice?: The portal to Pylea is at the Paramount movie-studio gates. Also, Lorne tells the gang that he and his buddy were "as close as a Torto demon and his parasite." In "Happy Anniversary," we saw a Torto demon and his parasite perform "Bye Bye Love."

Nitpicks: Wesley desperately searches through the books for a way to get into Pylea while Angel paces back and forth and yells impatiently for Wesley to hurry up. Since when did Angel lose the ability to read?

Oops: There's no way Gunn would have known where to find the guys. When the car arrives at the movie-studio gate, Angel says, "Here? Isn't this a movie studio?" so he clearly didn't know that's where they were headed when he left the phone message for Gunn.

Wolfram & Hart: When the muscle doesn't work, w&h fights back with . . . real estate law?

2.21 Through the Looking Glass

Original air date: May 15, 2001
Written and directed by: Tim Minear
Guest cast: Amy Acker (Fred), Brody Hutzler (Landok), Tom McCleister (Lorne's mother), Mark Lutz (Groosalugg), Michael Phenicie (Silas), Adoni Maropis (Rebel Leader), Brian Tahash (Constable), Andrew Parks (Priest #1), Danan Pere (Rebel #1), Joss Whedon (Numfar)

Cordelia is made the princess of Pylea, while Angel finds Fred and rescues her before becoming a demon that she'll need rescuing from.

Be careful what you wish for, yadda yadda yadda. In "Through the Looking Glass" everyone is subverted — when they finally get what they thought they wanted, they discover that it isn't what they'd expected. The episode title is taken from Lewis Carroll's classic sequel to *Alice's Adventures in Wonderland*, where Alice steps through a mirror and everything in the Looking-Glass world is the opposite of what it should be. People and institutions appear to be the same, but on closer inspection they are mirror versions of what she is used to. Similarly, Cordelia, who two episodes ago was mocked by a director and called "princess" in a sneering tone, now becomes a princess. However, she'll soon discover that her situation is only slightly different than it was in her own world; here she is wearing only a little more clothing than she was in the commercial, and she is still directed by a group of monks who despise her and use her to achieve their own ends.

Angel, who thought he loved Pylea because he seemed more human than vampire, discovers there's a dark side to the world, and to himself. Lorne explained in "Over the Rainbow" that in Pylea everything is black and white — there is no gray. Therefore, Angel can't be both a demon and a human at the same time. So he's a human at first, and then pure demon. Fred, who was brilliant in her world, is a raving lunatic in Pylea, constantly scrawling on the wall of a cave, trying to convince herself she's not dead yet. Wesley is finally the undisputed leader, but in taking charge he gets himself and Gunn in even more trouble than they were in when they started.

This episode is wonderfully written, and despite Angel's having to come to terms with his demon half, it has some of the funniest lines of the season, from Lorne calling Angel "Hans Christian Tarantino" and singing in the square to Cordelia almost accidentally beheading her friends and trying to escape the castle while loaded down with jewelry. But despite the episode's hilarity, it ends on a somber note. As Cordelia prepares herself to com-shuck with the Groosalugg, she's faced with a horrible surprise, and one of the most shocking endings on *Angel*.

Highlight: Numfar's dance of joy. Similar to Monty Python's "Ministry of Silly Walks" sketch, it's even funnier because it's going on in the background. And if you saw it and thought, "Now, that seems like something Joss Whedon had a hand in," you'd be right — Numfar *is* Joss Whedon. The night the episode first aired, writer Tim Minear posted the following on the Bronze: "The Dance of Joy and Honor both came from Joss. He did it in the room when we were breaking the story, and it was too brilliant to entrust into any other hands, so I asked if he'd do it in my episode — and sure enough, he did. It took a moment for the cast to even recognize him, as he was in full demon makeup. But then they noticed that I was letting an extra sit in my chair and saying nothing — the only extra on the set who could fire me!" Joss had actually tipped Bronzers to his appearance a few weeks earlier when he posted, "Yes. I will make my on-screen debut in Angel 21. No, I will not speak, and no, you will not see my face. But I will make my presence known! Just remember my watchword: Dignity. Always dignity." A sidesplitting series highlight.

Interesting Facts: Tim Minear explained that the triumvirate of books that Wesley discovers wasn't something he came up with and admitted that "Wolf, Ram, and Hart was Joss's notion from day one."

Mark Lutz Says: "When I was in the audition I was like, 'Oh, I *love* this show! *Angel*? It's fantastic. Della Reese is one of my favorites. Jessica Alba, isn't she great?' No, seriously, I had seen it occasionally while channel surfing, but I had a lot of friends back home in Toronto that were into *Buffy* and *Angel* and they told me they were great shows with great writing. I had only been in L.A. for about six or eight weeks, so I didn't know anyone yet. The character description was half man, half demon, other-worldly, and originally the name was "Galencie" and he would be a sort of Sir Lancelot character, very naïve. They were having trouble finding the right combination of what they were looking for. I went in to read and the casting director said, 'That was great; can you stick around for another hour?' and I said, 'Sure,' and I read for Tim [Minear] and David [Greenwalt], and they said, 'That was great; can you stick around for another hour?' and I said, 'Are you kidding? I have important things to do!' [Laughs] So I stuck around and I think I was the only one that really found the comedy in it. Everyone else was reading it very straight. The audition scene I had was the scene where he first comes in and tells Cordelia his heart is in the wrong place and look at all these muscles and he's putting himself down, and everyone was playing it straight, and I was playing it silly. In between the casting director would come out and say to the room, 'Okay, you need to find the comedy in it,' and I'd be like, 'Hey hey hey! Don't be telling them what to do — that's my schtick!' But ultimately it all worked out."

Did You Notice?: The first time Wesley describes Fred he calls her a "strange, wild girl." Also, this is the first time we see Angel's pure demon form.

Nitpicks: While Angel's reaction to his hair is pretty funny, he shouldn't be so shocked to see it standing on end; he saw his reflection in "I Will Remember You" and his hair was the same then. And since Lorne knows about this prophecy of a "sighted one" in Pylea, wouldn't he have mentioned it sooner, knowing about Cordelia's visions? Also, Wesley shows the rebels the photo of himself with Cordelia and they recognize her as the princess, but Cordy has never left the castle and it's unlikely the rebels would have known what she looked like. Finally, whether he's been told she's the messiah or not, it seems strange that the Groosalugg would be so taken with Cordelia considering he finds his own human features disgusting.

Oops: We see Angel rip one of the guard's legs off, but in the very next scene, both legs are intact.

Wolfram & Hart: w&h exists in other dimensions, not just this one. When Wesley finds the Pylean priests' books, he sees that they have a wolf, a ram, and a hart on their covers.

2.22 There's No Place Like Plrtz Glrb

Original air date: May 22, 2001
Written and directed by: David Greenwalt
Guest cast: Amy Acker (Fred), Brody Hutzler (Landok), Mark Lutz (Groosalugg), Michael Phenicie (Silas), Tom McCleister (Lorne's Mother), Lee Rehmerman (Second Rebel Leader), Alyson Hannigan (Willow), Jamie McShane (Rebel #2), Adoni Maropis (Rebel Leader), Danan Pere (Rebel #1), Alex Nesic (Slave #1), Andrew Parks (Priest #1), Whitney Dylan (Serving Wench)

When Angel finds out that Cordelia is with the Groosalugg, he's determined to fight it to save her. Meanwhile, Wesley has found a rebel army that he leads in storming the castle.

A great season ender. Cordelia must try to put Lorne back together again, and Angel faces the truth about his demon self while talking with Wesley and Fred. Picking up a technique used on *Buffy*, there are moments in this episode that foreshadow certain storylines for season 3: Fred moons over Angel, telling him the others might judge him but she wouldn't, and she reveals an adeptness at burying things she doesn't like when she offers to throw the dead guys into the Drokken gully "like I did the others"; Angel looks disappointed when Cordelia says she loves the Groosalugg and not him; Cordelia uses a sword, which Angel will teach her more about later; Groo tells Cordy that she's not equipped to handle the visions; and, for the first time, Cordelia chooses to keep the visions and sees them as a positive thing. She's come a long way from being the girl who would kiss any guy who came near her in an attempt to lose them.

Wesley finally makes an effective leader in this dimension (no one listens to him at home), learning the first rule about battle: some people will get killed, and the leader's job is to incur the least number of casualties, not to prevent casualties altogether. The priests become more powerful, but not more powerful than the gang when all the members finally come together. The only person who questions Wesley's direction is Gunn, but Wesley has the confidence to override him (although when Angel shows up he immediately offers to hand over the mantle of leader). Interestingly, Gunn is the only person who doesn't change because he actually views the world in black and white, while the others see the gray. He identifies with the rebels, seeing similarities between them and his old gang, which also fights for a good cause it believes in. Once again, we see that apart, everyone flounders with their personal demons and self-doubt, but together, they get things done right.

The battle between Angel and Groo is exciting and scary, especially because the gang believes that the Groosalugg is a beast, and Cordelia doesn't realize that the monster Groo is fighting is actually Angel. Angel proves just how strong he is, and even in this world of black and white he fights the demon within and finds the same nobility in himself that he's identified in his own dimension. By the end of the episode we realize that despite what Lorne has said, things *aren't* black and white in Pylea if you don't allow them to be.

The episode has a great ending. Everyone realizes that while things seemed like fun for a while in Pylea, they actually agree with Lorne: L.A. is a place for all of them because no one belongs there. But they realize just as quickly that things aren't all peachy at home, either. Especially when they return and a sorrowful-looking Willow is waiting there for them . . .

Highlight: Lorne's mother's "fond" farewell to her "vile excrement" son.

Mark Lutz Says: "Probably ninety or ninety-five percent of the fighting was me, but when Angel turns into the demon he takes poor Groo and he goes flying — that's about the only thing I didn't do. They put the actors on an air ramp that has compressed air, and it throws the actor about twenty feet into the air, and I was begging them, 'Oh, let me do it, let me do it! Oh, come on!' [Laughs] But I did everything else. I come from a very athletic background, so it was pretty easy. When I came back in the third season they had another stuntman come in and do stuff, and then Tim said, 'Well, you can probably do that stuff, can't you?' and I said, 'Sure,' so I ended up doing all of it.

"My dad was a big horseman growing up and I remember calling him the day I was riding around in a chariot and telling him. They ended up only using thirty seconds [of the] ride in the chariot but I got to ride it beforehand and I called my dad up and said, 'Well, I'm dressed up like Conan and driving around in a chariot.'"

Did You Notice?: All the knights are dressed exactly like John Cleese's Black Knight in *Monty Python and the Holy Grail.* Also, Wesley assures Angel that he'll come back from his beastliness but later admits he wasn't sure Angel would. Wesley will toy with Angel's beastly side again later, to Angel's detriment, in order to save himself and the others (in season 4's "Awakening").

Nitpicks: When Groo asks Cordy what she means by reconstruction, she tells Gunn to field the question. Way to point out the black guy as the only person who can make a comparison between Cordy's new proclamation and what happened in the United States after Emancipation.

The *Buffy* Connection: Willow has arrived at the Hyperion at the end of the episode to tell Angel that Buffy is dead.

Season Three

September 2001 • May 2002

Recurring characters in season 3: Andy Hallett (Lorne), Keith Szarabajka (Daniel Holtz), Stephanie Romanov (Lilah), Laurel Holloman (Justine Cooper), Daniel Dae Kim (Gavin Park), Jack Conley (Sahjhan), John Rubinstein (Linwood Murrow), Mark Lutz (Groosalugg)

3.1   Heartthrob

Original air date: September 24, 2001
Written and directed by: David Greenwalt
Guest cast: Ron Melendez (James), Kate Norby (Elisabeth), Matthew James (Merl), Koji Kataoka (Pilgrim), Sam Littlefield (Young Man Hostage), Dalila Brown-Geiger (Sandy), Christian Hastings (Vamp #1), Bob Fimiani (Codger Demon), Robert Madrid (Rough Man), Bob Morrisey (Dr. Gregson)

When Angel kills a vampire he knew in the 18th century, her boyfriend hunts him down and opens some emotional wounds.

It's been three months since the events of season 2, and the gang is having a tough time moving on. Cordelia pines for Pylea, where she had been worshiped; Fred has created a new cave for herself that she refuses to leave; and Angel is trying to deal with the loss of . . . "the B-word" by going to a monastery. But the theme of the episode is twofold: what it's like to have pain in your heart and how to move on.

For the duration of this incredible season, we will flash back in time to when Angelus and Darla were being hunted by Daniel Holtz, a vampire hunter first mentioned by name in "The Trial," and we will see how Angel's actions in the past dictate what happens to him in the present. While Angel has to deal with an angry, vengeful vampire in this episode, his bigger battle is with himself. Will he be able to move on from Buffy's death? And if so, will he betray her by doing so? The theme cleverly touches on the fact that *Buffy* and *Angel* are now on different networks and the fledgling spinoff must find its own way now, without relying on She Who Must Not Be Named.

The plot of two vampires who loved one another is an interesting one, and James is a great character, if only for the one episode. Like Spike was with Drusilla, James is truly in love with Elisabeth, even though he has no soul. We can only imagine the sort of man he was before he became a vampire.

While Fred tries to overcome her agoraphobia so she can pull herself out of her new cave, Cordelia is dealing with her excruciating headaches, which we see have become far more serious in a scene where she goes home and Dennis helps her out.

Wesley has a fine new haircut that makes him more of a heartthrob himself, and he's also developed more confidence than he had a year ago. In "Judgement," Wesley met with Merl in Caritas and paid him more money when Merl said the initial offering wasn't enough. In a parallel scene, Merl tells him the money isn't right in this episode, and Wesley begins removing bills from the table, showing how much he has changed. And, of course, there's the shocking ending, where we discover that Darla might have a little future of her own soon. An excellent start to *Angel*'s strongest season so far.

Highlight: Cordy asking if the "Amarra people" made cufflinks or belt buckles.

Interesting Facts: From this point on, *Angel* will air in widescreen.

Keith Szarabajka Says: "I had worked with David Greenwalt on *Profit* on Fox. They had originally hired me as a guest star on the pilot and they sort of recalibrated the show when they got picked up and used me as a main character for the nine lonely episodes. [Having watched *Angel* occasionally], I had heard Holtz mentioned on *Angel* prior to the third season, and I had no concept of me playing him and David called me up. My agent had submitted my reel and the casting director looked at it and saw there was someone from *Profit* in it. He told David, and David said, 'Just offer him the part.' I had a great time doing it."

Nitpicks: Wesley is thrilled by Angel's gift of a rare dagger from the 16th-century Chinese Murshan dynasty, but that dynasty never existed; it was the Ming dynasty. This fictitious name is strange considering in "I Will Remember You" Angel gave the female Oracle a Ching Dynasty vase from 1811, which is the real dynasty from that era. Also, Wesley says that Cordelia was in Pylea for a week before they made her princess, but it was more like two days.

Oops: Angel tells Fred that he can't enter her room unless invited. However, not only does he own the hotel, but in "The Trial" he explains that hotels are public accommodation and therefore he can enter rooms at will.

The *Buffy* Connection: This was the first episode of *Angel* to air after *Buffy* had moved to UPN, so using "the B-word" rather than saying her name was an inside joke about how the WB didn't want to hear the word "Buffy" on *Angel*. Also, when Angel held Elisabeth's locket and talked about love being forever, it might have made him think of Buffy and how he gave her the silver cross that she always wore.

Music/Bands: After Lorne sings, we hear "Blackjack" by the Morphic Fields, from their self-titled CD; The Crystal Method's "The Winner" (*Tweekend*) plays in the car the vampires are driving.

3.2 That Vision-Thing

Original air date: October 1, 2001
Written by: Jeffrey Bell
Directed by: Bill Norton
Guest cast: Frank "Sotonoma" Salsedo (Shaman), David Denman (Skip), Justin Shilton (Young Man), Ken Takemoto (Old Chinese Man), Alice Lo (Old Chinese Woman), Mitchell Gibney (Innocuous Man), Bob Sattler (Masked Man), Kal Penn (Young Man in Fez)

Cordelia's visions begin leaving physical marks on her body, and Angel vows to find out what's going on.

A very exciting episode right up to its graphic conclusion, "That Vision-Thing" features a storyline the writers had been leading up to throughout season 2. Cordelia has been suffering migraines, and worse, as the visions begin to take their toll, but she has quietly endured them, refusing to let the others know how serious they've become. As far as she's concerned, she's finally part of a team where she's not a hindrance or the screaming girl who always gets kidnapped, as she was in Sunnydale. Without her powers, she's nothing more than the flighty Cordelia she was in the first season of *Angel*, sitting around the office answering phones and buying donuts. In Pylea, she was given the opportunity to lose her visions through one good com-shuck, but she chose not to for fear it would make her less valuable. And again in this episode, despite being clawed, burned, and covered in boils, she holds on to those visions. The old, superficial Cordy is long gone.

For the first time she fears for her life, terrified that the powers that be are trying to kill her for reasons she can't understand. As she did in "Rm w/ a Vu" and "Expecting," she immediately assumes that terrible things are happening to her as a punishment for who she once was. Just like Angel, she seems to be holding on to her guilt as penance and cannot find a way to get past it.

Meanwhile, Angel is forced to sacrifice the greater good for someone who has become extremely important to him. The scene where he meets Skip — an absolutely brilliant character — is very funny, as they chitchat about commuting to work while standing around in a hell dimension. Skip explains that the man he is guarding, who is on fire, is silent because he keeps him that way: "My will prevents him from being heard. I mean, there is only so much 'Oh my god! The pain! Please make it stop!' you can listen to before it starts to bug the crap out of you." But despite the humor of the scene, what Angel does in the end isn't so funny, and his actions will have terrible consequences.

Highlight: Cordelia's response to Fred's stream-of-consciousness rambling about rain: "You know, next to you, I am downright linear."

Interesting Facts: David Greenwalt talked about the changes that Cordy has undergone since season 1 of *Buffy*: "Her character is really deepening. Think about the snotty cheerleader that she began as on *Buffy the Vampire Slayer*. Then, when she and Xander got together, she became more and more human. She will always be the Cordelia who always speaks her mind and that big, bright, wonderful creature that she is, but she is getting deeper and deeper. She's becoming kind of a superhero." Also, Lilah made the Fez Guy fill out a 1099, which is an IRS form that states the person has provided a miscellaneous service for which he or she was paid more than $600. Finally, the demon Skip was named after *Angel* co-producer Skip Schoolnik.

David Denman Says: "I'd auditioned for *Buffy* before for the part of Riley, but obviously didn't get that, and then I auditioned for this part. I just came in and read for them and they said, 'Great. Do you have a problem putting prosthetics on?'

"The thing I like most about Skip is he's so much fun. What's awesome about *Angel* or *Buffy* is, where else would you have a character like that? All it said in the script was "Powerful Demon Skip," and they just had a conversation that was, like, 'Hey, how's it goin'?' The tongue-in-cheek aspect was definitely in the writing and what they wanted. I think the only direction I got was to play him like a regular guy, a soldier talking to another guy, and I said, 'Okay' and I did that. He comes in and you don't know who he is or what he's going to say and the first thing that comes out of his mouth is such a great introduction. I don't know if we ever really got that back, because of the surprise of him. We were always trying to, but we never really had the right situation. It's such a conglomeration of everyone putting his or her two cents in. His makeup is amazing, the writing is great, the direction, the whole concept of the show, you put it all together and it's what you get. I can't take all the credit, you know."

Stephanie Romanov Says: "It's always really fun to have a nice little healthy competition, and I think as a character the healthy competition was great because it brings out that great sparring, and as an actress it's really fun because you have something you're going against. You work off the other one and make choices as to how you want to handle that. The sparring with Lindsey was more two people on the same level trying to one-up the other one. And then Daniel Dae Kim came in, and we'd never met before, and part of me was, like, 'I'm not going to banter with you the same way I did Christian' because she wouldn't. I really felt like she was, like, 'Okay, you shouldn't be here.' And so I played it like that in the very first scene I did with Daniel Dae Kim. I felt so bad because I'd barely just met him and we're rehearsing the scene and of course Lilah's a bitch, and she's a bitch in this scene. And Daniel didn't like me. When the scene was over I was, like, 'I'm sorry — it's not really me, it's not you, I'm not really mad at you.' [Laughs] And he and I ended up getting along really well. He didn't know me and he told me afterward he just thought, *What a f---in' bitch.* And I was, like, 'Good, I'm doing my job!'"

Did You Notice?: Cordelia's voice is so scratchy by the time she's suffering from her worst visions that one wonders if Charisma Carpenter had to do a lot of screaming to make it that way.

Nitpicks: Apparently all are welcome in the shaman's home, since Darla just walks right in without an invitation. And why doesn't Cordelia worry about sending Fred back to the hotel alone?

Oops: At the end of the fight in the herbalist's shop, Angel flips the Chinese man into the air and he lands facedown near a doorway, but when Angel removes the coin from the man's neck, the man is lying in the middle of the room on his back.

Wolfram & Hart: Real-estate lawyers can be promoted to Special Projects (as Gavin is, to Lilah's dismay) and Gavin has decided to come after Angel "in his own way." While the firm is capable of hiring people who perform supernatural stunts, it still needs a tax form filled out in order to cut them checks. And in this episode, what Lilah does crosses a line with Angel and makes things personal, and his vendetta against her officially begins.

3.3   That Old Gang of Mine

Original air date: October 8, 2001
Written by: Tim Minear
Directed by: Fred Keller
Guest cast: Jarrod Crawford (Rondell), Khalil Kain (Gio), Matthew James (Merl), Giancarlo Carmona (Gang Kid), Steve Niel (Huge & Horrible), Josh Kayne (Cowering Demon), Sam Ayers (Tough Guy Demon), Heidi Marnhout (Fury #1), An Le (Fury #2), Madison Gray (Fury #3)

When harmless demons around L.A. are found dead, Gunn worries it could be the work of his former gang members.

J. August Richards is a terrific actor, and it's great to see episodes that give us further insight into his intriguing character while continuing to show that Gunn is torn between his old gang and his new one. We also see that he's still haunted by Alonna's death, which replays for him constantly in his nightmares, and we can only imagine how difficult it must be for him to go to work with a vampire every day. Gunn is again taunted by his former gang, including a newcomer named Gio, who sees Gunn as a sellout and traitor. But while in "The Thin Dead Line" Gunn was torn between his past and his present, here the lines are more clearly drawn. His former gang members have lost their ability to fight what's wrong and instead paint every demon with the same brush. The episode brings up an interesting point: Which is worse — a human being who is a murderer, or a demon who is completely harmless? Why is it okay to slaughter demons just because they're demons, but keep human beings off-limits no matter what they do? It's an interesting argument, and one played here for irony, since Gio's remark to Gunn that he's a "demon lover" eerily echoes racist remarks that have probably been used against the street gang.

Although the episode focuses on Gunn, we get some insight into some other characters as well. While Fred is having trouble coming out of her shell (hiding in her room, eating under a table, talking to shrubs), when given the opportunity, she sings onstage and takes on a gang leader on her own. Her ramblings always seem like they don't make any sense, but in one scene in this episode we realize Fred is far more brilliant than she might seem at first. Wesley becomes a little more authoritative in his role as leader, but his comments to Gunn at the end of the episode are eerie, considering the source. He tells Gunn, "It's never easy, the pull of divided loyalties. Whatever choice we do end up making, we feel as though we've betrayed someone," which will hit a little too close to home very soon. But the real irony is in his next statement, when he tells Gunn that he will fire him if he withholds any information again, because keeping secrets will endanger the safety of the group. Both comments foreshadow a huge mistake Wesley will make.

While it is great to have another Gunn episode, it would be better if the writers could focus on something other than his gangster past for a change and show a different side of his history.

Highlight: The big, ugly, but oh-so-sweet Yarbnie demon sucking on a Slurpee: "Hello? Who's there, please?"

Interesting Facts: This episode was supposed to be the second episode of the season, with "That Vision-Thing" being the third, but the order was switched just before they aired.

Did You Notice?: Angel is wearing leather pants in the episode, a fashion statement usually reserved for Angelus.

Nitpicks: After the baby-killing monster is killed, Angel haughtily asks Gunn if he's next. Though Caritas is a sanctuary, isn't a world without a baby-killing monster a better place? Why would Angel equate himself with a creature like that?

3.4   Carpe Noctem

Original air date: October 15, 2001
Written by: Scott Murphy
Directed by: James A. Contner
Guest cast: Rance Howard (Marcus Roscoe), Paul Benjamin (Fellow Resident), Misty Louwagie (Christina), Marc Brett (Health Club Man), Paul Logan (Woody), Lauren Reina (Escort #1), Magdalena Zielinska (Escort #2), Steven W. Bailey (Ryan)

An elderly man switches bodies with Angel, who must find a way to contact his friends before succumbing to the ravages of aging.

"Carpe Noctem" is a lot of fun, if only to see David Boreanaz playing a rude, womanizing sex fiend. After being called a eunuch by Cordelia, Angel is tossed into the body of an elderly man, where he essentially does become a eunuch while Marcus goes wild with Angel's body. Meanwhile, Fred has developed a crush on Angel, believing him to be a white knight that has saved her from a life of torture and imprisonment. When Cordelia tells Marcus-in-Angel's-body that he must tell Fred there can be no office romances, the ensuing scene, displaying a *Three's Company* confusion, is hilarious. David Boreanaz is excellent in this episode.

"Carpe Noctem" also marks the only time on *Buffy* or *Angel* that the episode's plot stands as a metaphor for an issue pertaining to the elderly (usually the metaphors apply to teenagers or people in their 20s and 30s). As Angel-in-Marcus's-body wanders around the nursing home, trying to escape, the health-care aides and nurses naturally assume he's senile and doesn't realize the retirement home is his place of residence. We can only imagine that Marcus's previous victims would have been doing the same thing — insisting they weren't actually Marcus, but someone young.

The episode has its sad moments as well, such as when Fred catches "Angel" in a surprising moment and is completely devastated. This episode shows how easy it is to succumb to temptation, and how difficult it must be for Angel, day after day, to resist letting the demon in him come out — not just the vampire, but the sexually active man. Angel also gets to experience the ups and downs of living in a mortal body, whether it's the body's limitations (he has a heart attack) or the little things that he can no longer enjoy (his heart actually beating). He may never become an elderly man, so this might be his only taste of the sadness of growing old.

Highlight: When Marcus believes Fred is a man and Angel must have been gay.
Interesting Facts: Marcus is played by Rance Howard, who is Ron Howard's father (his late wife, Jean Speegle Howard, played the real Nathalie French in "Teacher's Pet" on *Buffy*). Also, the episode's title is Latin for "seize the night," a play on the traditional "seize the day." Finally, Steven W. Bailey, who plays Ryan, starred in the reality-TV show *My Big Fat Obnoxious Fiancé* as the title character (he is also the Cave demon on *Buffy* at the end of season 6).
Stephanie Romanov Says: "The on-screen sexual tension between Angel and Lilah just kind of happened. We definitely had a great chemistry together and our scenes were sexually charged, and I think that once the writers saw it and knew it was there, they used it. It had never been specifically written that way; it was more, like, I'm scared and he's mad, and I said, 'I'm not just going to play it like I'm scared. I work for

the evil people!' Also, when you're afraid, you have a heightened sense of breath like when you're excited, so the two emotions are closely linked."

Did You Notice?: This is the second time someone has called Angel a eunuch; the first time was in "Guise Will Be Guise," when Virginia's father says he hired Angel because he was a eunuch and Virginia would remain a virgin that way. Understandably, Angel isn't fond of the term. Also, when Marcus-in-Angel's-body looks through the Angel Investigations business cards on the front desk, Cordelia's cards are the only ones with an actual title.

Nitpicks: In the *Buffy* episode "Flooded," Angel calls Willow, yet in this episode it is Willow who calls Angel to tell him the news about Buffy. Perhaps Willow called Angel when Buffy wasn't around, and he had to call her back? Also, how was Marcus able to perform the spell on the previous guys? Since the retirement home has such heavy security, Marcus isn't able to actually leave, so if he could see his potential victims leaving the gym, how was he able to approach them to cast the spell? And why does Gunn automatically untie Angel when Angel reassures him it's really him in his body — it could have just as easily been Marcus. And finally, why didn't Angel-in-Marcus's-body try calling Cordelia's cell phone when he couldn't reach her at the hotel?

Oops: The business cards give the Hyperion's address as 1481 Hyperion Avenue, yet in several scenes throughout the series, when the gang is standing out front, we can see the address is 4121. Also, Lilah and "Angel" clear off Angel's desk, but when the gang shows up there are things back on top of it.

The *Buffy* Connection: The episode ends with a phone call from Willow, who tells Cordelia that Buffy is alive. Buffy and Angel decide to meet, but because of the touchy situation of *Buffy* moving over to UPN, it was impossible to show a crossover on either series, so we never see the meeting.

Wolfram & Hart: The lawyers work against each other if they think it'll help them personally. In this case, Lilah helps Angel protect himself against Gavin.

Music/Bands: In this episode, we hear "Galaxy Bounce" by the Chemical Brothers (*Come with Us*) and "Jaded Heart" by Limor (*LoveCat Music Catalog Highlights #2*).

3.5   Fredless

Original air date: October 22, 2001
Written by: Mere Smith
Directed by: Marita Grabiak
Guest cast: Gary Grubbs (Roger Burkle), Jennifer Griffin (Trish Burkle)

Fred's parents show up in L.A. and she tries to evade them, hoping they won't take her home with them.

"Fredless" features Amy Acker's best performance to date. Up to this point Fred's been a stuttering mass of nerves, but in this episode Acker shows a new side of her character. We discover that Fred has convinced herself her time in Pylea never happened, that it was all a figment of her imagination that is still playing out as a fairy tale in her head. She tries to stay away from her parents because she doesn't want to know the truth — that if they can see her, all her suffering was real. She doesn't want to cope with that reality.

The Burkles, who show up on the doorstep of the Hyperion like Rooster and Lily in *Annie*, are probably the first set of positive parents we've seen on either *Buffy* or *Angel*, which is why they immediately raise our suspicions. They are a breath of fresh Texas air on our dark L.A. show, and not only are they wonderful parents to Fred, but they become parental figures to the rest of the gang, all of whom had less-than-desirable upbringings (we never find out what Gunn's parents were like, but it's probably safe to assume he pretty much raised himself and his sister on his own, living on the streets). Wesley begins thinking aloud and inadvertently lets the gang know a little too much about how his parents treated him, something that will haunt him in the next episode.

This episode has some very funny moments, including Cordy's even-better-than-usual barbs, the increased flirtiness between Cordy and Angel, Angel's blubbering through his explanation of the severed head, and a dirty homeless guy shuffling away from Fred in the bus station because he thinks *she* looks crazy. By the end of "Fredless," Fred has become an undisputed member of the gang, earning Wesley's admiration for her deductive reasoning and Gunn's respect for her "tight" demon-fighting contraption. As the gang welcomes her into the fold, she literally erases the remnants of the fairy tale from her life with the help of her new friends in a beautiful final scene.

Highlight: Wesley and Cordelia playing the parts of Angel and Buffy having their long-awaited reunion.

Interesting Facts: As Angel and Mr. Burkle point out, Jack Nicklaus did indeed defeat Gary Player at the Bob Hope Classic in 1963, and since the tournament was first televised in 1961, Angel would have been able to watch it on television without turning to dust. However, the tournament was called the Bob Hope Palm Springs Classic in 1963. Both Angel and Mr. Burkle refer to it as the Bob Hope Desert Classic, which was its name from 1965 to 1983, before it was eventually called the Bob Hope Chrysler Classic. But considering they're only off by two years, I won't put this one under "Nitpicks." Also, Spiro Agnew (who Angel and Mr. Burkle believe was a Grathnar demon) was Richard Nixon's vice president from 1969 to 1973 until he was charged with tax evasion and stepped down.

Fred (Amy Acker) is terrified when her parents suddenly show up at the Hyperion.

Did You Notice?: Mrs. Burkle says that her husband loves the *Alien* films, although he dozed off in the last one. She's referring to *Alien Resurrection*, which was written by Joss Whedon but had changed so much by the time it hit theaters that he absolved himself of having had anything to do with it.

Nitpicks: Why is it that Angel's cell phone never rings or keeps a signal aboveground, yet deep in the sewers he has no problem talking on it?

Oops: Cordelia says that she's never ridden on a schoolbus, but in the *Buffy* episode "Inca Mummy Girl," she travels to the museum exhibit with the other students, presumably by bus.

The *Buffy* Connection: When Mrs. Burkle splats the big bug with the bus, she says, "Did I get it? Did I get it, y'all?" a play on Buffy's same repeated question at the end of the season-3 *Buffy* episode "Gingerbread" (minus the "y'all").

3.6   Billy

Original air date: October 29, 2001
Written by: Tim Minear and Jeffrey Bell
Directed by: David Grossman
Guest cast: Justin Shilton (Billy Blim), Richard Livingston (Congressman Blim), Jeniffer Brooke (Clerk), Cheri Rae Russell (Female Officer), Gwen McGee (Detective), Kristoffer Polaha (Dylan), Rey Gallegos (Sanchez), Charlie Parker (Guy), Joy Lang (Amber), Timothy McNeil (Cab Driver)

The gang must take action when Billy, the man Angel freed from a hell dimension, begins causing men to hate women.

"Billy" is a very creepy episode, showing us a new — and scary — side of Wesley while developing Cordelia's character even further. "Billy" explores the perceived helplessness of women and the men who prey on it. The show opens with Angel teaching Cordelia how to swordfight so she can defend herself. She questions having to wait to be saved and wants to learn how to protect herself. Not only is she a quick study, but soon she's overpowering him when he least expects it. Billy Blim, whom Angel had freed in "That Vision-Thing," reappears and begins to wreak havoc by causing men to become misogynistic psychokillers. Throughout the episode, we see Cordelia come to terms with the fact that Billy was freed so she could be saved, and Lilah discovers what helplessness really is. Will these women continue to be dependent, or will they be able to rely on their own strength to get them out of their predicaments? The thing is, when you target three self-sufficient women like Cordelia, Fred, and Lilah, you can't beat them down. This episode is perhaps a comment on how today's women are much harder to dominate because they've been raised to have minds of their own.

One of the best aspects of *Angel* is the transformation Cordy has undergone. Throughout season 3, you can't help but recall the über-bitch she used to be in Sunnydale and compare that with the incredible woman she has become. In this episode she makes her own decisions, uses her knowledge of bossy bitchiness (and spring fashion) to get information she needs, and refuses to run screaming from inevitable danger. While we definitely saw this side of her last season, it was still mixed in with her predominantly superficial exterior, but this season she finally puts the Cordelia of old behind her and becomes a mature woman.

An interesting thing to watch throughout the episode is how long it takes for Billy's power to rub off on each of the men. Gavin beats up Lilah within seconds of touching Billy, showing how quickly his own misogynistic tendencies can be brought to the surface. It takes longer to affect Wesley, who touches the blood and then makes it all the way back to the Hyperion before it changes him. Gunn touches it in the lobby and exhibits he's under the influence within a matter of minutes, yet he finds the power within himself to fight it, telling Fred that he can feel it coming on and she has to get away from him before it takes over. Angel is the only one to remain unaffected. But does he treat women and men equally? When he storms up to Lilah's door, he's furious with her and ready to take her on, yet when she comes to the door with a black eye and bruises all over her face, his demeanor immediately changes, and he shows genuine concern for her because she's been hurt. He never would have blinked an eye if Lindsey had come to the door looking the same way.

Meanwhile, Wesley succumbs to Billy's powers at the Hyperion, and the ensuing terror between him and Fred is suspenseful and frightening: it definitely borrows from the film *The Shining*, with Wesley hunting for Fred through the hotel corridors while wielding an ax. All work and no play might make Wes a dull boy, but in the end he's left with his own personal horror: he actually possesses within himself the power to be brutal and cold, just like the father he tried so desperately to please. His guilt over what he was able to become will fester throughout the season until it drives him to make the biggest mistake of his life.

Highlight: Cordelia going off on a tangent about Lilah's shoes, and the two of them going head-to-head in a scene that shows just how alike they really are.

Stephanie Romanov Says: "The ending to 'Billy' was one of my favorite Lilah moments. It was the only time Lilah was the hero. [Laughs] She came back and did the right thing. She'd had the sense knocked into her, I guess."

Did You Notice?: Wes's comment to Fred — "Lie to me again and we're going to have a problem" — could be Billy-induced, but it's an awful lot like what he said to Gunn in "That Old Gang of Mine," showing that Wesley has an issue with anyone being untruthful with him, even if it's a little hypocritical considering the source. Also, the Blims are clearly modeled on the Kennedy family — they're in politics, Lilah describes them as "the closest thing this country has to royalty," and she adds that they own half the Eastern Seaboard.

Nitpicks: How many times must Cordy remind Angel that someday she might have to kill him? I mean, what's that doing to the guy's self-esteem?

Oops: When Angel is holding the crime-scene photo, he says it's marked 11:24, 20 minutes before the crime happened, but when the camera points to the picture, we can see the time stamped on it is actually 10:52. Also, at the very end of the episode, when Fred leaves Wesley's apartment, she appears to bump into some production equipment or a camera in the hallway just as he's closing the door. Finally, when the camera shows an outdoor shot of the Hyperion, you can clearly see the Los Altos Apartments sign on the top (see "I Fall to Pieces"), which actually appears several times throughout the series in long shots of the hotel's exterior.

The Buffy Connection: Wes and Cordy's discussion about how they'll both probably end up alone echoes the discussion that Willow, Xander, and Buffy had at the end of "I Robot, You Jane."

Wolfram & Hart: At least one of W&H's clients is a very powerful congressman, and the firm will do anything to keep him happy. Lilah's grievance ramps up with Gavin, and he attacks her physically.

Music/Bands: When Billy visits his cousin, we hear "Clint Eastwood" by Gorillaz, from their self-titled CD; Elwood's "Slow" (*The Parlance of Our Time*) plays when Angel comes to the cousin's apartment.

3.7   Offspring

Original air date: November 5, 2001
Written by: David Greenwalt
Directed by: Turi Meyer
Guest cast: Steve Tom (Stephen Mills), Heidi Marnhout (Fury #1), An Le (Fury #2), Madison Gray (Fury #3), Robert Peters (Arney), Sergio Premoli (Monseigneur), Van Epperson (Bus Driver), Peyton and Christian Miller (Johnny), Kathleen McMartin (Mom), Theresa Arrison (Johnny's Mom)

Darla arrives in L.A. and announces to Angel that he's about to be a father, which disappoints Cordelia and worries Wesley.

This is a fantastic episode that sets in motion everything else that will happen in season 3 and lays the groundwork for the pivotal events of season 4. "Offspring" gives us another flashback to the 18th century, when Holtz was chasing Angelus and Darla was intent on causing Holtz more pain and misery. In the present, Darla returns to Angel, looking very pregnant, which shocks and hurts Cordelia. Angel had earlier reassured Cordelia that nothing had happened between him and Darla, and after he's spent the last several months regaining Cordy's trust, it's gone in an instant when she realizes he's betrayed her. This scene is a perfect manifestation of the potential repercussions of a one-night stand.

This episode also sees Angel become aware of his feelings for Cordy, and while she seems oblivious to the fact that she feels the same way, there is definitely chemistry between them. The contrast between his relationship with Darla in the past — when they banded together on a destructive killing spree across Europe and didn't love each other so much as enjoy mutual emotional torture — and his healthier, more loving and equitable relationship with Cordelia shows how far Angel has come. But a visit from his lover of the past — carrying their child of the future — forces his worlds to collide.

While Angel marvels at the possibility of having a child (and also acknowledges that he might have to kill it when it's born), Wesley stands back from the action and asks the more technical questions: What could the child be? How could two vampires have possibly created a living thing? Could this child be the destructive force predicted in the Nyazian scrolls? When Wesley begins to find answers, everything falls apart. What no one counted on, of course, was the reappearance of Angel's arch-nemesis. The last few minutes of this episode are amazing.

Highlight: Angel's awkward talk with Cordelia, pointing to her, then himself, while explaining how they're fundamentally different: "Human — vampire. Woman — man . . . pire."

Keith Szarabajka Says: "David Boreanaz would always look at me and just start laughing, and I really enjoyed working with him. We got along great . . . although he's, like, eight inches taller than I am! I would say, 'Hey, should I be standing on an apple box here?'"

Did You Notice?: We find out in this episode that Holtz chased Angelus to North Africa, where he lost him, and then found him in Rome.

Nitpicks: Why are all the ancient prophecies about things happening in L.A. when L.A. didn't exist at the time the prophecies were recorded? And it's interesting that Angel tells Fred and Cordelia they can't go near Darla unless he, Gunn, or Wes is with them. It's only one episode after "Billy" and already the women are back to being treated like they're helpless.

The *Buffy* Connection: The comparison between Buffy (the girl that Angel loved who died and was brought back to life) and Darla (who had the same fate) is made here for the first time. The main difference, of course, is that Buffy and Angel were actually in love, and Angel and Darla were more in lust.

3.8   Quickening

Original air date: November 12, 2001
Written by: Jeffrey Bell
Directed by: Skip Schoolnik
Guest cast: José Yenque (Vampire Leader), Matt Casper (Cyril), Bronwen Bonner-Davies (Caroline), Michael Robert Brandon (Psychic), William Ostrander (Captain), Kasha Kropinski (Sarah), John Durbin (Dr. Fetvanovich), Angelo Surmelis (Tech Guy)

The gang tries to figure out what they will do when Darla's baby is born, and Angel's old enemy is in town to deliver some vengeance.

The good just keeps getting better. "Quickening" is like part two of "Offspring," with "Lullaby" rounding out the trilogy. Each episode takes place immediately after the one before it, building up the suspense, and this one ends on a major cliffhanger. In fact, if you look at all the episodes of season 3 from this point on and mark them on a calendar, the rest of the season takes place over about a month.

"Offspring" brings together all the elements of Angel's life and current predicament: Darla, the baby, the gang, Holtz, and Wolfram & Hart. Darla wants to get rid of the baby, the gang ponders how to kill it when it's born, Holtz doesn't realize the baby exists, and Wolfram & Hart want to dissect both it and Darla. Connor's birth is in some ways a parody of the Christ birth: the child is a miracle of sorts because he never should have happened; Darla eventually gives birth in a very primitive place; and the vampires are a warped version of the Magi, bringing gifts and wanting to protect the baby. It's also interesting how, even when faced with the possibility of carrying a demon child, parental instinct always kicks in on this show. In "Expecting," Cordelia became so attached to her unborn demon that she hurt her friends and jeopardized her own life. In this episode, Angel wants to believe that his son might be a chance for life that he never thought he would have.

For anyone who follows that other sci-fi show, the one featuring a butt-kicking gal, a very similar storyline occurred on *Xena: Warrior Princess* when Xena wanted to kill Gabrielle's child and the Greek gods tried to destroy Xena's daughter. On *Angel*, both those elements come together. Angel wants to believe that the child will be fine, while his friends are convinced it's an evil thing that could destroy them. Just as he did in "That Vision-Thing," Angel lets his heart get in the way, opting to save someone close to him and possibly sacrificing the greater good in the process.

Holtz gets caught up on the last 228 years he's missed with the help of Sahjhan, the time traveler that brought him to L.A. (a great character who is very funny), but he's so intent on killing Angel and Darla that he doesn't care about anything else happening around him. The parallel is perfect: Angelus killed Holtz's wife and children, and Holtz is determined to kill Angel the father. They're both about to get a surprise, one that will compromise Angel's new mission and Holtz's religious sense of right and wrong.

Highlight: The hilarious answering-machine greeting when Cyril calls his Master: "[Female voice] Hi, you've reached the Tittles. We can't come to the phone right now. If you want to leave a message for Christine, press one. [Male voice] For Bentley, press two. [Dark, deep voice] Or to speak to or worship Master Tarfall, Underlord of Pain, press three."

Interesting Facts: Jack Conley, who plays Sahjhan, played the werewolf hunter Cain in "Phases," the *Buffy* second-season episode in which Oz discovered he was a werewolf. Also, the term *quickening* refers to the movements that a mother feels from her baby when it's in the womb, and it's usually through these movements that a pregnant mother begins to bond with the child.

Keith Szarabajka Says: David Greenwalt just kept saying to me, 'Don't do any yelling,' like I'm going to go off and do an Al Pacino on Angel or something, which I would because I'm a theater actor and I don't mind blowing my top if I'm asked to. But he told me to be very quiet and to just use my voice all the time. They would yell, 'Cut!' and I would say, 'Can I yell now?'"

Did You Notice?: Holtz was a vampire hunter before Angelus and Darla massacred his family even though it's insinuated a few times in the series that he became one as a result of their actions.

Nitpicks: The transcriber at Wolfram & Hart refers to Cordelia as "female one." If he's been transcribing every conversation for weeks, why doesn't he know her name yet? Also, why do a bunch of vampires know about the prophecy, yet Wolfram & Hart *and* Angel Investigations are totally in the dark about it? And like other vampires, Darla doesn't feel pain the way humans do, so why are the contractions so painful for her? This is a woman who's been thrown across rooms and through plate-glass windows.

Oops: Sahjhan tells Holtz that 227 years have passed since they made their deal, but the deal was made in 1773, which would have been 228 years earlier.

Wolfram & Hart: The lawyers at the firm quite literally sign their names in blood on the contracts. Despite knowing every apocalypse and prophecy to date, they seem to be clueless about the Nyazian scrolls. Gavin has planted bugs at Angel Investigations and Lilah finds out about it. Linwood reassures his underlings that should anything go wrong, he'll pin the blame on them.

Music/Bands: In this episode, we hear Ministry's "Corrosion" (*Psalm 69: The Way to Succeed and the Way to Suck Eggs*).

3.9   Lullaby

Original air date: November 19, 2001
Written and directed by: Tim Minear
Guest cast: Jim Ortlieb (Scroll Translator), Robert Peters (Arney), Bronwen Bonner-Davies (Caroline), Kasha Kropinski (Sarah)

As the evil forces close in on Darla and Angel discovers that Holtz is back, Darla prepares to give birth to the baby.

Each episode in this arc is better than the one before it (no surprise, considering the heavyweight writers at the helm of each episode). "Lullaby" explores the pain of losing a child and what it's like to be a parent. Once again we go back to the 18th century, and just when the viewer is hoping Angel will drive a stake through Holtz, we see what it was like for him to come home and discover that Darla and Angelus not only massacred his family, but turned his daughter into a vampire. We see the pain and rage that Holtz felt, and we sympathize with him entirely. He was tortured in the way that Angelus loved to torture people — killing just wasn't satisfying enough. Keith Szarabajka is terrific in the role of Holtz, making him the most complex character of the season. He's a villain who isn't a villain — he's a man whose world was destroyed by Darla and Angelus, and now he's come back, not for revenge, but to balance the scales of justice. He's a religious man who wants to do what's right, which is why he's momentarily halted when he discovers the major difference between Angelus and Angel.

Darla is a sad character in a way. She never experienced love of any kind in her first life and was used by men as a prostitute. In her second life she wandered the earth alone until she found Angelus, who merely lusted after her — they never knew love because neither had a soul (it's interesting that in "Heartthrob," James and Elisabeth don't have souls either, yet they love one another) — and he ultimately dusts her. When she's given a second chance to become human, she's dying once again, Angel tells her he never loved her, she's turned into a vampire once more, and Angel has rough sex with her and tells her it didn't mean anything to him. In the end she admits that having Connor was the only good thing they ever did together, despite there being no love in the situation. The only time she's ever felt love in her life was in "The Trial," when she realized the lengths to which Angel would go to save her.

In the present, Darla is shocked to discover that she loves the child inside her, and for the first time she doesn't want to get rid of it. But she doesn't want to give birth to it either, because she knows that once the baby's soul has left her body, she'll be the same ruthless, soulless creature she was before. She begs Angel to keep her from hurting the baby when it comes. When Caritas — ironically, the bar's name is Latin for "mercy" — blows to bits (again), Darla and Angel are forced into an alleyway, the same sort of place where Angelus was "born," so to speak. As Holtz comes face-to-face with the two vampires he despises more than any other, the viewers are treated to one of the most incredible sequences ever seen on *Angel*, and the image of a solid hand turning to dust in Angel's grip is devastating. Darla discovers what a mother is and acts accordingly, and Holtz devises a new plan that will cause Angel infinitely more pain than death would.

Highlight: Gunn asking if they should get some Vaseline and a catcher's mitt when Darla suddenly goes into labor.

Interesting Facts: John Rubinstein, who plays Linwood Murrow at Wolfram & Hart, is the son of famous piano virtuoso Artur Rubinstein and a composer and singer in his own right. Also, Jim Ortlieb, who plays the scroll translator, is a character actor who is probably best known to genre fans as Nasedo from the television series *Roswell*.

Keith Szarabajka Says: "I liked the idea that Holtz wasn't a pure villain. I have this belief that people don't act from a sense of being wrong, they act from a sense of doing right. Adolf Hitler, for instance: he acted from a sense of what he believed was improving Germany. What he did was heinous and utterly unforgivable, but I don't believe he thought he was doing evil. And Holtz didn't act out of a sense of doing evil, he acted out of a sense of trying to right what was a perceived injustice, which was a heinous crime that was committed against his family. 'Lullaby' was my favorite episode."

Did You Notice?: Darla calls the baby "my darling boy," the same endearment she always used to use on Angelus. Also, the prophecy stating that there will be no birth, only death, is similar to the prophecy of the Weird Sisters in *Macbeth*, who state that Macbeth will be killed by a man who is not born of a woman. He is eventually killed by Macduff, who was delivered via C-section (a rather unflattering loophole, if you ask any woman who's gone through a Cesarean section).

Nitpicks: Holtz's men don't have English accents, and even Holtz's accent sounds more like he's from New England than England.

Oops: Although the lullaby that Holtz sings to Sarah, "All Through the Night," is based on a traditional Welsh air that would have existed at the time, the English words that he sings were written in 1884 by Sir Harold Boulton, 120 years *after* Holtz was singing them.

Wolfram & Hart: Linwood again says he'll tell the Senior Partners he knows nothing. Lilah gets her hands on the Nyazian scrolls and hires an in-house interpreter to translate; the interpreter works much faster than Wesley (although he has a lot more incentive from Lilah).

3.10 Dad

Original air date: December 10, 2001
Written by: David H. Goodman
Directed by: Fred Keller
Guest cast: Kira Tirimacco (Doctor), Stephanie Courtney (Gwen)

Angel becomes fiercely protective of his newborn son as demons move in to try to kill the infant. Meanwhile, Holtz recruits a woman for his new gang of warriors.

After the last three episodes built to such a stunning conclusion, it's only natural that this episode seems a little slower and not as enjoyable. Not only that, but we have to listen to a 240-year-old vampire making baby talk with his son, and the goo-goo's and ba-ba's, funny for about two minutes, are sickening by the end of the show. I prefer my Angel broody, thank you. That said, the writing is still very strong, full of a lot of pop-culture references and funny asides.

"Dad" is where the gang finds out that raising a baby who plays an important part in an ancient prophecy isn't as easy as it might seem. Web sites have gone up offering rewards for his capture; biker demons have shown up to kill the baby; Wolfram & Hart has installed cameras throughout the Hyperion to watch the goings-on — and boy, can that kid fill a diaper. Angel won't let anyone near the baby, instead developing a "serious mama-bear vibe," as Lorne observes.

Holtz chastises Sahjhan for hiring a bunch of stupid minions whose sole purpose is to maim and kill without any passion and goes off to find his own helper, someone whose heart is really in the fight. He finds the ultimately loathsome Justine, a girl whose twin sister was killed by vampires. The ensuing scenes, which are a little too similar to Buffy being trained by Merrick, show that sometimes a vampire slayer doesn't have to be chosen by the powers that be in order to fight. But can she actually win?

David Boreanaz is a proud dad in real life as well, to his son, Jaden Rayne.

While Wesley tries to decipher the text to discover exactly what the child's part in the prophecy will be, Angel must learn to trust his friends and understand that raising a baby is a group effort.

Highlight: Justine asking if Holtz wants to be a Mr. Miyagi to her, teaching her to wax on, wax off, and Holtz's blunt reply: "You'll find your references to modern popular culture tend to be lost on me."

Interesting Facts: Lilah says the partners are at "DEFCON, like, a thousand." A common misconception is that DEFCON levels indicate an increased threat when the numbers are higher, but the opposite is actually true. The DEFCON (Defense Condition) scale, which determines the U.S. military's likelihood of going to war, ranges from five through to one. Five indicates a normal peacetime state; four is when the military is put on alert and security measures are tightened; three indicates an increased readiness for war; two is a more serious readiness; and one indicates maximum readiness, which usually means war. Today the U.S. government has developed the color-coded system to indicate to citizens the likelihood of a terrorist attack, although it has been criticized for creating undue panic.

Keith Szarabajka Says: "Holtz is definitely a religious man. I think he still wanted to destroy Angel, but there was a dilemma in that now there's a soul and this soul must be saved. To be honest with you, I think he never really believed that Angel had gotten a soul back. I think he believed that he was still a soulless, vile vampire, and it was all an act."

Did You Notice?: Both Gunn and Wesley's pop-culture interpretations of the impending vampire attack are appropriate to what is happening. As they await the siege, Wesley tells Gunn he's imagining himself as John Wayne in *Rio Bravo* (a film in which John Wayne plays a sheriff who, with his deputies, tries to stave off an attack of ranchers trying to free a murderer being held in the station) and Gunn says he's picturing himself as Austin Stoker in *Assault on Precinct 13* (an early John Carpenter film about gang members attacking a police station that is about to be closed and how the last few officers must band together with the criminals to fend them off).

Nitpicks: How is it that Lorne immediately hears the hum of the Wolfram & Hart cameras, but Angel's highly attuned vampire hearing never picked up on it? And why does Angel talk to the "baby" in the car; there's no one actually inside his car that he has to convince, so it doesn't make sense that he's pretty much talking to his arm.

Oops: Sahjhan says that he can't do the Heimlich on the minions in this dimension because his arms will go right through them, meaning he hasn't figured out how to actually touch things. Yet in "Offspring" we see him sprinkling powder on the statue containing Holtz and smoking and holding a cigarette, and in "Quickening" he hands

Holtz a jacket. Also, the scratch on Connor's cheek keeps appearing and disappearing. Finally, when Angel climbs out of the sewer, the hole is square, but it has a round manhole cover.

The Boy Ain't Right: Connor only stops crying when he sees his dad's game face.

Wolfram & Hart: While it seems like most of the lawyers at W&H have sold their souls to work there, Linwood Morrow handed over his children to the Senior Partners to get his position. Also, the firm has an entire section of file cabinets devoted to Angel's history, and their files and records woman appears to be a demon with all the records stored in her memory.

3.11   Birthday

Original air date: January 14, 2002
Written by: Mere Smith
Directed by: Michael Grossman
Guest cast: Patrick Breen (Nev), Max Baker (Hyperion Clerk), David Denman (Skip), Heather Weeks (Tammy), Aimee Garcia (Cynthia)

When Cordelia receives a powerful vision that puts her in a coma, she has an out-of-body experience in which she's told that she has to give up the visions or she'll die.

Another excellent episode from Mere Smith. We're given a what-if scenario that shows what could have happened if Cordelia hadn't met up with Angel at the party in "City Of." It also allows Cordelia to take yet another step away from the Cordy of Sunnydale and become more mature.

Skip returns (it is great to see him again), this time in the role of the guide, or the Clarence part of this *It's a Wonderful Life* takeoff (or all three ghosts in *A Christmas Carol*, from which the episode also borrows). We're shown the past, when another young woman from 1630 gives Cordy a graphic illustration of what will happen if, like her, she ignores Skip's warning that a human being cannot handle the visions.

Cordelia is torn, though. She's come a long way from the woman in "Parting Gifts" who was kissing every guy she saw in an effort to give up the visions. Back then she said to Angel, "I didn't ask for this responsibility" and wanted the powers that be to get out of her head. But now, for the first time in her life, she fits into a group of real, genuine people, completely unlike the phony clique she had had in high school. She feels like these people care about her, and as she matures, she sees her personal growth reflected back to her through the admiration from those around her.

It's only when Cordy overhears Angel telling the conduits that she is nothing more than a flighty rich girl that she steps back, aghast, and chooses a life of fame over goodwill. But the fates are at work here, and we've watched her overcome her previous life

Manifestations of Phantom Dennis

In "Rm w/ a Vu," Cordelia discovered a friendly ghost in her apartment that seemed to have a bit of a crush on her. Viewers fell in love with Phantom Dennis immediately. Here is a list of all his "appearances" on the show:

★ Tries to take Cordelia's root beer and turns on the television ("Rm w/ a Vu")

★ Turns the lights up when Cordelia brings home a date and then switches the radio station from romantic music to polka; pulls the covers up around Cordelia's head and floats a box of Kleenex over to her so she can wipe her tears after she wakes up pregnant ("Expecting")

★ Pulls out a chair for Angel and gives him a beer ("She")

★ Closes the front door when Cordelia tries to come home, to save her from the danger within the apartment ("Five By Five")

★ Throws a book at Wesley to help him with his research ("Judgement")

★ Turns up the thermostat when Cordelia complains about how cold it is in the apartment and hands her the phone when she's incapacitated after a vision ("First Impressions")

★ Slams Cordelia's bedroom door to wake her up and warn her that Harmony is in the room ("Disharmony")

★ Closes the bathroom door after Cordelia has a particularly harsh vision and turns on a lamp; fills the bathtub with hot water and bubble bath and hangs up Cordelia's clothes when she drops them on the floor; scrubs Cordelia's back with a loofah brush once she sinks into the tub ("Heartthrob")

★ Opens Cordelia's front door to let Fred out after Cordy's made it clear she doesn't want Fred around ("That Vision-Thing")

★ Puts up a happy birthday sign in Cordelia's apartment and comes to the door with a party hat on his head, throwing confetti; tries to hide Cordelia's medications from Gunn and Fred, but when he realizes he's not actually helping her, he pulls out the box from under Cordelia's bed ("Birthday")

★ Keeps unpacking Cordelia's things (which Fred boxes up when Cordy goes missing) because he doesn't want to believe that she's gone ("Ground State") as vacuous Cordy, the cheerleader who wanted to be an actress. She's realized that that's not who she is, and even when she decides to try out that other life again (the sitcom idea is hilarious), something will always draw her back to her true path. We soon discover that despite the powers that be saying Doyle's "parting gift" was a mistake, perhaps it was fated after all.

Meanwhile, with the help of dear Dennis (who had his own little birthday surprise planned), the rest of the gang discovers that Cordelia has been keeping medical records, medications, and her condition a secret, and she'll need to re-establish some trust with them. Throughout this season, everyone will keep a secret from the others, and season 4 will be about trying to regain that lost trust.

Highlight: When Tammy praises Skip and he smiles and says, "Aw, get out of here. Really. Get out. I've got work."

Interesting Facts: The theme song to Cordelia's sitcom, Cordy!, is written by David Greenwalt and sung by Marti Noxon and Greenwalt. Also, Skip was brought back because of an enormous fan reaction to him in "Billy." "People are insane for Skip," says Angel executive producer David Greenwalt. "Not since Angel appeared on Buffy have I seen people go wild for a character like this." Also, the season-3 dvd contains a deleted scene from Cordy's actual sitcom, but the scene goes on for a long time and it's clear why they chose to cut it out of the episode.

David Denman Says: "Charisma was great; we had a good time. When I came on to do that second episode, she was so excited I was there. I thought she was kidding with me. She was, like, 'Oh my GOD I'm so excited to be doing these scenes with you. This is gonna be great — everyone loves your character!' and I'm, like, 'O . . . kay . . .' I couldn't quite get if she was really that excited or if she was just messing with me and it turns out she was just really that excited. And while we're doing that episode, people are coming up, going, 'Can we get pictures with you? This is my family — they came down to see you,' and I was, like, 'Okay,' and they said, 'Haven't you been looking on the Web site?' and I hadn't been. I was just so clueless to it all and how popular Skip had become. I had some friends who watched the show and they would go on about how my character was so great, so it was pretty funny to find out how many people were such fans of the character."

Did You Notice?: In Cordelia's alternate universe, Wesley tells Cordy that he lost his arm fighting a Kungai demon, a reference to the demon he was chasing when he ran into Angel in "Parting Gifts." He followed it into an apartment where Angel was standing and the two of them fought it until it ran away. Presumably, without Cordelia's vision, Angel never would have been at that apartment and Wesley would have lost an arm. The problem is, Angel would have actually received the vision himself, so he *would* have been in the apartment. Unless, of course, he was so devastated by Doyle's death that he didn't act on the vision.

Nitpicks: We're never told how the Hyperion suddenly became a flourishing hotel again. Did someone else find the money in the basement? And why are the visions now painless for Cordelia when Doyle always had blinding pain despite having been half demon? Is it her reward for choosing the visions when Doyle just wanted to be rid of them? Also, she tells the gang at the end of the episode that the 171 Oak vision has been taken care of, yet that happened in an alternative world where Wesley had one arm and Angel was insane. Why does she think the victim has been saved in the real world?

The *Buffy* Connection: In season 3 of *Buffy*, in an episode called "The Wish," Cordelia wishes that Buffy had never come to Sunnydale, and she finds out what life would have been like without her, a similar plot to this one. In "Amends," which aired that same season, Angel is visited by three ghosts who show him his life, another similarity to this episode. Also, Cordelia refers directly to the sloppy kiss that she has with Wesley in "Graduation Day, Part Two," and it's funny that she mentions him drooling on her chin, because in that episode she immediately wipes her mouth and chin after kissing him.

3.12   Provider

Original air date: January 21, 2002
Written by: Scott Murphy
Directed by: Bill Norton
Guest cast: Jeffrey Dean Morgan (Sam Ryan), Eric Bruskotter (Brian), Sunny Mabrey (Allison), Tony Pasqualini (Harlan Elster), Alan Henry Brown (Head Nahdrah), David Ramirez (Pizza Chef), Brett Wagner (Nahdrah Prince), Benjamin Benitez (Tat Vamp #2)

In an attempt to boost business and raise money for the new Connor Fund, Angel instructs the gang to take on any case and nearly gets them all hurt.

While this episode has its funny moments, it is pretty much filler. Angel begins to move away from his path of atonement and toward his new path: a college fund for his son, Connor (despite declaring two episodes ago that Linwood would be the one to pay for Connor's education). When you watch how greedy Angel becomes in this episode, it's amazing to think this is the same guy from season 1 who refused to take money from clients, telling Cordelia that it was wrong to charge people for help. As Wesley and Gunn try to chase off one girl's zombie stalker boyfriend while Fred and Lorne try to help the Nahdrahs by deciphering their puzzle and Cordelia plays babysitter, Angel clears out a vampire nest for a guy who can't exactly pay up. Angel's flip attitude toward him — "You're a true champion!" "Yeah, yeah, whatever" — is hilarious, but the rest of the episode is taken up with more of Connor crying while Wes and Gunn fawn over Fred.

This episode is a metaphor for new parenthood. Often when people become parents they become so focused on their newborns that they are blind to everything else around them. Money often becomes a serious issue, and some parents choose to leave their work to raise their children. Unfortunately, Angel's job is also his mission, a very important one that he can't walk away from. Allison is a woman whose dead boyfriend is stalking her, which is a metaphor for abusive relationships in which one side asks for help but then ends up going back to the abusive party anyway.

Meanwhile, outside the Hyperion, Holtz is teaching his new charge, Justine, a thing or two about obeying orders and fighting demons. At first it appeared as though he was trying to train her to become a Slayer, but after this episode there are no further scenes in cemeteries. Holtz's mission to do the right thing has definitely changed to hell-bent vengeance, and the way he treats Justine — a woman whose heart has grown cold after the loss of her sister — is pretty shocking, but it foreshadows the way he'll treat another protégé.

The final scene of Cordelia, Connor, and Angel in bed together is a beautiful shot that looks like a family planning their son's future, but it's an eerie picture in the context of season 4.

Highlight: When Wesley says he's working on an article about genome mapping and Lorne says they can all go download it at "I'll never know the love of a woman dot com."
Interesting Facts: Triplets Jake, Connor, and Trent Tupen play Connor on the show.
Did You Notice?: When Angel says making money is his number-one priority, then making money and finding Holtz are his two number-one priorities, and then helping the helpless, making money, and finding Holtz are his three number-one priorities, the scene is an homage to the classic Monty Python sketch "The Spanish Inquisition," where the cardinal keeps bungling his entry line. As he runs into the room after someone says the clichéd line "I didn't expect the Spanish Inquisition," he shouts, "*Nobody* expects the Spanish Inquisition! Our chief weapon is surprise . . . surprise and fear . . . fear and surprise. Our *two* weapons are fear and surprise . . . and ruthless efficiency. Our *three* weapons are fear, surprise, and ruthless efficiency . . . and an almost fanatical devotion to the Pope. Our *four* . . . no. *Amongst* our weapons . . . amongst our *weaponry* . . . are such elements as fear, surprise . . . I'll come in again."
Nitpicks: Why is it that one episode ago there were hundreds of demons after Connor, and now the gang just leaves him in the hotel with Cordelia? And why, after finding out what really happened between Brian and Allison, are Gunn and Wesley completely

unconcerned and don't seem to feel any moral responsibility to do something about a murderer in their midst?

Oops: When Gunn hits Brian for the first time with a wooden stake carved from a baseball bat, you can see the stake bend against Brian's body as if it were made of rubber.

3.13   Waiting in the Wings

Original air date: February 4, 2002
Written and directed by: Joss Whedon
Guest cast: Mark Harelik (Count Kurskov), Summer Glau (Prima Ballerina), Thomas Crawford (Manager), Don Tiffany (Security Guard)

The spirits of two lovers take over Angel and Cordelia at the opera, causing them to act out a love scene that happened over 100 years before.

A beautifully directed episode by the one and only Joss Whedon, "Waiting in the Wings" incorporates lush music, gorgeous costumes, and some of the finest acting we've seen yet. Normally that wouldn't be a surprise coming from the master, but on *Angel*, Whedon's work sometimes falls flat. Borrowing from the second-season *Buffy* episode "I Only Have Eyes for You," Joss uses the concept of two present-day people succumbing to the will of former lovers in trouble. He aptly uses *Giselle* as the ballet backdrop for the story. In *Giselle*, a nobleman who falls in love with a peasant girl is exposed as a liar by the gamekeeper, who is also in love with the girl, and she dies of a broken heart. In the second act, the two men visit her grave, and as night falls, the wilis appear. The wilis are vengeful spirits of virgin brides who died the night before their wedding days, and they find young men and force them to dance themselves to death. Giselle's spirit rises from her grave to join them; the gamekeeper is killed and the nobleman is saved by her love, although she now realizes she'll be a wili forever.

ALBERT L. ORTEGA

Summer Glau, who plays the ballerina, later starred in Joss Whedon's *Firefly* as River.

In "Waiting in the Wings," the roles

have been switched. When Kurskov discovered his favorite ballerina was in love with another, he trapped her into dancing forever in a ghostly ballet performance that is the same night after night. But because she's a spirit, her essence traps Cordelia and Angel, forcing them to do a dance of their own. The ensuing love scenes between Cordelia and Angel are hot and steamy, but their love, like the ballet, is not real — it's "an echo." The scene between Angel and the ballerina is touching.

Meanwhile, both Wesley and Gunn make plays for Fred: Gunn says she laughs at all the same jokes he does, while Wesley is thrilled that he's finally found someone who reads the same science journals and understands difficult mathematical problems like he does. But when it comes to love we act with our hearts, not our heads, and when Wes discovers that Fred has chosen Gunn, his depression and sadness are almost overwhelming from this point on. Just as the ballerina hesitated and lost her lover, so too did Wesley hesitate, and now he'll be waiting in the wings while Fred begins her new life with Gunn.

Season 3 definitely belongs to Alexis Denisof, who turns in one great performance after another. This season his character develops from the sort of bumbler whose lack of grace covers up his true pain to a tormented man whose troubled past catches up to him and encroaches on his present. We're only given clues about his upbringing, but the clues are enough to round out the character and insinuate that terrible things have happened to him. As the episode comes to an end, Wesley is not alone in his unrequited love — an unexpected blast from the past arrives just in time to whisk Cordelia away from Angel, who also waited too long to tell her how he feels.

Highlight: Angel becoming annoyed with Lorne's suggestion that he and Cordy get together: "Stop that. And stop calling me pastries."
Interesting Facts: Summer Glau, who plays the ballerina, later played the slightly loony but fascinating River Tam on Joss Whedon's *Firefly*. Also, Joss had originally come up with this idea when Amy Acker told him that she used to be a ballerina. He filmed a dream sequence where Fred is dancing on-stage and Wesley comes out and dances with her (with rather hilarious results). Unfortunately, the sequence was cut due to time constraints, but it's on the DVD.
Amy Acker Says: "I was actually really surprised when Fred ended up with Gunn because I had been playing that I was going to get together with Wesley, and all of a sudden I got a script where I was kissing Gunn, so I thought, *Oh, maybe I should have been doing this differently.* [Laughs] As for the deleted ballet scene, it was supposed to fit in while we were watching the ballet, and it was supposed to be Wesley's daydream, but it just sort of stuck out because the rest of the episode wasn't really like that. Also, the episode was really long and it was the most obvious thing to cut. It didn't take that

long to film — we only did a couple of takes. I don't know if they have the one on the DVD where Wesley comes out in a red G-string, but I couldn't do the scene because I was laughing so hard, so we had to remove it. Even as it was, I couldn't look at him the whole time."

Mark Lutz Says: "I wasn't allowed to tell anyone, but I already knew I was coming back in season two. Joss told me, 'Yeah, you're going to be coming back about halfway through next season as the big surprise,' so I wasn't allowed to say anything in interviews. People would ask, 'So will you be coming back?' and I had to say, 'Well, I don't know.'"

Nitpicks: Cordelia says if she can't return her dress to the store they'll have to take on a lot more cases. Did they somehow blow through the $50,000 from "Provider" already?

3.14   Couplet

Original air date: February 18, 2002
Written by: Tim Minear and Jeffrey Bell
Directed by: Tim Minear
Guest cast: Bernard K. Addison (Monster), Fanshen Cox (Anita), Steven Hack (Lionel), Marisa Matarazzo (Susan), Scott Donovan (Jerry), Bob Rumnock (Business Man), Vanie Poyey (Pillow Fight Woman), Michael Otis (Pillow Fight Man)

Angel feels jealous when the Groosalugg can do things he can't, and Wesley ponders the consequences of office relationships.

"Couplet" begins immediately after "Waiting in the Wings," with everyone trying to pick up the pieces of their lives. Gunn and Fred couldn't be happier, but Wesley quietly stews in his office, wondering why he wasn't chosen. The scenes between Angel and Groo at the beginning of the episode are amusing: Angel stands on his tiptoes to look taller, complains that Groo is too bulky to fight alongside, and makes fun of his tactics. But when the two fight together, Angel realizes Groo can do certain things that he can't — including com-shuck with the girl he loves. Where Wesley cannot see any reason why Fred would want to be with Gunn, Angel — the more mature of the two, even when he's joking around — learns to accept what has happened and only wants Cordelia to be happy.

Cordelia is thrilled that Groo has come to L.A., but the viewer sees that maybe Cordy has feelings for Angel, too — she just doesn't acknowledge them or even realize they're there. Sometimes it's rather disappointing that the writers choose to make Cordy as clueless as she is; it undercuts her maturity and intelligence, which have recently flourished. She cuts Groo's hair and makes it short and spiky, and she dresses him up in Angel's clothes. She is physically attracted to Groo but worries she'll lose her "visionity" and won't be valuable to Angel anymore.

Meanwhile, Gunn and Fred make a near-fatal error because their newfound love has them making googly eyes at each other rather than focusing on the mission. The relationship between Gunn and Fred had a lot of potential, but it's never convincing. The two actors have little chemistry on-screen and seem to be going through the motions whenever they're together. Wesley, on the other hand, comes off as a bad loser, and his comments to Gunn at the end of the episode are insulting. He worries that an interoffice relationship will be dangerous to Fred if it's with Gunn, yet somehow believes that one with him would be perfectly fine.

But when Wesley makes a grisly discovery within the scrolls at the end of the episode, suddenly everything else seems unimportant.

Highlight: Groo finding a man in shackles in the demon brothel and, thinking he's a prisoner, shouting, "Fear not, friend; we are here to save you!" and rushing over to free him.

Interesting Facts: When this episode first aired on the WB, Verizon Wireless did one of those annoying "Can you hear me now? Good" commercials that took place on the Hyperion Hotel *Angel* set. Interesting, considering Angel's cell phone never works *anywhere*.

Mark Lutz Says: "In 'Couplet,' when we were shooting in downtown L.A. and I'm dressed up as Groo in those animal skins, that was a great episode for me. I'm running around with a sword, chasing and beating up demons, and there are crowds forming, watching us in this park. And I'm thinking, *What a job; here I am running around in animal skins and a scratchy wig while people are staring at us . . .*"

Did You Notice?: When Angel and Wesley first walk into the bookstore, the camera pans by the "Wolf" part of the Wolf, Ram, and Hart books from Pylea that are sitting on one of the shelves.

Nitpicks: First of all, Angel leaving Lorne behind in the last episode to babysit while everyone else went to the ballet was insulting, but now again he's at the hotel babysitting while the others are out necking in trucks or discussing com-shucking. Second, why did it take Gunn and Fred so long to check the camcorder to see how Jerry disappeared? And the suggestion that the tree is evil and has a DSL connection and lures people underground is just lame, and Tim Minear and Jeffrey Bell are capable of so much better. Finally, Groo tells Angel that his phone is "singing," but having lived all his life in the music-less Pylea, Groo wouldn't be very familiar with the concept of singing.

3.15   Loyalty

Original air date: February 25, 2002
Written by: Mere Smith

Directed by: James A. Contner
Guest cast: Wendy Davis (Aubrey), Enrique Castillo (Doctor), Susan Martino (Mother #1), Annie Talbot (Mother #2), Marci Hill (Nurse), Chris Devlin (Holtzian Man), Thom Scott II (Holtzian Man #2)

When Wesley discovers the prophecy that Angel will kill Connor, he exhausts every source he has trying to prove it wrong.

The first of a trio of stunning episodes, "Loyalty" moves away from the lovebird theme and gets back on track with the Angel/Holtz/Connor/Sahjhan saga. Holtz's army is becoming more powerful, and because it's made up of ordinary people who have lost loved ones (giving them a desire for vengeance), they can blend in more easily without raising the suspicions of Angel and the gang. Holtz is an interesting character because of his complexity, and in this episode, as with others, his touching speeches about losing his family raise our sympathies, and we can't help but feel like we might do the same if we were in his situation.

The episode looks at the definitions of good and evil, and we realize that the lines aren't so clearly drawn here. Holtz says that things aren't black and white or good and evil, but when Justine asks about Angelus he says, "He's evil" without hesitation. Angel says that Holtz is one of the good guys, yet Holtz isn't purely good. The point is that Holtz isn't wholly good and Angel isn't wholly evil — they both represent the gray areas of reality.

Angel seems to be drinking a lot more blood than usual, Fred and Gunn have decided they won't break up just because Wes is uncomfortable, and Cordelia is not around (Angel sent her on vacation with Groo, and she won't reappear until "Double or Nothing"). But the focus of this episode is Wesley. He alone bears the weight of his new knowledge, and he's so convinced it's wrong he can't bear to share it with anyone. His quest throughout the episode is heroic, although the seriousness of the prophecy is undermined by that stupid drive-thru hamburger he talks to. He refuses to believe that Angel could be capable of what the biblical-like prophecy is suggesting, yet by the end of the episode he won't be able to deny the signs any longer. When Wes finally confronts Holtz and Holtz tells him that Angelus is always in Angel, Holtz puts in motion the events that will change all their lives forever, and Wesley's path is determined when Angel utters his astounding comment at the end.

Highlight: Holtz telling Wesley that a child's coffin weighs nothing — a sadly beautiful, but frightening, line under the circumstances.
Stephanie Romanov Says: "You try to create a whole history for your character so you know what you're working from, and in the third season they revealed that I had a

mom I was taking care of who was in a home. But prior to that knowledge I kind of thought Lilah was orphaned and had to make her own way in the world. By virtue of that, that's how she wound up where she was. It was either kill or be killed. She was a survivor, and now she was in a company full of these men and she was a powerful woman and again, kill or be killed. It had to have started really young with her — blocking off love and not getting love and making everything about power — and that had to have come from her childhood. And then I found out I had a mom and I was, like, 'Hmm . . . okay.' But I used that because now that I had a sick mom, I played it still like it was kill or be killed because I'd had to take care of her. [Laughs] She was a loner who wasn't abandoned but just had to survive in the world."

Did You Notice?: Wes's dream shows that he has blood on his hands, which is an ominous foreshadowing of what is to come.

Nitpicks: Did I mention that annoying hamburger? It would have been funny in another context, but considering the seriousness of what is happening — a man fighting for revenge after the brutal and vicious deaths of his beloved family members and the possibility that Angel could hurt Connor in some way — the hamburger didn't belong in this episode and it's too bad they didn't keep that joke for a more lighthearted one. Also, why doesn't Sahjhan use his less conspicuous street face when walking into the bar?

Wolfram & Hart: Sahjhan turns to w&h when he seems to be getting nowhere with Holtz, but Lilah's already on the case. She seems to have made her vendetta with Angel a personal one and is willing to go against the wishes of her company to see Angel dusted. w&h is still tailing Angel to get some clues about Connor. Lilah has a mother in a home whom she's taking care of.

3.16 Sleep Tight

Original air date: March 4, 2002
Written by: David Greenwalt
Directed by: Terrence O'Hara
Guest cast: Marina Benedict (Kim), Jeff Denton (Lead Guitar), Jhaemi Willems (Drummer), J. Scott Shonka (Commando #1), Robert Forrest (Warrior #2)

Wesley kidnaps Connor to prevent the fulfillment of the prophecy and sets in motion several tragic events.

"Sleep Tight" is the stuff season finales are made of. This episode has everything: suspense, intrigue, betrayal, loss — and vengeance. The special effects at the end of the episode are amazing (the portal Sahjhan opens literally looks like a tear in the sky). And with outstanding performances by David Boreanaz and Alexis Denisof, it is one of the

ALBERT L. ORTEGA

In "Sleep Tight," Wesley makes a huge mistake – will he ever find forgiveness?

best-acted episodes of the season. As Angel continues to chug down the blood like it's, well, blood, the others start to notice changes in him: he is talking and acting differently, getting a little too excited about killing demons, and becoming annoyed with Connor. When they discover the reason for his behavior, it's absolutely chilling.

Lilah turns out to be even more of a coldhearted bitch than we thought possible; Justine — who appears to be falling in love with Holtz — goes from being merely unsympathetic to downright despicable; Holtz takes his vengeance to a level even he didn't think he could manage; and Sahjhan reveals a long-standing feud with Angel (who has no idea who Sahjhan is).

Of course, the most interesting change in character happens to Wesley. Holtz gives Wesley 24 hours to deliver Connor to him to prevent the child's death at the hands of Angel, which is foretold in the prophecy. But Wes has plans of his own, and it's obvious by the way he packs up his vehicle that he has no intention of delivering the child to anyone. Throughout the season he has been battered, rejected, betrayed, and filled with pain, and he's no longer the prim Watcher he was in season 3 of *Buffy*. He's surrounded by friends whom he considers his family; they give him the only solace he's had in his life. But by the end of the episode, fans feared he would be no more.

As Wes lies bleeding to death, Angel watches his son disappear from his life at the hands of Holtz, and the look on his face is heartbreaking. On another show, the lead character would have been screaming, beating the ground, and crying, but David Boreanaz conveys a father so filled with grief that he's completely paralyzed and speechless. Not only is his son gone — to Quor-toth, the darkest of the dark dimensions — but Angel is filled with the pain of knowing that he had inflicted this very anguish on Holtz 230 years earlier, and that the demon inside him deserves this punishment. No matter how much good Angel does, he will always pay for the sins of Angelus.

Highlight: Lorne doing his stuffed-animal re-enactment of the Rat Pack for Connor.

Interesting Facts: David Greenwalt wrote the song that Kim sings at the beginning of the show, the third song he's written for the show (see "Dead End" and "Birthday").

Keith Szarabajka Says: "People recognize me because of the show, even now, saying, 'You're that guy on *Angel*, aren't you?' People hold on to their babies much tighter now when they see me coming."

Did You Notice?: Holtz offers Wesley an apple, like he's Eve tempting Adam to take the ultimate fall and leave the Garden of Eden, which in this case is Angel Investigations. Also, Angel wishes aloud that Connor would just stop being a baby and grow up. Finally, Holtz reassures Angel that Connor will never know he existed, an interesting foreshadowing of the end of season 4.

Nitpicks: What was with that "Texas doesn't hate the black man" speech that Fred was giving to Gunn? It almost sounded like Gunn was accusing Fred of being racist, or at least coming from a racist state, yet when they see each other they're all lovey-dovey again, as if the conversation didn't happen. And why isn't anyone bothered by the fact that Holtz's army was made up of human beings and the gang killed them?

Wolfram & Hart: Lilah makes a pact with Sahjhan but has plans of her own that might not mesh with his.

3.17   Forgiving

Original air date: April 15, 2002
Written by: Jeffrey Bell
Directed by: Turi Meyer
Guest cast: Kay Panabaker (Girl), Kenneth Dolin (Bum), Tripp Puckell (Holtzian), Sean Mahon (Truck Driver)

As Gunn and Fred search frantically for Wesley, Angel tries opening a portal to get his son back.

"Forgiving" is a whirlwind of an episode. Angel stares at Connor's empty, burnt crib, which mirrors his own soul. He becomes dark once again and tortures Linwood for information (although Linwood is someone from Wolfram & Hart, so technically he's only barely human). Angel ultimately turns to dark magick to rescue his son, and Lorne begs him not to because of what might be done that will be impossible to undo.

Fred seems to have taken the news of Wesley's actions the worst and is in disbelief that Wesley would ever do anything to hurt Connor or to separate him from the rest of the team. She's also heartbroken that they've lost Connor through a portal of all things, remembering how awful it was when she went through one. Fred and Gunn go to Wesley's house and find his diaries, discovering exactly why he did what he did.

An *Angel* Timeline

c. 1000 – The Master becomes a vampire.

1609 – The Master visits a dying Darla in the Virginia Colony and makes her a vampire.

1630 – A young woman receives the visions that Cordelia later gets but discovers that humans aren't equipped to deal with them.

1727 – Liam is born in Galway, Ireland.

1753 – Darla turns Liam into the vampire Angelus, and he kills his family.

1760 – Darla introduces Angelus to the Master in London, England, but the meeting doesn't go very well.

1764 – Angelus and Darla kill the family of Daniel Holtz in York, England.

1765 – In France, Holtz's army traps Angelus and Darla in a barn; Darla hits Angelus over the head and escapes on a horse.

1767 – With vampires James and Elisabeth, Angelus and Darla are surrounded by Holtz's men in Marseilles, France, but they escape.

1771 – Holtz captures Angelus in Rome, Italy, with the help of a monseigneur and begins to torture him, but Darla saves Angelus and shoots Holtz with an arrow.

1773 – The time traveler Sahjhan visits Holtz and makes a deal to take him to 2001, where he can kill Angelus and Darla.

1789 – Angelus meets the Beast in Prussia.

1791 – The L.A. branch of Wolfram & Hart is built on its present site, on deconsecrated grounds.

Late 1700s – Angelus turns Penn into a vampire, and Penn becomes his protégé; Angelus begins leaving a cross in the cheeks of his victims as a sign that he'd killed them.

1838 – Angelus kills a young man named Daniel in Dublin, Ireland.

1845 – Angelus is with a young woman named Rosaria in Tuscany.

1860 – Angelus stalks Drusilla, making her crazy by killing her family, and ultimately sires her.

1880 – Drusilla finds William (Spike) in London, England, and sires him; she soon introduces him to Angelus at the Royal London Hotel.

1890 – Angelus sees a performance of *Giselle* and weeps like a baby (*before* he had a soul!).

1894 – Angelus and Spike are caught by the Immortal in Italy and chained up.

1898 – Darla kidnaps a gypsy girl in Borsa, Romania, and Angelus kills her; the gypsies place a curse on him, giving him his soul; Spike, Dru, and Darla massacre everyone in the camp.

1900 – Spike, Darla, and Dru are in China during the Boxer Rebellion, and Spike kills his first Slayer; Angel rejoins them and tries to convince Darla he's still Angelus, but she knows he's lying.

1902 – Angel arrives in New York City.

1908 – Penn is possibly in Boston, as the murders there match his modus operandi.

Early 1920s – Angel is living in Chicago and saves a puppy from being hit by an oncoming car.

1920s – Angel is in Juarez, Mexico, with Boone.

1929 – Penn is in L.A.

1930s – Angel is in Montana during the Depression.

1943 – Angel is living in an apartment in New York City and sires another vampire.

1943 – Spike is in Madrid, Spain, when he's caught and put on a submarine.

c.1946 – Angel is in Las Vegas playing tennis with Bugsy Siegel.

1950s – Spike and Dru are in Italy.

1952 – Angel is staying at the Hyperion Hotel, where he rediscovers why he hates humans.

1953 – Numero Cinco's brothers are killed by Tezcatcatl.

1960 or 1963 – Angel meets up with the Rat Pack in Las Vegas and has dinner with Sammy Davis Jr.

1963 – Penn is in L.A. again.

1963 – Spike slaughters the residents of an orphanage in Vienna, Austria.

1967 – Angel is in Las Vegas crashing Elvis and Priscilla's wedding reception.

1967 – Angel attends the first taping of the *Carol Burnett Show*.

1969 – Spike attends Woodstock and kills a flower child.

c. 1976 – Angel enters a diner and drinks the blood of a murdered waiter.

1977 – Spike kills his second Slayer in New York City.

1989 – Spike and Drusilla are in Prague, Czech Republic, when she is attacked by an angry mob and weakened.

1995 – Charles Gunn trades his soul for something that means a lot to him.

1996 – Winifred Burkle opens a book in a library and reads aloud some words that send her into another dimension; Krevlorneswath of the Deathwok Clan sees a portal open in his home dimension and jumps through it.

1996 – Whistler finds Angel in an alleyway in New York City sucking blood from rats and shows him who Buffy is.

Searching for the diaries is Fred's idea, showing us how well she knows Wesley. Unlike the others, Fred has figured out that if Wesley had found something important, he would have written it down, like a good former Watcher would. Fred is overwhelmed with relief when they find the books; knowing that Wesley was only trying to act in Connor's best interest, she believes it'll be easier for everyone to forgive him. Gunn, on the other hand, echoes Wesley's very words in "That Old Gang of Mine" when he wonders why Wes kept such a huge secret from everyone else.

Justine continues her yawn-invoking rampage to destroy Angel, while Angel goes to "the white room" for the first time and discovers a way to deal with part of his problem. Through the advice of the being he finds in the room, he manages to use dark magick (and Lilah) to open up a portal, but his tunnel vision ends up putting other people in peril. He needs to make Sahjhan corporeal in order to threaten him, but as a corporeal being Sahjhan is now dangerous to the public at large — and the gang at Angel Investigations. When Angel finally comes face-to-face with him, Sahjhan reveals a devastating truth that makes Wesley's decision even more tragic.

The ending of this episode is the most powerful and unexpected thus far, and I defy any viewer to watch it without trembling. David Boreanaz is brilliant as Angel calmly reassures Wesley that he hasn't turned into Angelus and is not evil — but not for the reasons we might think. Just as with *Buffy* in season 6, our loyalties are now divided as we watch the cracks in the friendships become deep, impassable chasms.

Highlight: Boreanaz's performance in the final moments of the episode. He's shown a completely new side of Angel in the last couple of episodes and has really matured as a lead actor.

Stephanie Romanov Says: "The thing I loved most about Lilah was her sense of fun. I definitely think she has fun. Playing her, whether it was with Angel or with Lindsey, there was always an element of 'Let's play ball.' She was a real sportsman in the way that she attacked life; she was competitive, but fun. She really rejoiced in her role of being the only woman, being the underdog who was trying to go forward, and she always appreciated her competition. Lilah is *so* not in my nature, but so much fun to play. I got to say and do things I would *never* do in real life. I looked at some of those scripts and I was like, 'Ooohohoho . . .'"

Did You Notice?: Wesley must have crawled to the spot near the woods, where we see him in this episode, because Justine cut his throat in an area much closer to the sidewalk.

Nitpicks: Despite his grief, Angel puts Cordelia's holiday above all else, which is a little crazy. He would want her to know the truth about Connor so she could help. She might actually be able to lead them to Sahjhan quickly, but he refuses to get her help, which makes no sense given how desperate he is. Considering the woman was willing to have the back of her head explode so she could keep the visions to help the gang, she would want to be there to help him now. Also, in "Over the Rainbow" Wesley discovered that the gang could enter a portal together, but wouldn't end up together on the other side. We find out later that Holtz and Connor were together, so how did Holtz manage to zip through the portal without losing Connor in the process?

The *Buffy* Connection: Over on *Buffy*, Willow is dabbling in dark magicks that will forever change her life, and just like Lorne warns Angel about the consequences of such magick, everyone around her pleads with her to stop. She doesn't listen, either.

Wolfram & Hart: The white room is a place that only the top people have access to, and even Lilah hasn't been there before. It'll come in to play more prominently in seasons 4 and 5. Angel makes a mortal enemy of Linwood.

3.18   Double or Nothing

Original air date: April 22, 2002
Written by: David H. Goodman
Directed by: David Grossman
Guest cast: Jason Carter (Repo-Man), Patrick St. Esprit (Jenoff), John David Conti (Male Elderly Demon), P.B. Hutton (Female Elderly Demon), Nigel D. Gibbs (Doctor)

A soul sucker demands payment of Gunn's soul, which Gunn had sold to him seven years earlier.

In this episode, we flash back seven years to see Gunn selling his soul to Mr. Jenoff in order to obtain something he wanted. The theme of the episode "Double or Nothing" is pertinent to what is happening in the show's main storyline — just as Gunn believed he had no future "living in a gangsta's paradise" and therefore was able to sacrifice it for something that would make him happy at the time, Angel also believed he had no future until Connor came along. Gunn now sees that he was wrong seven years earlier and that his future now lies with Fred, while Angel has had his future ripped from him. Gunn used to live in the present, but now he lives with an eye on his future while recalling the things that have happened in the past so he doesn't repeat them.

Like Angel, Wesley has seen his future evaporate. For the rest of this season and part of the next, he'll begin to live in the present only, with no regard for the consequences of his actions. Fred goes to Wesley in this episode, partly to warn him not to return to the Hyperion and partly to chastise him for what he did, and her words are harsh. When the doctor asks him who will be picking him up from the hospital, he realizes he no longer has any friends and must face his new life alone. Like his father predicted, he's failed at yet another job, and by believing in the wrong thing, he's lost everything that's ever mattered in his life.

Groo is entertaining throughout the episode as he marvels at the small paper rectangles that people hand out so others remember who they are, tries to fit in with the gang, and learns to strategize with the team rather than just run into battle with his sword in the air. The writers are careful not to drop the other storyline, though, and keep us updated on Wesley's adjustment to his new life, Angel's grief and movement forward, and Cordelia's discovery of what has happened in her absence. The scenes between Cordelia and Angel are quiet and touching: she reads a book in the room just to be there for him and he tells her that's it's dawning on him that his son is gone for good. Before her vacation she seemed blind to his affections for her, but now, while comforting him in his grief, her jokiness is gone and she's beginning to realize that the feelings might be mutual.

"Double or Nothing" is an engaging episode, but it seems a little strange that Angel would be so gung-ho about helping Gunn when he's still suffering his own loss. The guy goes to a monastery in Sri Lanka for three months to work through his grief over losing Buffy, yet when his son is snatched from him and sucked into a hell dimension, he snaps back within a week and is playing cards in a casino. However, the move is consistent with Angel's character, since he identifies with what Gunn is going through. It also points to the fundamental problem within the gang: the keeping of secrets. Angel lied about sleeping with Darla; Cordelia didn't tell anyone about the impact the visions were having on her physically; Wesley discovered a horrifying prophecy and kept it to himself; and now Gunn, who suffered the consequences of keeping secrets once when he found out his gang was slaughtering innocent demons and didn't tell anyone, goes to the casino to hand over his soul rather than appeal to his friends for help. Thankfully, the gang will eventually learn that secrets hinder more than help, and they will begin to work together and be more open with one another.

Highlight: Groo welcoming the Repo-Man to the Hyperion: "Hail to you, potential client!"

Interesting Facts: Repo-Man is played by Jason Carter, the Terence Stamp sound-alike who is best known as Ranger Marcus Cole on *Babylon 5*.

Mark Lutz Says: "As a Canadian, there are certain times where I would have to go back into ADR [automatic dialogue replacement] sometimes because I'd said the word wrong. I kept saying 'out.' Everyone kept teasing me [in a Bob and Doug MacKenzie accent]: 'Oh, I've got to go out, eh? Get some coffee from Tim Horton's before I watch the Habs game, eh?' So I had to loop a couple, say 'owt' instead of 'out,' 'sari' instead of 'sorry,' 'pasta' instead of 'pahsta.' I would just say, 'Well, listen, it's not *my* fault that you're not pronouncing it properly!' I was reading something online not too long ago that was saying that English scholars say the most correct pronunciation in the English language is the Canadian pronunciation; we're the most phonetically correct."

Nitpicks: Some people go away on vacation and come back with their hair in corn-rows, but Cordelia returns with a god-awful haircut and dye job. And Gunn can pledge his undying love to Fred all he wants, but there's still no chemistry between Acker and Richards. Their kisses look staged, and their sentiments are forced.

Oops: When Cordelia and Gunn are talking on the stairs, every time the camera is shooting over Cordy's shoulder so we can see Gunn, her mouth isn't moving with the words she's saying.

Music/Bands: In the flashback to Gunn entering Jenoff's place, we hear Coolio's "Gangsta's Paradise" (*Gangsta's Paradise*).

3.19   The Price

Original air date: April 29, 2002
Written by: David Fury
Directed by: Marita Grabiak
Guest cast: John Short (Phillip J. Spivey), Vincent Kartheiser (The Destroyer), Wayne Ford (Kid), Waleed Moursi (Manager)

Angel discovers the consequences of practicing dark magick when the Hyperion is overrun with translucent, slug-like creatures.

"The Price" is a great episode that begins to set the tone for season 4. Throughout the episode, relationships are tested by the tension that has arisen in the wake of recent events. Groo overhears Cordelia telling Fred about her loyalty to Angel and he worries that it might supersede her love for him. Even when she later tells him that's not the case, we can tell that he's not convinced. Fred and Gunn have some minor tiffs about Wesley (who has usurped Buffy as the One Who Must Not Be Named on the show),

CHRISTINA RADISH

The Groosalugg (Mark Lutz), begins to wonder if Cordelia still has feelings for him.

and they have very different beliefs about how the situation should be handled. Despite Fred's harsh words to Wes in the previous episode, she believes that he thought he was acting out of Connor's best interests, but neither Gunn nor Cordy agree with her. As far as they're concerned, what Wesley did was take Angel's son away from him for good, and their loyalties lie with Angel. Lorne hangs around in a Quentin Crisp hat not doing much of anything, as has been typical of the character for the entire season. While season 3 is by far the best of the seasons of *Angel*, the lack of development in Lorne's character has been a big disappointment.

But the finest moment belongs to Wesley, who has been shunned by the only people he loves — though they are quick to use him when the situation calls for it. Gunn asks for his help but never returns to say thank-you or even just to talk. Wesley's impassioned speech about staying alive for his friends is a touching moment, one that seems wasted on Gunn. Wes took a bullet to save Gunn and his friends, and when Angel pulled away from everyone in season 2, Wesley stepped up to the plate to help lead his friends in a new investigations agency. After everything the trio has been through, the way Cordelia and Gunn both turn their back on Wesley is sad. Cordelia's behavior is even more shocking given her extended history with Wes, and while Gunn at least shows some emotion about what happened, she seems too wrapped up with Angel to notice anything else happening around her.

While Angel still retained a hint of depression in the previous episode, he actually borders on being giddy in this one, excited that they finally have a case to work on. He does have some serious moments, however, when he realizes that it's because of his rash behavior when he lost Connor that an innocent man has died and Fred may be next. Cordelia finally shows her "demon" side, putting both Groo and Angel in awe of her and leading her closer to where she'll end up by the beginning of season 4.

But, as with "Forgiving," the ending of this episode will make you forget everything that came before it.

Highlight: Groo giving Angel advice on paint colors: "Sunburst splendor is a hue more worthy of a champion."

Mark Lutz Says: "I got invited to a couple of conventions and I had no idea the show was as big as it was. You don't see *Friends* or *ER* having conventions, and I'd never done the convention circuit, and I was really surprised at the response. I get a lot of fan mail and the response I got was really gratifying and much appreciated."

Did You Notice?: Not only does Connor come through the spot where Angel conducted the dark magick, but he also appears in the place where Angel, Gunn, Wesley, and Cordelia killed the Thessulac demon in "Are You Now or Have You Ever Been?" It's appropriate, not only because Connor was kidnapped as a result of Wesley's paranoia that Angel would kill his son, but because the scene of Angel's biggest revenge against humankind becomes the biggest revenge against him.

Nitpicks: The gang has been at the Hyperion for two years now and not one of them has realized there is a huge lounge *and* a pool? Also, if the creatures really wanted out of the building and they were thirsting for water, why not jump in a toilet, go down the drain, and try swimming into the sewer system? There are a lot of ways in and out of the Hyperion, and if large monsters seem to find their way in all the time, why can't a slug slip out through one of the many passageways? And we see Fred's skin split from the dehydration, yet as soon as the slug is out of her body, all the marks disappear as if nothing happened.

Oops: The pentagram on the floor has perfect dimensions, but when Angel first painted it, it was lopsided and looked more realistic. Also, when Angel and Cordy walk back into the lobby at the end of the episode, the lights come back on even though no one has turned the power back on.

The *Buffy* Connection: The term *thaumogenesis* is from the *Buffy* episode "After Life," in which the gang discovers that when Buffy returned from the afterlife, she brought something evil back with her.

Wolfram & Hart: When W&H lawyers get confidential e-mail, they have to pull out a mystical tarantula that walks on the keys and types in the correct password. The partners believe that Lilah is partly responsible for the disturbance at the Hyperion because she helped Angel open the portal. Linwood wants Angel dead despite the Wolfram & Hart policy to keep him alive.

3.20 A New World

Original air date: May 6, 2002
Written by: Jeffrey Bell
Directed by: Tim Minear
Guest cast: Vincent Kartheiser (Connor), Erika Thormahlen (Sunny), Anthony Starke (Tyke), Deborah Zoe (Mistress Meerna)

Connor is back in town, but he's suddenly a teenager — and he's pretty pissed off.

"A New World" is a good episode, although it lags a bit as Connor shows up and then immediately leaves again, and afterward it seems like not much happened. We see him wandering the streets of grimy L.A. and hooking up with a drug-addicted girl, and while the plot is a little slow when Connor (now called Steven, but for the purposes of the episode guide I'll call him Connor) is with her, it picks up in the scenes at the Hyperion. Connor's hesitant discovery of his new world is interesting to watch considering he's been raised almost like an animal.

Sunny makes Connor's metaphor clearer. She's a teenager who's lost her way: she hates her father and her parents probably have no idea where she is; she is living like an animal, squatting in an old, dirty abandoned room while shooting heroin and living off junk food from vending machines; and she is at the mercy of brutal drug dealers and pimps. She doesn't survive long in this world. Connor can relate, as he lived in a world of monsters, too.

When Angel does catch up to his son he gains some of Connor's trust by saving his life and telling him he is not alone. But as someone who has had to work out difficult situations himself, Angel understands Connor's need to be alone. Angel moves into the fatherly role easily and is so elated to have his son back that he doesn't seem to register the shock of what has happened. He doesn't seem to know where to start the relationship and asks Connor a million questions, but they're all thrown back in his face and he realizes that Connor hates him. Angel is forced to admit that he's part monster, a horrible thing to have to tell his own son.

Fred, on the other hand, becomes increasingly annoying throughout this episode, telling everyone that only Wesley would know what to do in the current situation. This coming from the person who in "Double or Nothing" visited Wes in the hospital and told him never to come to the hotel again. No one will listen to Wes's side of the story, yet Fred believes he would help them in their time of need? *Again?* Cordelia and Groo stay behind as warriors to watch the hotel, and Groo regales her with stories about standing perfectly still for 11 days to avoid being "coupled" by an engorged Bur-beast. But when they take their eyes off the Quor-toth portal for one moment, something comes through, and by the end of the episode we find out what that is.

Lilah has swooped in on her broomstick to recruit Wesley for Wolfram & Hart by brilliantly comparing him to Judas Iscariot — she's at her evil best in this scene. Lilah has just gotten better and better throughout the season and has proven to be an even more intriguing character than Lindsey. And she's just so much fun to hate. Her words to Wesley are pretty convincing; he's been abandoned by everyone he's ever loved and who has ever loved him, and the thought of doing a 180 and playing for the other team doesn't seem out of the question.

Highlight: Mistress Meerna putting on a welding mask to avoid getting "schmutz" in her eye.

Keith Szarabajka Says: "I wasn't surprised that they turned me into an old man. David [Greenwalt] had known that I had done Stephen King's *Golden Years* and Tim Minear said, 'I had no idea we were going to do that with you' and I kind of figured David was going to do that because he knew that I'd done this before and it just seemed natural, that somehow I would become aged. In the world of the WB, as soon as you become old, you're dead. It's teenage land; everyone over thirty, you've got one foot in the grave! [Laughs]"

Nitpicks: While the monster that comes through the portal and the slugs that preceded it in "The Price" are amazing special effects, the opening scene, a *Matrix* rip-off, is laughable, and I hope the entire budget wasn't blown on it. It would have been slightly fascinating if we hadn't already suffered through countless takeoffs of the same special effects in dozens of other movies and television shows. Unfortunately, it won't be the last time the writers pay homage to their favorite film. Every fight scene in this episode, in fact, has too many slow-motion moments that are atypical of the direction of the series and are therefore distracting.

Oops: During the bad opening fight scene, you can tell that the ax Groo throws is CGI, since his hand never looks like it is actually holding the weapon. Also, "The Price" takes place in the middle of the night, yet at the beginning of this episode, which occurs about 10 minutes later, it's midday.

The Boy Ain't Right: Connor jumps off a bridge without hurting himself, and he tracks people by smell. He's also survived 17 years in a hell dimension.

3.21   Benediction
Original air date: May 13, 2002
Written and directed by: Tim Minear
Guest cast: Vincent Kartheiser (Connor)

Angel continues to vie for Connor's trust and discovers things they have in common, but Holtz has other plans.

By the time this episode aired, David Greenwalt had announced that he would be leaving the show by the beginning of *Angel*'s fourth season, which was unfortunate, but his departure left Tim Minear with more responsibility. And with this, another stunning episode, Tim Minear proves he's the best man for the job. In "Benediction," everyone is losing someone: Groo is losing Cordelia, the gang is losing Wesley, and Angel is losing his son after just having gotten him back.

Holtz returns, and with him comes a complicated moral conundrum. His need for vengeance often borders on being repugnant, yet we cannot blame him for it because we know what he's been through. He lost everything that meant something to him at the hands of Darla and Angelus and has just spent 17 years in a hell dimension. He began his hunt for Angel 229 years ago as a quest to do the right thing, seeking to dole out Old Testament "eye for an eye" justice. But when Sahjhan brought him back, Holtz realized there was a kink in the plan — if Angel has a soul, then, as Wesley told Holtz, he's no more responsible for the crimes of Angelus than Holtz is. Holtz was torn: if he didn't kill Angel, he would be letting down his family and his entire mission would have been in vain. Instead, he buries his doubts and convinces himself that Angel is evil, thus changing his quest for justice into a quest for vengeance. Now it doesn't matter if Angel and Angelus are two separate beings — Holtz knows that Angelus still resides somewhere within Angel, and for that he will punish him.

In "Benediction," Holtz wears the ravages of time and torture on his face, appearing to have aged about 40 years. He encourages Connor to be with Angel, telling him he belongs with his real father, but he's lying. Connor will become the final pawn in Holtz's complex plan to avenge the deaths of his family members. Despite truly believing that he himself loves Connor, what Holtz chooses to do will destroy Connor's life as well as Angel's, a path that will culminate in the events of season 4's "Home."

Connor, who is filled with rage and bewildered by his new surroundings, attacks Angel's "demon" friends, and we catch another glimpse of Cordelia's rather confusing new power. Skip had told her she would have to be part demon, but she appears to be part angel instead, and her soothing "Let it go, honey" is so out of character for the original Cordelia that we can't help but look upon this woman's growth with awe. She's also able to return to a vision to watch what happens in real time. It's a shame that this fascinating new power of hers that can destroy evil and hatred isn't further explored after this season.

The best parts of the episode take place between Angel and Connor. The fight scene involving Angel and Connor is superb and shows just how much they really do have in common, but the subtlety of their uncomfortable moments together at the hotel are even better. Connor desperately wants to know his biological father, but he loves Holtz so much that he doesn't want to hurt him as a consequence. The episode plays with the allegory of a child who has been adopted and finally gets the chance to meet his real parents, but is worried that he might offend his adoptive ones in doing so.

The final few moments of the episode — Holtz's voice-over reading the letter he has just given to Angel, Justine aiding Holtz in putting his vengeance to rest, and Connor beginning a quest for retribution of his own — are spectacular.

Highlight: Fred's skewed but charming logic: "So he survived an unspeakable hell dimension. Who hasn't? You can't just leave him alone on the streets of Los Angeles!"

Keith Szarabajka Says: "I don't think Holtz ever really changed; I think he was always pursuing the same goal, which was to get justice against Angel for the loss of his family, and he finally figured out the way to do it near the end. You don't always have a plan; sometimes the circumstance changes and you have to go with the circumstance. I think in this case he snatched the baby, took him to Quor-toth, trained him, altered him greatly, and brought him back, and what he did, essentially, was take Angel's child from him in the same way Angel took his daughter from Holtz. He turned Connor into Angel's nemesis just as Angel turned Holtz's daughter into a vampire that was his nemesis. It was poetic justice if you think about it. I'm not saying it was kind. I think he had great respect for Angel — the way an American general would have respect for a Nazi general."

Did You Notice?: Fred tells Connor that when she first returned from Pylea she felt completely lost, like she was looking at the world from the bottom of the ocean. Could that have put a particularly evil thought into Connor's head? Also, despite being raised in Quor-toth, Connor still eats an Oreo by taking it apart first, which is a great little on-screen touch.

Nitpicks: If Connor has such highly attuned hearing, why doesn't he hear Angel telling Gunn and Fred to take him out somewhere to distract him? And Holtz says he forgets the details because of his age and what he's been through, yet he opens the newspaper and seems to remember the exact day he entered Quor-toth. First of all, he has traveled through time almost 230 years, so just adjusting to the 21st century would have been difficult. Second, while he was in L.A., he was too busy assembling his vampire-hating army to pay attention to a calendar. Yet now, after 17 years of suffering in a hell dimension, he still remembers when he left? Seems unlikely.

The Boy Ain't Right: Connor displays highly attuned hearing, picks up a vending machine like it weighs nothing, and says that he must be a demon if he's the son of two other demons. Holtz tells Connor to find out how much of Angel is within him, and Angel tells Connor his fighting instincts are in his blood.

Wolfram & Hart: Lilah lures Justine into a vampire ambush and invites Wesley to watch.

3.22   Tomorrow

Original air date: May 20, 2002
Written and directed by: David Greenwalt
Guest cast: Vincent Kartheiser (Connor), David Denman (Skip)

As Angel begins to make plans for Connor's future, Connor secretly plans Angel's. Meanwhile, Cordelia realizes she loves Angel and races to meet him and tell him so.

Until this season, there was a sort of unwritten rule about the season finales of *Buffy* and *Angel*: never end them on a cliffhanger. Finish all of the storylines, bring the arc to a close, and use the first few episodes of the next season as a transition from the previous one before launching into a new story arc. But "Tomorrow" drops many surprises into our laps and leaves the people we love in limbo, forcing us to suffer through a long, excruciating summer for resolution.

The Groosalugg finally confronts Cordelia about her love for Angel, and when she is unable to reciprocate Groo's undying love for her, he leaves. Groo was rather annoying when he first showed up, but by the end of the season he had become a delightful character similar to Anya on *Buffy*, who was trying to fit into the L.A. scene. As if his departure isn't bad enough, Lorne — many fans' favorite character — announced his impending departure for Las Vegas. He complains that the fang gang is always ruining his club and there's no sense in going back there, but why not restore the dance hall in the other wing of the hotel, a space that the gang discovered in "The Price"? It's as if the writers wrote that detail in with the intention of making the hall a place for Lorne in season 4, but it never works out and the concept is dropped.

But the biggest changes happen to Cordelia and Angel. These two characters have been moving toward their destinies all season, and while Cordy's has allowed her to move up, so to speak, Angel's torture has sent him down into the depths. The punishment that Connor and the despicable Justine subject Angel to is a clever plot device, while Cordy's fate had some fans scratching their heads — which they will continue to do for most of the next season. The ending leaves us hanging with a ton of unanswered questions, and despite being a season finale to cap off what has been a whirlwind for the viewers, it is a pretty disappointing finish. And considering *The Adventures of Gunn & Fred* would be canceled after about 30 minutes, it is inevitable that most of the main characters will still be central in season 4.

Season 3 proved the strongest season yet. Holtz was a brilliant invention by the writers, played beautifully by Szarabajka, and his hell-bent vengeance and heartrending sadness came together in such a way that our sympathies kept moving back and forth throughout the year. His painful background story allowed the writers to show us more of Angel's past, which is always a highlight on the series. No one could have guessed way back in season 1 that Cordelia would demonstrate enough goodness and purity to be deemed a higher power by the powers that be; that Angel would have a son; that Wesley would become sufficiently dark and serious to be abandoned by the entire gang and literally start sleeping with the enemy. Yet every journey

ANGEL

DATE: **Mon. 04/15/02**

20th Century Fox Television
Paramount Studios

"Tomorrow"

Episode 22 (3ADH022)

CREW CALL
10:30A
Report

DAY: **7**	OF **9** DAYS
CREW CALL:	10:30A
SHOOT CALL:	11:30A
REHEARSAL :	10:30A
SUNRISE 6:22A	SUNSET 7:23P

Director: **David Greenwalt**

Exec. Prods: **David Greenwalt, Joss Whedon, Tim Minear, Sandy Gallin, Gail Berman, Fran & Kaz Kuzul**   2

Producers: **Kelly A. Manners, Jeffrey Bell**   Latest Script Revision: Yellow

Co-Prods.: **Skip Schoolnik**   Consulting Producer: **Marti Noxon**

SET	SCENES	CAST	D/N	PAGES	LOCATION
	•SHOOTING ORDER SUBJECT TO CHANGE•				
INT. ANGEL'S HOTEL ROOM	17	1,6D	N-2	1 2/8	Paramount
The Host tells Angel that Cordy has the same feelings that Angel does					Stage 7
INT. ANGEL'S HOTEL ROOM	19,21,23,25,29	1,6D	N-2	1	
Host-Angel side of the intercut dialogue sequence					
• **Move to Stage 5** •					
INT. ANGEL'S HOTEL-Connor's Rm.	7	1,2,6D	N-1	3 3/8	Stage 5
The Host tells Angel & Cordy he is going to Las Vegas					
INT. ANGEL'S HOTEL-Connor's Rm.	13	1,7,26	D-2	2 3/8	
Angel wants quality time w/ Connor; Connor wants to learn to fight					
				8	TOTAL PAGES

#	CAST & DAY PLAYERS		PART OF	P/U	M/U	REH.	SET	REMARKS
1	David Boreanaz	W	ANGEL	-	10:15A	10:30A	11:30A	Report to make-up
2	Charisma Carpenter	W	CORDELIA	-	12N	tbd	1P	Report to make-up
4	J. August Richards	2U	GUNN		See 2nd Unit			
5	Amy Acker	2U	FRED		See 2nd Unit			
6	Andy Hallett	SW	LORNE	-	7:30A	10:30A	11:30A	Report to make-up
7	Vincent Kartheiser	W	CONNOR		W / N @4:30P			From 2nd Unit
8	Mark Lutz	H	GROOSALUG		HOLD			
10	Keith Szarabajka	H	HOLTZ		HOLD			
11	Laurel Holloman	2U	JUSTINE		See 2nd Unit			
12	John Rubinstein	2U	LINWOOD		See 2nd Unit			
13	Daniel Dae Kim	2U	GAVIN		See 2nd Unit			
26	Mike Massa	W	STUNT COORDINATOR		W / N @4:30P			

The crew call report for one of the shooting days on "Tomorrow."

taken by the major characters has been a believable one. Season 4 will lag slightly, not being nearly as strong as this season, but at the same time it's saved by the strength of season 3, which created such a powerful storyline that it'll take two years to resolve it.

Highlight: Fred noticing Angel's happiness and nudging him with a stake to make sure it's not *pure* happiness.

Mark Lutz Says: "There was talk about bringing the Groosalugg back at the end of season 5, but now that it's been canceled that was nixed. But I believe that he's like Cain, wandering the Earth, doing good, you know?"

David Denman Says: "I don't watch the show that often (I don't watch TV much at all), but I have this friend who's a total fanatic fan, so I'd call him every time I would do the show again and I'd go, 'Oh hey, what's goin' on?' and he'd say, 'Well, what are you doing?' and I'd say, 'Well, I don't know, I'm coming back and I have this scene with Cordelia' and he'd go, 'OH wow! Well, this is what's happening!' and would start telling me everything that had happened since I was last around. It was always very helpful.

"I find being unidentifiable outside the makeup to be a very good thing. I like to be as anonymous as possible. I'd rather not be recognized, because the moment you're recognized, you're 'that guy.' If they don't really know who you are, you can work in this town for a long time. The second they know what you do they either love it or you're typecast as 'Oh, that's what you do' and then all of a sudden they get bored with you and someone else comes along. I think the trick is to stay recognizable enough with casting directors that they know me and like me and like my work and will keep bringing me in, but if I get to a point where the public knows, it makes it a lot more difficult. But I've been lucky enough to play a variety of characters, so that's been good."

Did You Notice?: Skip says to Cordelia that deep down she knows she's ready to move on, and Groo points out that deep down Cordy's always known she's loved Angel. The theme of someone knowing something "deep down," even if they've never admitted it to themselves, will be the overriding theme of season 4, beginning with the first episode, appropriately titled "Deep Down."

Nitpicks: When the gang is at the drive-in, they're suddenly ambushed by helicopters, a Wolfram & Hart SWAT team, and other goons, and yet no one else in the entire drive-in seems to notice? You don't see cars squealing out of there in a panic or anyone else getting out of their cars to see what's going on. In a post-9/11 world, you'd think most people would be hightailing it out of there.

The Boy Ain't Right: When Connor fights Angel, the two seem evenly matched.

Wolfram & Hart: Lilah has clearly reported back to W&H on her discovery in the previous episode that Connor is alive, and the firm's associates come to the drive-in to kidnap him.

Season Four
October 2002 • May 2003

Recurring characters: Stephanie Romanov (Lilah Morgan), Daniel Dae Kim (Gavin Park), Vladimir Kulich (The Beast), Gina Torres (Jasmine)

4.1   Deep Down
Original air date: October 6, 2002
Written by: Steven S. DeKnight
Directed by: Terrence O'Hara
Guest cast: Laurel Holloman (Justine Cooper), John Rubinstein (Linwood Morrow), Noel Gugliemi (Driver Vamp), Rod Tate (Bruiser), Ingrid Sonray (Marissa)

With Cordelia still missing, Wesley searches for Angel while the gang tries to continue fighting baddies and dealing with a moody adolescent.

With last year's season ending on a cliffhanger, we fans were hoping "Deep Down" would answer a lot of questions — for us and for the characters. The episode gets the season off to a bit of a slow start, but it still shows how the characters have evolved (or devolved) over the summer. Angel has become hallucinatory, while trapped in his watery tomb, imagining what life *could* have been like if only he had met Cordelia at their appointed spot.

While Angel's in the deep, Wesley's gone off the deep end, sleeping with Lilah and keeping a human being locked in his closet, threatening, "I'll take away your bucket." He's no longer the awkward rogue demon hunter of season 1; he's tired of being the bumbler. At the beginning of season 5 on *Buffy*, Xander finally declared that he was sick of being everyone's butt monkey and things were going to change. But they didn't. He continued to be the butt monkey. Wesley, on the other hand, has made a conscious decision to change his life. His Angel Investigations "friends" might have turned him away, but he is intent on finding his boss no matter what it takes, even if he has to lower himself to the point of acting like the scum that he tries to eradicate. The way he talks to Justine (despite her deserving every word) is so unlike Wesley it's scary, but he's a new man. An unhappier man, but one who won't be as easily dismissed. The relationship between Wesley and Lilah seems to have deepened over the summer as well, and there actually seems to be an ounce of caring between them. Where before they just had sex, now they're kissing, which is a more personal gesture.

Fred and Gunn have their hands full trying to deal with Connor (a problematic teenager if ever there was one) and being the only remaining people at Angel Investigations. When they find out the truth about Angel, Fred's reaction is one of anger and betrayal, and Connor becomes the latest Angel Investigations expatriate. His behavior for the rest of the season will divide fans — is he nothing but a petulant child, or has he been wronged to such a horrific degree that his actions are understandable?

Highlight: Fred trying to use street slang and Gunn telling her she can't say "bro." "Can I say dawg?"

Interesting Facts: There's a sly in-joke in this episode when Linwood tells Lilah that the Special Projects Division at Wolfram & Hart is his corner of the sky. John Rubinstein, who plays Linwood, played the lead role in *Pippin* on Broadway in 1972. Pippin's signature song is "Corner of the Sky" (the original cast recording featuring John Rubinstein is still available).

Christian Kane Says: "When I was on the show I was talking to [David] Greenwalt and he would say, 'We might kill you . . . we might have Lilah come up and decapitate you' and it didn't happen to me . . . as far as I know it happened to somebody else. . . . But then again, you have to die to become a series regular on that show anyway. [Laughs]"

Did You Notice?: When Angel is underwater he pictures Gunn with a goatee, Connor with long hair, and Cordelia with chin-length brown hair, yet Gunn's chin was smooth, Connor had short spiky hair, and Cordy had short blond hair when Angel saw them all last. Also, in the dream sequence, Cordelia's wearing the same outfit she would have been wearing had they met, but he never actually saw her in it. Perhaps Cordy is sending him some of these visions from on high, where she can see these physical changes? Also, Angel throws Connor out of Angel Investigations the same way his own father had thrown him out of his house.

Nitpicks: Wesley has clearly spent all summer searching the ocean depths for Angel (and we later find out he's been trying to uncover the whereabouts of Cordelia), and when he shows up at the Hyperion with him and promptly leaves (as per Fred's original instructions, I might add), she snottily retorts, "You really don't care anymore, do you?" It's like the gang can't even hear themselves talk. Also, Gunn says they can't find Holtz or Holtz's "psycho girlfriend." How did he know Justine was involved again? As far as they knew at the end of season 3, Holtz was back but Justine was working only with Connor, and she would have been completely below their radar.

Oops: When Wesley pulls the cage up out of the water, we see the water drain out of it, proving it's not airtight (which makes sense, considering the lid slid on). Yet at one point Angel screams under the water and it sounds like he's in an empty room, not gargling, which is what he would have been doing.

The *Buffy* Connection: Angel says to Connor that being underwater for three months is nothing compared with being sent to Hell for 100 years by his girlfriend. This is a reference to the season-2 *Buffy* finale, "Becoming, Part Two," when Buffy is forced to send Angel to Hell in order to close a portal. Because time moves more quickly in Hell, he toils for 100 years despite reappearing in Sunnydale a few months later. There is some discrepancy, however, when Angel says in "Deep Down" that he was sent there for 100 years; the assertion on *Buffy* was that he had, in fact, been there for several centuries. Perhaps he's just remembering it differently or time moved a little more slowly in the particular demon dimension he was in.

The Boy Ain't Right: Gunn suggests that Connor might not be completely human. Considering he's the product of two vampires, has superhuman hearing, and seems to be able to withstand blows that would kill a normal person, the response to this suggestion might be, "Well, *duh*." We see Connor jump out a sixth-storey window and remain unharmed.

Wolfram & Hart: Linwood wonders if Lilah is sleeping with Wesley to get information from him. The Senior Partners *do* talk to the lawyers and apparently aren't happy that Linwood has gone against their agenda and wants Angel dead. They give Lilah some advice that makes her the official head honcho of Special Projects.

4.2   Ground State

Original air date: October 13, 2002
Written by: Mere Smith
Directed by: Michael Grossman
Guest cast: Alexa Davalos (Gwen Raiden), Rena Owen (Dinza), Tom Irwin (Elliot), Belinda Waymouth (Ms. Thorpe), Heidi Fecht (Mrs. Raiden), Michael Medico (Mr. Raiden), Jessica M. Kiper (Nick), Easton Gage (Young Boy), Megan Corletto (Young Gwen)

Angel tries to retrieve the Axis of Pythia in order to bring Cordelia back, but a woman with an electric touch is after the same thing.

While the introduction of Gwen Raiden is a little derivative, she is still an exciting character, and one that will surely be back. She's clearly modeled after Rogue from *X-Men* (she goes to a school for "special" children, she cannot make human contact without hurting people, and she develops a strange white patch of hair when she gets older) and dresses like Elektra from the *Daredevil* comic. But Alexa Davalos handles the character with a gravity that keeps her from being just another monster-of-the-week comic-book rip-off. She puts up a tough exterior, never gets close to anyone, and acts out of desperation and sadness. She immediately exhibits chemistry with all the characters, whether or not they like her.

Phantom Dennis makes his last "appearance" on the show (sniffle) and he clearly misses Cordelia and doesn't want the others to be messing with her stuff. Interestingly, they never return to give Dennis any updates later on (then again, he probably wouldn't want to hear what ultimately happens). Wesley has apparently begun his own more brutal and primitive version of Angel Investigations, and he and Angel have a serious talk about what happened last season. However, when Angel tells him they're okay again as far as he's concerned, the look on Wesley's face clearly indicates that things are not okay. It's going to take a lot more than a half-hearted "sorry about that" from Angel for Wesley to feel welcomed back into the fold. When he hands Angel a certain file, though, it's clear he still does care about the gang, despite what Fred may think.

One of the most intriguing moments of the episode occurs when Gwen touches Angel. In a very csi moment, the camera zooms into his chest to capture a miraculous event, one that's never mentioned again. Was the effect permanent or only temporary? It would appear to be the latter, and considering the last time he felt his heart beat, in "I Will Remember You," he immediately exclaimed, "I'm alive!," wouldn't this be a pretty big moment for Angel?

Highlight: Angel asking if he should send Dinza an unholy fruit basket.

Interesting Facts: Raiden is the Japanese god of thunder and lightning, often portrayed as a red demon with sharp claws. Also, the actress playing Dinza is Rena Owen, the acclaimed New Zealand Maori actress whose best-known performance is as the battered wife in the excellent but disturbing *Once Were Warriors*.

Did You Notice?: *Finally* someone makes a joke about how Angel is such a spot-on sketch artist (everyone on *Buffy* is as well). Also, no one seems to be worried about what happened to the Groosalugg (only Cordelia knows he's gone). They all go to Cordy's apartment, where he *should* be staying, but everyone just assumes it'll be empty. Perhaps he sent a postcard over the summer? "Greetings, fine warriors. Having a most delightful time. Thank you for wishing you were here."

Actress Rena Owen poses with a sculpture of Dinza, her unholy character in "Ground State."

Nitpicks: Why does Angel climb a ladder when in "Deep Down" we saw a vampire scale the side of a building like Spider-Man? Also, while Cordy's one-liner at the end of "Deep Down" was hilarious, ending this episode in exactly the same way is just repetitive.

Oops: In the scene where Gwen melts Elliot's watch, she has one glove off in order to do so. But one second later when she walks away from the table, both gloves are back on.

Wolfram & Hart: Lilah keeps an eye on Connor because she doesn't know why the Senior Partners haven't captured him yet.

4.3 The House Always Wins

Original air date: October 20, 2002
Written by: David Fury
Directed by: Marita Grabiak
Guest cast: Clayton Rohner (Lee DeMarco), Morocco Imari (Spencer), Jennifer Autry (Lornette #2), Matt Bushell (Security Guard #3), Tom Schmid (Well Dressed Man), Sven Holmberg (Delivery Guy), Brittany Ishibashi (Vivian), Diana Saunders (Bejeweled Woman), John Colella (Croupier), Rod Tate (Bruiser)

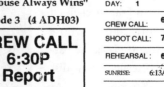

ANGEL

20th Century Fox Television
Paramount Studios

"The House Always Wins"

Episode 3 (4 ADH03)

CREW CALL
6:30P
Report

DATE:	Fri 08/16/2002
DAY: 1 OF 8 DAYS	
CREW CALL:	6:30P
SHOOT CALL:	7:30P
REHEARSAL:	6:30P
SUNRISE: 6:13A	SUNSET: 7:41P

Director:	**Marita Grabiak**

Exec. Prods: **Joss Whedon, Sandy Gallin, Gail Berman, Fran & Kaz Kuzui**

Supervising Producer: Jeffrey Bell	Producer: Kelly A. Manners	Latest Script Revision: Pink
Co-Prods.: **Skip Schoolnik, Steven S. DeKnight**	Consulting Producer: Tim Minear, David Fury, David Greenwalt	

SET	SCENES	CAST	D/N	PAGES	LOCATION
	·SHOOTING ORDER SUBJECT TO CHANGE·				
EXT. ROOFTOP	1pt, 2, 3pt,5,6pt,7	1,1X,4,5,6X,	N1	2 3/8	**740 S. Los**
Angel watches Connor fight w/ Gunn & Fred +(Cordy POV of Angel)		8,26			Angeles St.
· **Move to alleyway** ·					
EXT. ALLEYWAY-Burly Guy POV	4pt	1	N1	1/8	
POV of Angel on rooftop					
· **Burly Guy in Vamp** ·					
EXT. ALLEYWAY	4pt	6,6X,8,26	N1	5/8	
Connor does a dusting					
EXT. ALLEYWAY	1pt	6,6X,8,26	N1	3/8	
They fight					
· **Burly Guy Non-Vamp** ·					
EXT. ALLEYWAY	1pt	6,6X,8,26	N1	4/8	
Connor chases a burly guy					

> **There will be Digital Photos taken of Lorne at approximately 11A Friday at Paramount.**

		4	**TOTAL PAGES**

#	CAST & DAY PLAYERS		PART OF	P/U	M/U	REH.	SET	REMARKS
1	David Boreanaz	SW	ANGEL	-	6:15P	6:30P	7P	Report to make-up
4	J. August Richards	SW	GUNN	-	5:45P	6:30P	7P	Report to make-up
5	Amy Acker	SW	FRED	-	5:30P	6:30P	7P	Report to make-up
6	Vincent Karthheiser	SWF	CONNOR	-	12M	tbd	tbd	Report to make-up
7	Andy Hallett	SW	LORNE	-	8A	-	11A	Report to MU at Paramount
8	Matt Mc Colm	SWF	UTIL STUNT-Burly Guy	-	5:30P	6:30P	7P	Report to make-up
26	Mike Massa	SW	STUNT COORDINATOR	-	-	-	6:30P	
1X	Mike Massa	SWF	STUNT DBL-Angel	-	5:45P	6:30P	7P	Report to make-up
6X	Zack Hudson	SWF	STUNT DBL-Connor	-	5:45P	6:30P	7P	Report to make-up

The crew call report for one of the shooting days on "The House Always Wins." Notice how much longer Lorne is in makeup than the other characters.

(K)= Minor	NO FORCED CALLS	WITHOUT PRIOR APPROVAL OF PRODUCTION MANAGER		

ATMOSPHERE AND STAND-INS		SPECIAL INSTRUCTIONS			
1	Angel SI (Joel)	Rpt at 6:30P	**PROPS:** [1pt, 4pt] Stake		
1	Gunn SI (Thom)	Rpt at 6:30P	**CAMERA:** Steadicam, Hot Head		
1	Fred SI (Heidi)	Rpt at 6:30P	**SPECIAL EQUIPMENT:** Phoenix Crane, 1--Balloon Light, 1--80' Condor, 1--750 Towplant		
1	Connor SI (JT)	Rpt at 12M	**SPECIAL FX:** [4pt] Crashing mortar gag		
1	UTIL SI (Joe)	Rpt at 6:30P	**ADDL. LABOR:** 4--Addl. Lamp Ops, 4--Addl. Grips, 1--Lense Tech,		
			1--Hot Head Tech., 1--Balloon Tech		
			MU/HAIR: Lorne MU for Digital photos, [1pt,4pt] Vamp MU, blood, Bleeding arm wound		
			LENSES: [1pt,4pt] Burly Guy=Yellow Vampire		
			GRIPS: Phoenix Crane		
			ART DEPARTMENT: [1pt, 4pt] Graffitied Dumpster		
			VISUAL FX: [1pt] Dusting of Burly Guy		
			PICTURE VEHICLES: [1pt, 4pt] Junker car		
			TRANSPORTATION: Water truck, Picture vehicles see above		
			·No Meal Penalties w/out prior approval·ND Breakfast provided for early calls		
0	Tot. BG		THIS IS A CLOSED SET — NO VISITORS WITHOUT PRIOR APPROVAL		

ADVANCE SCHEDULE						
DATE	SET	SCENE	CAST	D/N	PAGES	LOC.
Monday 08/19/2002 Day 2	INT. BACKSTGE HALL-Post Show	12	1,4,5,7,11,12,13, 16,26, Atmos	N1	2 1/8	Stage 5
	INT. HALL-Outside Lorne's Room	A13	7,12,13,19, Atmos	N1	2/8	
	INT. HALL-Outside Lorne's Room	20	4,5,18,18X,19, Atmos	N1	5/8	
	Fred goes to into Lornette make-up					
	INT. HALL-Outside Lorne's Room	14	7,12,14, Atmos	N1	3/8	
	INT. HALL-Outside Lorne's Room	22	4,5,18,19	N1	1 3/8	
	INT. HALL-Outside Lorne's Room	25	4,5,7,18,19,26	N1	1 4/8	

UPM: Robert Nellans   Approved _RN_   Ass't. Directors: Ian Woolf, Rich T. Sickler, W. Scott Wolf, Michelene Mundo

The gang travels to Las Vegas to talk to Lorne and discovers that his new gig isn't as glamorous as they thought it was.

"The House Always Wins" is entertaining and has moments of excitement, but it is more of a throwaway episode meant to achieve certain ends plot-wise. The episode is more or less a vehicle for the writers to get two of the characters back into the series while still giving fans an entertaining hour.

Lorne's Las Vegas revue is filled with tacky fabulousness (including the horned, high-kicking "Lornettes") and leads to the main plot twist of the episode — that Lorne's destiny-reading ability is being abused by the hotel owner, who is forcing Lorne to trap people against their will. Cordelia comes into play in her own little way as she watches Angel and Connor at the beginning of the episode and tries to effect change from on high when Angel runs into trouble in Vegas. Her comments to Angel throughout are classic Cordy, and they make the ending of the show a surprising one. She also links the metaphor of the episode — that people who become addicted to gambling in casinos are throwing their lives away and becoming slot-machine zombies — to the main story. Cordelia's destiny has been chosen for her, even more so than it might seem at this point in the storyline, just as Lorne aids in helping people lose theirs.

While the show has its funny moments, it's more of a caper episode that lacks the depth of more serious and arc-driven *Angel* episodes.

Highlight: Angel hinting that two of the three members of the Blue Man Group are actually blue demons.

Interesting Facts: Benjamin "Bugsy" Siegel was one of the most ruthless killers in Mob history. He is known as the man who built Las Vegas as a gambling mecca, which is a bit of an exaggeration; he moved there shortly after World War II and realized that if gambling was legal in Nevada, the Mafia could make a lot of money off casinos there. He decided to build a lavish casino hotel called the Flamingo, and work began at the end of 1945 with the Mob investing the money to make it happen. A year later the casino had racked up costs in excess of $6 million (it was originally supposed to cost $1.2 million), and the Mob was not happy. When Siegel finally opened the hotel in 1947, it began losing more money, but it finally turned a profit later that year. It was too late, however, and on the evening of June 20, 1947, Bugsy Siegel was shot five times while sitting in his home. No one was ever charged with his murder, but it's generally assumed he was killed by someone seeking revenge for his having lost so much money.

The "Rat Pack" was the nickname given to Dean Martin, Frank Sinatra, Sammy Davis Jr., Peter Lawford, and Joey Bishop, and it became interlinked with Las Vegas. The quintet starred in the 1960 caper movie *Ocean's Eleven* (which was remade in 2001 with George Clooney and Brad Pitt) and they would film the movie during the day and perform at the Sands Hotel at night. The Rat Pack returned to the Sands in 1963 for a much-anticipated show, the recording of which is still available on CD.

Did You Notice?: In "The Shroud of Rahmon," Angel tells Cordy and Wesley about the Vegas vampire, "Jay-Don," mentioning that he ran with the Rat Pack and never quite got over it. Angel then says that he never actually met Jay-Don, and when he walks up to him, Jay-Don doesn't seem to recognize him. It seems strange that the Rat Pack had such a thing for vampires, yet Angel and Jay-Don never actually met.

Nitpicks: Angel, Gunn, and Fred leave L.A. at night and arrive in Las Vegas later that same night. The trip would be somewhere between four and five hours (and Fred and Gunn have clearly changed their clothes before leaving), and Lorne is the star attraction at the Tropicana, yet when they see him in what must be the wee hours of the morning, he says it's his first show of the night. Why would the hotel bury him in the program so late at night if it's put a huge marquee out front trumpeting that he's performing there? Also, Angel boasts that he played tennis with Bugsy Siegel (which must have been under floodlights at night, and considering Las Vegas was a desert at the time, it's a highly unlikely scenario), hung out with the Rat Pack, and crashed Elvis and Priscilla's wedding. But countless flashbacks throughout the 20th century have shown that Angel wasn't exactly a fun guy. Why is he suddenly a party animal?

Oops: Elvis and Priscilla's wedding reception was at the Aladdin Hotel in Las Vegas, not the Tropicana, so the room Angel is in at the Tropicana couldn't have possibly been the same one. Also, while the menu at the reception boasted food such as candied salmon, roasted suckling pig, lobster, and oysters Rockefeller, there were no peanut butter and banana sandwiches. Finally, Gunn refers to Angel's visit to Tibet, but it was actually Sri Lanka.

The Boy Ain't Right: The vampire fighting Connor at the beginning of the episode says that Connor moves too quickly to be human and asks him what he is. Connor says he doesn't know yet.

4.4   Slouching Toward Bethlehem

Original air date: October 27, 2002
Written by: Jeffrey Bell
Directed by: Skip Schoolnik
Guest cast: Thomas Crawford (Eater Demon), David Grant Wright (Minivan Dad), Carol Avery (Mom), Steven Mayhew (Minivan Teen), Nynno Ahli (Carlo)

Cordelia has returned with a bad case of amnesia, and Angel must convince her that she can trust all of them.

"Slouching Toward Bethlehem" gets its title from the William Butler Yeats poem, "The Second Coming." The terrifying and powerful poem was written in 1921, when many people of Yeats's generation were disillusioned by the destruction of World War I, and the opening stanza of the poem describes a world that has lost its innocence:

> Things fall apart; the centre cannot hold;
> Mere anarchy is loosed upon the world,
> The blood-dimmed tide is loosed, and everywhere
> The ceremony of innocence is drowned . . .

Within this terrible new world, the narrator speaks of a second coming, although rather than being Christ-like or a figure of salvation, the narrator believes this thing that is coming will be a horrible beast, one that will bring the ultimate apocalypse upon the Earth. He describes a creature that looks like a Sphinx — with the body of a lion and the head of a man — who is slowly creeping through the desert toward humankind. At one time the world had destroyed itself to such a point that Christians believe God sent His Son, Jesus, to save them, but now, in the wake of a war that devastated a generation, Yeats's narrator claims the only being that could come now would wreak more destruction upon the earth and destroy it once and for all:

> . . . but now I know
> That twenty centuries of stony sleep
> Were vexed to nightmare by a rocking cradle,
> And what rough beast, its hour come round at last,
> Slouches towards Bethlehem to be born?

The use of the birthplace of Christ indicates that this second coming will feature an Antichrist, a symbol of the new mystical, primal, non-Christian world. Many scholars have interpreted Yeats's poem as his belief that the world was moving away from Christianity and toward paganism (something that Yeats himself began studying around the time of the poem's publication).

The poem is evoked in the title of this episode because of what Lorne sees when he reads Cordelia. When he shakily tells Angel that evil is coming and it's planning to stay, the season finally gets started. Cordy is back, but she's . . . a little different, shall we say. Her complete amnesia might seem a little soap opera-ish at first, but what sets her experience apart from those plot lines is that while most amnesiac characters must adjust to family and friends, Cordelia must adjust to many worlds, several dimensions, creatures of all kinds, and her various lives (and haircuts).

Unfortunately, seeing all the crossbows, horned green demons, and crazy creatures chasing her through the Hyperion, she's not exactly comfortable and takes off with Connor. Her decision to trust this stranger over the people who seem to know her seems fishy, but we'll later discover why she did it. There's also something to be

ALBERT L. ORTEGA

Cordelia is back, but she's not the happy Cordy that we remember from previous seasons.

said for the fact that she trusts Connor because he tells the truth; everyone else lies to her or keeps things from her, which is typical of the Angel Investigations gang. As we learned last season, everyone on this show keeps secrets and ends up putting themselves and others in danger.

Wesley shows where his true loyalties lie, even if, once again, he makes a mistake and his friends pay the price. Wesley has definitely developed feelings for Lilah and is upset when she betrays him, but he had betrayed her, too. Their relationship is a mutually destructive one in which they both care about each other but are loyal to their companies and previous friendships, for which they will constantly betray one another. The episode ends with Angel staring at the bed where he had been with Cordelia and Connor at the end of "Provider." At that time Angel and Cordelia seemed like the happy parents of his baby boy, and now she has amnesia, his son is 17 and estranged, and Angel can only dream of what might have been.

Highlight: Cordelia seeing an old picture of herself with Monica Lewinsky hair and saying, "Yikes."

J. August Richards Says: "If I had to choose my favorite storyline, I liked it when Wesley and Lilah were sleeping together. I thought that was pretty cool; it was very inspired. I thought ironically they were really good together."

Nitpicks: If Lorne knew that his client ate people, why would he let it in the building with his human friends and not keep an eye on it? Also, Lorne's character has become pretty unnecessary on the show. Sadly, the writers can't seem to find anything useful for him to do anymore. He sits around in loud outfits and tosses out the occasional quip, but he's no longer the lovable and wonderful guy he was in season 2. As soon as he packed his bags and moved into the Hyperion, the character was doomed. It almost makes you wish the gang had left him in Las Vegas. Watch how many times this season (and next) he *almost* has a use (like reading Cordelia or listening in while Angelus is singing in his cage) and then the writers gloss over it or stage an event, making Lorne worthless again. It's a sad waste of a character, and why they chose to keep him around rather than just write him off is a mystery.

The *Buffy* Connection: Cordelia sings a botched version of "The Greatest Love of All," a song that we first suffered through in the season-1 episode "The Puppet Show," when she performed it for the school's talentless show. Also, all mentions of the Sunnydale high-school graduation (replete with its flaming arrows, giant snakes, and the school burning down) and the yearbook Cordy looks through are from the season-3 episode, "Graduation Day, Part Two."

The Boy Ain't Right: Connor scales the side of a building like the vampire in "Deep Down." Later, Angel enters Connor's apartment uninvited, which would suggest

Connor has demon in him (or perhaps because he's squatting Angel can enter; the rules about vampire entry have become pretty lax).

Wolfram & Hart: Two lawyers are outside the hotel, clearly casing Connor's movements, and the firm has a demon that can suck the thoughts out of someone's head.

4.5 Supersymmetry

Original air date: November 3, 2002
Written by: Elizabeth Craft and Sarah Fain
Directed by: Bill Norton
Guest cast: Randy Oglesby (Professor Oliver Seidel), Jerry Trainor (Jared), Jennifer Hipp (Laurie)

When Fred delivers a physics paper and almost gets pulled into another portal, she finally discovers the shocking truth about how she went through the other portal to Pylea.

As the title suggests, this episode is about symmetry, but not so much the scientific properties of it as the human ones. Are Gunn and Fred meant to be together? Or is she perhaps more suited to Wesley, the one who not only read but understood her complex physics article? Is Cordelia meant to be with Angel? Or will she end up with Connor (a possibility that definitely sent the "ick" factor soaring this season)? Throughout this episode the relationships of the key characters are tested, and there are few conclusions to be drawn. However, one thing is for certain: they won't be the same by the episode's end. "Supersymmetry" is a great episode that not only explores these emotions but also explains how Fred got to Pylea and examines the concepts of vengeance and mercy.

Connor and Cordelia get comfortable at his place, and her ease around him is still puzzling to viewers. In the previous episode Angel caught Cordelia up on what her life has been like, yet he strangely left out the most important part — Connor growing from a baby to 17 years old in a matter of weeks. When Connor insinuates to Angel that he and Cordelia have been getting a little closer, Angel expresses the same revulsion that many fans did at the thought of Connor falling in love with his mother figure.

Gunn proves that while he might not be one for reading lofty physics papers, he still has a big heart when it comes to Fred and the brawn to go after anyone who might be threatening her. But by the time the two discover who is guilty of trying to send Fred to another dimension, their emotions are running high. Fred has been hanging by a string for some time. In Pylea she was a rambling lunatic by the time Angel saved her, and once in her home dimension she stayed in her room for months, ate food with no cutlery, and hid in small places whenever she could. When her parents showed up she completely lost it, and then she worried excessively about Gunn's well-being at the ballet in "Waiting in the Wings" and had another mini-breakdown in "Ground State." It's not a surprise that she reacts to the new discovery in the way she does. When Gunn disagrees with her she turns to Wesley, who tells her what she wants to hear, making her the first person to reconnect with Wes since the Connor kidnapping incident.

Sadly, there is no right answer to the question of how Fred and Gunn can deal with this person. Gunn tells Fred not to seek revenge because it's not worth it. He could have offered her some words of support and maybe told her about how he felt when his sister was killed and how he was determined to make someone pay, but instead he gives her a figurative pat on the head and offers her some cocoa, like she's two years old. He realizes what a silly thing it was to say later, but it's too late. Gunn isn't strong when it comes to talking through a situation, and while he loves Fred with all his heart, sometimes a person needs more than that. Each ends up lying to the other, and the decision made at the end of the episode is a disturbing one that will have long-lasting effects on both of them — and their romantic symmetry.

Highlight: When Angel finds out that people talk about him in "the chatty rooms" online.

Interesting Facts: What I understand about physics could be written out on Fred's thumbnail, but supersymmetry is an actual physics concept involving string theory. It describes how microscopic particles that transmit a force relate to the particles that make up matter.

Nitpicks: Cordelia looked at the photo of Angel holding the baby in "Slouching Toward Bethlehem" and in this episode just accepts that the baby in the picture is suddenly 17, which doesn't make any sense on the purely literal level and is confusing — why didn't Angel explain everything about Connor? She also sees a picture of Fred and Gunn, taken at the opera. When was that picture taken? No one had a camera (they wouldn't have been allowed to take one into the theater), and they were too close to the balcony railing for a proper picture to be taken anyway. Also, Gunn tells Angel that they'll find the guy in the Thwack! T-shirt in a comic-book store, and they end up at the right one. There are so many comic-book stores in L.A. that they would have been looking for days, although we don't know how many they checked before finding the correct one. Speaking of which, this is the first time Gunn has even mentioned comic books on the show, yet he quotes from *Daredevil* like he's one of the Troika on *Buffy*. Wouldn't he have been full of references in "Ground State"? Finally, considering how hard the gravitational force of the portal is pulling on Seidel and his desk, why don't Gunn and Fred seem to be in danger of being sucked in, too?

Oops: Fred says she'll be appearing between two speakers, but she's the first one on the stage, with no one preceding her.

4.6   Spin the Bottle

Original air date: November 10, 2002
Written and directed by: Joss Whedon
Guest cast: Sven Holmberg (Delivery Guy), Kam Heskin (Lola)

When Lorne's memory spell goes awry, the entire gang loses their memories of the present and believes they're 17 again.

"Spin the Bottle" is the funniest episode of the season — one of the funniest ever, actually — and in the hands of the master, we wouldn't expect anything less. Joss Whedon is as adept a director as he is a storyteller, and the episode features some very funny and beautiful camera movements that draw us into the story. He also places an actual narrator at the center of the episode, something that the writers over on *Buffy* tried later that season for "Storyteller," with equal success.

The concept of the episode is borrowed from a season-6 episode of *Buffy the Vampire Slayer* titled "Tabula Rasa." In that episode, everyone's memories are wiped clean (through another memory spell that goes wrong) and they create their own personas to try to fight evil. This episode is different in that everyone's personalities remain the same, but they've reverted to their teenage selves. Before doing the spell, Angel refers to Cordelia as his dearest friend (but she can't remember anything), something is sparking between Wesley and Fred, Gunn and Fred are having problems, and Cordelia is growing increasingly frustrated by her ability to remember frivolous things but not anything that matters. Though these characters have worked together as a team before (if not now), this episode highlights why they just can't get along: because they come from different worlds. Gunn grew up in a different lifestyle, Fred is from a different state, Wesley is from a different country, Angel/Liam is from a different time period, and Cordelia is . . . just different. The spell they perform is a mystical form of spin the bottle, so it's no surprise that they all end up as teenagers.

The episode is perfect for letting Alexis Denisof show off his brilliant slapstick skills again ("Nobody scream . . . or touch my arms!"); for allowing Angel to be more of a humorous character ("You stopped the tiny men from singing!"); for revisiting the old Cordy that we know and love ("You two want to pause the homoerotic-buddy cop session long enough to explain this?"); and for seeing what Fred and Gunn were like at one time (pothead and high-school dropout, apparently). As all the characters instinctually regress to behaviors and attitudes typical of their younger years, their actions show clearly how much they have evolved. Wes is smart but awkward, has no confidence around women, and can't fight. Liam is cowering one minute and acting like Angelus the next. Cordelia is vacuous, mean-spirited, unsympathetic, and snobby. Gunn believes all demons are bad and has no tolerance for these people, who didn't grow up on the streets with him and clearly don't understand how bad things are. (We didn't know Fred before, but she's babbling and nerdy, the way she was when she returned from Pylea.)

Put in the same room, these 17-year-olds can barely tolerate each other for a few moments much less get a job done, but eventually, when the situation forces them to work together, they do. As a contrast, when Connor enters the scene as the only *actual* teenager, we discover just how similar he and his dad are: they both hate their fathers and wish they had never been born. These are two people who might have actually been friends had they known each other at the same age, but alas, at the end of the hour, the spell must wear off, and as in "Tabula Rasa," everyone is forced to face their own bitter realities and the realization that there's an apocalypse they need to fight.

Highlight: While there are countless comic highlights in this episode, the most memorable moment is a sad, poignant one. At the end of yet another argument with Wesley, Gunn asks, "What happened to you, man?" and without missing a beat, Wes turns and answers quite stonily, "I had my throat cut and all my friends abandoned me." Whoa.

Did You Notice?: In flashback episodes where we've seen Liam, he's been cocky, loud, and obnoxious, yet here he displays none of those characteristics and is innocent and almost sweet (of course, he is disconcerted by the time-period change). Perhaps he was quiet when he was 17, but by the time he was 26 (the age he is when he's turned into a vampire), something had happened along the way that made him a lout.

Nitpicks: Angel is freaked out by many miracles of modern science but seems to take the electricity in the hotel for granted. And why is Lorne unaffected by the memory spell?

Oops: Cordelia met Angel when she was 16, so she should have recognized him in this episode if they are 17, as Fred says they are.

The *Buffy* Connection: There are several references to earlier episodes of *Buffy*. When Cordelia "first" sees Angel, she says, "Hello, salty goodness," which is exactly the same thing she says when she sees him for the very first time way back in season 1 of *Buffy*, in "Never Kill a Boy on the First Date." Also, Wesley refers to a test where someone is locked in a house with a deadly demon, a test that Buffy undergoes in "Helpless." Finally, Fred refers to government tests where examinees are asked if they want to be florists. That's a reference to the *Buffy* episode "Doppelgängland," in which Buffy tells Willow that the Watcher's Council administers all sorts of tests to figure out if you're crazy, asking if you hear voices or ever wanted to be a florist.

4.7 Apocalypse, Nowish

Original air date: November 17, 2002
Written by: Steven S. DeKnight

Directed by: Vern Gillum
Guest cast: Tina Morasco (Mrs. Pritchard), Molly Weber (Waitress)

The Beast appears in L.A., and the gang knows they're in for one hell of a ride.

The end is near. Angel Investigations is receiving a record volume of strange phone calls from people suffering severe psychic phenomena. Birds are flying into windows in a scene that is like Alfred Hitchcock meets Paul Thomas Anderson. Fire is falling from the sky. And Lilah is ticked that someone else is muscling in on her apocalypse.

As Fred and Gunn deal with the fallout of what happened to them in "Supersymmetry," Cordelia begins having more destructive visions about something big that's coming. In a nod to the season premiere, Cordelia says that something from "deep down" is making its way back up. Connor is so worried about her that he actually lowers himself to appealing to Angel for help, but things have changed between Cordelia and Angel — when Cordy was a higher being, she received a visual on Angel as Angelus. No matter how many stories the group hears about what Angelus is like, nothing is like having it right there in front of you, re-enacted in Technicolor. Just think of how viewers felt seeing Angelus massacre Holtz's family. Angelus wasn't exactly a sympathetic character in *that* little play.

In the end, Angel won't be able to help Cordelia, and Cordelia won't be able to help anyone else. In a great fight sequence (*Matrix* rehash notwithstanding) where Wesley gives up on the medieval weaponry John Woo–style, the battle still amounts to nothing. There's a new Big Bad in town, and the gang is going to have to go a long way to fight it. But in the meantime, the whole Oedipal subplot is in full swing over at Connor's apartment. He's always wanted to kill his father, but now he . . . I can't even say it. What happens at the end of this episode is just painful for the eyes — and the brain. The writers took a big risk with this little twist, and it disgusted a lot of fans and tarnished the character of Cordelia Chase that Charisma Carpenter had worked so hard to establish.

Highlight: Lorne's *Jaws* reference when he sees the size of the Beast's activity area: "I'm gonna need a bigger arrow."

Stephanie Romanov Says: "I loved when I dressed up like Fred. That whole [puts on a Texan accent] 'Hey!' I just thought it was so cheeky, and so kind of bold of her to just do something like that. That was fun, but then the moment after when they're gettin' down and she goes to take off her glasses and he says, 'No, leave them on,' the pain of that moment was just heartbreaking. It was wild; I really liked that scene."

Did You Notice?: From this point on Charisma Carpenter will be shot from the chest up or will have her midriff obscured in various ways as the directors try to cover up her real-life pregnancy. In this episode she wraps herself in blankets (although in the scenes where we see her walking around it didn't appear that she needed to quite yet).

Nitpicks: While I appreciate that every writer and director on *Angel* seems to be a big fan of *The Matrix*, the constant "homages" are tiresome. Why not brand your own unique directing style rather than stealing someone else's?

Oops: Several times during the battle with the Beast, you see Boreanaz's stunt double instead of him.

The *Buffy* Connection: While this episode was airing on *Angel*, over on *Buffy* the characters were discovering that something apocalyptic was happening as well and kept receiving the cryptic message "From beneath you it devours," just as Cordelia is saying that something from deep down is clawing its way up. Also, Cordelia's eyes go white at one point and she has a vision of the Beast coming immediately. On *Buffy*, living characters who were being taken over by the First had similar white eyes, leading some fans of both shows to speculate that the Big Bad might be doing a crossover.

The Boy Ain't Right: Cordelia wonders if Connor's ability to sneak up on people unheard is genetic. The Beast rises up out of the very spot in the alleyway where Connor was born.

Wolfram & Hart: The firm has removed information from Lorne's head and somehow translated it onto paper. Despite the attempts of several psychics to decipher it, they haven't made any progress because every time they get close, their heads explode.

4.8   Habeas Corpses

Original air date: January 15, 2003
Written by: Jeffrey Bell
Directed by: Skip Schoolnik
Guest cast: Kay Panabaker (Little Girl)

When Connor is held captive by the Beast at Wolfram & Hart, the gang must try to find a way to save him.

Several relationship changes take place in "Habeas Corpses," some subtle, some obvious. Wesley makes a decision about his tryst with Lilah. For once Lilah actually shows some concern about him; the relieved look on her face upon seeing him after the rain of fire speaks volumes. But it's too little too late. She's realized she loves him, but he's realized once and for all that he can't be with her because of what she represents. He's fighting with the good guys and believes the Beast is giving him a choice, and he chooses to stop cavorting with the enemy. While Wesley has made the right decision, we actually feel sorry for Lilah for once. Her speech about black-and-white morality is one of the best of the series, and it applies to just about every character.

Vladimir Kulich plays the Beast, a demon who threatens to unleash hell on earth unless Angel and the gang can stop him.

She explains to Wesley the problem with black and white: when you mix the two you get gray, and no matter how much white you try to put back in, it'll always be gray. It's why Angel will never escape Angelus, Gunn now has Professor Seidel's murder hanging over his head, and Wesley will always be reminded of what he did to Connor.

The one who reminds Wesley the most about his past transgression is Gunn, and at points Gunn's behavior borders on annoying. Gunn used to be someone who had a fair sense of right and wrong, and he treated people with respect if they deserved it and like dirt if they didn't. But lately every word that comes out of his mouth is brutal, and he's constantly angry with Wesley because he believes he's losing Fred (and blames Wesley) and he's still upset about Connor. Regarding the latter, however, the only person who needs to forgive Wesley is Angel, and he has. The old Gunn would have forgiven Wesley after he saved Fred's life in "The Price," but we must remember that Gunn never forgives himself, and he rarely forgives others. It's too bad he's forgotten how much "white" Wesley has put back into his gray mix: he saved Gunn's life in "The Thin Dead Line" by taking a bullet for him; he saved Fred; and he pulled Angel out of the ocean in "Deep Down." Though we can see where Gunn is coming from, Angel pretty much speaks for all of us when he finally tells Gunn to shut up.

Cordelia tells Connor that what happened in the previous episode was a one-off thing and cannot happen again, but what she doesn't know is that Angel was being a bit of a voyeur that night. Judgement Day has arrived for many of the characters, and the Beast will be either the catalyst that forces people to change, or the judge that decides their fates. As it stomps its way into Wolfram & Hart and begins the lawyerly slaughter, however, we can't help but wonder — can the Beast be *all* bad?

Highlight: Lorne calling the rain of fire a "Cirque du Flambé."

Interesting Facts: The term *habeas corpus* is Latin and literally translates to "you must have the body." It is used in law to describe a writ that requires prisoners to be brought before a judge to determine if they are being held lawfully.

Stephanie Romanov Says: "When you're an actor playing a character you don't think things will come up and surprise you, but with that whole storyline with Wesley, I felt like they actually reached a point of really caring for each other. I just thought, *I'll play it like she wants something from him; she's never going to go to the good side — it's business.* And then I found that it wasn't, but it happened quite naturally; it was quite interesting. I do think that she loved him, and I think he surprisingly brought her back to a more tender part of herself, which came out unexpectedly. It was really kind of cool playing that, I have to say. She always knew they couldn't be together unless she could drag him over to her side, but when he left there was jealousy and a lot of hurt."

Did You Notice?: Angel says he has a photographic memory, which would explain why he can remember everything he's done as Angelus in such detail.

Nitpicks: Ignoring that Angel is in a very bad mood, wouldn't everyone question his logic of leaving Cordelia behind when going to save Connor (Cordelia, the one who is the trained fighter and has the strength to back him up) and instead taking Fred (Fred, the one who looks like she'd snap like a twig if she turned too suddenly)?

Oops: Angel pushes the buttons on the elevator and then clears them to try again. How did he do that? Elevators don't have clear buttons like calculators do.

The Boy Ain't Right: The Beast immediately knows Connor's name when he confronts it in Wolfram & Hart. Connor is buried under rocks but somehow survives intact.

Wolfram & Hart: Gavin is officially afraid of Lilah and is pandering to her every need. The L.A. office is annihilated.

4.9   Long Day's Journey

Original air date: January 22, 2003
Written by: Mere Smith
Directed by: Terrence O'Hara

Guest cast: Alexa Davalos (Gwen Raiden), Jack Kehler (Manny), Michael Chinyamurindi (Ashet)

The gang learns about the RaTet, an ancient quintet of beings that the Beast is hunting down, and they wonder why the Beast is targeting these entities specifically.

"Long Day's Journey" is an episode that *finally* sheds some light on what's been going on this season. The RaTet is named after Ra, the Egyptian sun god. The ancient Egyptians believed that Ra was the creator of the universe, but he never quite lived in harmony with the world around him. He first appeared as the sun and created moisture and air. From his tears he then formed land, on which he put humankind, and every night he was swallowed by a serpent (therefore nighttime has no sun), who also created clouds to try to hide him during the day. Eventually Ra grew old and Isis overpowered him when she tricked him into telling her his real name (see "Peace Out"). In time, Ra left the world, but he still sailed his boat across the sky during the day to give the people the sun, and at night he was swallowed by the serpent and traveled to the underworld to be worshiped by the dead. He is often depicted with the head of a ram; hence the Beast's appearance.

In this episode, Gwen Raiden is back, and Wes discovers the existence of the RaTet, a group of five entities, each of which possesses a certain essence the Beast wants. Manny seems like a good guy, but at least two of the others seem evil (and one works at Wolfram & Hart). Just as the RaTet is a quintet that is being dismantled, so too is Angel Investigations a group of five that is falling apart (Angel, Wesley, Fred, Gunn, and Cordelia — Lorne's never really been part of the core team). While the RaTet members are being taken out one by one, the fang gang is crumbling as the friends alienate themselves from one another. Angel is *very* angry with Connor and Cordelia, and he tells Cordy to stop pretending to give a damn, to which she replies, "Get over it." Her words might sound harsh, but Angel is losing sight of the mission again, something that happened in season 2, and Cordy knows better than anyone what happened as a result. Lately Connor has been reaching out to Angel, and Angel doesn't even seem to notice because of his own pain. Fred is still being cold to Gunn, who hates Wesley.

If the Beast can put the pieces together, what it will create will destroy the world slowly and painfully. Cordelia finally has a vision that suggests only one creature can stop the Beast — a creature that fans have been waiting for since the beginning of the series.

Highlight: Manny's profound words to the gang, telling them the Beast will "blot out the sun for all of eternity. [Pause] You guys got a john?"
Interesting Facts: Someone on the writing staff definitely knows literature. The title

of the episode is taken from the Eugene O'Neill play *Long Day's Journey into Night*, about a family breaking down. Also, this episode sadly acknowledges the death of Glenn Quinn, who had played Doyle in season 1. Quinn died on December 2, 2002. He had had a long battle with drug and alcohol abuse and is believed to have died of a heart attack at the age of 32, although the family kept private the details of his passing other than to say he did not take his own life.

Did You Notice?: The Beast is putting its hand into the members of the RaTet to find their "toy surprises," and apparently it thought Lilah was a member, since that's exactly what it did to her in "Habeas Corpses."

Nitpicks: The RaTet members have existed around the world at various points and when they find out the Beast is in L.A. . . . they all go there? Why? To make their deaths that much quicker? Also, Fred opens a portal within seconds in "Supersymmetry," yet Fred and Wesley seem to be chanting a long time before one opens here. And Gwen knocks over the assembled totems that the Beast has set up, but later, during the fight, they're intact again. Did Angel stand back and let the Beast reassemble them?

Oops: When the sun goes out we see a sunset, but if the sun had been blotted out it wouldn't have actually set, and there wouldn't have been a dark sky with a lighter horizon.

The Boy Ain't Right: Connor wonders aloud how he got his superhearing, super-strength, and superspeed. He also survives a fall from a very high window.

4.10   Awakening

Original air date: January 29, 2003
Written by: David Fury and Steven S. DeKnight
Directed by: James A. Contner
Guest cast: Roger Yuan (Wo-Pang), Larry McCormick (Himself)

Angel decides to bring forth Angelus, but the spell goes awry and the gang has to come up with a new plan.

"Awakening" is a fun episode full of twists and turns that recalls the opening scene of "Deep Down." After Cordelia uses reverse psychology on Angel to convince him to become Angelus (you'd think Angel would see right through her plan but he doesn't appear to), Wesley fetches a shaman to extract Angel's soul and bring forth one of the worst vampires that ever existed. Interestingly, while Wesley has definitely seemed like the wronged one this season, he doesn't hesitate to rush off to find a shaman despite the protests of everyone else (including Angel), as if he didn't learn anything from the *last* time he rushed off to do something on his own. But in the end it's an Angelus-less event, and everyone has to band together to come up with a plan B.

One thing this episode shows is how Angel's priorities have changed since he was in Sunnydale. At that time, it took having an intimate moment with the one woman he loved more than anyone to bring about his moment of true happiness and, subsequently, Angelus. But now his life seems far more complicated. Wesley doesn't trust him anymore and despite what Angel might say, he's not sure he can trust Wesley. Cordelia, the woman he is now in love with, has slept with his son. Connor hates him and wants him dead (well, *more* dead than he is). And there's a big, rocky Beast walking the streets of Los Angeles, and it has just blotted out the sun. If Angelus can be brought forth only by a moment of true happiness, a lot of threads would have to be neatly tied up before that could happen. Many wrongs would have to be righted, many friendships healed, and an apocalypse thwarted.

But the mind is a dangerous thing, and happiness is subjective. Six years ago Angel turned into Buffy's worst nightmare after he realized that they were soul mates and she was a person he could be truly happy with. Now it'll take a little more creativity and work, but there's still a chance that he could be convinced he is happy. After all, he believed it when he was trapped underneath the ocean.

Highlight: The ending, and the delicious sound of that evil laugh.
Interesting Facts: Larry McCormick is an actual anchor at KTLA, the Los Angeles WB station that airs *Angel*.
Did You Notice?: The blotted-out sun is an image that is very similar to a symbol the gang will discover at the end of season 5.
Nitpicks: When Wesley apologizes to Angel for bringing the shaman to him, Angel retorts that it's the first time Wesley has ever apologized for anything. Yet Wesley used to apologize for *everything*, even if he happened to be breathing in the same room as someone else. His tough, unapologetic exterior is a more recent development. Also, after Wesley's hand is run through with a knife of some kind, wouldn't Angel have picked up a rock to push the remaining letters? Finally, while Cordy's presence in the cave is necessary for events to take place, wouldn't it have made more sense for Angel to have taken Gunn, especially since they need brute strength and in the previous episode he wouldn't allow Cordy to accompany him at all?
The *Buffy* Connection: If you listen carefully, right before Angel rolls off Cordy he says, "Buffy?"

4.11   Soulless

Original air date: February 5, 2003
Written by: Sarah Fain and Elizabeth Craft
Directed by: Sean Astin

Angelus is back, and Cordelia wants answers about his former relationship with the Beast.

He's ba-ack. Ever since *Angel* began in 1999, fans have wondered when Angelus would return. We've been taunted with it — in "Eternity" there was an Angelus moment, and there have been several references to the evil that exists within Angel at all times — but he's never made a permanent reappearance. Until now. However, he's different; this is not the Angelus of season 2 of *Buffy*, folks. This guy is the more crass, adult version of Angelus, full of smutty remarks and literary references. And while he has his moments, he just isn't as amusing as the original Angelus was.

As all the characters have been warned, Angelus immediately begins

ALBERT L. ORTEGA

Angelus has finally returned, but will he be able to provide the gang with the help they need?

to dig away at their insecurities (and he's returned at a prime moment to do so). He taunts Gunn about how Fred is more suited to Wesley. He reminds Wesley about all his failures. He reveals to everyone that Cordelia slept with Connor. And worst of all, he tells Connor *exactly* what Connor has been waiting to hear — that he doesn't care about him, that Angel doesn't care about him, and that Darla and Holtz never loved him, either. Connor, who has become more and more annoying with every episode (his whining is becoming almost unbearable), is nonetheless an angry, confused teenager who's been raised like an animal, and his primal hatred for Angel can finally come to the fore when he's faced with his most hated enemy. Just as Holtz couldn't kill Angel last season when he realized he had a soul, so too has Connor been held back from true revenge by realizing that Angel isn't the person he's been trained to hate. He is a "good guy" with plenty of friends and loyal companions, not the evil, sadistic vampire that massacred Holtz's family. But now he *is* that vampire, and Connor revels in the possibility that he might be able to fulfill the mission Holtz couldn't.

After hearing plenty of Angelus's references to Shakespeare (comparing Gunn and Fred to Othello and Desdemona), Yeats, and Oedipus, the gang has finally had its fill, and so have we. While the prospect of getting Angelus back was exciting, the result is a little disappointing. Gone is the clever, biting Angelus who could fell Buffy's confidence with one glance, and in his place is this lesser version, who makes references to sex and masturbation. Of course, part of the problem is that he's locked in a cage, and it's hard to be witty and superior when everyone else is roaming free while you're imprisoned. In Sunnydale he was gleefully wicked because he could create fear; now he can only feed on everyone's doubt and paranoia. Because of *Buffy*'s younger demographic, the writers had to keep Angelus's barbs a lot cleaner, and it's too bad they had to change that here. David Boreanaz has proven he is brilliant as Angelus, but we'll have to wait until the next episode to see the true re-emergence of Angel's dark side.

Highlight: Angelus asking Cordy if she brought him back a stray baby toe from the Svear slaughter.

Interesting Facts: Although at one time he was best known as the son of Patty Duke and John Astin (who played Gomez on television's *The Addams Family*), the director of this episode, Sean Astin, has since made a name for himself starring as the heroic Samwise Gamgee in the most successful movie trilogy of all time, Peter Jackson's *The Lord of the Rings*. He had known David Greenwalt ahead of time and shadowed him on the set for a few weeks during season 3 to watch how things were done. "As a director, when you're working with David, and he's into Angelus, he's got so many layers and so many different shades and qualities, you want to keep exploring them and mining them and pulling them out," Astin said at the time. "It's such a rich, meaty character for him to do."

Also, Angelus saying that Wesley lives in the "foul rag-and-bone shop of the heart" is a line from Yeats's poem "The Circus Animals' Desertion," in which the poet laments that he's gotten older, is a broken man psychologically, and can no longer rely on his intellect.

Did You Notice?: Before, Connor would only call his father "Angelus," and now he insists on "Angel," as if always reminding his father that the other half of himself is in there.

Nitpicks: In the previous episode, the monk was still in the cage with Angel when he turned into Angelus, and Angelus was strapped to a steel table. But by the beginning of "Soulless" Angelus is wandering around in the cage and the monk and table are gone — how was he able to open the cage door without Angelus getting free? Also, at one point Angelus sings "Teddy Bear's Picnic," which would have been a perfect opportunity for Lorne to read him and possibly get the information about the Beast the gang is looking for, but Lorne does nothing and just says that they don't want to know what Angel's thinking, which is an opportunity wasted. And Wesley says that he's waited a long time to meet Angelus, but he's already seen a rather authentic version of him in "Eternity." Finally, Wesley cleverly stabilizes Angelus with tranquilizer darts, making me wonder why the Scooby gang never thought of something as rudimentary as that in season 2 on *Buffy*.

4.12   Calvary

Original air date: February 12, 2003
Written by: Jeffrey Bell, Steven S. DeKnight, and Mere Smith
Directed by: Bill Norton
Guest cast: Roger Yuan (Wo-Pang)

When Angel's soul goes AWOL, *the gang is forced to try a spell to restore it.*

Ah, now *this* is the Angelus we know and love. David Boreanaz is finally allowed to play Angelus to the fullest, and the vampire sits back and revels in the messes he's created in everyone's relationships. With the exception of his transgression at the beginning of the episode (where he disgustingly threatens to rape Fred to death), Angelus is much funnier and a lot more exciting to watch. And the end of the episode is reminiscent of Angelus rampaging through Sunnydale in season 2 of *Buffy* — you never know what will happen next.

Interestingly, Angelus acts as a much-needed catalyst in the romantic love triangle between Fred, Gunn, and Wesley. Despite the lack of chemistry between Fred and Gunn, what they went through together in "Supersymmetry" was no doubt going to tarnish their relationship forever. Romantics often say that "opposites attract," but Fred and Gunn had nothing in common but a physical attraction. We rarely saw them discuss anything besides work and how much they loved one another, and that can only last so long before the honeymoon is over and you're stuck staring at a wall with nothing to say. Wesley, on the other hand, respects Fred's brain, believes she's a beautiful woman, and has a lot in common with her. Like Fred he's been through hell, and his knowledge can probably help him imagine a little more clearly what Pylea must have been like for her.

Unfortunately, there's the matter of the little tryst with Lilah, and Angelus doesn't fail to mention that one to Fred. Lilah and Wesley meet in the sewers, and Wesley brings her back to the Hyperion to try to help her.

Cordelia has been getting stranger and stranger as the episodes go on. When you think back to "Long Day's Journey," it was Cordelia who first suggested that Angelus was necessary, and she's the only one with proof that he met with the Beast. Then she backhandedly convinced Angel to give up his soul to help the gang, and she seems to be rather unharmed emotionally by all of Angelus's taunting (that said, she *is* the only one who has previously encountered Angelus in the flesh). In this episode, when Angel is back and saying that he should stay in the cage for everyone's good, she is the one who mocks him for being cowardly and opens the door. What happens at the end of the episode is a shock for its suddenness and graphic nature, but it's not exactly surprising in the greater scheme of things.

Highlight: Lilah joking about becoming one of the good guys: "Well then braid my hair and call me Pollyanna!"

Nitpicks: Wesley says that Angel's mind has been wiped clean, just like the books in this dimension, which would explain why he doesn't remember where he met the Beast. However, Angelus and Angel have the same memories, so why does Angelus remember it? Angelus isn't in another dimension — he's in the same one as everyone else. Fred explains that Angelus's mind "wasn't here" when it happened, but he and Angel share the same mind (which is why they share the same memories), so that explanation doesn't work.

Oops: Lilah says at one point that nothing can save Angel, not even the 42nd "cavalry." Her comment points out a fundamental mistake in the title: the episode should have been called "Cavalry," not "Calvary." Calvary is the hill upon which Jesus Christ was crucified, but that reference has no place in this episode, no matter how you try to twist it.

The *Buffy* Connection: Fred mentions the Orb of Thessulah, which is what Willow used in "Becoming, Part Two" to re-ensoul Angelus (see "Orpheus").

Wolfram & Hart: Lilah knows how to get items on the pan-dimensional black market.

4.13 Salvage

Original air date: March 5, 2003
Written by: David Fury
Directed by: Jefferson Kibbee
Guest cast: Eliza Dushku (Faith), Kara Holden (Young Woman), Billy Rieck (Paco Vamp), Joel David Moore (Karl Vamp), Alonzo Bodden (Prison Guard), Joshua Grenrock (Demon in Bar), Addie Daddio (Rosaria Vamp), Brett Wagner (Bong'dar Demon), Spice Williams (Debbie)

With Angelus loose, the gang has more than just the Beast to deal with, and Wesley decides to get the one person who might help them — a Slayer.

While "Salvage" is a strongly written episode and features some great moments, the overall arc of the season is a little disappointing, mainly for the way it changes the character of Cordelia. First we had to watch her in bed with Connor (ick). Then we watched her spear Lilah in the neck. And now we have to suffer through her necking with the Beast and saying, "Give mama some sugar," which is just degrading. And it doesn't stop there; what she pulls next will trump all the other embarrassments that preceded it. It seems the writers of *Buffy* and *Angel* have a serious problem with their fourth seasons. Both shows had some of their best moments in their fourth years, but both had bumpy overall arcs, questionable Big Bads, and character directions we'd rather not have seen.

Despite the Cordelia material, this episode has some wonderfully funny and wonderfully painful moments. Angelus goes to a demon bar and the experience is like David Boreanaz walking into a fan convention: "Could you sign something for my hellspawn?" Los Angeles has turned into a demon playground, but while that could have been a lot of fun for Angelus, we're reminded that what he loves most about being a vampire is the challenge of killing people. When Jenny ran away from him in "Passion," it excited him, and he said, "Oh good, I need to work up an appetite first." Now it's too easy, and he's not having any fun.

The best part of the episode, however, is Wesley. First he has to face the daunting task of decapitating his now-dead former lover, and the scenes where he imagines himself talking to her are quiet and touching. Did she really love him? Did he love her? He'll never know, but there was definitely tenderness between them, and he brought out the little good that was left in her. She brings up the season's recurring theme of "deep down" when she tells him that deep down he always wanted her dead, but it doesn't undercut the pain he's feeling.

Once he finishes the task at hand, he turns to the bigger one — retrieving Faith. Having Eliza Dushku back in the Whedonverse is a breath of fresh air. Faith has always been a fantastic character, and Dushku plays her to the hilt (the scene where Wesley catches her up on what she's missed is very funny and is a parody of what would happen if a fan tuned in now after missing seasons 2 and 3 — it also suggests that Angel didn't keep up his regular visits with her). Whether she's fighting vamps, giving Connor a much, *much*-needed scolding, or confessing that she won't kill Angelus no matter what, she turns in a fine performance in every scene. Faith brought out a lot of humanity in Angel, and he's never turned his back on her since season 1, so Angelus will *really* hate her.

Highlight: Angel calling Dawn when he hears a Slayer's in town, and Dawn telling him Buffy's at home. "It's the other one," he says disappointedly as he hangs up.
Did You Notice?: This episode marks the first time Connor complains about magick, something that seems to come out of the blue but will be a major pet peeve of his from this point on.

Nitpicks: While Faith is a Slayer and can withstand a lot of pain, there's no way Wesley would have made that jump out the window without some serious consequences. Also, Angelus meets "Rosaria" in a bar and she reminisces about their time together in Italy and tells him she just flew in, yet she has an American accent, not an Italian one. It would be understandable if, like Angel, she'd been living in the U.S. for over a century, but she made it sound like she was still living in Italy. And, by the way, how did she survive a flight with the sun shining through the airplane windows? Did she travel via cargo?

The _Buffy_ Connection: The knife that the inmate uses to attack Faith is a Bringer's knife. The Bringers are the First's minions over on _Buffy_ in season 7, and they are systematically killing all Slayers. Since they couldn't get into the prison, they've obviously paid the inmate to do the job for them.

The Boy Ain't Right: Faith fights Connor and says, "I get it, you're a superhero." Also, when Gunn, Fred, and Lorne stand in the sun and revel in its return, Connor walks past them and admires it from the shadows, as if the sun bothers him.

4.14   Release

Original air date: March 12, 2003
Written by: Steven S. DeKnight, Elizabeth Craft, and Sarah Fain
Directed by: James A. Contner
Guest cast: Christopher Neiman (Froter Demon), Eliza Dushku (Faith), Darren Laverey (Lackey Vamp #1), Sam Stefanski (Lackey Vamp #2), Catalina Larranaga (Vamp Waitress), Peter Renaday (Master's Voice), Becka Linder (Drugged Girl #1), Chris Huse (Drugged Vamp #2), Ian Anthony Dale (Drugged Vamp #3), Randall Rapstine (Reg), Andrew McGinnis (Mullet Head Vamp)

Wesley and Gunn continue their search for Angelus while Connor tries to deal with Cordelia's shocking revelation.

"Release" is an apt title for this episode because it's something several of the characters are seeking. Angelus wants to be released from his soul and from the annoying goodness of Angel. Gunn and Fred are gradually releasing themselves from their relationship. Cordelia has told Connor she's pregnant, and what she will eventually release we can only imagine. And Faith must find a release within herself if she is to fight Angelus effectively.

Fred and Gunn take a good look at their relationship and the kiss that happened between Fred and Wesley in "Soulless." Life has become so complicated for both of them and they wish they could go back to when life was simpler, when they were fighting the weekly baddies side-by-side, sharing a bed at night, and being too much in love to notice they had nothing else in common. But when Gunn kisses Fred, it's in that moment of intimacy that both realize things have irrevocably changed between them. They can't go back to being Gunn and Fred. The world has changed, circumstances have changed, and their feelings for each other have changed. Ironically, it's in this moment of realization between them that we feel on-screen chemistry between J. August Richards and Amy Acker for the first time.

Cordelia has begun contacting Angelus through telepathy, and the scenes of him going crazy with her bellowing in his head add humor to an otherwise dark episode. The voice of the "Beastmaster," as Angelus keeps calling her, is rather stereotypical of horror films and over-the-top (as Angel later says), and she has that little problem of people wandering into the room while she's trying to contact him, but her threats and constant badgering eventually break him down.

Faith is back, and now it's time for her to help Angel the way he saved her in season 1.

Wesley is trying to do the opposite with Faith. She's back, she's strong, but whereas before she could fight without any emotion, now she's so filled with remorse and caring that she can't fight Angelus effectively. The scene at the beginning of the episode, of her beaten and bloody, stepping into a shower to wash away the signs of her failure, is a gruesome but poignant one, showing that she still has the anger in her, but it needs to come out. Where other criminals might find that being in a penitentiary has deadened their emotions, Faith has had time to reflect on what she's done, and she's discovered an emotional kinship with Angel that prevents her from being able to attack Angelus. Wesley finally becomes Faith's Watcher after having failed before, and he must help her find that primal anger within herself and use it when it's most needed. But Angelus has a few tricks up his sleeve, too.

Highlight: The demon in the bar taunting Angel for bringing the sun back, and then immediately backpedaling and blaming the comment on Tourette's.

20th Century Fox Television
Paramount Studios

ANGEL

"Release"

Episode 14   (4 ADH14)

CREW CALL
1:30P
Report

DATE:	Wed 01/15/2003
DAY: **8**	OF **8** DAYS
CREW CALL:	**1:30P**
SHOOT CALL:	**2:30P**
REHEARSAL :	**1:30P**
SUNRISE: 6:58 A	SUNSET: 4:57 P

Director: **James A. Contner**

Exec. Prods: **Joss Whedon, Sandy Gallin, Gail Berman, Fran & Kaz Kuzul**   65

Co-Executive Producer: Jeffrey Bell	Producer: Kelly A. Manners	Latest Script Revision: Green
Co-Prods.: Skip Schoolnik, Steven S. DeKnight	Consulting Producer: Tim Minear, David Fury, David Greenwalt	

SET	SCENES	CAST	D/N	PAGES	LOCATION
	· SHOOTING ORDER SUBJECT TO CHANGE ·				
INT. OCCULT SHOP-Reading Area	21 pt	1,13,17,25	N1	2 2/8	Los Altos
Angelus hears from the Master again; he is threatened w/ his soul					Apartments
					Mid-Wilshire

· *Move outside to front Courtyard* ·
· *We will shoot directionally---please be prepared to shoot Sc. 15 and 17* ·

EXT. ANGEL'S HOTEL-Courtyard	15	1,1X,3,3X,8,	N1	1 2/8	
Angelus faces Wes and Faith..."Let the games begin"		8X,25			
EXT. ANGEL'S HOTEL-Courtyard	17	1,1X,3,3X,4,	N1	1	
Faith does not sacrifice Wesley's life to capture Angelus;		4X,8,23,24,25			
Angelus escapes					

• Entertainment Weekly will be on set today doing Cast Interviews •

| | | | | | 4 4/8 | TOTAL PAGES |

#	CAST & DAY PLAYERS		PART OF	P/U	M/U	REH.	SET	REMARKS
1	David Boreanaz	WF	ANGEL	-	1:15P	1:30P	2P	Report to make up
3	Alexis Denisof	WF	WESLEY	-	4:15P	4:30P	5:30P	Report to make up
4	J August Richards	WF	GUNN	-	5:30P	tbd	tbd	Rehearse then make up
8	Eliza Dushku	WF	FAITH	-	3:45P	4:30P	5:30P	Report to make up
13	Peter Reneday	WF	MASTER'S VOICE	-	-	1:30P	2P	
17	Randall Rapstine	SWF	Reg (Occult Bookman)	-	12:45P	1:30P	2P	Report to make up
23	Nick Brandon	SWF	UTIL STUNT-Rigger 1	-	-	-	7P	
24	Clark Tucker	SWF	UTIL STUNT-Rigger 2	-	-	-	7P	
25	Mike Massa	WF	STUNT COORDINATOR	-	-	-	1:30P	
1X	Mike Massa	SWF	STUNT DBL-Angel	-	4:15P	4:30P	5:30P	Rehearse then make up
3X	Mike Gaines	SWF	STUNT DBL-Wesley	-	4:15P	4:30P	5:30P	Rehearse then make up
4X	James Pearson	WF	STUNT DBL-Gunn	-	5:30P	tbd	tbd	Rehearse then make up
8X	Karen Sheperd	WF	STUNT DBL-Faith	-	3:45P	4:30P	5:30P	Report to make up

(K)= Minor   NO FORCED CALLS WITHOUT PRIOR APPROVAL OF PRODUCTION MANAGER

ATMOSPHERE AND STAND-INS		SPECIAL INSTRUCTIONS
1	Angel SI (Joel) Rpt at 1:30P	**PROPS:** [21] Angelus slams into bookshlf knocking stuff over, Hero book that blocks dart,
1	Wesley SI (Cary) Rpt at 1:30P	multiple Occult texts, Soul jar, W&H brain extraction papers; [15,17] Bag of weapons, Tranq.
1	Gunn SI (Thom) Rpt at 5P	guns + rubber tranq guns

The crew call sheets for "Release." Check out the note about *Entertainment Weekly*.

1	Faith SI (Heidi)	Rpt at 3:30P	CAMERA: Steadicam, Addl. Loader, Arri 435						
			SPECIAL EQUIPMENT: Steadicam, Arri 435, 2–80' Condors, 2-500 A tow plants, 1--15 Ton Stunt crane						
			ADDITIONAL LABOR: 3-Addl. Lamp Ops, 4--Addl. Grips (2 to Rig), 1--Loader, 1--VSFX Rep, 1--Addl. MU, 1--Addl. Hair, 1--F S O						
			MAKE UP: [21] Reg bleeds as he tries to crawl away; [15,17] Faith wounds						
			GRIPS: Tent frame and solids						
			SPECIAL FX: [21] Atmos smoke, practical fireplace; [17] 15 ton Crane for stunts to rig, Heaters for exterior night work						
			STUNTS: [21] Angelus slams into bookshelf; [15,17] Angelus kicks Faith; she flies into Wes, Angelus swings Wesley into something, Angelus jumps the wall, Angelus throws Wes into Gunn						
			SET DRESSING: [21] Lamps, side tables and winged back chairs						
			VISUAL FX: [21] Angelus's hand passes thru Soul Jar, MUO-PING does its thing						
			LOCATIONS: Fireplace to be working in the "Occult Shop" set, lane closures as needed for stunt crane and condors						
			TRANSPORTATION: 15 ton Crane for stunts to rig from for wall gag						
			· No Meal Penalties w/out prior approval · ND Breakfast provided for early calls ·						
0	Tot. BG		**THIS IS A CLOSED SET — NO VISITORS WITHOUT PRIOR APPROVAL**						
			ADVANCE SCHEDULE						
DATE	SET		SCENE	CAST		D/N	PAGES	LOC.	
Thu. 01/16/2003 Day 1	· *Begin Episode 15--Work T B D* ·							Universal Back-Lot	
UPM: Robert Nellans Approved			Ass't. Directors: Ian Woolf, Rich T. Sickler, W. Scott Wolf, Michelene Mundo						

Interesting Facts: Gunn says Angelus pulled a "*Dark Shadows.*" *Dark Shadows* was a daytime soap opera that ran from 1966 to 1971 on ABC television about a 175-year-old vampire and other supernatural characters, like werewolves and ghosts.

Did You Notice?: Gunn is suddenly taking orders from Wesley again. Gunn always becomes closer to people when they're aligned against someone else; notice how close he and Wesley were in season 2 when Angel had turned his back on them, and how he never had a bad word to say about Angel after they had all turned against Wesley. Now that Angelus is back, he seems to get along with Wesley again.

Nitpicks: Why doesn't Connor seem to notice that Cordelia is behaving very differently now? Her voice has taken on a tone that's not hers, she's acting strangely, and she addresses him in a way she never used to. And when Angelus attacks Faith in the courtyard, rather than sneaking up behind him to pull him off Faith, Gunn yells from across the yard. Nice stealth there, Gunn.

The *Buffy* Connection: The back room of the demon bar where Angelus hangs out is the opposite of the demon crackhouse in season 5 on *Buffy*. Riley would go there to have female vampires suck on his arm to give him a weird high. Here, female "prostitutes" take drugs and vampires pay to suck on their arms to get high.

The Boy Ain't Right: Connor is prevented from stopping Angelus because of Lorne's protection spell, but the spell only stops demons from fighting. He begins looking for fangs on himself and tells Cordelia he doesn't know what he is.

Music/Bands: When Angelus is in the demon bar at the beginning of the episode, the song playing is "Here" by Vast (*Visual Audio Sensory Theater*).

4.15   Orpheus

Original air date: March 19, 2003
Written by: Mere Smith
Directed by: Terrence O'Hara
Guest cast: Alyson Hannigan (Willow Rosenberg), Eliza Dushku (Faith), Adrienne Wilkinson (Flapper), Nate Dushku (Armed Robber), E.J. Callahan (Old Craps Man), Jeremy Guskin (Cashier), Peter Renaday (Master's Voice)

With Faith in a coma (again), the gang calls the only living person who has successfully re-ensouled Angel — a redheaded witch from Sunnydale.

Orpheus is one of the most celebrated and symbolic figures in Greek mythology. A singer and musician, he had a voice that could charm the wildest beast, and he accompanied the Argonauts on their expedition, saving them from certain doom by outsinging the Sirens. The most beloved story of Orpheus is his descent into the Underworld to retrieve his bride, Eurydice. Eurydice was killed when a snake bit her, and Orpheus, who was inconsolable, traveled to the Underworld to beg a second chance for her. He sang to the gods of the Underworld to win an audience with Hades, who agreed he could have Eurydice back, but only under one condition: he had to walk out of the Underworld ahead of her and could not look back until they were safely out. Orpheus agreed, and just as he could see the light from the entranceway, he was overwhelmed by a feeling that he might have been tricked, and at the last moment he looked back. Sure enough, Eurydice was right behind him, but she was immediately pulled back into the Underworld and died a second time. Although Orpheus tried to get her back again, he was denied the chance and had to live without her.

In this episode, Orpheus is the name of the drug that people take to make vampires high. It turns out that right before Angelus bit Faith, she had injected herself with the drug, and it rendered Angelus momentarily unconscious. But the drug has far more serious consequences for Faith. Faith makes an Orpheus-like journey to the underworld of Angelus's mind and talks to him there while their actual bodies lie unconscious. Angelus is forced to watch Angel's life, starting with his arrival in New York in 1902 and ending somewhere around 1996. Faith argues with Angelus, reminds him of his past, and shows him how similar he and Angel really are when Angel commits a shocking crime in one of several flashbacks. But when they get to the present

Faith looks forward, and unlike Orpheus, she does not make a final glance backward, allowing her to achieve her prize.

While Faith and Angelus are unconscious, the rest of the gang tries to do a re-ensouling spell on him with the help of Willow Rosenberg (who had put his soul back in the second-season finale of *Buffy*, "Becoming, Part Two"). The scenes of her chatting about books with Fred (who has *far* more chemistry with Willow than she ever had with Gunn), catching up with Wesley and Cordelia, or meeting Angel's "handsome yet androgynous son" are hilarious. Lorne and Fred are angry with Wesley for making Faith take Orpheus, but Connor, of all people, tells Wesley that he believes Wes did the right thing. The story unfolding at the Hyperion alongside Angelus's various reactions to the painful flashbacks to goody-goody Angel make this episode one of the best of the season. It's a great hour full of serious revelation, humorous asides, and really, *really* bad hair.

Highlight: Angelus's horrified reaction to seeing Angel wander into a diner in the mid-1970s complete with David Cassidy hair, plaid pants, and a brown leather coat: "Bring on the pain!"

Interesting Facts: When this episode first aired on the WB on the east coast, the newscast cut into the episode five minutes before the end to announce that war had been declared in Iraq. Also, Adrienne Wilkinson, who plays the flapper in the flashback to Chicago, is best known as Xena's daughter, Eve, on *Xena: Warrior Princess*, and the armed robber who comes into the diner in the 1970s flashback is played by Nate Dushku, Eliza's older brother. Finally, Alexis Denisof and Alyson Hannigan had gotten engaged over the Christmas break in 2002 and were married on October 11, 2003.

Did You Notice?: Cordelia tells Connor, "Sometimes one death can spare infinite pain," which is prophetic considering what Jasmine's credo will be later in the season.

Nitpicks: Buffy's dealing with her own apocalypse over on the other show, but Willow is refusing to help because she doesn't want to go all black-eyed and out of control. Yet somehow she can travel to L.A. and do it with no problem?

The *Buffy* Connection: This episode is similar to the season-3 episode of *Buffy* called "Amends," where Angel once again encounters a Jacob Marley–type ghost who shows him his transgressions of the past to help him understand his present. In that episode, however, the ghost was trying to kill Angel. Interestingly, the ghost was an incarnation of the same evil that is happening over on *Buffy* in season 7, which is concurrent with this season of *Angel*. Also, this episode confirms that Angel lied to Buffy. Back in season 1 of *Buffy*, in the episode "Angel," where she first discovered he was a vampire, he assured her that after he got a soul, he never fed on a human being. Finally, Willow mentions that she tried a standard locator spell to find Angel's soul, but it didn't work, a reference to Willow's locator spells almost never working on *Buffy*.

The Boy Ain't Right: Connor knocks Gunn unconscious with one blow. Cordy reveals her large belly for the gang, which contains a child she had conceived with Connor only a few weeks earlier. She's obviously not Cordelia any longer and sought out Connor specifically to help bring whatever is in there into the world.

4.16 Players

Original air date: March 26, 2003
Written by: Jeffrey Bell, Sarah Fain, and Elizabeth Craft
Directed by: Michael Grossman
Guest cast: Alexa Davalos (Gwen Raiden), Dana Lee (Takeshi Morimoto), David Monahan (Garrett), Hope Shin (Little Asian Girl), Wendy Haines (Over-Jeweled Woman), Michael Patrick McGill (Checkpoint Guard), John Fremont (Security Guy)

Gwen Raiden returns and asks for Gunn's help, and Lorne prepares to read Cordelia's belly to find out what's inside her.

While "Players" can be accused of sidetracking just when the season's momentum should be heading toward the finale, it's actually a fantastic episode that brings back the best guest character on the show along with a suspenseful conclusion. Gwen is back, and she needs Gunn's help to save a little girl who has been kidnapped. J. August Richards shows what he's capable of in this episode, and he's amazing in every scene. From cleverly charming the host of the party to get them in to taking on several samurais at once to helping Gwen change her life in the final scene, he just sizzles, and you can't help but notice how much he's been wasted all season bumming around the Hyperion worried about Fred. Alexa Davalos is equally remarkable, and the final scene between the two of them has a sensuousness that has been missing from this show for ages.

Meanwhile, Connor begins to question who Cordelia is (*finally!*). How could a gestation period of a few weeks be normal? Why is she suddenly urging him to kill Angel, whom she used to care about so much? Why did she tell him in the last episode that Willow was bad news and was only trying to open another demon dimension? Unfortunately, Connor's powers of deduction are weak and he backs off quickly. Connor might not be the sharpest knife in the drawer, but his confusion is ramped up another notch by this unexpected pregnancy. It's understandable that his head is swimming with questions, but his sense of finally being part of a family, of possibly being the father that he himself never had, is outweighing all his doubts at the moment. As Fred and Gunn speculate about the creepiness of Connor and Cordy's coupling and Angel tries to work through his fury about it, Wesley is the

Gwen Raiden (Alexa Davalos) discovers that Gunn (J. August Richards) has a little electricity in him as well.

only one who won't judge what they've done because he doesn't want to be judged for his affair with Lilah.

Finally, Lorne has his powers back again and gets ready to find out once and for all what is inside Cordelia. This isn't the first time she's had a mystical pregnancy (see "Expecting"), and he assumes that if he can read what's inside her they'll be able to pinpoint why Cordelia has been targeted yet again. But Cordelia has worked too hard to let Lorne thwart her now.

Highlight: Gunn's reaction to Angel when Cordelia reveals her pregnancy to everyone: "Congratulations! You're gonna have a grandspawn."
Interesting Facts: After the electricity (no pun intended) between Gunn and Gwen, this is the last time we'll see her character. While it's too bad that such an intriguing character will never be used again, Alexa Davalos had moved on to movies and was no longer available to play the character.
J. August Richards Says: "In the episode 'Players,' where I had to beat up six samurais, that was probably the most fun I've had on the show ever. [Laughs] There was talk of bringing Alexa Davalos back, but she's in the *Pitch Black* sequel and she's an amazing, amazing, amazing actress and I had a blast working with her. I've been really lucky on this show because the women they've paired me with have really made me better. Amy,

Alexa — any sort of relationship I was in was one that pushed me to the next level."

Did You Notice?: Gwen tells Gunn that he's brainy and shouldn't be relegated to being the "muscle" of the group, a foreshadowing of what will happen next season. Also, perhaps in a nod to the futility of Lorne's character, he seems annoyed all the time and calls himself the equivalent of a cheap fortune cookie. When Angel asks Lorme to do something for him, he mutters, "I'm your demon" with no conviction or enthusiasm.

Nitpicks: Where did Cordelia get that outfit? Bondage Maternity Clothes R Us?

4.17 Inside Out

Original air date: April 2, 2003
Written and directed by: Steven S. DeKnight
Guest cast: David Denman (Skip), Stephi Lineburg (Girl), Julie Benz (Darla)

Connor helps Cordelia put the finishing touches on the impending birth of their child, and Angel imprisons Skip and demands some answers about Cordelia.

"Inside Out" is an episode that brings back events from long ago and sets in motion the events that will hurtle the season toward its conclusion. It also asks the question, What will a mother do for her child?

Angel goes back to the underworld to find Skip, who has always been a fan favorite. Unfortunately, in this episode we discover that Skip isn't who we thought he was and instead has been part of this whole scheme. In fact, none of the events in this series has been by chance — each has been preordained, from Fred's journey to Pylea to Gunn's sister dying to Darla and Angel's tryst to Wesley's liaison with Lilah. When Gunn protests that there's no way someone else could have been pulling the strings all this time, Skip asks him what free will really is. It's an interesting question that will be more relevant by the end of the season. While it's a little disconcerting that one of our favorite demons is actually a bad guy, what's even more disturbing is Skip's suggestion that Cordelia was chosen to become a higher being not because she had overcome who she was in the past, but because that bitch of yore will always be a part of her. The implication undercuts Cordy's incredible transformation of the past three years.

Meanwhile, Connor is having more doubts than ever before. He played the hero and got Cordelia out of a potentially dangerous situation, but for what? He's only now realizing she's acting strangely, and when she tries to use what should be a fairly simple psychology on him — that his father is evil and is trying to stop her because he hates him — it falls flat. The sudden appearance of Darla is thrilling and suspenseful, and it shows that despite Connor's belief that she doesn't care about him, her spirit is connected to his and she loves him. Vincent Kartheiser puts in a wonderful performance (and he'll have a few more great scenes before the end of the season), showing the

Seasons with No Sun

While *Buffy* and *Angel* are two very different shows, they share many of the same writers, and they have one overseeing master: Joss Whedon. Perhaps it's because of this commonality that their corresponding seasons have some creepy parallels (season 4 was the weakest on both shows; during season 4 of *Buffy*, Joss was focused on starting up *Angel*, and during season 4 of *Angel*, Joss was working on *Firefly*). Maybe the writers always follow the same patterns?

Season One
The first season took a while to get off the ground on both shows. Season 1 of *Angel* was mostly a monster-of-the-week series that had very little overall arc, no real Big Bad, and the terrible plot device of a detective tailing Angel. But it established the characters (L.A. detective Angel, Cordelia, Doyle, Wesley), and by the end of the season the show had gained some momentum. The discovery of the Shanshu prophecy gave Angel motivation for his mission to help the helpless, and it set up the events of season 2. Season 1 of *Buffy* (which only had 12 episodes) was similar. We learned who Willow, Xander, Buffy, Giles, Angel, and Cordelia really were, and there was a Big Bad in the season – the Master. But overall the episodes were mostly stand-alone installments that helped us get to know the characters, and the first season is probably the weakest of all in terms of an overall arc. But the fantastic season finale left Buffy with a realization about her mission in life and us on the edges of our seats, waiting for season 2.

Season Two
On *Buffy*, the show began to hit its stride. The focus was on the relationship between Buffy and Angel, and how it went horribly wrong partway through the season. New secondary characters like Spike and Drusilla spiced things up, and the ending was one of the best season finales of the series. Similarly, on *Angel* the focus was on Angel coming to terms with his new motivation, and he went all dark and broody midway through the season. Darla and Drusilla made great side characters, and the four-part season finale was fantastic, introducing Lorne and Fred. Gunn joined the cast as a major character and added a new dimension and excitement to the show.

Season Three

The best of the *Angel* seasons, season 3 saw *Angel* finally find its niche. With the incredible story of Holtz and Angel's past, this season had an unmatched momentum. Lorne's Caritas offered a second setting for the series, and the show's mostly dramatic overtones added some much-needed comedy. The season finale left us breathless and in disbelief. *Buffy* had a similarly fantastic third year, which many fans consider the best season. Buffy and her friends grew up and prepared for the world post–high school, and the introduction of Faith brought in a darker, angrier nemesis for the Slayer (conversely, Fred's presence on *Angel* lightened the mood for everyone over there). Season 3 ended with a bang on both series, but for different reasons.

Season Four

For some reason the writers on *Angel* and *Buffy* have serious season-4 issues. On *Buffy* we suffered through a lame plot of government commandos coming to Sunnydale to do research on the monsters and quash the efforts of Buffy and her friends. The relationship between Buffy and Riley left a bad taste in many fans' mouths, and the bumpy ride the characters endured was explained away by the writers' suggesting it was paralleling the difficulties Buffy and Company were facing in the wake of leaving high school (the Frankenstein plot with Adam didn't help matters). On *Angel* the plot was also a little skewed, with a weird twist that saw Cordelia become a bad guy, a relationship between Connor and Cordy that left fans more than a little uncomfortable, and an up-and-down plot line that never seemed to know where it was going. That said, both shows aired some of their best episodes ever during season 4 – "Hush," "Restless," "Pangs," and "Wild at Heart" on *Buffy*, and "Spin the Bottle" and "Orpheus" on *Angel*.

Season Five

Both series provided a feeling of closure at the ends of their fifth seasons (*Angel* for more obvious reasons), which were characterized by a fair share of laughter and tears. Buffy grew up, gained a little sister, and lost her mother, and episodes like "The Body" and "The Gift" were heart-rending beyond words. Season 5 had an episodic feel, but the overall arc was a strong one that got stronger as the end of the season neared. Spike became a more prominent character in a way he hadn't been before, and Buffy made an ultimate sacrifice at the end of the season, similar to Angel's in "Not Fade Away." Season 5 of *Angel* was also episodic (the WB had ordered it so) and had hilarious moments ("Smile Time") followed by devastating ones ("A Hole in the World"). Spike was a prominent character again and became a thorn in Angel's side, although with both funnier and sadder consequences. The WB saw it fit to cancel *Buffy* and *Angel* in their fifth seasons, when the writing, directing, and acting on both shows were more exciting than ever. Go figure.

personal torture he's enduring. He's always been lied to, so why should this moment be any different?

When Cordelia walks back into the room and he must choose between her and Darla, it's not surprising which way he goes. One woman staked herself before he was born because, according to Angelus, she couldn't bear to see his face or know what she'd given birth to, and the other has been intimate with him and wants to start a family. Deep down (there's that phrase again), Connor knows that Darla is telling the truth and Cordelia is lying. But he fears he might be wrong, so he chooses what seems to him to be the easier path. Darla pleads for her son to listen to her, while Cordelia pleads for him to make a huge sacrifice for their baby. Motherhood has never been so complex.

Highlight: Lorne calling Connor "Kid Vicious."

David Denman Says: "That suit — [it] took three and a half hours to put it on, an hour and a half to take it off. I swore every time I did it that I'd never do it again, and then they'd call and I'd go, 'Oh, all right.' You've got to work a twelve-hour day and then you have to add the additional five hours of makeup on top of that so you're working seventeen hours on the set, and I'd get home and barely get five or six hours of sleep and then have to go back in again and work another seventeen hours. There were a couple of times, like the last episode we did, where I would literally lie down on the ground and fall asleep in that getup. I was exhausted; you can't do anything. It's like being in a wetsuit, kind of. You just have to get into a weird meditation zone where you just kind of hang out and know you've got to pace yourself, because it's a long day.

"When I found out Skip was actually a bad guy, I was surprised and very excited. I was, like, 'Oh great!' It's always fun to do something like that. I was really happy about that last episode. It was a bummer for all the fans because I was such a nice guy, but it was a really good script and a lot of fun, and I thought it was a great way to bring me back and just sort of seal up the entire season. I was bummed they cut me up and burned me in the incinerator, although I did ask, 'Can I come back? How can they bring me back?' That was the first time that I left and thought, *Well, god, I don't think I can do this again!* I'm sure there could have been ways — you know, Cordelia could have another vision and there I am. [Laughs] 'I thought we killed you the first time!' 'You did, but I'm his twin brother, Seymour.'"

Did You Notice?: Darla tells Connor that he is the one good thing she's ever done, an echo of her statement in "Lullaby": "Angel, it's the one good thing we ever did together. The *only* good thing."

Nitpicks: Angel's reasoning for how he figured out that Cordy is up to no good is lame. He noticed that she said "my sweet baby" and the Beastmaster had said "my sweet boy"; he put the two together and had his very own eureka moment. Right. Because the word *sweet* is an archaic form of English that no one uses.

The *Buffy* Connection: Skip tells Angel that no one comes back from Paradise, "except a Slayer once." He's referring to Buffy's death at the end of season 5, when she went to a place she thought was Heaven before her friends performed a spell that brought her back.

The Boy Ain't Right: Connor ends up coming through the glass ceiling of the warehouse and lands on his feet. Even though his mother was a vampire who died before he was born, there's a spiritual connection between them that brings her back when he's teetering on the brink of a momentous decision.

4.18   Shiny Happy People

Original air date: April 9, 2003
Written by: Elizabeth Craft and Sarah Fain
Directed by: Marita Grabiak
Guest cast: Sam Witwer (Young Man), David Figlioli (Vamp Leader), Suzette Craft (Teacherly Woman), Annie Wersching (Margaret), Steven Bean (Middle-Aged Man), Lynette Romero (News Anchor), Lyle Kanouse (Diner Counter Guy), Tawny Rene Hamilton (Host of *Good Morning L.A.*) Chane't Johnson (Martha Jane), Jackie Tohn (Woman #1)

The child of Connor and Cordelia is born as a full-grown woman whom everyone falls down and worships, and she says she will help them change the world for the better.

The special day has finally arrived, and Connor and Cordelia are the proud parents of a bouncing baby . . . woman. Of course, Connor seems to be in some trance and

Cordy has slipped into a coma, undercutting the happiness of the day. In "Shiny Happy People," all Skip's predictions come to fruition. We see why the powers that be aligned things in a certain way to bring forth Jasmine, and characters like Angel and Connor, who are never giddy, are suddenly very different — smiling and feeling oh-so-happy.

The Jasmine plot line, while starring the incomparable Gina Torres, is a shaky one and feels a little disappointing after the full season buildup. The premise is slightly over-the-top and pooped out so quickly that it made the entire season feel like a bit of a waste. What gives it meaning is that Jasmine enters the story at a time when the gang is at its most vulnerable and will be likely to follow her anywhere. Jasmine gives them hope of a better world, an idea they've been fighting for for years but have begun to doubt. One problem, however, is that Jasmine has arrived with easy answers for all, and human nature is such that we don't listen to easy answers, instead making things more difficult for ourselves and others.

Jasmine's symbolic meaning — if she has any — could be one of many things. Is she supposed to be a Christ figure? Is she based on another religion? Is her origin actually in ancient mythology? She seems to most resemble Isis in the myth of Ra, the Egyptian sun god (see "Long Day's Journey"). Isis is like Mother Nature, associated with the earth and the sky and believed to bring fertility to the land and people of Egypt. She is also known as the Black Virgin (which is perhaps the reason an African-American woman was cast) and was worshiped well into Christian times. There are still some "black virgins" in churches, since Isis was seen as the original Virgin Mary, conceiving her son, Horus, with only the phallus of her husband.

In this episode Fred has the unfortunate mishap of seeing something no one else can see, and it makes her a leper in this colony of happy people. The true face of Jasmine is horrific, hinting that she might not be everything she seems. The true terror of this episode comes when Fred tries to appeal to the others but realizes that the spell they are under will make them go all *Stepford Wives* on her, forcing them to see her as their enemy and to forget all allegiances they had prior to Jasmine.

Highlight: Angel's reaction when Jasmine tells them all they'll be able to change the world: *"Finally."*
Interesting Facts: "Shiny Happy People" is an atypically happy single by the Athens, Georgia, band REM. The song was a hit off their album *Out of Time*.
J. August Richards Says: "It takes eight days to shoot an episode, and someone like me would work an average of four days per episode. David would work seven days per episode. The hours are extremely long, usually fourteen a day; [you] come home, memorize the lines, and then go back. It's really hard to have a personal life while you're shooting, but it's ultimately worth it because you really enjoy what you do."

Did You Notice?: Angel is wearing white! Clearly he's starting to believe in the good within himself.

The Boy Ain't Right: Connor is the product of two vampires, but now he and another (Caucasian) half-demon have created an African-American child.

4.19   The Magic Bullet

Original air date: April 16, 2003
Written and directed by: Jeffrey Bell
Guest cast: Danny Woodburn (Creature), Patrick Fischler (Ted), Terrylene (Deaf Woman), Mia Kelly (Woman), Andre Hotchko (Man in Lobby), Ajgie Kirkland (Black Man), Michael McElroy (Young Boy), Chad Williams (Rock Dude), Phyllis Flax (Very Old Woman), Amy Raymond (Weeping Woman), Steve Forbess (Mexican Man)

Exiled from her friends and with a price on her head, Fred is determined to show the others what she saw in Jasmine.

In "The Magic Bullet," Jasmine becomes more of a metaphor for religious fundamentalism. There are those who are content reading their scriptures or worshiping their god(s), but others will kill in the name of their religion. Countless wars have been started in the name of holy love, and many, many people have died as a result. In a post-9/11 world, this fear of religious war has become even more real and makes the events of this episode more relevant. Jasmine, despite having some Christ-like features (and Cordelia's being enshrined like the Virgin Mother), doesn't stand for just one religion but for the fundamentalist side of religion itself. She represents the paradox of one willing to cause war and bloodshed in the name of love and peace.

Fred is now separated from everyone else, and Jasmine has blessed/infected the minds of millions of people to wage war against her. As with many fundamentalist movements, these minions believe that one person will be a threat to their religion and seek to destroy her. Fred is driven to desperate measures, and while she has a momentary reprieve when she talks to the Magic Bullet bookstore owner, those who used to love her eventually corner her. Luckily, Fred is too smart to go down without a fight, and her brilliant idea (sparked by the bookstore's name) gives her at least one more ally.

Jasmine has brought the gang together, though at a cost. We've watched them move further apart all season, and their biggest problem is keeping secrets from one another, but now they are all connected. Each knows what the others are thinking, and there's no way one person would be able to keep a secret from the others — nor would that person want to, apparently. Interestingly, Fred is the first one to break out of the pack, and she's the only one who has never kept a secret from the others.

Religious worship can be a beautiful thing, and many people find solace in it, but it can also be dangerous if it's in the wrong hands and if it becomes extreme. The moment someone is willing to kill in the name of their god, the message of peace and love is long forgotten.

Highlight: Connor and Angel singing "Jasmine" to the tune of Barry Manilow's "Mandy."

Interesting Facts: Danny Woodburn, who plays the creature Fred meets, is a versatile and very funny actor who is probably best known as Kramer's sidekick Mickey on *Seinfeld*. "The magic bullet" refers to the story that the U.S. public was fed after U.S. President John F. Kennedy's assassination during a motorcade in Dallas, Texas. According to the government, JFK was shot by a lone gunman (Lee Harvey Oswald), who fired three shots from the nearby Book Depository building. But, as later pointed out in reports (and the movie *JFK*), one shot hit the president in the head and one shot hit a man standing nearby, which left one bullet to do the rest of the damage. The theory that one "magic bullet" could have incurred such damage is rather ridiculous, because it suggests the bullet entered the president through his back, exited through his throat, then entered Governor Connally (who was sitting in front of the president in the car) through his back, exited through his chest, turned and hit him in the right wrist, with fragments of the bullet hitting in two spots on his *left* leg, creating a total of seven wounds.

Did You Notice?: When Lorne, Angel, and Connor sing during open-mike night, they are accompanied on guitar by Zakk Wylde, Ozzy Osbourne's guitarist.

Nitpicks: Both Fred's and Angel's blood mingles with Jasmine's and they remain her followers until they look at her face. Yet when Fred and Angel mix Lorne's, Gunn's, and Wesley's blood with Jasmine's, they don't need to see her face to know there's something wrong. Also, after we learn what we do about Connor in the next episode, it begs the question, Why couldn't Lorne read him when he was singing with Angel? Does the enchantment make Lorne blind to things?

Oops: Jasmine is in room 619, but in "Spin the Bottle" Cordelia says the hotel has five floors. Also, the creature Fred meets says he wants to start a fire, yet there's a flickering on the walls of the cave the whole time, like there's already one going.

The Boy Ain't Right: We discover in this episode how Connor developed his tracking skills.

Music/Bands: "Wouldn't It Be Nice" by the Beach Boys (*Pet Sounds*) plays during the opening credits.

4.20   Sacrifice

Original air date: April 23, 2003
Written by: Ben Edlund
Directed by: David Straiton

Guest cast: Avery Kidd Waddell (Golden), Michah Henson (Matthew), Jeff Ricketts (Insect Demon), Tristine Skyler (Holly), Bradley Stryker (Sculpture Vampire), Taylor Lundeen (Little Girl)

As Fred, Lorne, Angel, Gunn, and Wesley run from Jasmine's devout followers, Wesley encounters a giant insect that claims to have worshiped Jasmine for millions of years.

Whereas the last two episodes have been just weird, this one takes a turn for the better and provides an intriguingly creepy demon and a doubting Connor, two things that don't bode well for Jasmine's fate. As the Jasmine exiles head down into the sewers to try to escape her Orwellian "eyes everywhere," they encounter another group of people who don't know who Jasmine is but who are fighting for their lives just the same. These ragamuffins explain that they have been fighting a creature who is trying to kill them one by one. When Wesley finally comes face-to-face with the creature, he obtains another clue as to who Jasmine is and what can defeat her.

In this episode, even Jasmine tells Connor that he holds on to his anger, but we can't really blame him. His friends have left him, and Angel, in a shocking scene at the beginning, beats Connor to a pulp and leaves him for dead. Although he tells the others that he's only trying to suppress his emotions to keep Jasmine from infecting his mind again, what he does to Connor is practically unforgivable. In one brutal act he confirms everything Holtz told Connor and everything Connor himself has come to believe about Angel. Granted, Connor didn't hesitate to throw his friends to the angry mob, but we'll soon discover why he is the way he is, and no matter how many times the kid whines about wanting to kill his father and everyone hating him, even the hardest hearted among us will have to feel a tiny bit of sympathy for him.

The creature itself is one of the creepiest demons to appear on the show and is similar to the equally freaky Gnarl, who appeared earlier this season on *Buffy*. Making weird clicking noises, scuttling about on his insect legs, and referring to Wesley as "talking meat," the demon has the same voice as the Master did on *Buffy*, but he speaks in riddles. He is from a race of demons that has loved and worshiped Jasmine for centuries, and he is bitter and angry that she has chosen to grace humans with her presence rather than returning in a second coming to his world. As he grotesquely pulls body parts off one of his prey and wonders aloud why the victim just won't die, Wesley asks enough questions to find out that, like Rumpelstiltskin in the Brothers Grimm fairy tale, Jasmine can be destroyed if her true name is discovered. It's the same method Isis used to destroy Ra, bringing the Egyptian myth full circle. But first, Angel will have to go on a journey to find that name.

Highlight: The insect demon.

Did You Notice?: Jeff Ricketts, who plays the insect demon, appeared on *Angel* in season 1 as Weatherby, one of the rogue members of the Watcher's Council who was trying to capture Faith. Also, Jasmine says to Connor, "Let it go," which are the same words Cordelia uses in "Benediction."

Nitpicks: Why does Gunn need Fred to grab Matthew's feet and help carry him? Gunn is a strong guy, and he certainly wouldn't need help carrying a child.

Oops: While the gang is on the run, Lorne puts his hand over his chest because he's very tired, but we all know his rapidly beating heart is in his butt cheek, not in his chest.

4.21 Peace Out

Original air date: April 30, 2003
Written by: David Fury
Directed by: Jefferson Kibbee
Guest cast: Robert Towers (High Priest), Bonita Friedericy (Patience), Eliza Pryor Nagel (Susan), Bob Pescovitz (News Reporter), Gerry Katzman (Technician), Audrey Kearns (Young Woman), Kristin Richardson (Female Reporter), Kyle Ingleman (Jeremy), Jeff Scott Bass (Brent), Kimble Jemison (Cop #1), Angelica Castro (Telemundo Reporter), Brian Bradley (Grizzled Reporter)

Angel goes on a quest to find the thing that will destroy Jasmine, and Connor tries to find where Jasmine has hidden Cordelia.

"Peace Out" is a well-written philosophical treatise on world peace versus free will. Throughout history, rulers have tried to govern with an iron fist while maintaining peace within their lands, but the indomitable will of the human spirit has prevailed. Civil wars and coups d'état have disrupted peaceful times but allowed people a say in how they would live. Jasmine brings the promise of world peace with her, and while she eats people to remain powerful, she is sacrificing a few to save the many. But at what price? She has taken away all free will, and according to Skip in "Inside Out," none of the characters has been making his or her own choices this entire time. The suggestion is that ever since Eve made the decision to eat the apple, the powers that be have been conspiring to put all of humanity back into that mindless Garden of Eden. Skip also says in "Inside Out" that everything thus far has been preordained, and while he points specifically to events on *Angel*, these wheels had to have been set in motion many millennia before to ensure Darla and Angel's coming together in the first place, or Darla's being made a vampire, or the Master's being made a vampire, etc.

So what are these characters fighting for? *Real* free will, not the phony free will they've believed they've had all along. From now on, the decisions they make will be

CHRISTINA RADISH

Jasmine (Gina Torres) says she has come to bring peace to the world, but at what price?

their own, not persuasions by the powers that be. Or will they? Unfortunately, considering how long it's taken the powers that be to make everything align in order to bring forth Jasmine, her stay of only a few weeks proves they aren't really working very hard. Talk about big overture, *little* show. Anyone else thinking of Gachnar on *Buffy*?

The most moving part of this episode is Connor's talk with Cordelia. He doesn't trust Jasmine as much as he once did because she moved Cordy without telling him. Interestingly, Jasmine's minions don't worship Connor the way they do Cordelia (he's the Joseph to her Mary, despite the lack of a virgin birth), but through perseverance, he finds out where she is. As she lies on a slab, still as death, he talks to her, the only person he has ever had an intimate, physical, and emotional connection with. And it's in this scene that we finally find out what Connor is all about.

All season Connor has been a character toward whom we couldn't help but feel ambivalent. Sometimes you wanted to hug him and reassure him the world isn't as bad as he thinks, and other times you just wanted to drive a sword through him. But all his life he's been a pawn. Holtz used him for revenge against Angel. He treated him like an animal for 17 years while insisting that he loved him far more than Angel ever would. The story in "The Magic Bullet" about Holtz tying Connor to a tree and abandoning him, forcing him to break free before he would be killed, is gut wrenching. When Connor returned from the hell dimension he was confused, and Holtz and Justine used him as a pawn against Angel once more. This season he has tried to strike out on his own, but something keeps drawing him back to Angel and the others, and now, after believing that he'd finally made a human connection with Cordelia, he realizes he's been used again. After all, his birth was an absolute medical, scientific, and mythological impossibility; there was never any way he was going to have the privilege of making his own decisions — clearly someone has already determined why he is here and what his role will be.

In "Inside Out," Connor refused to believe Darla, the one who was telling the truth, and instead did what Cordelia asked him to. In murdering another human being in cold blood, he clearly lost the sympathy vote, but now that he pours his heart out to a comatose Cordy, articulating what he's really been thinking, it's harder to judge him. It is much easier on Connor simply to go along with whatever he's told, even when the consequences of being a follower will hurt him. But in "Inside Out" Cordelia assured him that a new world was coming, and when you've had a life like Connor's, could it possibly be any worse than this one?

Now he tells Cordelia that unlike the others, he could see Jasmine's face all along. He grew up in a hell dimension where humans couldn't survive and beasts ruled, so personal appearances have never been a major sticking point with him. However, in seeing her face, and despite being able to look past it, he knew that Jasmine, and everything she stood for, was a lie. She couldn't purge his hatred and anger as she did the others'. But, as he reveals in this speech to the unconscious Cordelia, he went along with it because his whole life has been a lie. Holtz raised him for 17 years on a pack of lies about Angel. He's lived in worlds where hatred was the only emotion and war the only climate, and along comes a lie that promises peace and love. Even if he can see past it and knows that people are being duped, he also realizes it is the best lie he's ever been told. Can we really fault him for wanting to believe it so badly that he became a follower once again?

Highlight: The shocker of an ending.

Interesting Facts: While Tracy Bellows is not actually an on-air personality at KTLA, she throws it back to Hal, referring to Hal Fishman, KTLA's news anchor.

Did You Notice?: In an outdoor scene we see a church with "God Is Nowhere" on its billboard, which is a shout-out to David Greenwalt's short-lived, but brilliant, show *Miracles*. On that show a character who has lost his faith sees the words "God Is Nowhere" written on a window and believes God has abandoned him until someone suggests the words could have actually said "God Is Now Here."

Nitpicks: When Connor is speaking to Cordelia you can tell Charisma Carpenter is holding her breath, because her chest does not rise and fall. But Cordelia's not dead — she's just in a coma and should be breathing normally. Also, Gunn ends up kicking open the door to a cell that was supposed to hold back Angelus, which is a little unbelievable.

4.22　Home

Original air date: May 7, 2003

Written and directed by: Tim Minear

Guest cast: Jim Abele (Connor's Father), Jason Winer (Preston), Michael Halsey (Sirk), Jonathan Woodward (Knox), Merle Dandridge (Lacey), Jason Padgett (Suicidal Cop), James Calvert (Surgery Patient), Anthony Diaz-Perez (Hostage Father), Adrienne Brett Evans (Connor's Mother), Stacy Solodkin (Connor's Aunt), Emma Hunton (Connor's Kid Sister), Ariel Baker (Angel Greeter #1), Michael Ness (Angel Greeter #2), Alex Craig Mann (Angel Greeter #3), Nichole Pelerine (Angel Greeter #4), Joshua Grenrock (Angel Greeter #5)

Lilah is back and makes the gang a shocking offer for their part in ending Jasmine's rule; Angel worries about Connor's mindset now that everything is over.

Lies. They're an essential part of life. All of us have told them; no one has been spared them. We tell white lies to make people feel better or to keep difficult things from them that they're better off not knowing. We tell purposely deceitful lies to betray people. We tell lies to save ourselves, to hurt others, and to protect everyone's greater good. But in this episode, all the lies that have been poured into Connor's head come crashing together, and he snaps.

Meanwhile, Lilah has reappeared and applauds the gang for their part in ending world peace. And then she makes them the most insane offer they could imagine — she offers them the L.A. branch of Wolfram & Hart, the very firm that has been their nemesis for four years. Could she be lying? Wolfram & Hart isn't exactly known for its sincerity. As the gang heads over to the law firm to find out what their roles would be — Wesley would be in charge of books and spells, Fred would be the head of the science department, Gunn's role is unclear, and "Mr. Angel" would head up the entire operation — they view this boon with suspicion. But when Gunn visits the white room and comes face-to-face with a black panther, he sees something immediately that tells him he has no choice: he must stay at Wolfram & Hart. Just as Angel is about to refuse the deal, Lilah makes him an offer that changes his mind.

Stephanie Romanov is excellent once again, making us realize how much she added to the show as Lilah. Lilah's wicked comments to everyone are hilarious, but there's also a softness to her. We know that Wesley and Lilah really did care for one another, and she's comforted by the knowledge of the lengths he's willing to go to help her, even if it's all for nothing.

The final scene between Angel and Connor is a difficult and moving one. Up to now Connor has tried to drown out the voices in his head by eradicating the world of his father's kind, but he can't avoid them any longer; now he has won back his free will, and he wants to die. He's been lied to his entire life, trusting the wrong people and distrusting the right ones. He can't tell the difference between right and wrong anymore, and his confusion has made him go slightly mad. Cordelia made a connection with him, but it wasn't really Cordelia. Angel tried to forge a relationship, but too many things have happened between them — they will never be a loving father and son. Fred and Gunn no longer trust him, Wesley barely knows him, and Lorne would rather not think about him. Holtz is dead, and along with him went any hope for Connor's rehabilitation. Connor finally admits in this episode that he believes Angel *did* love him when he was still a baby, but by letting Holtz take him away, Angel is responsible for all the things Holtz did to him.

So Angel does the only thing he can think of, a decision that leaves a series of questions in its wake. On the one hand, Angel sacrifices the one thing he's always wanted in his life — a son. On the other, he gives something to Connor that he's never had before — hope. Connor's existence will now be the opposite of Dawn's on *Buffy*; where everyone on that show had memories of Dawn inserted into their minds, those on this show will have all memories of Connor removed. Only Angel will live with the truth, a burden he's been carrying since "I Will Remember You."

Connor says he "can't be saved by a lie," but Angel does just that. In doing so, does Angel perpetuate the life that Connor already has, or is the lie Angel gives Connor so beautiful that he can be forgiven?

Highlight: Sirk asking Wesley how Wes knew that he had stolen the Codex from the Watcher's Council, and Wesley responding, "Something about Watchers and libraries."

Interesting Facts: The Wolfram & Hart office looks nothing like the one in season 5, but when this episode aired the cast and crew still didn't know if the show would be renewed, so it didn't make sense to build the set if it was only going to be used for one episode.

Stephanie Romanov Says: "My agent called me and said, 'They want to use you for another episode of *Angel*,' and I was, like, 'They chopped off my head!' She was dead when she came back, now playing with the undead. But I was very surprised, and I loved doing that episode. I really saw her as a game-show host — you know, you see those Bob Barker girls going, 'And then, look what's behind Door Number Two!' I thought it was fun playing it that way to add a little humor to it, but I think she's done everything. There's nothing they could do to her now that hasn't already been done. You know when you're so afraid of something happening that when it happens you're so relieved? It sort of felt that way when my character was gone for good."

David Fury Says: "*Angel* has always been on the bubble, but it always gets renewed. I can tell you this much: it's not so much a cliffhanger, but you'll see in episode twenty-two that Tim Minear wrote and directed, it'll set up the new premise for next year, a whole new paradigm for the show. While it's not a cliffhanger, it'll be an intriguing place to take Angel and his crew."

Did You Notice?: Jonathan Woodward, who plays Knox, appeared on *Buffy* earlier the same year as Holden Webster in "Conversations with Dead People." Also, when Lilah explains the perpetuity clause in the Wolfram & Hart contract, she shows the gang a wound she incurred during her life, the same thing Holland did when he first explained the clause to Angel in "Reprise."

Nitpicks: Where is the "files and records" woman we saw in "Dad"?

Oops: Sirk hands Wesley a book upside down, and Wesley doesn't turn it over when he looks at it. Connor is wrapped in TNT at the sporting-goods store, and Angel pulls off the trigger. In the very next scene, all of the explosives that had been duct-taped to Connor moments earlier have suddenly disappeared. As Angel's limo drives away from Sunnydale, it appears to be driving on the wrong side of the road.

The *Buffy* Connection: Sirk tells Wesley that there's no Watcher's Council any longer; it was blown up, along with the Watchers, earlier this season on *Buffy*. The amulet that

Lilah gives Angel will play a major role in the *Buffy* series finale, "Chosen."

Season Five
October 2003 • May 2004

Recurring characters: Sarah Thompson (Eve), Jonathan M. Woodward (Knox), Adam Baldwin (Marcus Hamilton)

5.1 Conviction

Original air date: October 1, 2003
Written and directed by: Joss Whedon
Guest cast: Dane Northcutt (Hauser), Jacqueline Hahn (Judge), Marc Vann (Dr. Sparrow), Michael Shamus Wiles (Spanky), Rod Rowland (Corbin Fries), Peter Brietmayer (Desmond Keel), T.J. Thyne (Lawyer), Keli'l (Sam), Jordan Garrett (Matthew), Marissa Tait (Woman), Daniella Kuhn (Notary), Chris Eckles (Special Ops Guy), Susan Slome (Cindy Rabinowitz)

As the gang tries to settle into their new surroundings, a Wolfram & Hart client threatens to unleash something on L.A. if Angel doesn't try to get his case dismissed.

Season 5 opens on a familiar note. There's a damsel in distress in an alleyway, with a vampire about to sink his teeth into her neck. In swoops Angel just in time to save her — as he did at the beginning of "City Of." Only this time, just as Angel is about to slink off into the night like he always does, he's stopped by an army of lawyers, publicists, and soldiers. The world of *Angel* has changed.

After four years of fighting against Wolfram & Hart, Angel has become its CEO, with Fred, Gunn, Wesley, and Lorne all taking jobs within the company. The question of whether or not the gang is doing the right thing will be the central theme of season 5, and being part of the machine will not only empower them, but force them to suffer devastating consequences. In "Conviction," Angel is uncomfortable about the decision he's made. He took the helm of Wolfram & Hart to save Connor (someone no one else remembers now, as part of the deal), but three weeks later he's wondering what kind of price he's really going to have to pay to save his son's life. Way back at the end of season 1, when Angel was first starting to get frustrated with his new nemesis, he said that the world at large belongs to Wolfram & Hart's world and it's the one that works, with no guilt or consequences, and sometimes he misses that clarity. Now he sees that perhaps clarity isn't the most important thing.

Wesley is head of the spells department and seems to be settling in to his new position.

Eve (Sarah Thompson) appears to be a sweet person, but when you're the liaison to the Senior Partners, just how sweet can you be?

Fred seems to have developed an edge she didn't have before, and while she can still be cute and sweet one minute, the next she's barking orders and lecturing her staff. Lorne revels in his new position because of the glitterati he now rubs shoulders with, but his only use to the gang — reading the employees and anyone else they might need to check out — soon wanes.

Gunn is the only one who embraces what they do wholeheartedly. We discover what really happened in the white room at the end of season 4, and Gunn's purpose within the group changes entirely. Before he was the muscle; now he's their link to the new world they're inhabiting and will be the one who will get them out of tight situations. Wesley and Fred used to be the brains, with one using magick and the other science, but in the world of Wolfram & Hart, it's the law that will either save you or bury you, and now Gunn has that knowledge — and it will do both.

The newest members of the group are both women. Harmony makes a very funny entrance, and all season long Mercedes McNab will do a great job of maintaining the comic element of the series while being a constant thorn in Angel's side — "Creatures of the night, unite!" Sarah Thompson, on the other hand, isn't as convincing as Eve. The liaison to the Senior Partners is supposed to be someone who grates on us, but in this first episode, her lines are wooden. She delivers asides as if they were part of the main sentences, and she doesn't seem to have a grasp of how to say Joss's words. Lines like "This is the catch. I'm explaining the catch so you don't have to stand around wondering what it is" fall flat when she delivers them and are no livelier than they would have been on paper. She'll be a lot more tolerable later in the season, although her disappearance partway through may indicate that the writers felt the same way about her as some of the fans.

With Corbin Fries, the members of the Angel team face what will be their typical clientele from this point on, and it eats away at their sense of morality. Fries is the opposite of Angel — where Angel sacrificed himself to save his son, Fries is willing to sacrifice his son to save himself. What they do have in common, however, is that they will risk the lives of several people they care about in order to achieve one goal. "Conviction" is a great start to the season, full of humor — Harmony revealing her secret ingredient in Angel's blood; Angel saying he has no problem spanking men; Lorne trotting out in his hilarious incognito outfit; and Harmony uttering, "Blondie bear?" — and poignancy. The issue of Cordelia's coma isn't dropped, although we won't hear about it again for most of the season. Whedon does a great job of tying together the loose ends from the end of season 4 while setting up the main themes of season 5. We've got the same cast, but they're all just a little bit different, and the surroundings are a nice change from the Hyperion. Watching them all grapple with their morals while trying to maintain their new employment will be fascinating throughout the year.

Highlight: Angel attempting to use the office phone and showing the same "expertise" he does with a cell phone.

Interesting Facts: This is the first time Joss has written and directed an episode of *Angel*.

Amy Acker Says: "Joss is always there. It's great to have all those different people and every episode is a new writer and they're always on set, so you talk about the script to the person who wrote the show. If you have a major issue you'll talk to Joss, though. He was on the set more often this year than in previous years, because he didn't have the other shows on the go, but all the writers were in Santa Monica and we were in Hollywood, so we could just call one up if we needed to talk about something."

Did You Notice?: As the scene flashes away from Gunn the first time, one of the flashes is the black panther from "Home." Also, the "Black Tomorrow" sounds very much like a more important cult that will arise by the end of the season. And Lorne's employee-evaluation sheet has five categories: Okay; On the Bubble; Evil; To Be Fired; and Yikes! (making one wonder why "Evil" and "To Be Fired" are two separate categories). Finally, Eve looks a lot like an adult version of the little girl who was the former white-room conduit in "Habeas Corpses."

Nitpicks: You can always tell when Joss Whedon has had a direct hand in creating an episode, because Fred appears in extremely short skirts and we have a lot of close-up leg shots.

The *Buffy* Connection: In the series finale of *Buffy*, Spike agreed to wear the amulet that Angel brought over from Wolfram & Hart (the one Lilah gave him in "Home"). As a result, he was able to destroy the army Buffy & Company were fighting but was disintegrated in the process.

Wolfram & Hart: Because the Senior Partners exist on another plane, they have a liaison that acts as a conduit between them and their offices in this dimension. The firm has a special ops team that "takes care" of problems.

5.2   Just Rewards

Original air date: October 8, 2003
Teleplay by: David Fury and Ben Edlund
Story by: David Fury
Directed by: James A. Contner
Guest cast: Victor Raider-Wexler (Magnus Hainsley), William Utay (Man Servant), Bill Escudier (Hainsley Demon), Joshua Hutchinson (Novac)

Spike returns as a ghost and immediately begins driving Angel crazy.

Although Spike's return lends credence to the "no one ever stays dead on *Buffy*" criticism often levied against *Angel*'s sister show, it's great to have James Marsters back. Throughout his tenure on *Buffy*, Spike was always a source of fun, full of childish spite, but he could switch to being a sad, sympathetic character in the blink of an eye. On the fifth season of *Angel*, Marsters is at his best, and in "Just Rewards" we receive an excellent reintroduction to his character. Spike's best moments are when he's going head-to-head with Angel, needling him about their past and their relationships with Buffy, or just annoying Angel until he can't take it anymore. David Boreanaz has always played Angel with one part humor and three parts broodiness, but when he's pitted against Marsters he steps up his performance, as if Marsters pushes him to be better. The plot twist of Spike about to enter Angel's body is appropriate seeing how much Spike and Angel are alike — despite their declarations to the contrary. Watching the two of them on-screen this year will provide many of the season's highlights.

"Just Rewards" is an episode about control. Magnus Hainsley is a necromancer who controls the dead, and he can put the soul of a demon into a human corpse, re-animating it. Angel is the head of Wolfram & Hart but has already realized he exercises very little control over anything there. But the main storyline of the episode is Spike — he is now a ghost with absolutely no control over his environment. He can't touch things, he can't affect anything around him, and he can't leave Wolfram & Hart. He seems to be tied to the amulet in some way, but even while he's at w&h he keeps disappearing and then reappearing when he least expects it. He finally reveals to Fred what is really happening to him and asks her to help him. Spike might have saved the world and changed his ways for Buffy and all humanity, but it doesn't erase the thousands of people he killed and tortured before he got to that point. Now he's discovered what his ultimate fate will be, and it terrifies him.

The addition of Spike inevitably changes the group dynamic, but we know about

Spike's past with Angel and can't help but question his loyalty. Sure, he has a soul now and has vowed to fight evil, but can he be trusted? If there's one person in the world he'd love to stab in the back, isn't it Angel?

Highlight: Spike calling Harmony "the littlest vampire."

Interesting Facts: The WB asked Joss Whedon to make season 5 more episodic. Consequently, while the season will have an arc that continues throughout the year, it'll feature more demons of the week than the previous three years did.

Did You Notice?: After several seasons of Spike incorrectly calling Angel his sire, he *finally* calls him his grandsire in this episode. Also, the mail guy in the Mexican wrestler's mask will appear in the background of every episode until "The Cautionary Tale of Numero Cinco."

Nitpicks: If Spike is tied to the amulet, which is at Wolfram & Hart, how was he able to leave the building to go to Hainsley's house with Angel?

Oops: Throughout the episode, Spike's dialogue has clearly been overdubbed: it doesn't always match the movements of his mouth, and it sounds like it was recorded afterward. Also, at the very beginning of the episode, Angel is standing with the rest of the gang with his back to the door, but as Spike appears in front of them, Angel is suddenly over by the desk. Finally, if Spike walks through desks and walls and can't intentionally touch anything, how does he sit in Angel's chair? Or in Angel's car? (For that matter, how does he manage to walk on the floor without falling through it, too?)

The *Buffy* Connection: Angel expresses his frustration that while he atoned for decades, Spike spent three weeks in a basement and seemed to be all better. He's referring to Spike's having been mad in the school basement at the beginning of the final season of *Buffy* only to rejoin the Scooby gang after a handful of episodes — he seemed to deal with his guilt rather well.

5.3   Unleashed

Original air date: October 15, 2003
Written by: Sarah Fain and Elizabeth Craft
Directed by: Marita Grabiak
Guest cast: Jenny Mollen (Nina Ash), John Billingsley (Dr. Royce), Heidi Dippold (Jill), Sascha Shapiro (Amanda), Braeden Marcott (Jacob Crane)

Angel must find a woman who has been bitten by a werewolf before the next full moon occurs, for fear she could hurt someone.

Although the thought of Angel falling for somebody new just seems wrong considering how recently Cordelia was put into a coma (on the show's timeline the events of "Home" occurred about three weeks earlier), "Unleashed" is an interesting foray into the new paranoia surrounding the gang, and it's also a look at how Angel copes with his past. He identifies with Nina and therefore vows to help her (something he's done with Faith, Gunn, and Judy in "Are You Now or Have You Ever Been?"). *Buffy* viewers watched Oz come to grips with his wolfiness in season 2 of that series, but because of his laid-back manner he rarely seemed to be overwhelmed by it. Only when he loses control over his wolf side in season 4 and hurts Willow in the process does he leave Sunnydale in a state of pain and confusion, but he eventually learns to deal with being a werewolf. Nina, on the other hand, is new to having a beast within, and she is terrified when she discovers what has happened to her.

Angel feels a kinship with her, and the heart-to-shriveled-heart talks they have are illuminating. Angel tells her she will learn to live with what is inside her, and he should know: he's had to keep his dark side in check, and we've seen what a struggle that has been, even for someone as strong as he is. Despite living with the agonizing knowledge of his past crimes, he has fallen off the wagon. What bothers Nina the most is the danger she poses to the people she loves — the very fear Angel lives with every day as he wonders if Angelus will rear his ugly head.

The title of the episode refers not only to Nina's story, but to the gang as well. At the beginning of the episode, they finally unleash their deepest fears on each other and wonder aloud if what they're doing is really helpful. When Gunn allowed Wolfram & Hart into his head, what information did the Senior Partners gain access to? Is Gunn a threat to the rest of them? Fred is keeping Spike's predicament a secret from everyone else, as he asked her to, and while she is keeping up with her daily duties, she's also trying to find a way to help him on the side. And Lorne finally approaches Angel to tell him about the detrimental effects his new attitude problem is having on the team, but Angel's not about to listen. It's interesting that Angel explains to Nina how to suppress the monster within her when his monster side is starting to show around his other friends.

Highlight: Nina immediately assuming Angel is Frankenstein when he says he's a monster as well, and the way he touches his forehead when she says it.

Interesting Facts: While John Billingsley has appeared in many television series and films, such as *Six Feet Under*, *White Oleander*, and *Out of Time*, he's best known to genre fans as Dr. Phlox on *Enterprise*.

J. August Richards Says [on Gunn taking the brain upgrade]: "I honestly feel that he was tired of being the underdog, tired of being powerless, tired of living hand-to-mouth and just fighting tooth and nail. For once, he just wanted a break. I could really relate to that prior to me getting this series, actually. I remember I was auditioning like crazy, which is great for an actor, but I felt like I was getting so tired fighting for every little thing, whether it was two lines, three lines, whatever. So when I got this job I remember feeling a huge sense of relief because it was, like, 'Ah, good, now I can relax.' But my career in some ways has been parallel to my character, because in some aspect I feel like I got too relaxed and now that I'm auditioning again I feel really out of shape. So I think that's why Gunn jumped so quickly to go with Wolfram & Hart — he was just so tired of fighting."

Nitpicks: While the main story of the episode is interesting, the whole werewolf-eating ceremony was cheesy and over-the-top. Besides, if a werewolf reverts to human form when it's killed, wouldn't parts of a werewolf revert to human form if they are cut off?

Oops: Nina walks into the kitchen, the hamburgers are frying on the stove, and Amanda turns them over. Yet when Nina looks down at them, they're pink side up rather than brown — the sides facing up should already be cooked. Also, when Nina holds her hand up as she first starts to turn into a werewolf, the stubby little fingers on the arms are a pretty good indication that it's not actually the actress's real hand.

Wolfram & Hart: There are in-house psychics who can find a person by getting into their heads, seeing what they see, and creating fuzzy photographs of the person's surroundings.

Music/Bands: When Nina returns home at the end of the episode, the song playing is Ryan Adams's "La Cienega Just Smiled" (*Gold*).

5.4   Hell Bound

Original air date: October 22, 2003
Written and directed by: Steven S. DeKnight
Guest cast: Simon Templeman (Pavayne), Dorie Barton (Claire), Willow Greer (Glass Woman), Peter Kanetis (Lawyer #1), Judson Pearce Morgan (Bloody Lawyer), Elliot Gray (Hanging Man), Allison Barcott (Armless Woman)

Spike begins seeing horrifying images and believes he's slipping into Hell and will soon be gone.

Angel has boasted its share of horror and graphic images, but few compare with the ones we see in this episode. "Hell Bound" is a terrifying look at what awaits Spike in the afterlife, as he encounters people with missing limbs or objects protruding from their bodies, warning him that the reaper is coming to get him. The reaper is Pavayne, who has ties to Wolfram & Hart and was a brutal doctor in the 18th century, when he conducted appalling experiments on his victims. Spike sees images of people who have died in the service of Wolfram & Hart, and it makes us wonder if the gang will suffer a similar fate. They are all in the service of Wolfram & Hart, so will their actions haunt them into the afterlife?

Spike seems to hold himself together well for someone who is being prepared for entering Hell, but since getting a soul he has been not only bombarded with the memories and images of the people he has tortured and killed but also taunted by the First, and what he went through in "Chosen" probably makes Pavayne's psychological torture seem like a walk in the park. Nonetheless, the guilt he feels over what he did for 120 years is something he can live with, whereas what Pavayne has in store for him is a mystery, and that's the scariest part of all.

After Fred comes through for him, Spike is forced to make a difficult decision, but he does so without hesitation. His choice will make him a full-fledged member of the team, whether Angel likes it or not, and shows all of them that despite his past, he's trustworthy now. The end of the episode is eerie, and Angel ends up inflicting upon Pavayne the very torture that he himself underwent for months at the hands of his own son. Also, Spike now knows about the Shanshu prophecy, and he will question its real meaning until the end of the season.

Highlight: Angel admitting to Spike that he liked his poems, and Spike replying, "*You liked Barry Manilow.*"

Interesting Facts: This is the only episode of *Angel* to have a warning of graphic violence and partial nudity before it (although there didn't appear to be any more nudity than we've seen before).

Wolfram & Hart: The firm does regular sweeps of the building to keep out spectral intrusions. The building was constructed on the site of a former religious building, so the blood of the evil Pavayne was spilled on the ground to deconsecrate it before construction began. There are permanent storage cells in the basement, from which it is impossible to leave.

5.5   Life of the Party

Original air date: October 29, 2003
Written by: Ben Edlund
Directed by: Bill Norton
Guest cast: Leland Crooke (Archduke Sebassis), Michael Maize (Artode), Jim Blanchette (Devlin), T.J. Thyne (Employee #1), Ryan Alvarez (Demon Slave)

The gang begins acting strangely at the annual Wolfram & Hart Halloween party.

Lorne's character has slowly been fading in importance since the beginning of season 3. He was ineffectual throughout that season, being used as Connor's babysitter and otherwise hanging around the Hyperion answering phones and drinking Seabreezes, and in season 4, when the babysitting gig went out the window, he was tied up and tortured and was pretty useless beyond that. Because the writers can't seem to find a way to make Lorne a useful member of the group, they instead write stand-alone episodes for him (like "The House Always Wins") in order to show off Andy Hallett's talents. "Life of the Party" shows us a different side of Lorne, however, one that will persist for the rest of the year.

Lorne has always been the guy who smiles when everyone else is down. He's one of those people everyone expects will stay happy indefinitely and will cheer them up if they're down, even if he doesn't feel like it. Inevitably, the perkiness turns out to be nothing more than an act, and he starts returning to his room to brood and drink. Lorne has become so used to wearing a mask for everyone else and only giving in to his true feelings in private that he's developed a split personality, one that manifests in this episode when he makes the grave mistake of giving up his sleep. Unfortunately, when the other half of him appears as an Incredible Hulk–like creature at the party, the episode moves from funny to ridiculous.

Lorne's ability to write the actions of those around him is too close to Willow's ability to exert her will on everyone around her in "Something Blue." Wesley eventually states that Lorne can write the destinies of those around him because he's an Empath demon, but he's not exactly writing their destinies — a destiny is the ultimate course of events of a person's life, not their falling over drunk or urinating on the house plants. While Amy Acker and Alexis Denisof are hilarious as drunks, for the most part the plot of this episode is a throwaway, from the "pee-pee" slave to Eve and Angel behind the couch. The only important aspect of "Life of the Party" is that it shows the effect Wolfram & Hart is having on the gang. Lorne is sleep-deprived and has become a danger to himself and everyone around him; Fred and Wesley have forgotten how to be friends; Gunn aligns himself with Lorne in thinking that keeping good faith with their evil clients is a number one priority; and Angel continues to worry about what Wolfram & Hart's endgame might be.

Highlight: "Positive" Spike grooving to the music.
Nitpicks: Knox talks about last year's Halloween party as if he was there, but if the Beast killed everyone at W&H in "Habeas Corpses" (which happened after Halloween), presumably Knox has been transferred from another branch and probably wasn't at the party.
Wolfram & Hart: The firm has the capability of taking certain needs and desires away from people at their request to make them more productive workers.
Music/Bands: At the party we hear Thelma Houston's "Don't Leave Me This Way" (*The Best of Thelma Houston*).

5.6 The Cautionary Tale of Numero Cinco

Original air date: November 5, 2003
Written and directed by: Jeffrey Bell
Guest cast: Danny Mora (Numero Cinco), Bruno Gioiello (Security Guard)

When Wesley receives word that three people have been found with their hearts cut out, Angel turns to a member of his staff — a former Mexican masked wrestler — for information.

"The Cautionary Tale of Numero Cinco" had a lot of potential to be an outlandish stand-alone episode, but instead it's a brilliant and original tale, filled with music that is very different from what we're used to on *Angel* and a story that takes us to a time and place we haven't yet seen.

Jeffrey Bell certainly knows his stuff when it comes to Mexican masked wrestling. It is believed the trend began in 1934 when El Enmascarado (The Masked Man), an American wrestler, moved to Mexico and fought only while wearing a mask. Since then, the most famous Mexican masked wrestlers have been El Santo, Blue Demon, and Mil Mascaras. The mask, which often features a letter or number, isn't just part of the wrestler's outfit — it represents his honor, identity, and attitude. Wrestlers such as Mil Mascaras never removed their masks, even outside the ring, maintaining their mystery and integrity, like Numero Cinco and his brothers do in this episode. El Santo was even buried in his silver mask. The mask can also be used to honor one's predecessors (another theme of this episode), as it is passed down through generations of wrestlers. In "mask versus mask" tournaments, the losing wrestler must remove his mask, thus incurring the ultimate humiliation. The best-known masked wrestlers also starred in B-movies on the side (wearing their masks, of course) — interestingly, El Santo starred in *Santo vs. the Vampire Women*, while Mil Mascaras appeared in *Las Vampiras*, where he played a heroic *luchador* who fights vampires by using wrestling moves.

Mexican wrestlers who fight in the *lucha libre* style (the style of Numero Cinco and his brothers) are considered more athletic and agile than American professional wrestlers. Because the high-flying daredevil tradition is passed down through the generations, the wrestlers are trained at very young ages and can perform incredible feats by the time they are in their teens. One of the most popular *luchadors* today is El Vampiro Canadienese (Canadian Vampire), who doesn't wear a mask but paints his face a ghostly white, making him resemble Brandon Lee in *The Crow*.

Numero Cinco and his brothers are an amalgamation of several famous Mexican wrestlers, including members of the Guerrero family, who have boasted several generations of *lucha libre* fighters. Cinco wears the number "5" on his mask, which is significant because it draws a parallel between him and Angel — just as Tezcatcatl killed Cinco's four brothers because they were heroes and left him behind because he was not, Angel has been a hero and champion for four seasons of the show, but now in the fifth he's given up hope. He no longer believes the Shanshu prophecy applies to him; after all, why would he be given the gift of life when he's heading up one of the most evil corporations in the universe? Wesley is starting to worry about Angel and realizes that hope is what has kept Angel going for the past three years. With Wolfram & Hart threatening to corrupt Angel every day, will he be a more susceptible target if he doesn't have a purpose keeping him straight?

Highlight: The look on Angel's face when Numero Cinco's brothers run past him.

Interesting Facts: The Mexican Day of the Dead is celebrated on November 2 (All Souls' Day), with some festivities taking place on November 1 (All Saints' Day), so the events of this episode are happening one day after "Life of the Party." On this day many families set up altars to their dead loved ones, much like the one Numero Cinco has in his apartment, and hope the spirits of those who are gone will visit them. On November 2 the families go to the graves with food and celebrate the lives of the people they have lost. The Day of the Dead was originally an Aztec custom, which is appropriate considering the events of the episode.

Did You Notice?: Lorne seems to be a wrestling fan. First, he calls Cinco "El Cid," which can be translated into "The Champion," meaning Lorne knows that Numero Cinco was actually a champion at one time. (El Cid is also the name of a professional wrestler.) Also, when Cinco throws Angel through his office window, Lorne comes around the corner, refers to the incident as a smackdown, and says he'd already read about the attack on the Web. This is a reference to wrestling fans who post information about fights while they are still in progress. Before the fights are even finished, fans start arguing about the wrestlers' strategies and debating who really attacked whom.

Nitpicks: When Wes shoots at Tezcatcatl the first two times and its armor withstands the blows, why didn't he shoot it in the face? It might take putting a sword through the heart to kill it, but Wes could have at least momentarily paralyzed it, allowing him to remove the armor and kill it properly.

Oops: Holland Manners's card reads "Attorney's at Law," which is a pretty big typo for such a prestigious law firm. Also, Numero Cinco's brothers were killed in 1953, and Cinco says that he tried to keep things going, but the phone calls stopped because people wanted heroes and he wasn't one. He makes it sound like he continued on for another year or so before people stopped calling, and then Holland Manners handed him his business card. However, in "Blood Money," we saw that Manners's dates were 1951–2000, which would have made him two years old when Numero Cinco's brothers died; even if Cinco had continued trying to help people for five years, Holland would have been seven at the most.

5.7 Lineage

Original air date: November 12, 2003
Written by: Drew Goddard
Directed by: Jefferson Kibbee
Guest cast: Treva Etienne (Emil), Roy Dotrice (Roger Wyndam-Pryce)

Wesley's father comes to town to visit and to lure Wesley back into the Watcher's Council.

Crappy dads are a mainstay in the Whedonverse, and Wesley's is one of the worst. Until now we've gotten some hints about who Wesley's father was — a harsh man who punished Wesley unduly, who belittles his grown son whenever Wes calls him, and who instilled in him such a low sense of self-worth that Wesley tried for years to gain the approval of those around him. Since the end of season 3, Wes has no longer sought that approval from people and has changed drastically from the Wesley we knew in the beginning. But as soon as his father shows up, he's tripping through doorways and bumping into others. The difference is that Wes's bumbling is not funny to us this time around.

Throughout the hour we watch Wesley suffer as his father tells humiliating stories about Wes as a child, chastises him for working for a vampire and leaving his books out on the table, reminds him of his past failures, and calls him the single biggest embarrassment to the Watcher's Council. Roger Wyndam-Pryce watches Fred yell at Wesley and Spike revel in hearing Wesley called "head boy," and he clearly thinks his son is worthy of no one's respect. Thankfully, Gunn — of all people — assures Roger that Wesley is good at what he does. Roger's constant belittlement of Wesley is not new — Wesley has lived with it all his life, from when he was growing up to the present, when he makes overseas phone calls to his parents. But now that he's endured what he has over the last two seasons, he doesn't take his father's taunts lightly.

The cyborg subplot is a little odd, and it doesn't actually seem to go anywhere. Why cyborgs? Why were they targeting Angel specifically? Why did Roger spend so long chatting with Wesley when he could have done the job quickly? Luckily, this thread pales in comparison with the far more interesting character development that Wesley undergoes, which still makes this a great episode to watch. What happens at the end is shocking, and Alexis Denisof is wonderful as Wesley reels in the wake of what he's just done until he discovers what really happened and quietly returns to his life. The discussion that he has with Fred at the end of the episode parallels the one they had at the end of "Billy," but the difference between the two is that this is a Wesley who has already lived through the events of seasons 3 and 4 and recognizes the dark side within him. The Wesley from "Billy" denied that he was capable of doing anything "evil" and was scared that admitting as much might turn him into his father. As Wesley sits down at his desk and makes an important phone call, he has learned something from the incident, and it's not pretty: he is capable of killing his own father. Sadly, the real Roger Wyndam-Pryce will never know what happened and won't learn a thing from the events that unfolded across the sea.

Highlight: Spike trying to console Wesley: "Don't know if you know this, but I killed my mum. Actually, I'd already killed her, and then she tried to shag me, so I had to [makes staking motion]." One of the best lines of the season.

Nitpicks: Roger had to sneak a gun into the building in the body of a cyborg, which presumably would have been caught by the metal detectors. But wouldn't Roger's very person be detected by the same metal detectors if he's made of metal?

The *Buffy* Connection: Spike's comment about sex with robots being more common than people think is a reference to the season-5 *Buffy* episode "Intervention," when Spike had a robot made to look like Buffy and turned it into his plaything.

5.8   Destiny

Original air date: November 19, 2003
Written by: David Fury and Steven S. DeKnight
Directed by: Skip Schoolnik
Guest cast: Juliet Landau (Drusilla), Michael Halsey (Sirk), Justin Connor (Jerry), Mark Kelly (Reese)

Spike and Angel fight to get to the Cup of Perpetual Torment, knowing that whoever reaches it first is the vampire mentioned in the Shanshu prophecy.

While season 5 has been a lot of fun so far, "Destiny" is the first masterpiece of the year. As soon as fans heard that James Marsters would be joining the cast of *Angel*, speculation began about his possible part in the Shanshu prophecy. Could it be that all this time the prophecy was actually intended for him? It would seem like a bit of a cheat if Angel doesn't get to be the vampire in question, especially since he is the one who has been chasing the prophecy for so many years (and, after all, it *is* his show). On the other hand, the prophecy is so vague and both have shown so much heroism that the vampire for which it was intended is still undetermined.

Through flashbacks we see the origins of the hostility between Angel and Spike. In the very beginning, Spike and Angel were pals, and there's even an element of homo-eroticism in what they say to each other (a suggestion that Spike confirms in "Power Play"). Angel views Spike as a kindred spirit — just as Darla and Drusilla make good playmates (or loony companions), Spike is a guy Angel can go on rampages and be macho with. However, Angel soon discovers that while Spike may be into the torture,

No Respect

Despite usually being the boss, Angel has been on the receiving end of his share of insults and good and bad nicknames, usually bestowed by his friends (and mostly from Cordelia and Spike). Here's a short list of some of the names Angel's been called over the five seasons of the show:

Angel-cakes (Lorne)
Big hunk of hero sandwich (Lorne)
Big hunk of nobody cares (Spike)
Captain Forehead (Spike)
Chairman of the boring (Spike)
Coward of the night (Denver)
Culturally retarded (Cordelia)
Daddy Dearest (Cordelia)
Darth Vampire (Gunn)
Dork (Cordelia)
Equal-opportunity saver (Fred)
Estupido (Numero Cinco)
Fang boy (Gunn)
Filthy man-whore (Vinji Demon Leader)
General Grumpypants (Spike)
Giant black hole of boring despair (Cordelia)
Gourmless tit (Spike)
GQ (Faith)
Great big sap (Lorne)
Hans Christian Tarantino (Lorne)
Joe Stoic (Cordelia)
Loser pining guy (Cordelia)
Mahatma (Spike)
Monkey boy (Skip)
Mr. Goodfang (W&H employee)
Mr. I-was-alive-for-two-hundred-years-and-never-developed-an-investment-portfolio (Cordelia)
Mr. "Oh, you're my big, fat hero!" (Cordelia)
Mr. Sunshine (Lilah)

Mr. Tall, Dark, and Rockin' (Lorne)

Our friendly neighborhood vampire (Lilah)

Psychotic borderline schizophrenic vampire (Anne)

Queen of the Winter Ball (Doyle)

Real-Psycho-Wan Kenobi (Cordelia)

Rocky and Rocky II and half of the one with Mister T (Lorne)

Selfish sod (Spike)

Self-righteous bastard (Connor)

Soul boy (Faith)

Stupid jackass (Polo the Puppet)

The Prince of Darkness (Gunn)

The Slayer's lap dog (Spike)

Wee little puppet man (Spike)

at the end of the night he just wants to go home to Drusilla. He's tied to Dru in a way that seems foreign to Angel; after all, if Spike is soulless, he shouldn't have feelings for anyone but himself. So Angel sets out to put Spike in his place and steals his very "destiny" from him. Now, 120 years later, Spike is back to steal Angel's.

The scene of the two vampires fighting has been a long time coming. While it might seem like we've seen them fight a million times, we have never seen anything like this. In "School Hard" on *Buffy*, Angel pretended to be Angelus and never really fought Spike. Then Spike was wounded and ended up in a wheelchair, where he stayed for the rest of the season. He was gone during season 3 and returned in season 4, but Angel had already moved to L.A. at that point. When Spike followed him in pursuit of the Gem of Amarra, he was accompanied by another vampire, who took care of the torture while Spike stood back and taunted. Until now in season 5, we've only seen verbal sparring between the two. The fight on the way to the Cup of Perpetual Torment, however, makes the wait worth it. It's colossal, like the Buffy-Faith fights used to be. These two vampires are equal in so many ways — they both have souls, they share a past, they're in love with the same woman, and now they both believe they have the same destiny. But only one will be able to claim that destiny, and neither wants the other to have it. In the end, the one who doesn't make it to the cup worries that the other vampire wants it more.

The last few moments of the episode are amazing, as an old enemy of Angel's resurfaces and we start to piece together the events of the season. From this point on, the season just gets better and better.

Highlight: The poignancy of Spike's comment to Angel that while Drusilla may have sired him, it was Angelus who turned him into a monster.

Did You Notice?: Sirk mentions a tree with a fork in the roots, and while he says it's a metaphor, it sounds similar to the forked tree Spike and Angel encounter in "A Hole in the World."

Oops: Spike jumps off Harmony while the two of them are having sex on a desk, but his pants are completely done up when he does so.

5.9 Harm's Way

Original air date: January 14, 2004
Written by: Sarah Fain and Elizabeth Craft
Directed by: Vern Gillum
Guest cast: Danielle Nicolet (Tamika), Jennifer Haworth (Brittany), Stacy Reed (Charlotte), David Gangler (Danny), Christopher Gehrmane (Rudy), Brendan Hines (Eli), Bryce Mouer (Tobias Dupree), Olga Vilner (Vinji Leader), Nick Jaine (Sahrvin Leader)

When Harmony wakes up next to a dead guy with bite marks on his neck, she must prove that she didn't kill him.

"Harm's Way" is a fun episode that focuses on Harmony, someone who has proven to be a welcome member of the Angel team. In many ways, it's similar to the *Buffy* third-season episode "The Zeppo," where we see what goes on in Xander's life away from the rest of the gang. Like Xander, Harmony is never appreciated by the others for the work she does every day, even though she deals with all the little things so the rest of them don't have to. She doesn't go out and kill demons or translate spells in an office; she doesn't have a vast knowledge of the law or the ability to work in the lab. But she brings Angel his blood in the morning to keep him from getting cranky (a task that's becoming increasingly difficult each day); she deals with his appointments and lets him know who is evil and who isn't; she researches the demon clans and knows how to keep the peace when Angel offends someone. But she works for someone who is getting grumpier by the minute, and all her work goes unnoticed.

While this episode does nothing to advance the arc of the season, it is nonetheless an entertaining and amusing hour, as Harmony desperately tries to cover up a murder, attempts to become buddies with the other girls in the lunch room, fights back tears as Angel ignores her once again, notices how Lorne's assistant is far more appreciated than she is, and has a bonding session with Fred. Harmony has always been fun to watch, and it's clear that she's never moved past being in high school, still with her pink outfits, unicorn collection, and cruel insults. Harmony is like Cordelia

CHRISTINA RADISH

Mercedes McNab, as Harmony, is a hilarious addition to the cast in season five, and she does an excellent job carrying "Harm's Way."

when she says nasty things to people, but where Cordelia usually meant to hurt her victims, Harmony is as clueless as Anya was on *Buffy*, and she doesn't realize she's actually insulting people. In the end she comes to an important understanding about where she stands in the greater scheme of things. And then it's back to the ongoing Spike-versus-Angel war.

Highlight: Angel looking extremely uncomfortable in the Wolfram & Hart commercial, mumbling, "If you don't kill, we won't kill you."

Oops: When Harmony is on the phone, checking off items on her to-do list, you can see she's written "To Do" in big bubble letters at the top of the sheet when it's on the desk and the items fill more than half a page, yet when the camera zooms in on the piece of paper, "To Do" is written in normal capital letters and there are fewer items on the list. Also, Harmony says that Toby was bitten on the left side, proving she didn't do it because she's a "right biter." Yet in "Destiny" she bites Spike on the left side, making her a left biter (and in "Restless" on *Buffy*, when she's in Willow's dream, she stands behind Giles and keeps trying to bite him on the left side, again showing her to be a left biter).

Wolfram & Hart: The firm conducts regular tests of the in-house vampires to make sure they're not feeding on humans — interesting, considering that the law firm is evil and in "Power Play" Angel offers someone human blood because they're a guest of the place.

Music/Bands: When Harmony wakes up at the beginning of the episode, the song playing while she gets dressed is "Hey Sailor" by the Detroit Cobras (*Love, Life, and Leaving*).

5.10   Soul Purpose

Original air date: January 21, 2004
Written by: Brent Fletcher
Directed by: David Boreanaz
Guest cast: Ciara Hughes (Blue Fairy), Rob Evors (Man), Jodi Harris (Woman), Carmen Nicole (Lana)

As Angel suffers through a series of paranoia-filled nightmares, Spike encounters someone by the name of Doyle who has visions.

"Soul Purpose" signals David Boreanaz's directing debut, and what an episode it is. The dream sequences are like something out of a Cronenberg film, while Spike's storyline is reminiscent of the first few episodes of *Angel*, drawing a finer parallel between Spike and Angel. Angel has been dealing with a sense of inferiority ever since he lost the fight to Spike in "Destiny," while Spike is upset that the mission was a ruse and is annoyed by everyone's assumption that Angel is the vampire in the prophecy.

On the surface Angel's dreams have a lot of meaning, but psychoanalytically they are even more fascinating. Many of the images in Angel's dreams are common symbols in the subconscious and signify larger issues. His dream in which Fred slices into him is a perfect example. She opens up his abdomen (seeing one's abdomen in a dream symbolizes repressed emotions) and pulls out his liver (signifying belittlement); kidneys (an illness is coming); a heart that is a dried-up walnut (which is what Numero Cinco called it; also, seeing one's heart usually signifies love, but since Angel's doesn't really exist it could mean that he needs to seek out the heart of things and discover what is going on around him); a string of pearls (which symbolize the human soul, oddly enough); raisins (denoting that just when one's hopes are about to come true, they are dashed); a license plate (which represents freedom to control one's life; appropriately, the license plate Fred pulls out is bent in half and ruined); and a goldfish bowl (goldfish represent impending wealth, but Angel's fish is dead, so the meaning is probably loss of wealth) before a bear carries everything away (bears signify aggression and overwhelming competition, bringing to the fore Angel's belief that he will lose his destiny to Spike).

Throughout all his dreams, Angel feels rejected by everyone around him as Spike becomes the hero of the day and he himself is reduced to being a mail clerk, a post he obviously views as the lowest on the totem pole (and it's another reference to Numero Cinco). He dreams of the apocalypse, which symbolizes not only the real one that's coming but also that his life has changed dramatically. And when Lorne enters his dream, Angel can't sing at all — having no voice represents a loss of personal power. While he might be the most powerful person at Wolfram & Hart in theory, he's losing the people around him as well as control over himself. The way that Gunn, Fred, and Wesley all stare at him as he tries to sing shows how unworthy he feels around them and that he's disconnected from the team of friends he once had.

His dream about appearing in the lobby with no shoes represents his feelings that something is missing in his life (it's also a reference to Spike's calling the prophecy the "sans shoes" prophecy). When Angel was Angelus he was the leader of the gang, even if Darla occasionally called the shots. For the last four years he's been the leader of Angel Investigations, even though Wesley was at the helm for a short while. But now that he's been offered the position of CEO at Wolfram & Hart, he's no longer sure of himself and suddenly feels powerless, especially next to Spike, who can come and go as he pleases and taunts Angel mercilessly in every episode.

While Angel is enduring these nightmares, Spike has met up with the person responsible for bringing him back to life. Lindsey has returned, but because Spike has never met him, he can play with Spike's mind for a while. In an interesting return to the first season of the series, Lindsey pretends his name is Doyle and tells Spike that he gets visions and Spike must be the champion who will carry them out. Lindsey describes his visions as being "like brain pictures, but they hurt. Like when you eat ice cream too fast." His description is eerily similar to Doyle's account in "City Of" when Doyle says, "I get visions. Which is to say great, splitting migraines that come with pictures." Lindsey claims he was just an average guy going about his business when suddenly the visions were foisted upon him, just as Doyle says that he'd just found out about his demon side and was trying to deal with that new knowledge when he suddenly had the visions as well.

Once Lindsey is able to convince Spike that he's telling the truth, Spike's first mission is a parody of the events in "City Of." That episode opened with Angel fighting vampires in an alleyway to save a girl, using the bat toys attached to his arms to do so, and here Spike uses the same contraptions and dusts the vamps as quickly as Angel did. But there's a difference: whereas Angel disappeared mysteriously into the night, Spike sticks around to taunt the victim, telling her she deserved to be chased because she was stupid enough to walk a dark alley in high heels. Angel never remained at a scene to receive compliments — it would have seemed rude. Spike proves that he's ruder. But in the end Spike must come to the rescue of the one person he doesn't care about: Angel.

Lindsey has clearly come back to wreak vengeance on Wolfram & Hart and Angel, and whether or not he'll succeed will depend on how much he can build up Spike's confidence while grinding down Angel's.

Highlight: Spike's *Miami Vice* reference when Wesley and Gunn show up at his door: "Well, look who's come to call — Crockett and Tubbs."

Christian Kane Says: "When I came back in the episode where I end up in bed with Eve, I went in at six in the morning with a couple of people I'd never seen before who I think they brought in just for that. Joss is very, very smart with what he does. He knew my character and James Marsters were going to be in a big strip-joint scene with a lot of extras, which is the first time I'm predominant in the show. Joss wanted me to go by the name Doyle, but they knew one of the extras was going to leak this stuff. One actually did. So when I'm talking to him, he says, 'What's your name?' and I said something like 'Tim' or 'Charles' — I can't even remember . . . they all went online and said, 'Christian Kane's back, but it's not Lindsey — his name is Charles' and we went into ADR and put Doyle back in over that line. If I'd said 'Doyle' in that scene it would have leaked out that I was going by the name of Doyle. Joss was very smart with that, and he fooled everyone."

Did You Notice?: Fred tells Angel he's nothing but a shell, which foreshadows the events of "A Hole in the World" and "Shells." Also, when Lindsey tells Spike that Angel failed on his first mission, he is telling the truth — Tina, the woman in Doyle's vision, was killed by Russell before Angel could save her. Finally, the appearance of the Blue Fairy references the episode "To Shanshu in L.A.," where Cordelia refers to Angel as Pinocchio.

Nitpicks: The scene of Buffy with Spike is so fake it's embarrassing they even tried it. The voice is so obviously overdubbed, and it's clearly not Buffy. By using stand-ins like this one, it emphasizes rather than hides the fact that Sarah Michelle Gellar didn't make an appearance on the show this season.

5.11 Damage

Original air date: January 28, 2004
Written by: Drew Goddard and Steven S. DeKnight
Directed by: Jefferson Kibbee
Guest cast: Tom Lenk (Andrew), Navi Rawat (Dana), Jasmine Di Angelo (Young Dana), David Brouwer (Stock Boy), Kevin Quigley (Dr. Rabinaw), Alex S. Alexander (Carol), Rebecca Metz (Young Nurse), Michael Krawic (Vernon the Creepy Psychic), Mesan Richardson (SWAT Team #1), William Stanford Davis (Security Guard), Mike Hungerford (Dock Worker), Debbie McLeod (Real Estate Agent)

When a psychotic woman with superhuman strength breaks out of a mental hospital, Andrew arrives at Wolfram & Hart to help find her.

"Damage" is a superb episode, especially for *Buffy* fans. It not only features the return of a *Buffy* regular but updates us on where Buffy and Dawn have been, and we see the consequences of Willow's actions in "Chosen." Sure, she made all potential Slayers powerful enough to slay demons, but what happens if someone is imbued with a supernatural power and is not mentally equipped to deal with it?

In this episode, that person is Dana. Her parents were killed when she was a child and she was kidnapped and tortured for months by a madman, and since her escape she has lived with the horrific nightmares of what he did to her. Now she's been turned into a Slayer, and with that responsibility comes the Slayer dreams that we saw *Buffy* endure for seven years. Considering Dana was already mentally unbalanced, her old dreams are mixing with her new ones, and she's becoming confused about who she really is. Buffy had a difficult time adjusting to her new life and duty as a vampire Slayer, but she had a mother who loved her and friends who helped her. She received guidance from Merrick and later from Giles; they were her Watchers and assisted her in understanding where she came from and what she was meant to do. Dana has none of those things: she is without parents, she has no friends, and she finds her new

ALBERT L. ORTEGA

Love him or hate him, Andrew (Tom Lenk) manages to bring a bit of the Sunnydale charm to *Angel* when he appears in L.A.

powers baffling. While Willow's spell seemed like a great idea at the time, we now see its downside.

Andrew is a breath of fresh air in an episode that suggests untold crimes have been committed against an innocent girl. From his overwhelming shock at seeing Spike alive to his condescending comments to Wesley and Fred to his expected geeky sci-fi references (and his unwittingness in getting Angel to say "vam-pie-ress"), Andrew brings Sunnydale to life for us once more. Thankfully, two former *Buffy* writers authored this episode, giving it a richness that might have been missing if it had come from a writer not as familiar with the characters. We discover that Buffy is rounding up Slayers in Rome while Dawn is going to school there. In the season-6 *Buffy* finale, "Grave," Buffy promised Dawn that they would see the world together, and now it looks like she's keeping that promise.

Sadly, the one major nitpick of this episode is that the *Angel* writers seem determined to be unfaithful to the memory of *Buffy*. Andrew is the only *Buffy* character who crosses over to *Angel* this season, and in this episode and again in "Spells," we discover that the Scoobies want nothing to do with Angel and his gang because they no longer trust him. This betrayal makes no sense considering Buffy forgave Angel for torturing and killing her friends while he was Angelus. The Scoobies always questioned things, and Giles, more than anyone, understands that the world is made up of shades of gray. He of all people should know that Angel wouldn't just turn his back so easily on what he believes in. Willow had been to the Hyperion last season and knows that Wesley, Fred, and Gunn are good people. Why is everyone so quick to condemn Angel and refuse to help him? It seems completely out of character for our Scoobies, and it's sad that this is the lasting impression fans will have of these characters.

However, it is Spike who figures out what is going on (despite being sidelined at the beginning by thinking Dana is a Chinese water dragon). Not only was he sired by someone whose head was as muddled as Dana's, but he knows what it's like to have many voices chattering away in his head. When he first got his soul back, he suffered the torment of hearing the screams of his countless victims coupled with being haunted by the First. It took him months to overcome his madness, and now he's faced with someone who is going through a similar experience. When he realizes how much he and Dana have in common, it leads to one of the most beautiful endings of any *Angel* episode. Spike's final line to Angel is heartrending but true, and it reminds us that Spike and Angel were once William and Liam before they, too, were wrenched into a world they never expected.

Highlight: Andrew saying Spike is like Gandalf the White when he's resurrected: "He's alive, Frodo, he's alive!"

Nitpicks: If the drugs had been hidden in a hole over 10 years earlier, would they still be potent enough for Dana to use them on Spike? And after he's realized that she was tortured for months, why would Spike refer to her torturer as "the man who *tried* to hurt you"?

Oops: We see Dana pull the door of the chain-link gate off as she comes down the hallway, but when Spike and Angel show up, the door is bent and hanging off its hinges.

The *Buffy* Connection: Andrew's plea for everyone to "gather 'round" and hear his tale, and his pronunciation of "vum-pyres," is from the beginning of the seventh-season *Buffy* episode "Storyteller." When Dana says she needs to get home to her son Robin, she's channeling the memories of Nikki Wood, a vampire Slayer that Spike killed in 1977 in New York City ("Fool for Love"), whose son Robin comes to town as the school principal in the final season of *Buffy* to seek vengeance on Spike ("Lies My Parents Told Me").

Music/Bands: When Dana leaves the grocery store, the song playing is White Zombie's "Blood, Milk and Sky" (*Astro-Creep: 2000*).

5.12 You're Welcome

Original air date: February 4, 2004
Written and directed by: David Fury
Guest cast: Charisma Carpenter (Cordelia Chase), Christian Kane (Lindsey), Ryan Alvarez (Demon Slave), T.J. Thyne (Lawyer), Mark Colson (Izzy)

Cordelia wakes up from her coma and warns Angel that something or someone is after him.
 In Sunnydale she was a vicious popular girl, cutting down the less popular around her, surrounding herself with vacuous yes-girls, and boasting about Daddy's money.

20th Century Fox Television
Paramount Studios

ANGEL

You're Welcome
Episode 12 (5 ADH12)

CREW CALL
8A
Report

DATE:	Tue. 12/02/2003
DAY **4**	OF **8** DAYS
CREW CALL:	**8A**
SHOOT CALL:	**8:30A**
REHEARSAL:	**8A**
SUNRISE: 6:31 AM	SUNSET: 4:46 PM

Director: **David Fury**

Exec. Prods: Joss Whedon, Sandy Gallin, Gail Berman, Fran & Kaz Kuzui

85

Co-Exec. Producer: Jeffrey Bell, David Fury | Supervising Prod: Ben Edlund | Producer: Kelly A. Manners, Steven S. DeKnight

Co-Producer: Skip Schoolnik | Consulting Producer: David Greenwalt

Latest Script Rev. - Pink

SET	SCENES	CAST	D/N	PAGES	LOCATION
	· SHOOTING ORDER SUBJECT TO CHANGE ·				
INT. W & H-Angel's Office	7	1,2,3,4,5D,Atmos	D2	2 1/8	Paramount
Angel says he is resigning...then he gets the phone call					Stage 5
INT. W & H-Main Lobby	A41	1,2,3,4,5D,6,7,8,10	N3	1 4/8	
Re-cap of sorts...Gang leaves...Angel and Cordy head to Angel's office					
INT. W & H-Angel's Office	41	1,10	N3	3	
Angel and Cordy alone...they kiss...a phone call -END EPISODE					
INT. W & H-Main Lobby	14	1,7,8,10,13D,Atmos	D2	7/8	
Izzy comes and goes...Cordy walks away					
· **Wall plug which hides elevators in place** ·					
INT. W & H-Hallway	22	9,Atmos	D3	2/8	
Lindsey gains access to restricted area					
· **Move to stage 17** ·					
I/E LINDSEY'S BEDROOM/BALCONY	19	7,9	N2	6/8	Stage 17
Lindsey and Eve snuggle..."We're going places"					
				8 4/8	TOTAL PAGES

#	CAST & DAY PLAYERS		PART OF	P/U	M/U	REH.	SET	REMARKS
1	David Boreanaz	W	ANGEL	-	7:45A	8A	8:15A	Report to make up
2	Alexis Denisof	W	WESLEY	-	7:30A	8A	8:15A	Report to make up
3	J August Richards	WF	GUNN	-	7:30A	8A	8:15A	Report to make up
4	Amy Acker	WF	FRED	-	7A	8A	8:15A	Report to make up
5D	Andy Hallett	WF	LORNE	-	5A	8A	8:15A	Report to make up
6	James Marsters	W	SPIKE	-	10A	tbd	tbd	Report to make up
7	Sarah Thompson	WF	EVE	-	9:15A	tbd	tbd	Report to make up
8	Mercedes McNab	WF	HARMONY	-	9:15A	tbd	tbd	Report to make up
9	Christian Kane	SW	LINDSEY	-	· 2:30P	tbd	tbd	· MU then to Zoic
10	Charisma Carpenter	W	CORDELIA	-	9:15A	tbd	tbd	Report to make up
13D	Mark Colson	SWF	IZZY (Devil)	-	1P	tbd	tbd	Report to make up
23	Jim Churchman	SR	UTIL STUNT-Rigger #1	-	-	-	12N	Rig and rehearse
24	Paul Leonard	SR	UTIL STUNT-Rigger #2	-	-	-	12N	Rig and rehearse
25	Hank Amos	SR	UTIL STUNT-Rigger #3	-	-	-	12N	Rig and rehearse
26	Mike Massa	R	STUNT COORDINATOR	-	-	-	12N	Rig and rehearse
1X	Mike Massa	SR	STUNT DBL-Angel	-	-	-	12N	Rig and rehearse
9X	Dave Leitch	SR	STUNT DBL-Lindsey	-	-	-	12N	Rig and rehearse

(K)= Minor **NO FORCED CALLS WITHOUT PRIOR APPROVAL OF PRODUCTION MANAGER**

THIS IS A CLOSED SET — NO VISITORS WITHOUT PRIOR APPROVAL

· No Meal Penalties w/out prior approval · ND Breakfast provided for early calls ·

SPECIAL INSTRUCTIONS

The crew call sheets for one of the shooting days of "You're Welcome."

PROPS:	[14] Izzy's briefcase; [22] Key card, key pad and access panel, light on key pad changes; [19] Blanket

CAMERA: Steadicam, 1-Addl. Loader

SPECIAL EQUIPMENT: Steadicam

ADDITIONAL LABOR: 2-Addl. Grip (Rigging), 3-Addl. Lamp Ops., 1-Lens Tech, 1-Addl. MU,1-Addl. Hair, 1-Addl. Loader

MAKE-UP: Lorne's MU, Wounds from fight, Izzy MU, Lindsey's tattoos, bare shoulders

SPECIAL FX MU: Izzy MU / elements

LENSES: Lorne's demon red, Izzy's lenses

COSTUMES: [14] Izzy's shiny suit; [22] Lindsey in janitorial jumpsuit

SET LIGHTING:

GRIPS: [22] Wall plug to hide elevators

ART DEPARTMENT: [22] Signage as scripted, wall plug to hide elevators; [19] Greens outside of balcony

SPECIAL FX: Elevator doors to operate; [19] E-fan breeze

SET DRESSING: [22] Key pad and access panel, signage as scripted

PARAMOUNT OPS: Stage 5,6,7,17 opened at 4:45 AM, Heat on at 5 A at 50 %

TRANSPORTATION: Cast trailers per deal memos

STAND-INS			ATMOSPHERE		
1	U-SI/Angel (Joe)	Rpt at 8A	15	W & H Folks	Rpt at 8A
1	U-SI/Wes (Cary)	Rpt at 8A	10	W & H Folks	Rpt at 4:30P
1	U-SI/Gunn (Thom)	Rpt at 8A			
1	U-SI/Fred (Liz)	Rpt at 8A			
1	U-SI/Lorne (TBD)	Rpt at 8A			
1	U-SI/F (Nat)	Rpt at 10:30A			
6	Tot. SI			25	Total BG

ADVANCE SCHEDULE

DATE	SET	SCENE	CAST	D/N	PAGES	LOC.
Wed. 12/3/2003	INT. CORDELIA'S HOSPITAL RM	A5pt	10	D2	1/8	Stage 7
Day 5	INT. CORDELIA'S HOSPITAL RM	11	1,2,10,Ph. Dbl. #10	D2	2 4/8	
	INT. W & H-Angel's PH Suite	18	1,10	N2	5 1/8	
Thu. 12/4/2003	INT. W & H-Antechamber	23	9	D3	2/8	Stage 6
Day 6	INT. W & H-Antechamber	34	1,1X,6,6X,10,10X,15,16, 17,18,19,20,26	D3	6/8	
	INT. W & H-Antechamber	A5pt	15	D3	-	
	INT. W & H-Antechamber	B24	9	D3	1/8	
	· **Move to Stage17 - "B" camera stays behind to shoot on video** ·					
	INT. W & H-Antechamber	A24pt	-	D3	1/8	
	· **Angel 100th Episode press event** ·					
	INT. W & H-Failsafe Chamber	35	1,1X,9,10,23,24,25,26, Atmos	D3	1 2/8	Stage 17

UPM: Robert Nellans   Approved _RN_

Ass't. Directors: Ian Woolf, Rich T. Sickler, W. Scott Wolf, Michelene Mundo

---

While she eventually became a part of the Scooby gang and "lowered" herself to date one Xander Harris, she always maintained an aloofness, as if she knew she was better than everyone else. When her father lost all his money because of tax fraud, she moved to L.A. to chase her dream of becoming a starlet, but the harsh reality of the big city quickly humbled her. She helped form Angel Investigations with Doyle and Angel, and the subsequent transformation she underwent was thrilling to witness. Gone was the selfish cheerleader who only cared about the latest hairstyles and shopping (although she maintained an encyclopedic knowledge of the latest fashions) and in its place was a self-assured, self-sacrificing warrior woman who gave up a part of herself to serve humanity. And then, in season 4, it all disappeared when her body was possessed by a higher being that allowed Jasmine into the world. It seemed as though the woman who had grown so much was gone, and we'd never see her again.

And now, in "You're Welcome," Cordelia Chase is back — the *real* Cordelia Chase from season 3, not the demonic one from season 4. With her she brings memories of Doyle, of Angel's mission, and of who Angel used to be. She couldn't have come at a better time. The burden of Wolfram & Hart has been weighing on Angel — he's worried that he has made a huge mistake in joining the firm, as his friends are now disconnected from him, Buffy has shunned him, and his clients are killing nuns and escaping through dimensional portals. Fred has millions of dollars of scientific equipment at her fingertips, Wesley has access to every book ever written, and Gunn has an exhaustive knowledge of the law, but their efforts seem more futile now than when Fred was answering phones, Wesley had a handful of books, and Gunn was wielding a battleaxe.

Having Charisma back on the show reminds viewers of the gap that was left when she disappeared. She imbues every scene with a characteristic haughtiness and brilliance, and she brings Angel back to the basics — grabbing a sword and fighting the enemy where he stands rather than waiting for a courtroom to take care of the problem. She and Wesley try "kicking it old school" with the books, and while their much-missed arguing has disappeared, it wouldn't have fit with the episode. Both Wesley and Cordelia have long moved past their characteristic bickering from the first two seasons. And when Spike shows up and claims that a man named Doyle who has visions has been helping him, it's perfect that the two people who would be shocked by that statement are standing right there.

It seems like Lindsey has just arrived and already his plan is ruined and he's gone, but his purpose on the show was to break down Angel's self-esteem, and he did that. Earlier, Angel simply assumed he was the vampire in the prophecy, but Lindsey brought Spike back to make Angel question that presumption. Lindsey forced Angel to question himself, something Angel had to do before he could return to his path of atonement. Similarly, in season 2, Angel had to hit rock bottom before he could realize the importance of his work and know that he really was deserving of the reward mentioned in the prophecy.

The ending of this episode is shocking for fans, and it is considered the most moving ending of the series. Joss Whedon always promised he would never kill off a *Buffy* original, but considering his track record with other regulars, the ending isn't surprising. The final scene between Charisma and David is heartbreaking, and they don't appear to be acting — they know what's coming, and they can barely deliver their final lines to one another. Cordelia Chase was one of the best things about this series, and she exits with a profound poignancy. In her wake she reminds Angel of who he is and that despite his new occupation, the powers that be are still looking out for him.

Highlight: Lorne asking why the gang always needs demon blood, and not demon urine, and seeing the look on their faces, adding, "Look, I'm making some right now."

Christian Kane Says: "I have no idea where Lindsey went [when he left in season two], and when I got back this year, they said nobody else knew either. Hell, Joss still hasn't told me. I think he went away. . . . I think he went home, and I think he stayed there for a while and then went overseas. He just studied fighting and studied magick. Why did he return? I think that he's in love with Eve, but I think he's still very upset about what Angel did with Darla. So I think he came back for revenge. I also think that in Lindsey's situation he'd probably better straighten something out with W&H because he's going to be running for the rest of his life, and if he doesn't straighten things out with W&H then he'd better get enough badasses on his side [so that] he can at least have enough power to fight them."

Nitpicks: Cordelia asks, "Who's Colin Farrell?" but he would have already been a star before she went into her coma, and she admits that she remembers everything that happened while she was possessed. Also, you'd think that Wolfram & Hart would have a more powerful demon guarding the failsafe rather than a bunch of mindless zombies. Finally, it seems strange that Angel realizes only now that he must be the one in the prophecy because the Senior Partners are protecting him. From the beginning of season 1 he's been aware that the Senior Partners believe he'll play a part in the apocalypse, and as recently as "Just Rewards" Magnus Hainsley told him that the Senior Partners have big plans for him.

5.13   Why We Fight

Original air date: February 11, 2004
Written by: Drew Goddard and Steven S. DeKnight
Directed by: Terrence O'Hara
Guest cast: Eyal Podell (Lawson), Lindsey Ginter (Navy Man), Scott Klace (Man in Black), Roy Werner (Heinreich), Bradley Snedeker (Tyler), Mikey Day (O'Shea), Matt Goodwin (Hodge), Camden Toy (Prince of Lies), Bart McCarthy (Nostroyev), Nick Spano (Spinelli)

A vampire who was sired by Angel during World War II returns to ask him why he did it.

"Why We Fight" is another flashback episode that gives us some insight into Angel's life in the 20th century, but it's not as effective as others have been. We return to the 1940s and discover that Angel played a part in WWII, when he was recruited by a secret branch of the U.S. government to bring back a submarine that contained demons so the government could study them. When he arrived at the sub, he met up with an enemy from the past and encountered a problem that made him do something drastic. The character of Angel is consistent with the one we saw in 1952 in "Are You Now or Have You Ever Been?" and perhaps his actions in this episode dictated his withdrawn and surly attitude in that episode.

This episode bounces between 1943 and the present, where Angel has once again been recruited to do something that he loathes, but he's taken on the job because he has no choice. His victim from the ill-fated submarine incident has returned to find out why Angel did what he did and now fights for good. He puts Angel's friends in peril, demanding an explanation for why certain things happened, but Angel never gives him the satisfaction of a response. Angel claims to act in the interest of the greater good, which is interesting given that he has possibly sacrificed the greater good for one person — his son, Connor.

While the episode has its moments, the scenes on the submarine aren't very gripping and feel like something we've seen before in war movies. The story of Angel being revisited by someone he damned has already been played out to much better effect in "Somnambulist," and it's sad that only one episode after the death of Cordelia, Angel doesn't seem to be taking the loss very badly and Wesley, Gunn, and Fred don't seem to be very shaken up over it. Luckily, the surprise that awaits us next week will make us forget this episode pretty quickly.

Highlight: Every time Angel says "Prince of Lies."

Interesting Facts: Camden Toy, who plays the Nosferatu-like "Prince of Lies" in this episode, has appeared on *Buffy* as several creepy demons: one of the Gentlemen in "Hush"; Gnarl in "Same Time, Same Place"; and the Übervamp in season 7. Also, the week this episode aired, the WB announced it was canceling *Angel*.

Nitpicks: If the Prince of Lies is as old as he says he is (which could just be another lie), why does he dust completely when the Master's bones remained in "When She Was Bad" because he was such an ancient vampire? And after Angel sires Lawson, why would he just leave him behind, unsupervised, to fix the ship? Wouldn't Lawson simply save himself and leave the others behind to die considering he's become soulless? Finally, in this episode Spike calls Angel "Angelus" and assumes he's still soulless, which is consistent with the *Buffy* episode "School Hard." In that episode, Spike sees Angel for the first time in years and assumes that he's still Angelus. However, within seconds he surmises that Angel has become an "Uncle Tom" and is working for the good guys. Yet in this episode he never figures out that Angel has a soul even though he's beside him the whole time. Moreover, why *wouldn't* Spike know that Angel has a soul? Darla would have told Spike and Drusilla about it in 1898, and they accompanied her to the Romanian gypsy camp to slaughter the inhabitants as vengeance for Angel's soul having been returned. Spike would have known then that something had happened to Angel.

The *Buffy* Connection: One of the officers who visits Angel in his apartment says he is from a new government agency called the Demon Research Initiative, which is "The Initiative" that Riley works for in season 4 of *Buffy*. When Spike says he'll never be experimented on, it foreshadows that he is eventually caught by the DRI and called "Hostile 17." Also, Nostroyev's comment that he was Rasputin's lover vindicates Buffy. In "Checkpoint," a season-5 *Buffy* episode, she questions aloud (in the middle of a university history class) Rasputin's being killed by any conventional methods and mentions reports of Rasputin sightings as late as the 1930s, insinuating he was a vampire. The professor ridicules her and the other students laugh.

5.14   Smile Time

Original air date: February 18, 2004
Teleplay by: Ben Edlund
Story by: Joss Whedon and Ben Edlund
Directed by: Ben Edlund
Guest cast: Jenny Mollen (Nina), Marc Vann (Dr. Sparrow), David Fury (Gregor Framkin), Ridge Canipe (Tommy), Jenny Vaughn Campbell (Tommy's Mother), Abigail Mavity (Hannah)

When Angel visits a television studio to find out the cause behind several children ending up in the hospital, he's turned into a puppet.

If one were to make a list of things one never expected to see on *Angel*, Angel's being turned into a puppet would be at the very top. The idea sounds preposterous — the execution is brilliant. "Smile Time" is easily the funniest episode of *Angel* and will have you laughing for the entire hour. Whoever built the puppet clearly watches the show, and the puppeteer who operates it perfectly captures every movement and nuance of David Boreanaz's face. From one scene to the next Angel's brow furrows deeper and deeper while his mouth forms a more severe grimace. Just looking at him will make you guffaw.

Boreanaz does a great job voicing the puppet, and Angel seems more frustrated with things than he normally is — "I do *not* have puppet cancer!"; "Stupid fingers . . . stupid string!" — and even the serious scenes can't be taken seriously. Angel goes to Nina to apologize for shunning her earlier and begins one of his legendary speeches, but you can't watch the scene without laughing because he starts off by saying, "I'm made of felt," then pulls off his nose and says, "And by dose cubs off."

While the episode might not seem to make sense on the surface, it's actually the perfect metaphor for the season. Lindsey tells Angel in "You're Welcome" that he used to have fire in his heart but now he's nothing but a corporate puppet. Roger Wyndam-Pryce tells Wesley in "Lineage" that Angel is a puppet for the powers that be and always has been. From the moment Angel took Lilah's offer in "Home," Angel has been at the mercy of the Senior Partners of Wolfram & Hart — they pull his strings and he does their bidding. Even when he thinks he's working against them, he can't escape the reality that his clients are demons hell-bent on destroying the world he has tried so hard to make better.

While the puppet plot line is so entertaining that it's hard not to wish Angel was in every scene, the scenes with the other characters are the ones that will carry over into future episodes. Wesley tells Angel to go after Nina while remaining blind to the signals that Fred has been giving him (although they do seem to come out of nowhere, because Fred hasn't been flirting with Wesley up to this point). Gunn, meanwhile, has been losing his mojo, and the humor in the episode might have obscured the seriousness of what he agrees to do for the doctor. These two peripheral events will take on enormous significance for the rest of the season.

Highlight: A tie between Spike calling Angel a "wee little puppet man" and Lorne yelling, "Is there a Geppetto in the house?"

Interesting Facts: Dr. Sparrow refers to Gunn's predicament as "Flowers for Algernon Syndrome," which is a pretty condescending reference. *Flowers for Algernon* is the novel by Daniel Keyes about a man with intellectual disabilities who undergoes an experiment that turns him into a genius. He becomes smarter and smarter as the story continues but suddenly peaks and begins losing his intelligence, regressing into the person he once was. The only person smart enough to figure out a cure for his condition is him, so it's a race against time as he tries to find a way to retain his new intelligence before it's too late. In 1968 the book was made into the film *Charly*, starring Cliff Robertson. Also, the actor playing Framkin is none other than *Angel* writer and executive producer David Fury (who also appeared in "Reprise"), which adds an extra irony to the episode — as a writer Fury is actually the puppet master, telling the actors what to say, but in this episode the puppet is running him.

Did You Notice?: Watch when Lorne, Fred, Gunn, and Wesley are in Angel's office and see him as a puppet for the first time — Amy Acker and J. August Richards keep cracking up. It actually works in the scene, as Fred and Gunn would probably laugh in this situation, but in reality the actors couldn't look at the puppet without bursting into laughter. Also, Ratio Hornblower looks like Grimace of McDonald's fame, and the dog looks like Rolf from *The Muppet Show* and talks like Dr. Teeth of Dr. Teeth and the Electric Mayhem. Both the little girl and Polo look like any number of child Muppets on *Sesame Street*.

Nitpicks: When Framkin sings "Courage and Pluck," why doesn't Lorne read him and realize he's not who he seems to be? Also, if you listen to the opening without actually watching it, it sounds completely perverse, as if the puppets are pedophiles. A child is watching TV, and you hear a voice talking to him, saying, "Get over here and touch it." The voice then makes loud, sexual groaning noises. Yikes.

Oops: Fred says to Knox at the beginning of the episode that 11 children have been hospitalized in the past three weeks and all are in comas, but she later tells Angel that it's 7 children. Also, during the big puppet fight at the studio, Ratio is in the toy chest one second and is standing next to a cameraman in the next shot.

5.15   A Hole in the World

Original air date: February 25, 2004
Written and directed by: Joss Whedon
Guest cast: Jennifer Griffin (Trish Burkle), Gary Grubbs (Roger Burkle), Alec Newman (Drogyn), John Duff (Delivery Man), Jeremy Glazer (Lawyer)

When an ancient sarcophagus is delivered to Wolfram & Hart and Fred accidentally breathes in some air from it, the gang exhausts all options to keep her alive.

Only on a Joss Whedon show could we mourn the loss of the original female member of the fang gang in episode 12, laugh until our sides hurt in episode 14, and cry as we fear the loss of the remaining female on the show in episode 15. This season has been an emotional roller coaster, but by "A Hole in the World," the ride gets even bumpier.

As usual, Spike and Angel are arguing in Angel's office, discussing the seemingly innocuous question of whether a caveman or an astronaut would win if pitted together in battle. While viewers love watching the two vampires face off in stupid disagreements, it's become too much for Angel to handle. Spike knows how to push all his buttons, and right now Angel is in a precarious mental state, as he's trying to figure out a way to get his mission back on track. When Fred ends up in the hospital after making a mistake in the lab, however, Angel forgets about Spike and rushes to her side, as do Gunn, Knox, Spike, Lorne, and her beloved Wesley.

Joss has set up this episode beautifully, right from the opening scenes of Fred in the mid-1990s, moving from Texas to L.A. and reassuring her parents that nothing will happen to her. Now she's dying, but her sweetness and innocence have rubbed off on those around her — Spike owes her his life, as she tried to make him corporeal again; Angel remembers her as the frail girl he saved in Pylea and is proud of the woman she's become; Gunn used to be in love with her; Lorne adores her generosity and that she once complimented the color of his skin; Knox worships her from afar; and Wesley has been in love with her since they met.

Spike and Angel travel to England to meet with Drogyn and stop what's happening to Fred. Gunn returns to the white room to try to get help there, and he's faced with a surprising new conduit. He's told the conduit's form is determined by the viewer (which doesn't make a lot of sense considering everyone saw the same little girl in season 4 and both Angel and Gunn see the black panther in "Hell Bound"). The scene of Gunn fighting himself foreshadows the way he'll punish himself for events in the upcoming episodes. Lorne confronts Eve in a great scene; watching it we realize that since "Life of the Party," he's started to let a little of his anger out in healthy doses.

But Wesley stays with Fred, and his role is the most important of all. The last 10 minutes of the episode are heartrending: Spike discovers there's a hole in the world; Angel is forced to make a deadly decision; and Fred suffers through her final, painful moments. Alexis Denisof and Amy Acker are at their series best in the scenes in Fred's apartment as she quickly slips from his grasp. Fred has the mind of a genius and the latest technology at her fingertips, but she's no match for an ancient god. The meaning of the seemingly stupid argument Spike and Angel were having at the beginning of the episode suddenly becomes clear, and Fred realizes (as do the viewers) that the caveman wins. One of the best episodes of *Angel*.

Highlight: Angel spitting out the words "It's not about what I want!" during his argument with Spike.

Interesting Facts: When Fred asks Wesley if his book can be any book, he begins reading to her from *A Little Princess*, by Frances Hodgson Burnett. Also, Mitchell Feigenbaum discovered the Feigenbaum constant in 1975, which is a number that governs the universal constant of chaos theory. It's interesting that Fred is aware of a number that can be used to measure chaos, but in the end, the chaos takes over and she can't see what's coming next.

Amy Acker Says: "Joss wasn't supposed to write or direct ['A Hole in the World']; he was supposed to do the finale. The *Firefly* movie ended up happening so he realized he wouldn't be able to direct again, so Alexis and I were begging him to please do this episode! For two weeks he kept saying, 'I can't, they won't let me,' and two days before Christmas he said, 'Okay, I can do it!' I think it would have been really hard to let go of Fred if it hadn't been under those circumstances — he really pushes us much farther than any other director because he knows how far he wants it to go. Where other people would be, 'Good, that's great! Okay, it looks good!' he makes you take it way farther. We did all of Alexis's and my stuff in that apartment in one day and started crying at seven in the morning and were still crying at nine at night. We were just exhausted at the end of the day, but it was really fun."

J. August Richards Says: "One of my biggest surprises was a scene I got to do this year when I was fighting myself. I wasn't expecting that, and it was so much fun. I knew that I was going to go visit the cat but I had no idea that I'd be beating myself up. It was one of the most fun things I've ever done on the show. I had to play both sides of the scene; I was so exhausted, and I've never come home from work so beaten up before. It was probably the most satisfying day on the show, creatively."

Did You Notice?: Like Cordelia does in "Rm w/ a Vu," Fred believes bad things are happening to her as a punishment for something she's done. Also, the song that Eve sings to Lorne is "L.A.," the song that Lindsey sang at Caritas in "Dead End." Finally, there's a real irony to Gunn's responsibility for Fred's death — in "The Price" he tells Angel that Fred could die because Angel runs headlong into situations without looking at the consequences.

Nitpicks: Joss Whedon is a master of the dramatic sentence, but occasionally his drama descends into cheesiness — Angel turning to everyone and saying, "Winifred Burkle" is one of those moments.

5.16   Shells

Original air date: March 3, 2004
Written and directed by: Steven S. DeKnight
Guest cast: Marc Vann (Dr. Sparrow), Jennifer Griffin (Trish Burkle)

Fred's body is inhabited by Illyria, an ancient god that has returned to the world.

Just when you thought Amy Acker was perfect for playing cute and perky, she does an about-face and astounds *Angel* audiences with the character of Illyria. Illyria is as cold and monotonous as Fred was lively and sweet, and this plot twist allows Acker to show us what a wide-ranging acting talent she has.

Illyria is an interesting character. In its time it ruled the world and was the most powerful of the ancient gods. It was so powerful, in fact, that it still has minions today — the most devoted one being Knox, which is almost as much of a surprise as finding out Skip was evil in season 4. Now in the body of a female human being, Illyria explains how inferior she believes humans to be, and how vampires and other powerful demons are like insects to her. She is appalled that Wesley and the others don't bow before her and is shocked to discover, via Wesley, that human beings rule the Earth.

Gunn has realized that he was responsible for Fred's death, and he immediately offers himself as a sacrifice to bring her back. In "A Hole in the World" he faced the conduit in the white room and tried to bargain with it, and he does so again in this episode, but to no avail. He's already made his bargain, and now he'll have to live with it. When Wesley discovers what Gunn has done, he actually tosses aside his gun — the only weapon he seems to use these days — and stabs him in a far more personal and vicious attack. Just as Angel put a pillow over Wesley's face in "Forgiving" and swore he'd kill

CHRISTINA RADISH

Gunn discovers that everything at Wolfram & Hart comes with a price, but what happens as a result of his upgrade is too much for him to bear.

him, Wesley seeks vengeance on a former friend in a similar way. While Angel's act forced Wesley to become the dark, solitary, and introspective person he is now, Wesley's act upon Gunn will give Gunn time to himself to realize who he really is and how his thirst to become a different person has only led to pain and suffering.

Angel's refusal to believe that Fred is actually gone makes him a voice for the fans. After all, we've seen Angel return after Buffy thrusts a sword through him in "Becoming, Part Two"; Faith lie in a coma for a year before suddenly waking up; Buffy die and come back to life; Connor return after he is assumed dead; and Spike disintegrate before our eyes only to show up at Wolfram & Hart. Why can't Fred return, too? Wesley is the one who finally tells Angel the bitter truth — that he saw Fred's soul destroyed, and therefore she can't come back. While Angel's soul was removed when he was turned into Angelus, Fred's soul no longer exists.

In the end, Fred's death seems to have been for nothing. Illyria is powerless in this world — her temple is destroyed, her strength diminished, her minions gone. Fred's soul has disappeared, and all that remains of her is the shell of her body, which houses this angry, bitter god. And the hearts of Wesley, Lorne, Gunn, Angel, and Spike become empty shells that ache when they realize they've lost someone who meant the world to them. At the same time, they're unable to mourn Fred properly because Illyria is standing before them, looking so much like her.

Highlight: The heartbreaking ending, in which an optimistic Fred Burkle heads off to L.A., with her entire future ahead of her.
Amy Acker Says: "Joss actually told me about [the Illyria storyline] in October [2003]. I was one of the rare people who found out about a plot twist earlier, but I had to keep it a secret from everyone. Leading up to Fred dying and getting to change to be Illyria

was certainly unexpected, but I really liked it. Fred was my main character on the show so I always enjoyed doing that. Illyria was a really fun character because I got to do something so different. The show was ending, and they were like, 'Oh, okay, let's show them you can do other things.' It took two and a half hours to put on the Illyria makeup. There are long takes of me not blinking in the episode — I was trying not to blink, so I was able not to do it, but the contacts definitely helped."

Nitpicks: Knox says he has sewn Illyria's holy sacraments in himself, but after he is killed she doesn't tear him open to retrieve them. And again, the writers unfairly have the Scoobies turn their backs on Angel as Giles refuses to send Willow to help bring Fred back (see "Damage").

Wolfram & Hart: Illyria says that in her time, Wolfram & Hart was weak, barely above vampires in the hierarchy of evil.

Music/Bands: Kim Richey's "A Place Called Home" (*Rise*) plays at the end as the gang realizes Fred is really gone, and we flash back to Fred leaving her home to go to L.A.

5.17   Underneath

Original air date: April 14, 2004
Written by: Sarah Fain and Elizabeth Craft
Directed by: Skip Schoolnik
Guest cast: Christian Kane (Lindsey), Nicholl Hiren (Trish), Christian Boewe (Zach)

Angel locates Lindsey while Wesley begins to deal with Illyria.

While "Underneath" is definitely a lighter episode after the preceding string of sad ones, it shows how Fred's death has caused each remaining member to question his purpose at Wolfram & Hart and finally gives the gang a reason to fight back against the evil that had begun to assimilate them. Gunn returns to the firm in jeans and a T-shirt, the way he used to dress before getting his legal upgrade. He might still have the knowledge, but he's starting to remember who he used to be, and he makes a sudden shift away from his acceptance of the gang's role at Wolfram & Hart and toward skepticism about why they're there and a desire to return to who they used to be.

Lorne completely withdraws from the group and takes on a gloomy demeanor that he'll keep for the rest of the series. He not only loved Fred but missed the opportunity to save her when he misread Knox. It seems he's finally realized that his empathic abilities don't work the way they used to (think of how Dr. Royce escapes a proper reading in "Unleashed"), making him of little use to the gang. In "Life of the Party" we saw that being at Wolfram & Hart was affecting him physically and mentally, and throughout this season Lorne seems to have mellowed, no longer the cheerful, always-ready-with-a-quip guy he was before. He's become less and less a presence on the show, but from this point on he keeps to himself (with the exception of joining the mission in "Time Bomb"), he mourns the loss of Fred, he begins to drink more heavily, and he realizes he's not cut out for this life any longer.

Angel becomes determined to make Fred's death mean something, and whereas Eve has been useless since she took a self-imposed exile from Wolfram & Hart, Angel knows that Lindsey can help. He and Spike find Lindsey in a warped *Truman-Show-meets-Groundhog-Day* hell dimension, and the scene of every person in that dimension opening fire on the gang (including the little boy) is hilarious. But when it's time to return, Gunn makes a huge sacrifice in order to save the others. Although he and Fred broke up a year ago, she remained a very important person and had a place in his heart, and she's been ripped out of it. Now the metaphor becomes a reality as Gunn endures having his heart ripped from his chest for all eternity. It seems as though Gunn is being far too harsh on himself for what he did. He never meant to hurt Fred and would never have taken the legal upgrade if he had known it was going to hurt her in any way. But he did what he did, and out of his ingrained sense of guilt (remember Alonna and Rondell) he's going to be much harder on himself than most people would. Lorne speaks for everyone when he reminds Angel that one never leaves a soldier behind, and then he pauses before saying, "I guess that's what we do now."

Angel has grown weary of playing games, and now he just wants answers. He knows he's the subject of the Shanshu prophecy, and he wants to know when the apocalypse is coming. What Lindsey tells him finally reveals the modus operandi of the Senior Partners — we realize why Angel and the gang were brought to Wolfram & Hart and how doing so has played right into the hands of the Senior Partners, weakening Angel for the impending fight. What Angel needs to do now is go back to the way he used to be in order to stand a chance in the apocalypse — which, according to Lindsey, has arrived.

Highlight: Illyria telling Wesley that she visited many worlds when she was a god: "And one world with nothing but shrimp. I tired of that one quickly."

Interesting Facts: Mercedes McNab was promoted to series regular as of this episode (which was a little disingenuous considering the WB already knew the show was going to be canceled). Also, Adam Baldwin is the third *Firefly* exile to come over to another Joss Whedon show, after Gina Torres (Jasmine on *Angel*) and Nathan Fillion (Caleb on *Buffy*). Baldwin played Jayne on *Firefly*.

J. August Richards Says [regarding Gunn's being so hard on himself]: "That's been the truth about my character from the very beginning; he even blames himself for his sister's death still. My character is *so* guilt-driven. I mean, he's either Catholic or Jewish. [Laughs] Everything Gunn does is out of guilt or the guilt he'll feel if things don't go his way. He's living with the weight of the world on his shoulders. That's just who he is and who he's been from the beginning. He does not forgive himself for *anything*. That's one of the things I love about my character — it's the thing I gravitate to when playing him."

The *Buffy* Connection: Illyria says, "I reek of humanity," which echoes the words of the Judge in "Innocence," who says Spike and Drusilla "stink of humanity" because they have feelings for each other.

Wolfram & Hart: Eve is not only the liaison but also "the immortal child of the Senior Partners." Her immortality can be signed away.

5.18   Origin

Original air date: April 21, 2004
Written by: Drew Goddard
Directed by: Terrence O'Hara
Guest cast: Vincent Kartheiser (Connor), Dennis Christopher (Cyvus Vail), Jack Conley (Sahjhan), Jim Abele (Connor's Father), Adrienne Brett Evans (Connor's Mother)

Angel is shocked when Connor suddenly shows up at Wolfram & Hart.

We knew it had to happen sooner or later. The *Angel* writers wouldn't leave a prophecy unfulfilled and the most important person in Angel's life (and the reason he's at Wolfram & Hart) out in the world without resolving the storyline. And now, much to Angel's shock and anger, Connor is back. Of course, Connor doesn't realize Angel is his father, but Angel knows he can't trust Wolfram & Hart and worries that they are letting go of their end of the bargain. The "Origin" of the title refers to not only Connor's true origin, but the origin of Wesley's dark side, the origin of Illyria, and the origin of the gang's move to Wolfram & Hart — all of which become clearer to the characters throughout this episode.

Unlike the Connor of last season, who was an angry young man bent on suicide and destruction, this Connor is healthy, happy, and funny. Who would have thought the kid could be so likable? In his former life, he was used as a pawn in the war between Angel and Holtz; now he's just a normal kid with no memory of what happened to him before. Unfortunately, he's part of a prophecy that's bigger than both him and the reality shift that Wolfram & Hart conjured, and he's brought back to complete his designated task. Upon his return he's the son Angel always wanted — he thinks it's cool that Angel's a vampire (although he offends Angel slightly by asking if he's 500 years old), having gotten his knowledge of vampires through Anne Rice novels, which glamorize the beings, rather than through Holtz, who demonized them. He still has a thing for older women ("They were supposed to fix that," says Angel, annoyed) and he's gone to Stanford rather than Notre Dame, but otherwise he's the perfect son.

Wesley has been taking care of Illyria, agreeing in "Shells" to help her adjust to her new world because she looks like Fred. Sadly, that very likeness is causing him to slowly unravel. Illyria looks like Fred, but she isn't. She's wearing Fred's body, but she is the reason Fred is dead. Although Angel talks with Wesley, assuring him that he doesn't have to take care of Illyria alone, Wesley does so anyway and begins to retreat into himself. Illyria, meanwhile, actually seems to start developing feelings for Wesley, showing a susceptibility to human emotions that she didn't have before. She inadvertently helps him by revealing that Fred's memories have been changed, a piece of information he uses to discover that Angel created a reality shift. She helps him on purpose when she protects him by sending Angel flying across the room, and she informs Angel that Wesley no longer works for him, as if she's now Wesley's personal bodyguard. Her attachment to Wes makes his emotional state even more precarious, however, because it's possible her memories of Fred are creating this affection for him. In "Damage" we saw what happened when a Slayer's memories got mixed in with the memories of someone who is mentally unstable, and in "Not Fade Away" Connor will explain the effects of having two sets of memories in his head. Because Illyria can detect a shift in Fred's memories, it would make sense that she also carries those memories alongside her own.

Wesley has seen the effect Wolfram & Hart has had on Angel, and now that he finds proof that Angel has messed with everyone's memories, he immediately assumes Angel has done something terrible to them. As he holds the Orlon Window above his head, demanding to know if it is Angel's 30 pieces of silver, we hold our collective breath in anticipation and fear. Perhaps it's best that Wesley have his real memories back in place of the fabricated ones, but at the same time, in the fragile state he's in, can he really stand to find out what he did two years ago? What will happen when his memories become jumbled like Illyria's and Connor's? The ensuing flashback that illustrates all the memories flooding back shows us exactly what has been changed or altered — not only Wesley's kidnapping Connor and getting his throat slit, but also Angel's trying to kill him, Lilah's dressing like Fred to seduce him, Jasmine's showing up to "save" the world, and Cordelia's becoming evil. Wesley probably retained memories of some of these events, but those memories have been altered and until now didn't include Connor in any way. The look of pain on his face is the same one we saw when his memories came back in "Spin the Bottle," and the jolt the moment gives to Connor makes us suspicious of him, too. When Connor comes out of the room and pretends not to have any new knowledge, he's actually thinking of someone besides himself for the first time on this series.

Highlight: Spike "testing" Illyria, calling her a "filthy harlot," and getting the snot beaten out of him.

Did You Notice?: Connor says he doesn't like people touching his neck, which is probably a reference to the fact that both his parents were vampires and would kill their victims by biting them on the neck. Also, while the last line Connor says obviously refers to Angel, it could also apply to Holtz.

Nitpicks: When Connor's father says his son was hit by a van while getting the paper, he makes it sound like the family lives in the suburbs, but in "Home" they appear to live in a cabin in the woods. And when Vail tells Angel about the incident in the mall that Connor remembers happening when he was five, Angel says with some shock, "You rebuilt his memories." Well, duh — how did Angel think Vail would give Connor a new life? And if the Nyazian scrolls still exist despite the reality shift, why didn't Wesley find them and become suspicious about a mention of a "child of two vampires"?

Oops: When Wesley discovers that Angel conjured a reality shift the day the gang took over Wolfram & Hart, the camera keeps cutting to the piece of paper in his hand. On the third cut, the page is different (there had been a gray line running through it that is gone the third time).

The Boy Ain't Right: A van hits Connor and speeds off, and he gets up and walks away as if nothing happened to him.

5.19   Time Bomb

Original air date: April 28, 2004
Written by: Ben Edlund
Directed by: Vern Gillum
Guest stars: Jaime Bergman (Amanda), Jeff Yagher (Fell Leader), Nick Gilhool (Fell Brother #1)

Illyria becomes unstable and starts moving between the past, present, and future; the gang has to stop her before she self-destructs, which could destroy the world.

All through season 5 there have been several time bombs. Lorne seemed like one in "Life of the Party"; the gang believes their work at Wolfram & Hart will eventually blow up in their faces; Angel has been getting moodier with every episode; Wesley is coming undone; and now Illyria is threatening to literally blow up the world on account of her instability.

In "Time Bomb," Wesley seems to be losing it completely. Lorne tells Gunn that Wesley has two modes — he's either jittery as hell or catatonic. When Wesley is addressing others, he's stony, emotionless, and eerily calm. But when he's in his office, surrounded by his books, he laughs maniacally, scuttles from one side of the room to

the other, and doesn't make any sense when he speaks. His five o'clock shadow is turning into a shaggy beard, his hair is standing on end, and his eyes are bloodshot. One can't blame him — within a couple of weeks he's lost a close friend in Cordelia; seen his boss turned into a puppet; finally found and then lost the love of his life; watched her return in flesh but not in spirit; and suddenly discovered that two years ago he kidnapped Angel's son, had his throat slit, and was shunned by everyone. That's enough to bring on more than a wee bit of stress.

CHRISTINA RADISH

David Boreanaz with real-life wife Jaime Bergman, who appears in this episode as Amanda.

Illyria, meanwhile, has been enduring problems of her own. She once ruled the Earth but has returned from the past to a present in which she has no place, and she now realizes that she has no future. She zips from scene to scene, doubling over in pain and confusion each time and reliving some moments over and over again. Just as Wesley has had his memories of the past suddenly restored to him, leaving him utterly confused, Illyria is having to experience events over and over again, even ones that haven't yet happened. She believes that Fred's body is a prison from which she can't escape and it's the reason she cannot live in this world. Interestingly, when we first saw Fred, she was trapped in a cave, going mad. Now an ancient god is trapped in the cave of Fred's body and is going mad, bringing her full circle. In a clever twist, the writers draw the audience into the turmoil by having us watch the horrific scene of Spike and Angel getting dusted and Wesley and Lorne dying — a scene shocking in its suddenness — before zipping us to the past as well. (That's something I *never* want to see again.)

When Angel inadvertently comes along on Illyria's ride, she understandably believes he's behind the transit, but the time-shifting allows him to put the pieces of the puzzle together and discover what's happening to Illyria — and what could potentially happen to the world if things get out of hand. More important, Illyria's vulnerability opens Angel's eyes to the possible weakness of the Senior Partners, and Angel sets in motion the plan that he will fulfill in the final two episodes of the season.

Highlight: The Fell Brethren acting like concerned parents and excited girlfriends rolled into one.

Interesting Facts: The woman playing Amanda, the mother of the unborn child, is Jaime Bergman, David Boreanaz's wife.

J. August Richards Says: "By the end of the series my character has come completely full circle, which is a really beautiful thing. He starts out so clear on what his mission is and over the course of working with Angel Investigations and especially going to Wolfram & Hart, his ideas about what he is doing become sort of corrupted. And then once Fred dies and he goes to the basement, when he comes out he has a much clearer direction and sense of self — a clearer idea of good and bad, right and wrong. So by the time the series is over, I look exactly the way I did when I started and Gunn is the same as when he started — he's back to his roots as a character. So it all comes full circle."

Did You Notice?: Marcus tells Wesley, "This is a business, not a bat cave," using a Batman reference with regard to Angel, which was a prominent allusion in season 1.

Wolfram & Hart: The Senior Partners have clearly been with the firm since its inception, as they already know Illyria.

5.20   The Girl in Question

Original air date: May 5, 2004
Written by: Steven S. DeKnight and Drew Goddard
Directed by: David Greenwalt
Guest cast: Julie Benz (Darla), Tom Lenk (Andrew), David Lee (Alfonso), Gary Grubbs (Roger Burkle), Jennifer Griffin (Trish Burkle), Carole Raphaelle Davis (Ilona), Juliet Landau (Drusilla), Vikki Gurdas (Bartendress), Dominic Pace (Bouncer)

Spike and Angel head to Italy to retrieve the head of a client's family, and while they are there they search for Buffy.

With only three episodes left in which to wrap up five years of storylines, sending Angel and Spike off on a bumbling caper made many fans uneasy, but in retrospect it was a great way to give us one last comic episode while finally putting to bed the whole Buffy-Angel-Spike triangle (sort of). David Boreanaz and James Marsters clearly had a great time filming this episode, and they come off like two of the stooges in Italy. From complaining about the little bottles of alcohol on the plane (an allusion to Spike's protest in "Shells"), to getting stuck in Andrew's doorway, to hitting each other by accident in the bar and then starting to fight for real, to engaging in one of the most ham-fisted chase scenes of all time, Angel and Spike illustrate how two men can become completely inept, unreasonable dolts when divided by a woman.

Throughout the hour they keep losing sight of their mission, misplace the head they've traveled so far to retrieve, return to Andrew's apartment several times looking for Buffy, and get themselves blown up for not paying attention to what they are doing. Spike loses his beloved leather coat (something fans everywhere mourned, not only for how it looked on him but for what it represented), and Angel winds up looking like an ass when he has to wear a red-and-white Italian-leather jacket. The whole time we get a series of flashbacks that reveal this isn't the first time the Immortal has driven these two guys insane. Just as they let the Immortal get to them over his conquests of Darla and Drusilla, they're now vowing blood vengeance on him for messing with Buffy.

Sarah Michelle Gellar was originally supposed to appear in this episode, but her schedule didn't allow it at the last minute and the writers had to make do without her. In the end, the episode is far more successful because of her absence, as watching Spike and Angel bicker for a solid hour is a far more entertaining use of our time. Besides, if Buffy had been there, with the way the writers have had the Scoobies acting all season, she no doubt would have behaved in a way fans wouldn't have liked and that would have been our final impression of her. The woman we get in her place is Ilona and Carole Raphaelle David is as funny as Boreanaz and Marsters. Ilona squeezes Angel's and Spike's cheeks, reassures them everything will be fine, and spits on the ground every time she says the word "gypsy."

However, the episode isn't all fun and games. Back in L.A., the Burkles have arrived at Wolfram & Hart, and after Illyria has spent time studying Wesley's grief, understanding the gang's actions and emotions, and grappling with Fred's old memories, she pulls off a feat even Wesley didn't see coming — she does a bang-on impression of Fred to convince the Burkles that their daughter is alive and well. While it thrills the Burkles to see that "Fred" is okay, Wesley is devastated. It was bad enough that the Smurf resembled Fred, but now she looks, acts, and talks like her, and it's too much for him. As Spike tells Illyria in the next episode, looking like Fred is the most horrible power she now possesses. Wesley struggles to keep it together in front of the Burkles in this episode, but for the first time since Fred's death in "A Hole in the World," he's on the verge of tears. As Spike and Angel continue to argue in Angel's office about whether or not they can let Buffy go, Wesley begs Illyria never to pretend to be Fred again, because he's already had to let the woman of his dreams go.

Highlight: That side-splitting chase scene, where the demon butler comes flying around the corner in a sports car, with several seconds going by before Spike and Angel pathetically round the same corner at a much slower speed on their sad little Vespa.

Interesting Facts: The quick scene of Spike and Dru in Italy in the 1950s is a reference to a routine by British comedian Eddie Izzard, in which he runs through an idiot's guide to world history and says that the Italians were always much happier riding scooters and saying "Ciao" than being Fascists.

Amy Acker Says: "The cast had always done readings of Shakespeare [at Joss's house] and Joss told me, 'I had all these other characters I wanted you to play and I wanted people to see you could do other stuff,' which was a huge compliment, and we felt like we had sort of gotten into a routine where it was, like, 'Okay, we're going to have Fred say the run-on sentence.' He was thinking about a different project and then thought, *Well, why not just have her play a different role on the same show?* He told me that he wanted me to do something different and we talked about, [for] season six, where there would be a Superman/Clark Kent–type thing where she would switch between the two characters a lot, so that was going to be really fun. Then the show got canceled, so he moved that idea into this season."

Nitpicks: Considering this is the last time we'll see Darla and Drusilla, it's a shame they didn't have more air time. Also, while this episode was great, Angel is completely out of character — it's as if the episode doesn't actually happen in sequence. At the end of "Time Bomb" he seemed to have embraced Wolfram & Hart wholeheartedly, just as he does at the beginning of "Power Play." As a result, "The Girl in Question" feels out of place between the two episodes.

Oops: Spike says he's been wearing his leather duster for over 30 years, but he took it from Nikki Wood after he killed her in 1977, which was 27 years ago. Also, Angel asks the bartender if she's seen a girl with blond hair and blue eyes, referring to Buffy, but Buffy's eyes are green.

The *Buffy* Connection: When Angel goes on his seemingly insane rant about the Immortal eating Buffy's cookie dough, he's alluding to her speech from "Chosen" about how she's still cookie dough that's waiting to bake, and some day she'll be ready to be eaten. (Yes, it was as bad as it sounds.)

Wolfram & Hart: The Wolfram & Hart offices around the world all look identical on the inside.

Music/Bands: When Spike and Angel fight in slow motion in the Italian bar, we hear Dean Martin's "Take Me in Your Arms" (*Italian Love Songs*).

5.21   Power Play

Original air date: May 12, 2004
Written by: David Fury
Directed by: James A. Contner

Guest cast: Christian Kane (Lindsey), Dennis Christopher (Cyvus Vail), Alec Newman (Drogyn), Jenny Mollen (Nina), Leland Crooke (Archduke Sebassis), Stacey Travis (Senator Bruckner), Mark Colson (Izzy), Elimu Nelson (Ernesto)

Angel begins to act strangely, and the gang suspects he's gone over to Wolfram & Hart's side.

If you can't beat 'em, join 'em. It's a phrase we've been dreading all season, but with this episode Angel seems to have given up on fighting the good fight and crossed over to the dark side. Angel is now a full-fledged member of the Wolfram & Hart team. In "Time Bomb" Gunn was disgusted that Angel would be so quick to hand a woman's baby over to the Fell Brethren and questioned Angel's loyalties (which was interesting coming from Gunn, since he was the one who embraced Wolfram & Hart quicker than anyone at the beginning of the season). Now Angel is offering human blood to visitors, agreeing to run a smear campaign on the political opponent of a Wolfram & Hart client, and playing squash with a devil. While the gang has their suspicions, they refuse to believe that Angel has been completely assimilated until Drogyn — the man who cannot tell a lie — arrives to inform them that he believes Angel planned to set Illyria loose, which is what caused Fred's death. Now Angel's conversion is personal.

Despite the gang's trying to talk to Angel, however, he ignores them and they have to turn to the person who knows more about the Senior Partners than anyone else: Lindsey. We hear about a secret society — the Circle of the Black Thorn, which is a purely evil version of the Masons (or the Stonecutters on *The Simpsons*). Several key characters we've seen throughout the season belong to the Black Thorn, showing that while many episodes seemed to stand alone, they were all leading up to these final installments. When we see Angel at the Black Thorn induction ceremony, it's like a darker version of the masquerade scene of *Eyes Wide Shut*, but he's successful. The question is, was the sacrifice he made worth it? Angel's clearly chosen Drogyn because he is the one person everyone would have to believe, but did Angel know Drogyn would have to die?

By the end of the episode, the gang — and the audience — will get answers to their questions and realize that Angel has been playing the Senior Partners all along. It's too bad he felt compelled to be *so* convincing, as he alienated everyone around him along the way, but he brings together Lorne, Wesley, Gunn, and Spike in one final circle of his own to plan their next move. In the same spirit as "Hero," we discover that the kiss between Angel and Cordelia was something more than a romantic gesture on her part, and she gave Angel one last gift before she left (a clever twist on the part of the writers to make her a part of the final battle after all). Angel has little hope that the gang will survive the plan he has in mind, but he knows that if they can execute it, the toils of the past year won't have been in vain. An excellent lead-in to the series finale.

Highlight: Drogyn and Illyria playing *Crash Bandicoot* and Illyria saying, in her typically monotonous voice, "I play this game. It's pointless and annoys me. And yet I'm compelled to play on."

J. August Richards Says: "The biggest thing I'll take away from this job is that I feel like I've come such a long way as an actor. I've learned a lot about what it means to be an actor in front of the camera, what it means to conduct yourself as a professional, what it means to understand the shots and your part in them. So I've learned a tremendous amount about my craft from working on this show and that's why this job will always be special to me. No matter how far my career goes, I will never forget this job because I've really learned an amazing amount about acting. I used to be ashamed of the fact that I would steal from my fellow actors from the beginning. Anybody that I've worked with I would absorb something from them but now I've taken it as a mission that I have to steal something, I have to learn something from everybody that I work with. And it would just be stupid to work with somebody like Alexis for four years, someone like Amy for three years, and not steal from them. [Laughs]"

Did You Notice?: In "Shiny Happy People," Jasmine told everyone that they needed to take hold of the world and strip away the thorns. Was that perhaps a foreshadowing of the Circle of the Black Thorn and what is to come in the next episode?

Nitpicks: In "Home," Sirk explained that the books at Wolfram & Hart could be any book Wesley wanted them to be: he just had to say the titles to them and they would become those books. However, throughout this season Wesley has been using them more like a Google search engine, saying keywords to the books and having all the information come up, which is not what they were originally supposed to do. Also, if Nina goes away like Angel asks her to, what will she do with herself once a month when she becomes a danger? And how will she keep the secret from her sister and niece?

5.22   Not Fade Away

Original air date: May 19, 2004
Written by: Jeffrey Bell and Joss Whedon
Directed by: Jeffrey Bell
Guest cast: Vincent Kartheiser (Connor), Christian Kane (Lindsey), Dennis Christopher (Cyvus Vail), Julia Lee (Anne), Leland Crooke (Archduke Sebassis), Stacey Travis (Senator Bruckner), Mark Colson (Izzy), David Figlioli (Bartender), Ryan Alvarez (Demon Slave)

The gang prepares for what could be their final battle: taking out the Circle of the Black Thorn.

After watching Angel's history unfold for eight years, it all comes down to this episode. Many rumors had been circulating ahead of time that Joss would end things on a cliffhanger, leaving the ending open the way he had originally planned to when expecting a season 6, which would keep the door ajar for a possible television movie. Many fans worried about what that might mean and also wondered how the writers would be able to take a plot twist they'd only unveiled in the previous episode (the existence of the Circle of the Black Thorn) and resolve it in one hour. But, as usual, we never should have questioned Joss. "Not Fade Away" is magical and perfect in almost every way.

After Angel admits to everyone that he killed Drogyn, they warily agree to his plan and hope that he's not going to stab them in the back. Gunn will take out the senator (he's given the task because of his aversion to her in "Time Bomb"); Lorne will accompany Lindsey on his mission to take care of the Sahrvin lair (the Sahrvin appeared in "Harm's Way"); Spike will save the baby that was taken by the Fell Brethren; Wesley will attend to Cyrus Vail; Illyria will deal with Azerial; and Angel will kill the kingpin, Archduke Sebassis. As Angel tells them all to go out and live their perfect day, we get the resolution to many of the characters' stories, and the series comes together beautifully.

Gunn goes to see Anne, the woman who runs the homeless shelter (see "Blood Money" and "The Thin Dead Line"). Despite reveling in his legal upgrade, his heart is still on the streets, the place where he grew up, discovered who he was, and found his calling in life. As he helps her pack up a truck (she's moving the kids to a new shelter), he wonders aloud what she would do if she discovered that there was a higher power controlling everything she did, rendering all her work futile. Her response goes right to the heart of what Gunn believes: that in the end, you have to live day-to-day and not worry about the bigger stuff. In her line of work, she says, all that matters is that her kids are safe for the day and have a place to go — she can't worry about other things. Gunn's fight with the senator is also fitting, because he gets to take out someone who would otherwise corrupt the common man. That her assistants are all vampires is just an added bonus for him. Gunn has gone back to being exactly the same person he was when he joined Angel Investigations. It's who he always was.

Lorne informs Angel that he no longer wants to be a part of the gang, that this life is no longer for him. He spends his final day, fittingly, in a karaoke bar, singing a Tony Bennett song of hope and longing that sums up what the world would have been like if he'd been given the chance to be in charge. Unfortunately, the world he lives in isn't like the one in his song, and he's lost the will to fight for a world that will never materialize. Lorne's mission is possibly the most difficult of all, as he has to kill Lindsey. This is the only really questionable plot twist of the episode — why does Lindsey have to die? Angel believes that Lindsey is only out for himself, that he's soulless, and that

The Shanshu Prophecy

The following is a list of key moments when Angel and the gang learn more about the Shanshu prophecy and Angel's role in it:

★   Not only does the Mohra demon tell Angel that a big apocalypse is coming, but Angel realizes that he must give up his newfound gift of life if he's going to play a big part in it. ("I Will Remember You")

★   Angel discovers the Shanshu scroll in the Wolfram & Hart vault and brings it back to Wesley. Wesley tells Angel he's involved in it somehow. ("Blind Date")

★   We discover the Oracles must die, signaling an end to the old order and a beginning of the new one. The prophecy mentions a "vampire with a soul" who is integral to the order of things, and it says he will endure a coming darkness, plagues, and fiends (most of which will come to pass in season 4) before finally becoming human. ("To Shanshu in L.A.")

★   Holland assures Angel that Wolfram & Hart doesn't want him dead, but he doesn't say why. ("Reunion")

★   Angel worries that killing a woman's protector might prevent him from getting the reward mentioned in the prophecy. ("Judgement")

★   Darla begins to wonder what W&H's true plan is for Angel, and she knows it's something big. ("Redefinition")

★   Nathan Reed tells Lilah and Lindsey that Angel will be a key player in the apocalypse, but the prophecy doesn't say which side he'll be on. As a result, W&H wants to keep him alive in order to get him on its side. ("Blood Money")

★   Lorne says the Nyazian-scroll prophecy is mystically unfair if Angel, who is supposed to be working toward the ultimate reward, will be spawning something evil. ("Offspring")

★ Lilah reminds Linwood and Gavin that the Senior Partners have been planning an apocalypse for some time, and Angel is to be a major player in it. ("Deep Down")

★ The manager of a casino finds out that Angel will be playing a huge role in the apocalypse and tries to take his destiny away from him. ("The House Always Wins")

★ Jasmine tells Angel that she knows he worries about what side of the apocalypse he'll be on when it comes, and now she'll reveal the answer — because of him, she's going to wipe out humanity. ("Peace Out")

★ Magnus Hainsley tells Angel that he can't kill him because the Senior Partners have big plans for him. ("Just Rewards")

★ Fred tells Spike about the Shanshu prophecy, and Spike wonders if it might refer to him rather than Angel. Angel tells Spike he no longer believes in the prophecy because there's no way he'll be rewarded after working at Wolfram & Hart. ("Hell Bound")

★ Spike asks Wesley about the prophecy and tells Wes that Angel no longer believes in it. To show Wes the possible phoniness of the prophecy, Angel mutters "the father will kill the son" to him, but of course Wesley has no idea what Angel is talking about. Wes tells Angel that he's worried about Angel's losing hope. Angel returns to his office, takes out the prophecy and reads it, and regains his belief. ("The Cautionary Tale of Numero Cinco")

★ Sirk tells Angel and Spike that the vampire referenced in the prophecy will be the one to drink from the Cup of Perpetual Torment, which will bind his limbs and grind his bones until he saves or destroys creation, but his past will be wiped clean nonetheless. Whoever drinks from the cup is meant to do so. ("Destiny")

★ Angel worries that Spike has a stronger passion for life than he does. He has nightmares that Spike is actually the vampire in the prophecy and that a Blue Fairy comes to make Spike a real boy. ("Soul Purpose")

★ Angel realizes definitely the Shanshu prophecy *is* about him when he discovers the Senior Partners and the powers that be have been trying to protect him. ("You're Welcome")

★ Lindsey tells Angel that the apocalypse has already arrived and is underway, and that being at Wolfram & Hart has forced Angel and the gang to accept the world for what it is rather than continuing to fight against it. Wolfram & Hart's purpose in bringing Angel over to its side was to take his heart out of the fight, making him a weaker person in time for the apocalypse. ("Underneath")

★ When Angel becomes a member of the Circle of the Black Thorn, Archduke Sebassis makes him sign away his future in the Shanshu prophecy, taking away Angel's final hope of becoming human. ("Not Fade Away")

he would just as easily stab Angel in the back as help him. But couldn't the same have been said for Faith? Angel believed in her and helped her on the road to redemption. In this final battle, Lindsey fulfills his mission exactly the way he promised to, and he fights on the side of the good guys. Angel forces Lorne to take a human life by being the one to kill Lindsey, presumably because Lorne read Eve's future in "A Hole in the World" and read Lindsey in "Dead End." However, if Lorne had picked up on something Lindsey was going to do way back in "Dead End," wouldn't he have said something then? It seems unlikely that Lorne would have let Lindsey walk out of that club if he honestly thought Lindsey was capable of wreaking apocalyptic destruction. And as for Eve's future, Lorne's been batting zero the entire season when it comes to reading people's auras. As recently as the previous episode he listened to Angel tell a complete lie before turning to the group and assuring them that Angel meant every word. So why would Angel trust Lorne now? It's sad that when it comes to Lindsey, Angel has deemed himself God and feels that it's up to him to decide who is worthy of redemption and who isn't.

Spike's story arc is the most satisfying for *Buffy* fans. In 1880, William was a man who was in love with a girl named Cecily. At a society function, he was writing a poem for her but couldn't find a rhyme for the word *effulgent*. When a cruel group of dandies took the poem and read it aloud, it was greeted with loud, vicious laughter, and Cecily told William she would never be interested in someone as low as he.

Devastated, he stumbled into the streets, ran into a vampire named Drusilla, and when she asked if he wanted a new life, he said yes and became Spike. Now, 124 years later, he faces what could be the final battle of his life, and he attends a poetry slam to read the same poem that led to his downfall so many decades before. This time, it's met with uproarious applause (showing he was a poet ahead of his time). It's a hilarious and wonderful moment on the series, and we realize that no matter how many people Spike has killed, no matter how tough he pretends to be, he's still looking for someone to love his poetry and to mend his broken heart by appreciating him for who he is. For his mission, he must save a newborn baby, which is apt considering he has shown a sensitive side that would make him sympathetic to the baby's plight.

Wesley's final day is as sad as Spike's is funny. He stays with Illyria, patching her up after her unsuccessful battle with Marcus, and she quickly surmises that there is no perfect day for him. All he's ever wanted out of life is Fred, and she's gone. As Wesley hints to Angel in "Smile Time," Fred is someone who makes the world worth fighting for, but now that she's no longer in it, neither is his heart. At the same time, he refuses to take one moment of happiness if that moment is a lie, and he asks Illyria not to transform. In his final battle, perhaps it's because of his lack of passion that Vail is able to overtake him so quickly, and in a shocking moment, Wesley is cut by a knife once more. Only this time, the wound is deeper than it was in "Sleep Tight." When Illyria enters the room and realizes what has happened, Wes realizes it, too, and despite his earlier protestations to the contrary, he now allows her to "lie" to him. The final scene between the two is heartbreaking. Wesley has been a stellar character on the series, and he has undergone such a radical transformation since his first appearance on *Buffy* that it's remarkable to think that this is the same person. After the events of season 3 it seemed that nothing worse could happen to Wesley — until he received blow after emotional blow throughout this season. As his mental and emotional states disintegrated, it almost seemed as if there was no future for him, and perhaps his fate in this episode is the only resolution for his character that is fitting. We can only hope that in death, Wesley will find the peace he was seeking in life.

Despite what happens to Wesley, the character who makes the biggest sacrifice in this finale is Angel. At the beginning of the episode he is called to a meeting of the Circle of the Black Thorn, and those gathered ask him to do the unthinkable: sign away his future. As they unroll the original copy of the Shanshu prophecy, we watch Angel struggle to maintain his composure. The Shanshu prophecy has been his impetus for four years. Earlier this season he suspected the prophecy was for Spike, which made him question everything he had done to that point. But he has since realized that the prophecy really is about him, and that knowledge renewed his appetite for the good fight. Now, faced with the possibility of never becoming human, of being

They say all good things must come to an end, but the end of *Angel* came too soon. L-R: J. August Richards, Sarah Thompson, Andy Hallett, Amy Acker, Joss Whedon, David Greenwalt (executive producer), James Marsters, David Boreanaz, Julie Benz, Alexis Denisof, Dana Walden (President, 20th Century Fox Television), and Christian Kane.

undead for all eternity, he hesitates ever so slightly before putting pen to paper. It's a sad moment for all of us to watch, but it also signals that Angel has come to understand his mission in a different way. He's no longer helping the helpless because it might ultimately help him — he's willing to destroy the baddies with no concern for himself. By walking headlong into battle at the end of this episode, he'll be fighting for the good of humanity because it's the right thing to do, not because it might lead him to a big reward. It's the most appropriate resolution to the Shanshu prophecy we could have expected.

Angel's perfect day consists of spending time with his son, and we get confirmation of what we suspected in "Origin" — that Connor knows who Angel is. Angel can take comfort in knowing that Connor doesn't hate him for who he is or what he did for him. Instead, Connor appreciates the sacrifice Angel made and is grateful to him. Angel's battle isn't with the Archduke after all (he's already taken care of that) but with the liaison to the Senior Partners, as if he intends to send them a personal message. When Connor shows up, we finally see father and son fight the way Angel has always wanted them to — side by side, watching each other's back, and working together to bring down evil. It's a lovely scene and a perfect way to resolve Connor's character.

The final scene is amazing and sad. Angel has asked the gang to gather in an alleyway near the Hyperion Hotel, bringing them back to the place where they all became friends in the first place. It's fitting that the series ends in an alley — it's where Liam became Angelus, where he often hunted his prey, where he spent almost 20 years scrounging for rats while atoning for his sins, where he first spoke to Buffy, and where his son was born. The very first scene of the series was in an alleyway. And now Angel might die in one. As Gunn, Illyria, Spike, and Angel meet up, they realize that they are down two more soldiers after already having lost Cordy and Fred earlier in the season, but while their numbers are diminished, they know they have completed the task at hand. However, the Senior Partners aren't happy with what Angel has done, and all the beasts of Hell suddenly appear at the end of the alleyway. Can the foursome possibly take on the thousands of hell beasts that now face them? Probably not, but they're going to try anyway. As Angel steps forward and announces that he wants to slay the dragon, the remaining three brace themselves for battle. And then the screen goes black. Our heroes might die 10 seconds from now, 10 minutes from now, or 10 years from now. But as viewers, all we will remember is them rushing headlong into battle. We never see them die, we never see them win; all we see is the group ready to fight the good fight.

In the end, every major death in this series had meaning. Doyle's death allowed him to pass on the visions to Cordelia. Cordelia's death allowed her to pass on an important vision to Angel. Fred's death gave the gang Illyria, who proved essential in this final battle. And Wesley's death gave Illyria the passion she needed to return to Angel in the alleyway rather than walk away from the fight. Angel came to L.A. five years ago to help the helpless, and with the assistance of many friends, he did just that. As the title of the episode suggests, he will not fade away — he will go out in a blaze of glory. It's a fitting final scene for our dark, tortured hero: despite signing away his future in blood, he really has become human after all.

Highlight: Spike readily volunteering to be the one to betray Angel, and when Angel says no, he adds, "Can I deny you three times?"

Interesting Facts: When this episode aired on May 19, the WB ran an ad at the end of it thanking *Angel* for five fabulous years on the network (which had about the same effect as a murderer sending a sympathy bouquet to the family of the victim).

Amy Acker Says: "I was happy with the final episode. It doesn't really feel like an ending; Joss didn't really want to end *Angel* so it's interesting the way it happened. It's a good finale."

Christian Kane Says: "There's definitely a completion of the arc, but I'm definitely not happy with the way my character finished off the season. I can't really talk about the episode [which hadn't aired at the time of the interview]. I've been on three sets so far that were closed except for a skeleton crew of maybe three or four people. They want to keep it really quiet."

J. August Richards Says: "Amy and I thought that we were going to be devastated the whole night that we were shooting [the last day of the finale], but we were shooting under this rainmaker and it was freezing cold. It just turned into this thing where we were just focused on getting out of there and not focused on it being the last day and how sad that was."

Did You Notice?: The final line of the episode is an allusion to the very first episode of the series. In "City Of," when Angel realizes how serious his mission is, he says to Doyle, "Let's get to work."

Nitpicks: Why doesn't Wesley simply cut Vail's oxygen line? When Angel came to see him in "Origin" and disconnected his oxygen momentarily, Vail was helpless. The same thing happens at the meeting of the Circle of the Black Thorn when Sebassis's demon slave messes with the line, so why didn't Wesley try that?

Oops: Harmony says she was turned into a vampire on graduation night. It was actually daytime, but the sun had been blotted out by the impending Ascension. Also, Angel tells Connor that he attended the first taping of the *Carol Burnett Show* and that "Tim Conway was on fire." The show began in 1967, and Tim Conway didn't join the show as a cast member until 1975. While he did make guest appearances before then, he didn't actually appear in the pilot.

"Thank you . . . Thank you very much"

Buffy Season Seven Episode Guide

This episode guide features season 7 only, as seasons 1 to 6 are in *Bite Me!* The sections that follow each episode summary are the same as in the *Angel* episode guide, with a few exceptions: **Willow Wicca Watch** catalogs Willow's development as a witch; **Restless Moments** points out scenes in the episodes that echo or have been prophesied in the season-4 *Buffy* episode "Restless"; and **Going Back to the Beginning** details all the references to earlier seasons of *Buffy*, since Joss Whedon said season 7 would be all about going back and bringing up things from the past.

Starring:

Sarah Michelle Gellar as Buffy Summers

Alyson Hannigan as Willow Rosenberg

Nicholas Brendon as Xander Harris

James Marsters as Spike

Emma Caulfield as Anya

Michelle Trachtenberg as Dawn

Season Seven
September 2002 • May 2003

Recurring characters in season 7: Anthony Stewart Head (Rupert Giles), DB Woodside (Principal Robin Wood), Tom Lenk (Andrew Wells), Adam Busch (Warren Meers), Danny Strong (Jonathan Levinson), Iyari Limon (Kennedy), Clara Bryant (Molly), Indigo (Rona), Felicia Day (Vi), Sarah Hagan (Amanda), Kristy Wu (Chao-Ahn)

7.1   Lessons
Original air date: September 24, 2002
Written by: Joss Whedon
Directed by: David Solomon
Guest cast: Alex Breckenridge (Kit Holburn), Kali Rocha (Halfrek), Mark Metcalf (The Master), Juliet Landau (Drusilla), Harry Groener (The Mayor), George Hertzberg (Adam), Clare Kramer (Glory), David Zepeda (Carlos), Jeremy Howard (Dead Nerd), Ken Strunk (Dead Janitor), Rachael Bella (Dead Girl), Ed F. Martin (Teacher), Simon Chernin (Student), Jeff Denton (Vampire)

Buffy takes Dawn to her first day of classes in the reopened Sunnydale High and realizes the school has a lot of similarities to the high school she remembers.

"Lessons" is a fantastic season premiere. It not only catches us up on how the gang has been doing after a particularly trying previous year and summer, but contains a plot that reminds us of the early seasons of *Buffy* and establishes an ominous feeling that something huge is about to happen. Usually the Big Bad isn't touched upon until the third or fourth episode, but in "Lessons" we see a murder happen in the first minute (which goes unexplained for a few more episodes) and both Willow and the vision at the end let us know that something big will rise and devour everything in its sight. Add to that a killer ending that incorporates ideas from all the previous seasons, and it's clear that this season will be not only a doozy but probably the last.

The biggest question fans asked all summer is: What will happen to Willow? While there won't be a reunion quite yet (see "Same Time, Same Place"), the one thing we do know is that she's been struggling with her guilt and her fear that there is something evil inside her. Like Spike, Willow is now afraid of the monster that threatens to emerge if she becomes angry or lets the magick take control of her. Giles has some lovely scenes with her in Westbury, England (near Bath, where Anthony Stewart Head actually lives), as he patiently helps her harness the magick within her (with the help of the coven he mentioned in season 6) and understand that the immense power she has can be controlled and used to do good things.

April 22, 2002

 # 3

"BUFFY THE VAMPIRE SLAYER"
2002 - 2003

7th Season
SHOOTING SCHEDULE

EPISODE	PREP	SHOOT	DIRECTOR	AIR DATE
1	7/16 - 7/24	7/25 - 8/5	SOLOMON	
2	7/26 - 8/5	8/6 - 8/15	MARCK	
3	8/7 - 8/15	8/16 - 8/27	CONTNER	
4	8/19 - 8/27	A 8/28 - 9/9		
5	8/29 - 9/9	9/10 - 9/19	SOLOMON	
6	9/11 - 9/19	9/20 - 10/1	GERSHMAN	
7	9/23 - 10/1	10/2 - 10/11	MARCK	
8	10/3 - 10/11	10/14 - 10/23	PETRIE	
9	10/15 - 10/23	10/24 - 11/4		
10	10/25 - 11/4	11/5 - 11/14	SOLOMON	
11	11/6 - 11/14	11/15 - 11/26	CONTNER	
12	11/18 - 11/26	B 11/27 - 12/10		
13	12/2 - 12/10	12/11 - 12/20	SOLOMON	

X-MAS HIATUS 12/21 to 1/5/2003

EPISODE	PREP	SHOOT	DIRECTOR	AIR DATE
14	12/12 - 12/20	1/6 - 1/15	GROSSMAN	
15	1/7 - 1/15	1/16 - 1/27	GERSHMAN	
16	1/17 - 1/27	1/28 - 2/6	NOXON	
17	1/29 - 2/6	C 2/7 - 2/19		
18	2/10 - 2/19	2/20 - 3/3		
19	2/21 - 3/3	3/4 - 3/13	CONTNER	
20	3/5 - 3/13	3/14 - 3/25	GROSSMAN	
21	3/17 - 3/25	3/26 - 4/4	SOLOMON	
22	3/27 - 4/4	4/7 - 4/16	WHEDON	

A	Labor Day	9/2
B	Thanksgiving & Day After	11/28 & 11/29
X-MAS HIATUS		**12/21/02 - 1/5/03**
C	Presidents' Day	2/17

Xander and Buffy have proven they're "all growed up," as Xander walks around in a suit and drives a new car and Buffy becomes a mother to Dawn (complete with "Mom hair"). Buffy takes on an unexpected job that will allow her to be closer to not only her sister but also the evil she believes is brewing underneath the school. Principal Wood is the latest principal to walk the halls of Sunnydale High (and seems to be doing so with full knowledge that the previous two principals were eaten), and immediately our suspicions are aroused. If he knows what's really happening at the school, why would he take the job? Why would he position himself so close to the hellmouth? Dawn appears to be much stronger than she was last season. Presumably she's had a much closer relationship with Buffy over the summer now that Buffy seems to have overcome her aloofness and depression, and with Buffy showing her the ropes on how to be a Slayer, Dawn has a new confidence and leadership skills, which she shows when under attack at the school. And then there's Spike, who has returned with his soul (the big cliffhanger ending of season 6) and is living in the school basement, as batty as Drusilla. Season 7 will definitely be James Marsters's year, as he'll play Spike with a range, emotion, and subtlety that he hasn't been able to before now.

Joss Whedon described season 7 as a year when everything will go "back to the beginning," and he begins the season with a bang. As the surprise ending shows us characters we thought we'd never see again on the show, it's clear that Joss still has a few clever tricks up his sleeve. This season will be a gift to the loyal fans who have stuck by the show from the beginning, and as it continues, with several references to seasons gone by, it will become virtually impenetrable to new viewers. Throughout season 6, fans were divided among those who loved it and those who longed for a return to the simpler formulas of the early high-school years. With season 7, we get a combination of the two elements: the gang has clearly grown up, which was the main theme of season 6, but in order to progress further, they must confront all of the outstanding issues of their past — including high school.

Highlight: Dawn's speech introducing herself to her classmates, and the humiliation that follows.

Interesting Facts: As Principal Wood watches the weirdness unfolding around him on the first day of school, he mutters, "Curiouser and curiouser" to himself. That line is from Lewis Carroll's *Alice's Adventures in Wonderland*, when Alice first arrives in Wonderland and eats something that causes her to become very tall. There are many references to *Alice's Adventures in Wonderland* and *Through the Looking-Glass* on *Buffy* and *Angel*, but the line is particularly appropriate to the beginning of this season, as there's no telling just how insane things are going to get.

David Fury Says: "Angel's been living with a soul for a hundred years and Spike is still struggling with it and I think it does make him interesting as a character. I love playing the gray areas with Spike — he does still want to be the badass, and he doesn't understand why it hurts to be that, why it's painful, and that's a much more interesting thing to play; it's more sophisticated than what we played before. We've lost some fans because the basic framework of good versus evil is lost. And Spike *did* go to the cave to get his soul, despite what some people say. I tell them what happened and they still insist it was a trick. He went to the cave to get a soul — he wasn't tricked. You were the ones who were tricked. If you want to believe it was a trick, go ahead, but as the writer I can tell you it wasn't a trick! He went to get a soul, he got a soul. We wrote it in such a way to make it look like he was going back to being a vampire."

Did You Notice?: Just like the Master says everything will go back to the beginning, the end credits list the actors in reverse order of appearance.

Nitpicks: Not only has Anya lost her vengeful edge, but she's clearly lost some of her fashion sense. What was with that frilly Mozart top she was wearing?

Oops: There's an awkward edit when Xander is in the bathroom and finds the talisman. He slowly begins to rise, but the scene suddenly cuts to him standing upright and clearly bracing himself for someone to jump on his back.

Willow Wicca Watch: Willow realizes that everything is connected in the world and fears that she won't be able to control the magick within her. She has a breakdown and begins hyperventilating when she can feel everything in the earth and senses the hellmouth opening up and devouring everyone within it. When Giles asks her if she wants to be punished, she responds with a characteristically sweet answer: "I want to be Willow." What she'll realize this season is that the magick is a part of her, and not necessarily a bad part.

Restless Moment: In Willow's dream, she pulls back the curtain to the bedroom and says, "There's something out there," the same way she tells Giles something is coming and everything is connected in this episode.

Going Back to the Beginning: Buffy teaches Dawn how to slay vampires, and Dawn's first time out is similar to Buffy's first time with Merrick ("Becoming, Part One"). Sunnydale High is back in business, and Buffy is back in the school (as is Xander). Dawn creates her own Scooby gang (although Kit is a little more Goth than Willow was), even though we'll never see the members again. Buffy is revisited by the ghosts of two students and a janitor who died, presumably, while Buffy was in high school. And finally, Spike's visions at the end feature the Big Bads of the last six seasons, shown in reverse order down to the Master, the original Big Bad who tried to open a hellmouth under the high school.

Music/Bands: The two people in the bar at the beginning are singing "So High" by Strange Radio (*Pop Radio*).

7.2 Beneath You

Original air date: October 1, 2002
Written by: Douglas Petrie
Directed by: Nick Marck
Guest cast: Kaarina Aufranc (Nancy), Tess Hall (Punk Girl), Benita Krista Nall (Young Woman), Jack Sundmacher (Ronnie)

The gang realizes Anya's back in business when a giant worm creature begins terrorizing a woman.

"Beneath You" is another great episode in which the characters worry that they might never overcome the things they've done in the past. Willow sits on her luggage, reluctant to leave for the airport because she knows that when she arrives in L.A., she must face the very people she hurt a few months earlier. She worries not only that she's not ready to deal with the magicks within her, but that her friends might not be ready to deal with her.

Anya has been told by Halfrek that the other vengeance demons believe she's gone soft, so she begins mini–wish sessions at the Bronze, luring wronged women to her table and trying to get them to wish bad things upon the men who have hurt them. The gang catches on and Buffy, Xander, and Spike confront Anya at the Bronze to ask her why she would do such a thing after having lived as a human with them for a couple of years. But Anya's return to a life of vengeance isn't just her problem, it's also Xander's, and he's another one who must confront his past. As usual, he immediately refuses to take any blame, shrugging off Anya's suggestion that if he hadn't left her at the altar she wouldn't feel like this: "And sooner or later, Anya, that excuse just stops working." The problem is, she has a valid excuse, and until Xander accepts that, things will never change between them. Anya is definitely responsible for her actions, but Xander is also responsible for his, and when he finally accepts that responsibility, he truly grows up and effects change in his life.

But the biggest moment of the episode involves Spike. He attempts to look and act normal for Buffy until something catastrophic jolts him back to his pacing, maniacally ranting self. The title of the episode not only evokes the ominous phrase we'll hear throughout the season — "from beneath you it devours" — but echoes the words Buffy used last season when she broke up with Spike and told him that he was beneath her ("As You Were"), which in turn echo Cecily's telling William in 1880 that he is beneath her ("Fool for Love"). It was Buffy's statement that first sparked the idea for him to get his soul back.

Buffy follows Spike to a church, and what we see is someone who has lost his mind and all hope. His psyche has been infected by what we'll discover is the Big Bad of the

ALBERT L. ORTEGA

James Marsters (performing here with his band, Ghost of the Robot), turns in an extraordinary performance in "Beneath You."

season. But even more important, he's gotten his soul back. We've seen what Angel is like after having had a soul (and lived with the guilt that comes with it) for over 100 years. Although we've seen flashes of what his life was like soon after being re-ensouled, we've never seen the day-to-day problems that he had to live with. But with Spike, we're watching a man unraveling with guilt before our eyes. While Willow is filled with a guilt that keeps her from her friends and Xander's guilt remains unacknowledged and buried below the surface, Spike's guilt is monumental. He has killed thousands of people, and now he must live with the pain and suffering that comes with having committed those crimes. On top of everything, he has done this for Buffy, who tells him in this episode that no matter what, they will never be together again.

Sarah Michelle Gellar does a great job in this scene as it slowly dawns on Buffy that Spike has somehow gotten a soul to be with her. But the episode belongs to James Marsters. As he moves from incoherent babbling to confusion to a disjointed explanation (with a few lucid moments in between) he steals the scene, making it positively Shakespearean. In Spike's weird way, he admits in this scene that he's looking for forgiveness and love, but now he realizes he might never receive either. As he drapes himself on the cross, whispering, "Can we rest now? Buffy, can we rest?" as he slowly burns, we see the remnants of a man who has been completely destroyed. An astounding performance by Marsters, and one of the best scenes on *Buffy* ever.

Highlight: The look that passes between Xander and Spike when Nancy asks, "Is there anyone here that hasn't slept together?"

Nitpicks: How did Anya think turning a crazed stalker into a giant Slugoff demon was revenge? She's made him far more powerful than he was before, and now he's able to not only terrorize his ex-girlfriend but devour her as well.

Restless Moment: When Spike begins to tell Buffy what he did, he is standing in the dark and you can only see parts of him in shadow. The scene looks very much like the one in *Apocalypse Now* when Kurtz first speaks to Willard, and in "Restless," there is a scene in Xander's dream from *Apocalypse Now* where Principal Snyder takes on the role of Kurtz. Also, Xander tries to talk Anya out of becoming a vengeance demon again and tells her people can't just do whatever they want.

Going Back to the Beginning: Principal Wood warns Buffy that she might be eaten alive by the students, which immediately makes her think of Principal Flutie and how he met his death in season 1 ("The Pack").

Music/Bands: At the beginning of the episode, when the German girl is being chased, the song playing is Stillste Stund's "Von der Tiefe" (*Ein Mensch, ein Ding, ein Traum*); we hear "David" by Gus Gus (*Attention*) when Anya is talking to the woman with the spineless boyfriend; "It Came from Japan" by the Von Bondies (*Lack of Communication*) plays as Anya and Spike begin fighting at the Bronze; and Joey Ramone's "Stop Thinking About It," (*Don't Worry About It*) plays while Xander talks to Anya.

7.3 Same Time, Same Place

Original air date: October 8, 2002
Written by: Jane Espenson
Directed by: James A. Contner
Guest cast: Camden Toy (Gnarl), Anthony S. Johnson (Father), Matt Koruba (Teen Boy), Nicholette Dixon (Sister), Marshe Daniel (Brother)

Willow returns to L.A., but she can't find Buffy, Dawn, and Xander, who can't see her, either.

In previous years the Big Bad has been vanquished by Buffy and the gang, but last year there was no clear bad. All that was clear was that one of their own had had her heart ripped out and turned evil, threatening to destroy the world and everything in it. And of all people, that "villain" was Willow. Buffy, Xander, and Anya watched Willow kill a man, and Xander risked his life trying to stop her from killing more. She almost killed Giles and tried to slay Buffy. How does someone come back from that? For the last two episodes the writers have explored Willow's guilt and worry that her friends might not accept her. She's finally built up the courage (with Giles's help) to return, and now we'll see what happens when she does.

"Same Time, Same Place" explores how detrimental silence and white lies can be. Willow worries her friends won't forgive her. Xander, Buffy, and Dawn are excited to see Willow, but each one of them carries the fear within them that she might wreak havoc upon Sunnydale once again if she's pushed too far. Until they are willing to show Willow their true feelings about her, she won't be able to see them at all. And until she accepts that she *is* in control of things and can explain that to her friends, she will be invisible to them. All three of them immediately wonder if Willow is responsible for the death they find in the school construction site, proving they aren't ready to see her yet. What everyone has to do is get ready to see the real Willow and accept that she's not the same Willow she used to be. Until they can see all of her, they won't see her at all.

Anya, on the other hand, who has always been known for speaking her mind — "Come in! Enjoy my personal space!" — can see Willow as clearly as anyone else. She identifies with what Willow has gone through — where Willow lost Tara and went evil, Anya lost Xander and returned to her old ways. She knows what it's like to do terrible things and then feel guilty about them, and to long for the others to accept her for what she is. When she says to Willow, "I wish it could be better for you," she means it, but she also means it for herself. Ultimately, it's Anya's honesty and consequent ability to see her that saves Willow's life.

Willow (Alyson Hannigan) knew it was going to be difficult returning to Sunnydale, but she has no idea what is waiting for her when she does.

This episode is a great way to reintroduce Willow to Sunnydale, and it also features one of the creepiest villains of all time in the Buffyverse. Gnarl has an eerie nursery-rhyme voice that is reminiscent of the Gentlemen in "Hush" and a method of killing his victims that is unparalleled in grossness. Don't watch this episode while eating spaghetti.

Highlight: Anya using Dawn as a posable action figure.

Interesting Facts: Camden Toy, who plays Gnarl, also played one of the Gentlemen in "Hush" and plays the Übervamp in upcoming episodes.

Jane Espenson Says: "Ooh. Gnarl was creepy, wasn't he? Much of that was because of the amazing work of the actor who was also one of the very scary Gentlemen in the episode 'Hush.' I wish I could remember where the skin-eating notion came from — probably Joss. It was such a nice parallel with Willow having flayed Warren and gave us exactly what we needed for that episode. I simply wrote him as creepy as I could, but I was still surprised when one of the actors auditioning for the role felt the need to ask if I saw him as an aggressive guy. Um . . . yeah."

Did You Notice?: When Willow asks Anya, "Spike's what in the whatment?" Anya only fills in the blanks for the "what"s when she answers, "Crazy. Base." Also, Dawn calls up the online database Demons, Demons, Demons, the same one that Cordelia regularly checks on *Angel*. Finally, Buffy puts her fingers in Gnarl's eyes to kill him, and Xander in particular is disgusted, a foreshadowing of what will happen later in the season.

Oops: As Gnarl makes his first cut into Willow, the camera angle from the side makes it look like she already has several slices taken out of her abdomen.

Willow Wicca Watch: Willow tries a locator spell to find her friends, but it goes kerflooey and burns Anya's carpet. She admits that by worrying she wouldn't see her friends, she caused the invisibility to happen.

Restless Moment: Tara tells Willow that they'll all find out about her and they'll punish her. In Giles's pep talk before the performance, he tells everyone the audience wants to "find you, strip you naked, and eat you alive, so hide." At the performance, Willow is scared that everyone will see her.

Going Back to the Beginning: Spike asks Buffy, "What's a word that means 'glowing'? Gotta rhyme." His question is a reference to "Fool for Love," probably the most referenced episode this season, when we see a flashback to William, the man Spike was before Drusilla turned him, and his life as a "bloody awful poet." He uses the word *effulgent* in a poem, which is mocked at a high-society party, and later, before Drusilla turns him into a vampire, she tells him he wants something glistening and glowing, "something effulgent."

7.4 Help

Original air date: October 15, 2002
Written by: Rebecca Rand Kirshner
Directed by: Rick Rosenthal
Guest cast: Azura Skye (Cassie Newton), Zachery Bryan (Peter Nicols), Glenn Morshower (Mr. Newton), Rick Gonzalez (Tomas), Kevin Christy (Josh), Beth Skipp (Lulu; her scenes were deleted even though she's credited), Anthony Harrell (Tough Boy), Jarrett Lennon (Martin Wilder), J Barton (Mike Helgenburg), Daniel Dehring (Red Robed #1), AJ Wedding (Red Robed #2), Marcie Lynn Ross (Dead Woman)

When a student comes to Buffy's office and tells her that she knows she'll be dead by the following Friday, Buffy does everything in her power to make sure that doesn't happen.

"Help" touches on a topic that was explored throughout season 5: what happens when someone is threatened with a death that is not supernatural in any way and nothing can be done to stop it. Near the beginning of the episode, there's a touching scene where Willow visits Tara's grave for the first time and says, "Hey, it's me" (try watching that scene with dry eyes). Willow has accepted that Tara is gone and nothing is going to bring her back because her death wasn't a supernatural one. Similarly, Buffy realized that she couldn't save Joyce from a brain aneurysm. Now Buffy is faced with a student who at first appears suicidal, but isn't, and Buffy is determined to keep her safe.

Cassie is a typical artistic teenager: on the outside, she wears all black, writes depressing poetry, and eschews all high-school social functions because she thinks they're lame. People believe she's either suicidal or pretending to be, but on the inside she's incredibly intelligent, full of life, and exploring her feelings in ways that most people her age would be afraid to. Buffy and Xander investigate several possibilities of how she might die: her alcoholic father may become overly violent; a spurned boyfriend might seek revenge; a school cult could ritualistically murder her (this is Sunnydale, after all). But in the end they're wrong, showing that maybe they were looking too much on the outside, and not enough on the inside.

While the episode is entertaining, it's important for the impact of Cassie's character on the others and their fight. She tells Buffy that she will make a difference, and she says to Spike, "Someday she'll tell you," prescient words for both that will ring true in "Chosen."

Highlight: Buffy telling the guys that to complete their ritualistic atmosphere they should be listening to the music of "Blue Clam Cult."
Interesting Facts: Leaving stones on a loved one's grave is a Jewish tradition that not

only signals to the next person that someone else has visited the deceased but hearkens back to an older tradition. Grave monuments used to be made from mounds of stones, and leaving a stone behind shows that we are never finished building a monument to the deceased. It also symbolizes that love and memory are as strong as a rock. Also, Zachery Bryan, who plays Peter Nicols, is best known as Brad Taylor from *Home Improvement*. And finally, the Web site that Willow finds with Cassie Newton's poetry is real. Go to www.geocities.com/newcassie and you'll find the same site; the poetry on it was written by Rebecca Rand Kirshner.

Jane Espenson Says: "Every season our titles would change. The titles are very non-descriptive and they're built into your contract. Usually writers work under a three-year contract that specifies a promotion to each successive title in each year. But the duties vary very little. On some shows, the higher titles imply a greater involvement in the production aspects of the show like casting, editing, observing the director or the sound mix . . . but on other shows, these never become part of the writers' duties. I personally enjoy writing, and I'm very happy to enjoy the higher pay that comes along with the higher titles without taking on the extra responsibility. For the sake of completeness, here is the whole array of titles that writers work their way up through, from lowest to highest: staff writer, story editor, executive story editor, co-producer, producer, supervising producer, co-executive producer, executive producer, and except for that last one, they're all just writers."

Nitpicks: There doesn't seem to be a particular time lag between being bitten by a vampire and reawakening as a vampire. Often Buffy sits around in cemeteries waiting for the vampires to rise, yet in this episode she, Dawn, and Xander sneak into a funeral home to stake the vampire the night before the funeral visitation. How did she know it would rise then? And why don't more vampires rise before they're actually buried in the ground? Also, as the gang is looking through Cassie's file they find personal photos of Cassie with her friend Mike. Where did they get those photos?

Willow Wicca Watch: Willow worries that when the time comes for the Big Bad to rise, she won't be able to help.

Going Back to the Beginning: The scene of Xander, Dawn, and Buffy in the funeral home ready to stake the vampire is similar to the scene in "Phases" where Buffy goes to the visitation of a girl who's been killed and ends up having to stake her. Also, the parade of students coming into Buffy's office looking for help confirms her experience in "Earshot," when she discovered that no matter how popular or unpopular, smart or athletic, pretty or plain, every student has problems. At the time, she could hear what the students were saying by reading their minds, but now the students are coming to her voluntarily and opening up. The crazy ritual in which a bunch of stupid boys in robes tries to call forth a large demon and offer up a female sacrifice for riches is the same as the one in "Reptile Boy," where Cordelia and Buffy were the prey. Finally, Cassie's speech to Buffy and Xander about how she wants to get older and see things happen, experience love, and wear a silly dress to the formal dance is similar to Buffy's tearful confession in "Prophecy Girl" when she first hears the prophecy that she'll die before prom night.

7.5 Selfless

Original air date: October 22, 2002
Written by: Drew Goddard
Directed by: David Solomon
Guest cast: Abraham Benrubi (Olaf), Andy Umberger (D'Hoffryn), Kali Rocha (Halfrek), Joyce Guy (Professor), Jennifer Shon (Rachel), Taylor Sutherland (Villager #1), Marybeth Scherr (Villager #2), Alessandro Mastrobuono (Villager #3), Daniel Spanton (Viking #1), John Timmons (Viking #2)

When Anya wreaks vengeance and leaves a dozen frat boys dead, Buffy realizes she'll have to do something drastic to stop her.

Flashback episodes are always fan favorites, and now we finally see Anya as she once was, way back in her early days — 1,120 years ago. Filmed in a hilarious format reminiscent of *I Love Lucy*, we see her joking around with her husband, Olaf, preparing his meals for him, and showing some jealousy about his hanging out at the local bar with its loose barmaid. We see why she became a vengeance demon, how much she enjoyed it, and what partial responsibility she had in the 1905 Russian Revolution. Throughout, Anya comes across as someone who truly believes in her work, who feels no remorse for the thousands of men she has tortured and killed. What makes these flashbacks so powerful is that they cut back to the present, where Anya can barely live with herself after what she's done at the frat house. She puts up a brave face to everyone else, trying to prove to them that she's a demon first and foremost, but viewers know that she's racked with guilt.

Though this is an Anya-centric episode, the most important part of "Selfless" is Buffy's reaction to what Anya has done and the passionate argument she has with Xander. When she announces calmly that she has to kill Anya, not only does Xander react with shock, but the viewer raises an eyebrow as well. Isn't this the person who forgave Angel after he killed Jenny, tortured Giles, and tormented her friends? Hasn't she given Spike a pardon after he's murdered and tortured thousands? Xander brings up these points and more, but Buffy retorts that despite what he might think, she is the law and has been forced to make decisions that she doesn't want to make. She will always feel alone because of her vocation, and tells him she's cut herself off from

"Selfless" takes us back to Anya's (Emma Caulfield) origins, when she was "Aud" (pro-nounced, fittingly, "odd").

8A

CREW CALL

Twentieth Century Fox Television

DAY: Wednesday   DATE: September 4, 2002
DAY 6 OF 8
SHOOTING CALL: 8:45A
WEATHER: partly sunny; HI 73, LO 61
SUNRISE: 6:29A
SUNSET: 7:14P

EPISODE: Selfless   EPISODE#: 7ABB05   DATES 8/27-9/6/02, 2U 8/19&9/9/02
EXEC. PRODUCERS: Joss Whedon, Marti Noxon, Gail Berman, Sandy Gallin,
                 Fran Kuzui & Kaz Kuzui
CO-EXEC. PRODUCERS: David Fury, Jane Espenson, David Solomon
SUPERVISING PRODUCER: Doug Petrie
PRODUCERS: Marc Alpert, Gareth Davies   CO-PRODUCER: John Perry
DIRECTOR David Solomon

SETS	SCENES	CAST	D/N	PGS.	LOCATION
REHEARSAL AT CALL					
INT XANDERS APARTMENT-LIVING ROOM	24,B25,D25	2,6	N-flshbk	2 4/8	*Stage 3*
ANYA has a musical moment (FLASHBACK)					
EXT XANDER'S APARTMENT-BEDROOM	A25	6	N-flshbk	2/8	
ANYA smooths bed, gets blanket (FLASHBACK)					
EXT XANDER'S APARTMENT-KITCHEN	C25	2,6	N-flshbk	2/8	
ANYA sings and dances (FLASHBACK)					
EXT XANDER'S APARTMENT-BALCONY	25	6	N-flshbk 2	2/8	
ANYA sings on balcony (FLASHBACK)					
MORE VIKING FITTINGS TODAY!					
NOTE: LIMITED TECH SCOUT TO GLENDALE AT WRAP TODAY					
FOR 2ND UNIT EXT GERMANY TO SHOOT TUES 9/10				total pages:	3 2/8

CAST & DAY PLAYERS		CHARACTER	STATUS	MU CALL	SET CALL	REMARKS
1	Sarah Michelle Gellar	BUFFY	H			HOLD
2	Nicholas Brendon	XANDER	W	7:45A	8:45A	Report to SM Stages
4	Alyson Hannigan	WILLOW	H			HOLD
5	James Marsters	SPIKE	~~	~	~	
6	Emma Caulfield	ANYA	W	7A	8:45A	Report to SM Stages
7	Michelle Trachtenberg	DAWN	~~	~	~	
8	Andy Umberger	D'HOFFRYN	H			HOLD
10	Abraham Benrubi	OLAF	H			HOLD
X	John Medlen	STUNT COORDINATOR	H			HOLD
1X	Michelle Waitman	STUNT DBL BUFFY	H			HOLD
99	Anne Fletcher	CHOREOGRAPHER	SWF	~	8A	Report to crew parking

STAND INS & ATMOS		MU/WARD	SET CALL	REMARKS
2	UTILITY STAND-IN(S) (John, Rikki Rae)	~	8A	rpt to crew parking
7	VIKING FITTINGS (2 women, 5 men)	1P-4:30P	~	rpt to crew parking
	(to see wardrobe, hr/mup, ads, director)			
	(from 1P-4:30P)			
9	TOTAL			

INSTRUCTIONS

Camera: sc 24, B25, D25, 25: Technocrane w/ hot gears

Sound: Playback for sc 24 etc

Props: sc 24 etc: Engagement ring, hard hat and tool belt, blanket, lunch box, dinner remnants, coconuts sc 25: Engagement ring

Makeup/ Hair: sc 24 etc: Blonde everyday wig; sc 25: wedding hairdo
          More VIKING fittings today.

Costumes: sc 24 etc: XANDER in construction worker outfit w/ workboots to take off sc 24 etc: everyday look, sc 25: wedding dress
          More VIKING fittings today.

Set Dressing: sc 24 etc: Bedroom Dresser Drawers dressed
          sc 24 etc:Coconuts, dinner remnants w/ candles,orange recliner, ANYA smooths comforter on bed

Art Dept: sc 25: finish balcony, backing
          sc 25: balcony doors are thrown open,

COURTESY JENNIFER KAPLAN

The crew call sheet for one of the shooting days on "Selfless." Notice the line about Viking fittings.

others because of these feelings. The problem is, Xander is right. When Buffy was younger, she always found a way around things if it would help save the love of her life. She's saved Spike because she has feelings for him now that she's older. When Oz was dangerous they found a way to protect him and others from the wolfy side. But now that Anya has killed a group of people, Buffy seems to have made a decision that will impact everyone, and she doesn't seem to feel any remorse for it.

There was a time when, despite what all the Watcher history books said, Buffy refused to cut herself off from her friends. She's always carried a certain burden quietly without telling anyone, but now that she's gotten older and apparently more "mature," she's become a lot more emotionless about certain decisions and doesn't treat the Scoobies like a consultation committee the way she once did. She makes the decisions (even if they involve saving Angel's life and not Anya's), Scoobies be damned, and it's this cold mentality she has developed that will be her undoing by the end of the season. Buffy would like to think that this "leadership" is proof of her maturity, but an utter lack of respect for those around you does not equal adulthood.

Highlight: D'Hoffryn stating that the fraternity house looks like somebody slaughtered an Abercrombie and Fitch catalog.

Did You Notice?: When Anya goes to the window during her "I'm the Missus" song, you can hear the Parking Ticket Woman and the Mustard Man singing a duet below her window.

Nitpicks: While we're shown that Anya's house was overrun with rabbits when she was human, it doesn't explain her extreme bunny fear. Also, when Willow calls Buffy to give her the details about the dead fraternity guys she's found, Buffy takes down the information and then says, "Hey, did you get that physics class you wanted?" It's not like Buffy to casually joke after hearing that a dozen people have just been slaughtered. And Anya killed the frat boys early in the day, but in the evening when Buffy shows up to kill her, they are all still lying there. Aren't there ever any drop-in visitors to the fraternity? Didn't any of their friends wonder where they were and come by to check on them? Finally, the homage to the musical episode was a nice touch, but the song was pretty weak in comparison with the songs from "Once More, with Feeling."

Oops: In the flashback to the musical episode, the wig on Emma Caulfield is far too blond; her hair was red at the time.

Willow Wicca Watch: Willow uses magick as a shield to hold back the spider, but it momentarily takes over and she goes all black-eyed, telling the girl at the frat house to shut her whimpering mouth.

Restless Moment: Xander dreams that his father ripped his heart out. In this episode, Anya gets revenge on the frat boys by removing their hearts.

Going Back to the Beginning: Ah, frat houses. We've seen them in "Reptile Boy" and throughout season 4 (the Initiative lived in one), and while the fraternity boys are always loathsome creatures who probably deserve to have their hearts ripped out, in this episode we realize that *maybe* that would be wrong. More important, a thread that has always been left hanging in the series is addressed here (although it's still hanging) when Buffy reminds Xander that he and Willow had told her to kick Angel's ass ("Becoming, Part Two") and Willow responds in a shocked manner, "I never said that!" Finally, the 2001 flashback is to "Once More, with Feeling."

Music/Bands: Joseph Haydn's String Quartet no. 2 in F Major plays during the first flashback to Anya and Halfrek in 1905.

7.6 Him

Original air date: November 5, 2002
Written by: Drew Z. Greenberg
Directed by: Michael Gershman
Guest cast: Thad Luckinbill (R.J. Brooks), Brandon Keener (Lance Brooks), Yan England (O'Donnell), Angela Sarafyan (Lori), David Ghilardi (Teacher), Riki Lindhome (Cheryl)

Dawn falls in love with a football jock at school, and before long, Buffy, Anya, and Willow have fallen for him as well.

Well, the streak of excellent episodes had to end somewhere. "Him" isn't a terrible episode, but it's a little silly and doesn't live up to the standard that the first five episodes of the season have established. Also, there's an underlying chauvinism to the episode that's a little disturbing. The premise of "Him" is that women are drawn to a particular guy in the school because he's wearing a jacket that puts them under a sort of love spell, making them want to do whatever they can to make him theirs. The metaphor of the episode is the power of the uniform — in high school, it's the football uniform that drives the women crazy; in later years, it could be the uniform of a doctor or a police officer. Unfortunately, the episode suggests that only women fall for uniforms and all the power (or lack thereof) that they embody. None of the men in the episode falls under the spell of any uniform, and that's unfortunate. Considering Willow is *gay*, why exactly does she fall under its spell and not Xander?

Dawn (Michelle Trachtenberg) goes off the deep end when she believes she's found the man of her dreams.

"Him" has its moments — the *Charlie's Angels* homage with the 1970s music and four-way split screen; the scene of Spike and Xander visiting R.J.'s brother (whose pizza-delivery uniform evokes the opposite reaction of R.J.'s football jacket); Anya's lie about writing an epic poem comparing R.J. to a daisy; Spike and Xander stealing R.J.'s jacket like a couple of hoodlums. But overall, the silliness of the episode — Willow saying she'll just try to work past the fact R.J. has a penis; Buffy straddling R.J. in the guidance office — outweighs the good, and the suggested misogyny is a little bit much.

Highlight: The scene of Buffy with the rocket launcher outside Principal Wood's office, and Spike attacking her.

Did You Notice?: In "Earshot," Xander makes a joke about who the culprit might be, and it turns out he's right. In this episode he makes a similar joke, and he's right again.

Nitpicks: Just one episode before this one, Buffy tried to kill the woman that Xander loves. Now she has the nerve to show up at Xander's house and insist that he take Spike in? That takes a lot of chutzpah. Also, when the gang shows up at the trainyard, why does Xander just calmly point to Dawn lying on the tracks and say, "Oh look" like it's not a big deal she's about to get hit by a train?

Oops: Xander spots Dawn lying on the tracks and when the camera shows us the Scoobies' point of view, she looks fairly close. Yet Buffy runs toward her, jumps onto a train, rides it for a while, and then leaps down onto the tracks, making it seem like Dawn was a mile or more away.

Willow Wicca Watch: Willow decides to use magick to prove her love to R.J., and later she uses it more practically to do a locator spell.

Going Back to the Beginning: Dawn auditions for the cheerleading squad wearing Buffy's cheerleading outfit from "The Witch." The spell cast over the women is reminiscent of the one Xander conjured up in "Bewitched, Bothered, and Bewildered," and there is even a flashback to it, with Xander's nostalgic comment, "Good times."

Music/Bands: Whenever someone goes into a trance watching R.J., we hear Max Steiner's "Theme from *A Summer Place*"; when Dawn is looking for Buffy's cheerleading outfit, we hear "New Slang" by The Shins (*Oh, Inverted World*); King Black Acid's "School Blood" (*Loves a Long Song*) plays as Dawn lies on her bed and tells Buffy she's in love with R.J.; at the Bronze, The Breeders play "Little Fury" and "Son of Three" (*Title TK*); Coldplay's "A Warning Sign" (*A Rush of Blood to the Head*) plays as Dawn looks for R.J. in the school hallways; Tamara Silvera's "Let You Know" (*Sink or Swim*) plays at the end of the episode as the gang talks in Buffy's living room.

7.7 Conversations with Dead People

Original air date: November 12, 2002
Written by: Jane Espenson and Drew Goddard
Directed by: Nick Marck
Guest cast: Jonathan M. Woodward (Holden Webster), Azura Skye (Cassie), Kristine Sutherland (Joyce Summers), Stacey Scowley (Young Woman)

Buffy, Dawn, Willow, and Andrew all encounter dead people from their past who help them understand who they are now.

"Conversations with Dead People" is considered by many to be the masterpiece of the season. It explores the deepest fears of all the characters as they talk to people who they knew at one time but are now dead. Jonathan and Andrew return to Sunnydale, with Andrew conducting a secret mission and Jonathan hoping he can win back the respect of Buffy and the gang and be asked to be part of the Scoobies.

How a Script Is Written

When I was interviewing Jane Espenson for this book, I asked her about the writing process on Buffy *and* Angel *and how a script goes from start to finish. The following is her very detailed answer.*

The first part of the process of creating an episode is called "breaking the story." This includes everything from coming up with the idea all the way through determining the rough content of each scene. The initial idea for a story can come from anywhere, but it usually begins with us contemplating the next logical step for Buffy along her emotional arc for the season. That arc has been clearly laid out for us at the start of each year by Joss. Sometimes, though, an episode idea will come from left field – the episode "Superstar" had its start when Joss came to work and just described the entire Cold Open (the part of the show before the opening credits) in its entirety. But even then, the next step was to come up with what the emotional reality of the episode would be for Buffy.

The next step is to figure out the big events of the story, including the biggest moment that turns the story in an unexpected way. These big events will turn into the Act Breaks of the story (the things that happen right before each commercial break). The entire staff is usually working together at this point, unless one or more writers are out actually writing a script. Joss leads us through the process of picking the scenes that are necessary to telling the story and figuring out where they fit in the show's four-act structure. Television dramas vary a great deal in how much detail is specified at this point. Some shows create very detailed descriptions of the content of each scene, writing them out on a whiteboard in complete sentences. At *Buffy*, the process was looser, with scenes described as to their emotional content but often with all the physical and structural detail left out, which allowed each writer to make a lot of decisions during the writing of the script. This is part of what makes writing on *Buffy* such a joy. The whiteboard of a *Buffy* episode might describe a scene only as: "Int. The Bronze. Buffy tells Anya about her feelings re: monster attack."

After the entire episode is "broken" in this way, the individual writer is sent out to turn the rough whiteboard notes into an outline. They convert the thumbnail descriptions into actual structured scenes. A *Buffy* outline might be anywhere from nine to fourteen pages, I'd say. It might take anywhere from an afternoon to several days to produce an outline. Joss then reads the outline and gives the writer notes. On some shows, the entire staff would weigh in with their opinions, but on *Buffy*, only Joss or the amazing Marti Noxon would give us notes on our outlines. At that point, the writer rewrites the outline to address the notes and heads out to write a first draft. This might take anywhere from a weekend to a full two-week writing session.

The first draft is usually a little long, maybe fifty-eight pages. The final shooting drafts are usually fifty-two pages or perhaps less. Joss reads each draft of a writer's script and sends them back out to do rewrites based on his notes. A writer may end up working on as much as a fifth draft of a script if there's time. Joss gives very specific notes, which usually means that the writer is allowed to keep working on the script until it requires only a small rewrite pass from Joss himself. This is a particular delight to a writer used to the world of sitcoms, in which each script is rewritten by an entire staff and very little or nothing might remain of the writer's original draft.

Buffy encounters Holden Webster, a guy she went to high school with (but who didn't leave much of an impression), and he stops her before she stakes him and begins chatting with her, helping her to psychoanalyze her life. He brings up her parents' divorce (and we discover her father had had an affair before he left her mother), Buffy's conflicting superiority and inferiority complexes, and her relationships. The scene is a clever wink to the many scholars who have psychoanalyzed several characters on the show, but it also allows Buffy to express her regret over having done terrible things to her friends. Whereas in "Selfless" she seemed cold and uncaring toward Xander's pleas that she not kill Anya, here she confesses that she has behaved like a monster to people while at the same time believing she's better than the rest of them. She can't say any of these things to her friends, but Holden — "I'm here to kill you, not to judge you" — provides an objective voice through which she can express her innermost feelings to the audience.

Dawn, on the other hand, is visited by someone she misses terribly — her mother. Seeing Joyce on the show again is a thrill, although the scenes with her are very brief. Dawn shows an incredible amount of ingenuity and courage throughout her scenes, not only standing up to the monster that is hurting her mother but also doing a spell, suffering emotional and physical torment, and figuring out a yes-or-no system of communication for talking to Joyce. Her scenes are the most frightening, and many elements of horror films are used brilliantly, including "Mother's Milk Is Red Today" written in blood on the walls, the television still running after she's unplugged it, and an ominous knocking on the door and walls. What Joyce ultimately tells Dawn, however, will haunt Dawn for the rest of the season and will seem to ring true in "End of Days."

Andrew is back, but he's been talking to Warren for months, and what he ends up doing is shocking, especially coming from Andrew. The death of Jonathan is a sad moment on the show considering how long he's been around. He's yet another link to the high-school days, and the writers create a final sympathy for him when he says how much he misses high school. Jonathan Levinson, the guy who was bullied day in and day out, who was treated like dirt by the jocks and cheerleaders alike, who never had a date, and who holed himself up in the school clock tower with a rifle to commit suicide because he couldn't take it anymore, *misses high school*. The words might seem pretty unbelievable, but they could be more an echo of fan sentiment rather than the character's true feelings. Many *Buffy* viewers fell in love with the show because they had the same hatred for their high-school years as the writers and characters did, yet by season 6 we longed for the high school years on the show, and perhaps Jonathan's words are an expression of that nostalgia.

The final person who is visited is Willow (this is simultaneously the most heartrending and the least convincing of the sections). As she sits in the school library she is visited by Cassie from "Help," someone she's never even met. Cassie ends up being a conduit for Tara, and if you thought that something seemed off in this scene, you were right. Originally, Amber Benson was supposed to reprise her role of Tara, something that would have been devastating for Willow, and shattering for fans, yet it would have been a much more powerful scene. Unfortunately, despite wanting to return, Benson was unable to do so because of a commitment in England at the time, and the writers had to change the scene to bring back Azura Skye as Cassie. As a result, it doesn't make much sense that Willow would be visited by someone who meant nothing to her in life, and there's no chemistry between her and Cassie (we find out later what it is that is visiting everyone and that this entity had the power to be Tara, which would have been more hurtful). That said, Alyson Hannigan still makes the best of it, and as it dawns on Willow that she's actually speaking to Tara, she reacts in such a way that our heartstrings are pulled nonetheless, and we begin to believe that Tara might actually be speaking to her. Hannigan is brilliant in these scenes; Willow cries and begs Tara to believe in her, apologizing for what she did last season. Willow realizes she's been duped when "Tara" tells her to stop the magick and kill herself. The Big Bad of the season has finally revealed itself, and Willow is left alone in the library, shaking with anger, sadness, and a knowledge that what "Tara" has suggested is what she herself has probably considered doing.

But after all is said and done, the biggest shock involves Spike. We've seen scenes of him sitting at the Bronze throughout the episode, chatting up a girl, and Holden tells Buffy something at the end of the episode that she doesn't want to believe at first. But when Spike walks the girl home, we realize with sinking hearts that what Holden said is true.

Highlight: Andrew saying that he didn't like it in Mexico because everyone spoke Mexican and that he is upset with the dream they keep having, which he translates as "It eats you, starting with your bottom."

Interesting Facts: Holden tells Buffy that it's been rumored Scott Hope came out of the closet after he dated her. This tidbit is an inside joke; the actor who played Hope, Fab Filippo, later starred on *Queer As Folk*, playing a gay character. Also, this is the only episode of *Buffy* ever where Nicholas Brendon has not appeared at all. Finally, the song that Angie Hart sings at the beginning and end of the episode was written by Hart and Joss Whedon.

Jane Espenson Says: "[When we found out Amber wouldn't be able to appear], Marti Noxon was given the unenviable job of rewriting the scene for Cassie, because she had written the original Tara version. I imagine it was difficult, but she did an incredibly good job. Cassie had just been introduced, and she was a character that we liked and that the audience would recognize, and who was conveniently dead. She seemed like a good choice, and we were pleased with how it turned out. I should make clear that although Drew and I have our names on this episode, Joss and Marti were also involved in the writing of it. I believe one long weekend was all we had to write the episode, so we needed to break it up by storyline. I wrote the Dawn bits, Drew did the trio bits, Marti did Willow, and Joss did Buffy. This episode won a Hugo award, and it's important that credit is given where it's very much due."

Did You Notice?: "Conversations with Dead People" featured the only time on *Buffy* the episode's title appeared on-screen before the show.

Nitpicks: This is a nitpick with the whole series: Why is it that the vast majority of vampires are male, yet females would be far easier for them to attack? Considering that the act of turning into a vampire requires drinking another vamp's blood, it seems there's a lot of homoerotic behavior going on in those cemeteries.

Willow Wicca Watch: "Tara" tells Willow that the magick she's using will kill everybody if she doesn't control it by stopping completely, something that is Willow's deepest fear.

Restless Moment: Joyce is living in the walls, and in this episode she writes on the walls to contact Dawn.

Going Back to the Beginning: Holden tells Buffy it would be cool if they became "nemeses" and Buffy responds, "Is that how you say the word?" She's referring to the time when she first saw the Troika in season 6 ("Gone") and Warren referred to them as her "arch-nemesises."

Music/Bands: At the beginning of the episode, we hear Angie Hart sing "Blue" (*Buffy the Vampire Slayer: Radio Sunnydale*); as Dawn plays with Buffy's weapons, the song playing is Scout's "The Never Never" (*Drummer on the Cover*); as Dawn dances in the kitchen, we hear "Nicolito" by Los Cubaztecas (*Collection Dansez, Vol. 7*).

7.8   Sleeper

Original air date: November 19, 2002
Written by: David Fury and Jane Espenson
Directed by: Alan J. Levi
Guest cast: Robinne Lee (Charlotte), Rob Nagle (Robson), Lisa Jay (Linda), Kevin Daniels (Bouncer), Stacey Scowley (Young Woman), Lindy Christopher (Nora)

Buffy faces a dilemma when she suspects that Spike might be killing again.

"Sleeper" immediately follows "Conversations with Dead People" time-wise, as we see Dawn struggle to comprehend whether or not she actually saw her mother and Buffy wonder if Holden has told her the truth about Spike or if it was just another lie from the Big Bad. The gang realizes they've come face-to-face with the Big Bad, even though they don't yet know what it is. Buffy begins following Spike and asking the others to keep track of him, but eventually she just asks him straight out if he's killing again. Spike denies it without hesitation.

For Spike, this suspicion is even harder to bear than it is for Buffy. He's gone to hell and back to get his soul, and he's lived with a chip in his head for three years that has prevented him from hurting anyone. He feels he is beginning to pay his dues for the things he has done, and as he says to Buffy, the guilt he's living with now is so enormous that he would never willingly add to it. However, the Big Bad, which appears to him as a version of himself or as Buffy (for want of the Big Bad's real name, fans were referring to it online as "Morphy the Wonder Villain" at this point), is controlling him and using him to create an army of vampires that will kill. Considering the magnitude of what the Big Bad has up its sleeve, using Spike to turn a few people into vampires seems to be pretty small potatoes, and it doesn't make a lot of sense that it would be using him in this way.

Interestingly, when Buffy finds out that Spike has turned at least seven people into vampires (and dusts them in a dazzling display of her fighting skills) she immediately assumes someone must be controlling him and vows to help him. Funny she didn't have this sort of sympathy with Anya a few episodes ago.

The most shocking thing about this episode is the ending — could this be the end of Giles?

Highlight: Buffy's response when the bouncer asks if Spike is the Billy Idol wannabe: "Actually, Billy Idol stole his look from . . . never mind."

Interesting Facts: "Early One Morning," the song that we can hear Spike humming throughout the episode, is a traditional English song. If it sounded particularly familiar to Canadians it's because it was the theme song to the Canadian children's television show *The Friendly Giant*, which ran from 1958 to 1985.

Jane Espenson Says: "When co-writing episodes, I don't always write the comic parts. I wrote the scary bits of 'Conversations,' while Drew Goddard wrote the funny bits, but that was sort of a later development in my career at *Buffy*. Early on, I was often chosen to write the funny episodes, which suits me just fine. I was surprised to discover that I ended up enjoying other kinds of writing too. Splitting episodes was usually not done in terms of storyline, however, even though this is how it was done in a few cases. Usually it was done by acts. (I'll take acts one and two, you take acts three and four . . .) Doug [Petrie] and I also tried another method, in which one of us wrote a whole draft and then we alternated rewrites. But that didn't work as well.

"I loved writing for Cordelia and Anya because they were both so brutally honest. I adore Jonathan because he's so vulnerable and oddly insightful. Willow was fun because she had such a unique way with language. Buffy was hard to write because her character was so complex, but it was very satisfying when you felt you really got her words right."

Did You Notice?: When Buffy follows Spike through the crowd of people, it appears to be exactly the same location where Angel tracked Darla in "Dear Boy" on *Angel*.

Nitpicks: If Spike is really turning all these people into vampires, why in the previous episode did we see him bite the girl on the neck and her only fall to the ground? We should have seen her drink his blood as well. Also, why was Holden buried in the cemetery in "Conversations with Dead People" when Spike has been dragging victims to a basement and burying them there? Also, the writers have never explored what it must be like for the family of a vampire. Think of the people who've come to put flowers on the graves of their loved ones and found the ground disturbed, with big holes there. Or the families of vamps that Buffy has dusted in funeral homes. Or, in this case, the families who have listed their loved ones as missing persons. Their loved ones are dead, and Buffy can't exactly tell them what has really happened, so they'll continue waiting to hear news about those people for the rest of their lives.

Going Back to the Beginning: Anya coming on to Spike is a reference to their sexual encounter in "Entropy."

Music/Bands: Aimee Mann sings "This Is How It Goes" and "Pavlov's Bell" (*Lost in Space*) at the Bronze.

7.9   Never Leave Me

Original air date: November 26, 2002
Written by: Drew Goddard
Directed by: David Solomon
Guest cast: Cynthia LaMontagne (Lydia), Oliver Muirhead (Phili), Kris Iyer (Nigel), Harris Yulin (Quentin Travers), Donald Bishop (Butcher), Camden Toy (Übervamp), Bobby Brewer (Hoffman), Roberto Santos (Grimes)

Andrew's return to Sunnydale is discovered by the Scoobies, and when the Bringers attack Buffy's house, Buffy finally realizes what they're up against.

This episode begins as a hilarious, well-written story of how Andrew is captured by Willow and interrogated by Anya and Xander after he fails in his mission for "Warren." But it shifts into a fast-paced episode that charges into the main dilemma of the season by changing everything. Andrew's back, Xander figures out what's wrong with Spike, Principal Wood appears to be a villain, Buffy discovers who the Big Bad is (and that she's fought it before), the Watcher's Council meets an unhappy end, Spike is captured by the Big Bad, and the hellmouth begins to open. Whew!

The funniest part of the episode involves Andrew. He's useless when "Warren" tries to make him evil (making us wonder why the First actually chose him in the first place), he walks around in a long black coat to make himself feel more powerful (causing the butcher to call him Neo — hilarious), and his reaction upon spotting Willow is priceless. The last time he saw her she was black-eyed, black-haired, had just killed his best friend in the most gruesome manner possible, and was attempting to kill him. Naturally, there are some uncomfortable moments when he sees her again. Willow cleverly uses his fear to her advantage and shocks everyone when she shows up at the Buffy household with Andrew in tow. The ensuing good cop–bad cop interrogation by Anya and Xander is a riot — "The weasel wants to sing, he just needs a tune"; "I'll be pumping him in no time" — and is the first time the two have worked together on something since "Hell's Bells." It's great to see them together again.

Spike continues to be a threat to everyone and begs Buffy to kill him because he can't live with the knowledge that he's killed more people. Buffy believes in him, however (and as hypocritical as her belief in him seems after her actions in "Selfless," it proves correct by the series finale), and raises his spirits by telling him so. When he suddenly becomes violent again it's confusing for everyone, most of all himself, but eventually Xander figures out what has been going on, which will eventually help the gang stop Spike's outbursts.

But the last few minutes of the episode are when everything happens. We get a glimpse of the Watcher's Council preparing for a huge war (and, as usual, not telling

ALBERT L. ORTEGA

Andrew (Tom Lenk) is back, but he must reckon with a former vengeance demon and a witch, two women you do *not* want to mess with.

Buffy a thing) and incurring a surprise attack of its own. When the Bringers attack the gang, Buffy immediately recognizes them as something she's fought before. She's referring to the season-3 episode "Amends," where Angel starts to believe that he was brought back from Hell to do evil things and asks Buffy to kill him (in the same way Spike asks her to kill him in this episode). Angel is visited by ghosts of the people that Angelus had killed — a man he'd killed in Dublin, a servant girl, and Jenny Calendar — who convince him that he is a terrible man, not a good man with a demon trapped inside him. He discovers that he is being haunted by the First Evil, a.k.a. the First, something that had come before everything else in the universe and is responsible for the evil within it. The Bringers, the eyeless monk-like followers who are the corporeal thugs for the First, fought against Buffy, and it's when she sees them again in this episode that she realizes she's about to go up against the First again. This time, however, the First is much more powerful. It had tried to get Angel to kill himself, but failed. Now it has Spike's blood, and what emerges from the hellmouth as a result is a terrifying sight.

Highlight: Andrew's attempted pig slaughter: "That'll do, pig!"
Interesting Facts: In his speech to the Watcher's Council, Quentin says, "We are still

masters of our fate, still captains of our souls," which is a quotation from Sir Winston Churchill, from a speech he read in the House of Commons on September 9, 1941. He had just returned from a meeting with Franklin Delano Roosevelt, during which they drew up a Joint Declaration between England and the U.S. Churchill told the House, "This is no time for boasts or glowing prophecies, but there is this: A year ago our position looked forlorn, and well nigh desperate to all eyes but our own. Today we may say aloud before an awe-struck world: 'We are still masters of our fate. We are still captains of our souls.'"

Nitpicks: Why is it that on the eve of what will inevitably be the biggest battle the world has ever known, the Watcher's Council is keeping all its information from Buffy? She was reinstated as a Slayer in season 5 ("Checkpoint"), and with her, Giles was reinstated as an official Watcher. Therefore, it's the job of the Watcher's Council to keep her and Giles informed. Not only is she the only active Slayer who's not in prison at the moment, but she's actually *on the hellmouth*, thousands of miles closer to the Big Bad than the stuffy Council is. It's safe to say that few tears were shed by viewers watching this episode when the Council went boom.

Restless Moment: In her dream, Buffy asks the Primitive if she's a Slayer, to which the Primitive responds, "The First," drawing a parallel between this season's Big Bad and Buffy.

Going Back to the Beginning: Willow refers to Andrew as "whatshisname," and when Buffy tells Spike he took a chunk out of Andrew, Spike says, "Who?" This is a running joke — the Scoobies have had to stop Jonathan ("Superstar") and Warren ("I Was Made to Love You"), but it was Andrew's brother, not Andrew, who caused the third problem ("The Prom"). As such, the gang never remembers Andrew's name. Andrew will later give a "shout-out" to his brother, Tucker, in the series finale. Xander's memory that a trigger is used in sleeper agents is a reference to his brief time as a soldier ("Halloween"), which has been used many times since. (Oddly enough, Buffy doesn't seem to have any memories of what it is like to be an 18th-century damsel in distress.) Lydia, Phili, and Nigel were all Watcher's Council members who previously appeared in "Checkpoint"; Lydia had written her Ph.D. on Spike. Finally, Buffy realizes what they're fighting because she's already fought it before in "Amends" (see above).

7.10   Bring On the Night

Original air date: December 17, 2002
Written by: Marti Noxon and Douglas Petrie
Directed by: David Grossman
Guest cast: Kristine Sutherland (Joyce Summers), Courtnee Draper (Annabelle), Juliet Landau (Drusilla), Camden Toy (Übervamp), Chris Wiley (Roger)

Giles (Anthony Stewart Head, seen here with his daughters Emily Rose and Daisy May) returns to Sunnydale with several new houseguests for Buffy.

As Spike is tortured by Drusilla/the First, Giles returns with some new houseguests, and Buffy finds out how powerful the new enemy is.

Giles is back! Oh, thank goodness. Or is he (see "Showtime")? In this episode, Buffy receives her mission — she is no longer the follower, allowing a Watcher and a Council to dictate what she will do to save the world. Now she's a mature adult who is given her own army to lead and teach. For six years we've seen Giles and her friends teach her. Now she has learned what being a Slayer is all about, and we meet several potential Slayers in this episode (with many, many more to come), some who are eager to fight, others who are scared but willing, and still others who wonder why this horrible destiny has been passed to them. Watch how, despite becoming increasingly annoying, the Potentials actually echo the many stages of Buffy's denial, reluctant acceptance, and embrace of who she was born to be.

Meanwhile, Spike has become the puppy dog of the First, which now looks like Drusilla. Juliet Landau is once again back and at her glorious nutcase best, and she plays Drusilla with all the weird mannerisms and speech patterns that we've grown to love. The First switches between being Drusilla and Buffy (although, understandably, never Harmony) and taunts Spike, but ultimately Spike is able to look at the Drusilla incarnation with contempt and tell it that he will survive these trials because Buffy believes in him. The strength that simple statement has given him is enormous, making his re-ensoulment seem worth it while giving him a new reason to go on.

Buffy, on the other hand, goes up against the Übervamp and realizes what a powerful foe really is. The Übervamp, or Turok-han as Giles calls it, is an original vampire. It looks like the Master, who once explained that because he had been around so long, his face lost the curse of human features, something that has apparently happened to the Turok-han as well. Giles explains that the First is the source of all the evil in the world, insinuating how impossible it will be to defeat (how can one defeat evil itself?). He tells

Buffy that the First is able to morph from one form to the next, but its manifestations are of people who have died (in Buffy's case, she's being haunted by Joyce). The First is non-corporeal, and while it cannot be touched, it also cannot touch anything else, hence its henchmen in the Bringers. Buffy finds out the hard way that a Turok-han is even harder to kill than a Bringer, as it can't be staked and fights harder than any vampire she's ever encountered. But after getting her butt kicked all over Sunnydale, Buffy returns to her house, bruised but not defeated, and in an astounding speech (one of several more to come) she tells the others that the First might be powerful, but it's nothing compared with them, and they will defeat this thing. An amazing ending.

Highlight: Andrew saying he went over to the dark side, but it was just to pick up a few things and now he's back.

Interesting Facts: Xander jokes that if they can just trap the Bringers in the pantry it'll be all over, a reference to M. Night Shyamalan's *Signs*. In that film, aliens come to earth and a local man (played by Shyamalan), traps one in the pantry where it can't get out.

Nitpicks: Spike doesn't have to breathe, and even Drusilla admits as much when she says that vampires "make such good dollies" because they can be held underwater and don't die. But if he doesn't have to breathe, why does he struggle at all when his head is held under? Why not just lie there completely still?

Willow Wicca Watch: Willow tries to do a spell, but it takes her over completely, turning her black-eyed, black-haired, and fierce, and the essence of the First goes into her, frightening her.

Going Back to the Beginning: Xander says he's doomed to replace windows for the rest of his life, like it's his mummy hand, a reference to the mummy hand that tormented Buffy in "Life Serial." Buffy takes Giles back to the site of the Christmas tree lot where she found the entrance to the First's lair in "Amends." Andrew says his "spidey sense is tingling" and Giles seems to understand what he means. This is an echo of "I Robot, You Jane," when Buffy tells Giles that her spider sense is tingling and then apologizes to him for using a pop-culture reference.

7.11 Showtime

Original air date: January 7, 2003
Written by: David Fury
Directed by: Michael Grossman
Guest cast: Amanda Fuller (Eve), Camden Toy (Übervamp), Lalaine (Chloe)

With more Potentials arriving each day, Buffy takes charge and shows the girls what a real Slayer looks like.

ALBERT L. ORTEGA

Talented actor Camden Toy has appeared on *Buffy* as one of the Gentlemen in "Hush," Gnarl in "Same Time, Same Place," and as the Übervamp, seen here.

"Showtime" feels like a continuation of the previous episode, with the same themes and problems. The Potentials are more restless than they were before and are beginning to whine and complain. Rona is already bellyaching and acting more sarcastically than the others, and unfortunately, she will continue to do so for the rest of the season. We're up to six of them now, and as they sit together at the table moaning about how they're all going to die and this isn't fair and wasn't Buffy supposed to be protecting them (shut UP, Rona), Kennedy suddenly stands out as the only person who actually wants to fight. She's eager to be given weapons and has accepted her role as a potential Slayer (mostly because she doesn't realize just how dangerous it is; she'll be singing a different tune when she finally comes up against real danger). She's also been giving Willow the eye.

Anya and Giles go to see Beljoxa's Eye, a mystical entity that can only be accessed by a demon and can offer insight into the current situation (why no one has ever consulted this thing before is never explained). The Eye tells them that the First has come back more powerful than before because something has been shaken up and there's a rift in the cosmos. Anya realizes the disturbance is that Buffy was supposed to have died, but she, Tara, Willow, and Xander brought her back. The First is going to destroy the world because Buffy is in it.

Buffy, however, is still the hero, as she proves in her own little Thunderdome battle with the Turok-han. Throughout the battle she lectures her charges on what it's like to be a Slayer, how they have to fight what appears to be an invincible foe, and how they have to be prepared for what's coming, even though they don't know what it is. This is the second of her many, many long-winded speeches, and while the first one was a great moment, showing just how far this woman has come from the young girl she was in season 1, here she starts to come off as arrogant, holier-than-thou, and a sermonizer.

Throughout, Giles is becoming a more suspicious character. Despite six Potentials arriving, he's still wearing the same clothes he was the day he showed up with Kennedy, Annabelle, and Molly — even his coat. Fans on the Internet began worrying that Giles was actually the First, that in "Sleeper," when the ax came down near his neck, it actually sliced through it, and now he has arrived as the epitome of evil, with Buffy none the wiser. In the last episode he explained that the First can only morph into dead people and that it can't touch people. Fans began noticing certain details: he didn't hug Buffy — or anyone else — upon his arrival, as he usually would; he hasn't changed his clothes; and later he'll ask someone to grab his briefcase rather than pick it up himself. The thought that one of the most beloved *Buffy* characters could actually be the First Evil is painful beyond imagination. But isn't pain what this show is all about?

Pain is exactly what Spike has been feeling. Not only physical (the First's Über-vamp has been wearing him down by beating him constantly), but emotional (the First has been playing on his worst fears and has convinced him that Buffy doesn't care about him and will not come to get him). The final scene, where he is convinced he is being tortured again only to realize his dream has come true, is beautiful and touching. The subtle look of overwhelming relief and happiness that comes over his face is worth the entire episode.

Highlight: The sarcastic response of Beljoxa's Eye when it tells Giles that the First will always be here and Giles refuses to believe it: "What, am I talking to myself here?"

David Fury Says: "My whole thing is just to write the best episode. Regardless of what anyone's personal convictions are I just try to execute the story as best I can. The only thing I *do* try to do [is] if there's any part of the story that can lean a certain direction that might be opposed to my own personal philosophy on the character's development — with Spike: whether he's good, whether he's bad, whether he's really in love with Buffy or thinks he's in love with Buffy — I try to be true to that, true to my own convictions, even if some action that he's doing is a little bit opposed to it. I try to justify it in the script to what I want to make it fit within my own perspective on what it all means. As absurd as it all is — and my god, is it absurd — the important factor that people seem to overlook [regarding the rape scene in "Seeing Red"] is that the creature that tried to rape Buffy is not the man that we see on the show. To equate the Spike who attempted to assault Buffy as being morally culpable we'd have to make Angel morally culpable for everything Angelus did. It's absurd for me when people just feel "Well how could she be with the guy who tried to rape her?" That wasn't him; that was the demon that was in him that went to that place."

Nitpicks: Here's a huge nitpick of the entire season: Buffy, Giles, Dawn, the Potentials, and even Faith persist in the assumption that in order for one of the Potentials to become the Chosen One, Buffy must die. But that's not true. She died in "Prophecy Girl" and was brought back to life, meaning she was no longer the active Slayer. Her first death (the only one that counts to the powers that be) brought on Kendra, whose death in "Becoming, Part One" brought forth Faith. Now Faith is sitting in a prison, and it's *her* death that would trigger the next Chosen One. Buffy has since died in "The Gift" and possibly in "Villains" when she momentarily flatlines, and neither of those events brought forth a new Slayer. So why now, after living with the knowledge that only Faith's death can bring forth a new Slayer, is Buffy, and everyone else, insisting that Buffy's death will call forth the next Slayer? Also, how is Buffy able to talk to Willow telepathically and Xander able to hear the silent conversation? Before, Willow could only talk to people separately. And finally, if decapitating the Turok-han kills it, why not take a sword to its neck in the first place? Buffy's killed many a vampire smarter than the Turok-han by doing just that.

Oops: At one point Buffy/the First touches Spike's cheek.

Willow Wicca Watch: Willow puts up a shield to protect everyone against the Bringers, but she can't hold it. She also talks to Buffy and Xander telepathically.

Going Back to the Beginning: When Buffy slays the Bringers and walks up to Rona, she says, "Welcome to the hellmouth," the title of the first episode of the series. Willow's ability to speak to Buffy telepathically was first demonstrated in "Bargaining, Part One." And at the end of the episode, when she says to the gang, "Here endeth the lesson," she echoes Spike's final words to her in "Fool for Love" when he teaches her how he's killed two Slayers.

7.12 Potential

Original air date: January 21, 2003
Written by: Rebecca Rand Kirshner
Directed by: James A. Contner
Guest cast: James C. Leary (Clem), Derek Anthony (Imposing Demon)

When the coven tells Buffy there's another Potential in Sunnydale, Willow does a spell to find her, and it points to Dawn.

"Potential" is an excellent look at an individual who is a constant in the Buffyverse and is only occasionally touched upon: the underdog. Xander has been the one left behind for many years ("The Zeppo" was a great episode that explored his loneliness as such), and since season 5, Dawn has been the one who's forgotten. She is seen as too young and immature, and Buffy fears she might get hurt. This season Dawn has certainly learned to fight for herself, and we saw her display some amazing fighting skills in "Conversations with Dead People" and "Never Leave Me." But now that Buffy has the First, a house full of Potentials, and Spike to worry about, she's once again forgotten that Dawn is there. Add to this Dawn's warning from "Joyce" in "Conversations with Dead People," and her lack of confidence is completely understandable.

This episode also explores Dawn's maturity. When faced with the unenviable knowledge that she is a potential Slayer, she assumes Buffy won't be pleased and leaves to gather her thoughts. When she encounters danger, she uses her new position as a Potential to step up and take charge of the situation. And when she makes a surprising discovery, she calmly steps back and never lets on how disappointed she is. Dawn has come a long

CHRISTINA RADISH

In "Potential," we discover why bullies probably shouldn't choose Amanda (Sarah Hagan) as their target.

way from the annoying adolescent she was in season 5 and the screechy, difficult teen she was in season 6 ("get out, Get Out, GET OUT!"). She is a mature young woman, the same age as Buffy was in season 1, but she is handling her problems with even more grace and acceptance than her older sister did.

The final scene between Xander and Dawn is one of the best moments of the season. Thankfully, writer Rebecca Rand Kirshner recognized how important Xander was to the scheme of things, and despite his being lost in the shuffle of so much else going on this season (and last season, for that matter), she gives him a speech that shows what an incredible person he is. When he first found out that Dawn was a Potential, he accepted the news with excitement and support, rooting her on. Willow was also excited, although she insisted they tell Buffy, while Anya was, well, Anya, and told Dawn that she would die a premature and horrible death. When the reality of the situation comes out, Xander is the only one who notices Dawn is still standing there, her world having been turned upside down twice in a matter of hours, and he feels for her. In Dawn, Xander sees himself, the guy who's always forgotten in the heat of battle,

Potentials

Starting about midway through season 7, it seemed that every week the number of Potentials in Buffy's house was increasing exponentially, and it became impossible to remember who was who. The following is a list of the most prominent Potentials who were referred to by name, although there were dozens more who were extras in the background:

★ Girl with long, dark hair in Istanbul; killed by the Bringers in "Lessons"
★ Red-haired punk girl; killed in Frankfurt, Germany, by the Bringers in "Beneath You"
★ Kennedy – comes from a wealthy family; falls in love with Willow
★ Annabelle – British; ends up running away out of fear and is killed by the Übervamp in an alleyway
★ Molly – British, long dark hair; shows up with the first batch of Potentials
★ Vi – American, short red hair; often wears clothes and knitted hats with brightly colored stripes on them
★ Rona – African-American; first encounters Buffy at the bus station and is saved by her; has a complaining whine that persists throughout the season
★ Eve – mousy-colored long hair, southern accent; killed in hotel room before she actually makes it to Buffy's house (the First shows up looking like her instead)
★ Chloe – arrives at the same time as Eve and Rona; spends a night in her room alone with the First, who preys on her fears and causes her to hang herself
★ Amanda – a tall girl with straight brown hair from Sunnydale High; is a bit of a bully with people who try to bully her first
★ Chao-Ahn – Asian, doesn't speak a word of English; is lactose intolerant and finds Giles terrifying
★ Shannon – never becomes part of Buffy's army; chased by Bringers, she jumps into Caleb's truck, where he brands her with his ring and throws her out
★ Caridad – Latina, light-colored layered hair; she has very few lines and we don't know exactly where she comes from, but she's the first Potential in Xander's fantasy in "Dirty Girls"
★ Colleen – dark-haired; is the second Potential in Xander's fantasy
★ Dominique – we never actually see her; Rona mentions at the beginning of "Dirty Girls" that Dominique has the stomach flu and the toilet is backed up

the "butt monkey" of the group for many years, the one who's there to cower in the corner and fix the windows afterward, the only Scooby who has never been given the opportunity to come forward and be in the spotlight. Over the years we've seen Xander evolve from a sex-crazed teenager to an angry, emotional person to a confused husband-to-be to a quiet, mature adult who has accepted his position in the group. Fans and critics alike rarely talk about his development as a character, instead focusing on the more obvious and radical changes in Buffy, Spike, and Willow. But Xander has come a long way, too, and despite his share of heartache, he never gives up. Just like Dawn, Xander isn't special — he's extraordinary.

Highlight: Amanda saying that kids in the school have been wondering if Buffy is a high-functioning schizophrenic.

Jane Espenson Says: [Regarding whether or not Joyce was a ghost or the First in "Conversations with Dead People"] "Here is my memory of what was intended, and believe me, there was a lot of discussion of this issue in the writers' room, but some of it took place without Joss there and thus cannot be trusted. I believe that what was intended was that that was not Joyce. That it was the First. BUT that Dawn's erroneous suspicions that it was in fact Joyce were to be fueled by the events of the episode in which she thinks she's the next Slayer and she is not."

Nitpicks: As much as I like Dawn in this episode (and throughout this season, in fact), she occasionally still shows her immaturity. Anyone remember when Dawn escaped in "Real Me" and Anya ended up with a broken arm? Why, with the Bringers and the Übervamp and the First all targeting Buffy and the Potentials, does she stupidly go out the window? Also, Amanda tells Dawn that she's trapped the vampire in a classroom, but the classroom has windows. Considering we've seen many a vamp jump through plate-glass windows (and these windows probably have ways of opening), why doesn't he just escape? Finally, this episode is where Buffy's speeches begin to grate on the nerves. All this "death is what a Slayer breathes" stuff, spoken with no emotion whatsoever, is incredibly pompous considering it's taken her seven years to get to the same emotional state she needs the Potentials to be in in a matter of weeks.

Willow Wicca Watch: Willow performs a locator spell (it seems to be the only spell she does these days).

Restless Moment: Xander sees himself on the outside throughout his dream, working as an ice-cream clerk. Snyder tells Xander he's a whipping boy.

Music/Bands: When the Potentials go to the demon bar, we hear Citizen Bird's "I Love You" (*Citizen Bird*).

7.13   The Killer in Me

Original air date: February 4, 2003
Written by: Drew Z. Greenberg
Directed by: David Solomon
Guest cast: Elizabeth Anne Allen (Amy), Megalyn Echikunwoke (Vaughne), Rif Hutton (General), Terence Bernie Hines (Shop Keeper), Anna Maria Maccarrone (Waitress)

When Willow and Kennedy kiss, Willow turns into Warren, causing her to remember what happened to Tara.

"The Killer in Me" is an interesting title for a *Buffy* episode, considering how many members of the Scooby gang have actually killed people. Willow killed Warren, Spike and Anya have killed countless people, and Giles killed Ben. But in the case of this episode, it refers mostly to Willow and her fear that she was somehow responsible for Tara's death. She and Kennedy have become closer, and until now Willow has seen herself as a one-girl woman. When she and Kennedy kiss, her guilt that she is betraying Tara's memory gets the better of her, and she turns into Warren. The ensuing scenes that switch back and forth between Willow and Warren are very well done, usually showing Willow when we're hearing something from her perspective and Warren when we're seeing the responses of those around her.

This episode was necessary to address "Seeing Red," probably the most controversial episode in *Buffy* fandom. Fans were divided on Tara's death among those who thought it was sad but necessary; those who thought it wasn't necessary and the writers should have found another way around it; and those who thought the episode showed an inherent homophobia among the writers, who created a lesbian character just to kill her off and show that lesbianism is wrong (they seem to forget that it was those same writers who

ALBERT L. ORTEGA

Kennedy (Iyari Limon) helps pull Willow back from the brink by showing her she can find love again.

created such an amazing, gentle, and realistic portrait in the first place; that Tara is certainly not the first character to be killed off on the show; and that Tara was a lot more than just "the lesbian," and her character deserves better than that). Some fans stopped watching the show completely in their anger over Tara's death and were upset that it was never seriously addressed on the series. This episode shows that Willow feels incredible guilt over it. She also worries that the demon inside her that killed Warren is still there, and that if she gets close to Kennedy, Kennedy may die as well, possibly because of her.

Amy reappears for the last time in the series (she'd made appearances in seasons 1, 2, 3, and 6 and spent seasons 4 and 5 as a rat) and admits she's upset that everyone forgave Willow for doing what she did. What seems a little shaky about this premise is that Amy was never one of the Scooby gang, so it's not like they were her best friends and shut her out for doing a little magick. Also, considering that while Amy was a rat Willow became a very powerful witch and yet failed to look for any sort of spell to change Amy back, you'd think *that* would be the root of her anger.

Meanwhile, Spike's chip has started to act up, causing severe shooting pain in his head and seizures. His chip has been the thing that has kept the killer in him at bay for many years, and Buffy might be forced to find out if his soul is enough to keep his inner demon in check. Anya, Xander, and Dawn follow Giles into the desert as soon as their suspicions catch up to those of the show's fans, and they wonder if he might be the First. Giles's reaction to them — "You think I'm evil if I bring a group of girls on a camping trip and *don't* touch them?" — is priceless. A good episode to close the Willow-Tara chapter, although Kennedy is a poor substitute for the "awesomeness" of Tara.

Highlight: Spike saying to Buffy, "Who you gonna call? [Pause as Buffy looks at him] God, that phrase is never gonna be usable again, is it?"

David Fury Says: "It's actually kind of cool to be the one to kill off a character because there's a real feeling of power, this god-like omnipotence when you can end the life of a character that you've lived with for a couple of years, who you've written and filled in the voice for and know the actors or actresses, and then to be able to end their life and do it in a shocking or moving way. I don't think anybody resists it; I think we're often naïve in terms of how it'll be responded to. Joss had decided to kill Tara because he thought it was a story that was right for the story. We knew she was going to die really early on in that season, if not before, because we knew that Willow was going to become evil and we knew it would happen because of the death of Tara, and yet shortly before we were breaking the story Joss said, 'You know, should we really kill her? I don't know if we should kill her' and began to second-guess himself. And I said, 'No! Kill her! We're all prepared to kill her and so let's kill her' and that resulted in the backlash and we were all like, 'Whoops, sorry.' I mean, we don't regret having done it;

it's the way things unfold. We don't sit there going, 'Who does everybody like, who do they not like. . . .' If you wanted us to cater to the community at large, the show would never have been interesting, it never would have gotten the response it did. The thing is, it served the story well, it was tragic from a story point of view, it was sort of necessary for the time. There was only a year left, and the other thing people don't seem to realize is, it's not like we killed this character and you have to live years without this character; we knew we'd be wrapping up the story and we were hoping to wrap it up this year. And we were hoping to see more of Tara this year, but unfortunately, Amber just wasn't available. Tara was going to be a big part of this year. The First was going to take one single form this year and it was going to be Tara."

Nitpicks: For someone who takes being a Slayer so seriously, Kennedy playing hooky from Giles's excursion was a pretty immature thing to do. Does she really think she's so far beyond the other girls that she doesn't require any guidance from Giles? And when the gang thinks back to Giles and whether or not he touched anything, they realize he didn't. Hasn't he eaten anything the entire time he's been there?

Oops: If the writers were trying to make it seem like Giles never touched a thing, they didn't count on Anthony Stewart Head taking his glasses off when he sat down to talk to Buffy.

Willow Wicca Watch: Willow puts up a mystical barrier that prevents Kennedy from following her as they leave the school.

Going Back to the Beginning: This episode contains references to the past three seasons. Giles confronts Buffy about her telling the Potentials that the vision quest is about going out into the desert, "doing the hokey-pokey until a spooky Rasta-Mama Slayer arrives and speaks to them in riddles." Buffy was referring to the season-5 episode "Intervention," when Giles took her on the same Slayer quest into the desert (interesting that he waited five years to do it with her but assumes these girls are ready in as many weeks). As he jumped into the circle and out again, shaking his magick gourd, Buffy joked, "I know this ritual! The ancient shamans were next called upon to do the hokey-pokey and turn themselves around." Giles was not amused. Willow goes back to the WannaBlessedBes from university and asks them about their bake sales, something they discussed when Willow was first interested in joining them in "Hush." The room where they are meeting is the same lecture hall in which Professor Maggie Walsh taught in season 4. The remnants of the Initiative are left after the huge explosion that happened there at the end of "Primeval." Riley referring to Spike as "assface" is a result of what he discovered in "As You Were" about Buffy and Spike. The scene Willow/Warren re-enacts in Buffy's backyard is from "Seeing Red."

Music/Bands: On-stage at the Bronze, Aberdeen plays "Sink or Float" and "Cities and Buses" (*Homesick and Happy to Be Here*).

7.14 First Date

Original air date: February 11, 2003
Written by: Jane Espenson
Directed by: David Grossman
Guest cast: Ashanti (Lissa), K.D. Aubert (Nikki Wood)

Buffy and Xander each go out on dates, and they both encounter big surprises when they do.

CHRISTINA RADISH

Principal Wood (DB Woodside) knows more about Buffy than she realizes, and his presence allows her to understand more about a certain former Slayer.

We were *so close* to the end of seven years without a really awful guest star brought in as a publicity stunt. And then they cast Ashanti. If you can look past that annoyance, "First Date" is a great episode that's not only hilarious but sheds a new light on Principal Wood. We discover that the reason he took a job working in the "bidet of evil," as Buffy puts it, was because he knows about the coming fight, and he knows who Buffy is. In fact, he's linked pretty closely to Slayerhood, being the son of a slain Slayer. Buffy is ambivalent about discovering his news — on the one hand, it saddens her to meet someone who knows a Slayer who has died, but on the other hand, she never realized that any Slayer had lived long enough to have a child. Fans with good memories will immediately remember who Wood's mother was and that we've seen her death in a previous episode. And, with a shudder, we realize who killed her, even before she appears at the end of this episode.

Giles finds out that Buffy had Spike's chip removed, and it infuriates him that she would do something so selfish, in his opinion. She knows how potentially dangerous Spike is and that the chip is the only thing stopping him, but for Giles (who has been tortured by one re-ensouled vampire) it seems like a black-and-white issue — he doesn't see the gray area that Buffy does.

Xander, who by the end of this episode has given up on women, once again finds himself with a beautiful woman who isn't what she seems. On the date he expresses his discomfort with being so close physically to Anya all the time, when sometimes he feels like he needs some space from her. Lissa convinces him that he's better off without Anya, but afterward he has to consider the source. Anya is jealous that Xander is out on a date, but it's not clear whether she's jealous of someone else having Xander or Xander having someone else. Willow and Kennedy are closer, and when Xander sees this he begs Willow to "gay him up" and says he's mentally undressing Scott Bakula, which sends Andrew off into fantasyland momentarily. But Giles, tired of all the dating and joking around, insists that the gang become more serious. Perhaps his insistence is a comment on the show, which will become much darker from this point on, with only one more comic episode to come.

Highlight: Giles unknowingly terrorizing Chao-Ahn, from giving her ice cream and offering her milk (causing her lactose intolerance to flare up) to drawing graphic, explanatory flashcards that leave her completely frightened.

Did You Notice?: Anya tries to clean the blood from Buffy's shirt and then says it might actually be pizza, a reference to Dawn's squirting pizza sauce all over Buffy's shirt in "Conversations with Dead People" and shrugging, figuring Buffy will just assume it's blood anyway.

Nitpicks: If Wood was able to track down Buffy, why couldn't he track down Spike? There are numerous references to him in the books that Giles reads, which are presumably the ones he would have looked up in order to find the Slayer. Also, it's never explained just who Lissa is. Does the Seal of Danthazar close every time it's been opened? Since Buffy is determined in "Storyteller" to close it, the insinuation would be that it was already open, so why did Lissa need Xander's blood? And speaking of Lissa, Ashanti should stick to singing.

Oops: There appears to be a continuity error in this episode. In "Potential," Giles was away because he went to Shanghai to get a new Slayer. He shows up with her in this episode, yet he was also in the previous episode, without her. Did he find her, inform her, and leave her to come back on her own? Also, as Wood, Buffy, and Spike are driving to the high school, Wood continually glares at Spike in the rearview mirror. But Spike has no reflection, and Wood wouldn't have been able to see him (it can't be explained away by reasoning that Wood is glaring because Spike casts no reflection: at the high school Wood says, "You're a vampire" with some surprise when Spike begins fighting).

Going Back to the Beginning: Poor Xander. Lissa is just the latest in a long line of demon women he's fallen for. In "Teacher's Pet" he fell in love with a praying mantis who wanted to implant her eggs in his head; in "Inca Mummy Girl" he kissed a girl who tried to suck the life out of him, being an ancient mummy and all; in "Something Blue" he had every female demon after him when Willow accidentally called him a demon magnet and cast a spell; and the love of his life was Anya, a 1,120-year-old vengeance demon whose résumé included removing a man's entrails and wearing them as clothing. The only woman he's loved who wasn't actually a demon was Cordelia (although Willow might disagree), and even Cordy became part demon in season 4 of *Angel*. Also, Jonathan taunts Andrew and tells him it's no wonder his jet pack screwed up, referring to Andrew's less-than-graceful jet-pack exit in "Seeing Red." And we've actually watched the scene of Spike killing Robin's mother, Nikki, in "Fool for Love," in the New York City flashback scene. Finally, Giles's anger that everyone is out on dates when they should be paying attention to the impending apocalypse mirrors his disgust in "Never Kill a Boy on the First Date," when he forbade Buffy from eschewing her duties and insisted she cancel her date.

Music/Bands: During Xander's date, we hear "Ammunition" by Trembling Blue Stars (*Alive to Every Smile*) and Patty Medina's "Still Life" (*Happy Hours and Heartaches*).

7.15 Get It Done

Original air date: February 18, 2003
Written and directed by: Douglas Petrie
Guest cast: Lalaine (Chloe), Camden Toy (Übervamp), Sharon Ferguson (Primitive), Geoffrey Kasule (Shadow Man #1), Karara Muhoro (Shadow Man #2), Daniel Wilson (Shadow Man #3)

Buffy receives Nikki Wood's Slayer bag and within it finds the answer to a question she's been asking for years.

Finally, after seven years, the fans have been given what they want — a history of Slayers and how they came to be. In this episode, three characters have to face their fears: Spike must embrace who he used to be in order to become a better fighter; Willow must control herself while doing a difficult and dark spell; and Buffy must find the courage to find out who she is and why she's been chosen. All three are tested, and when they take control and embrace who they are, they win.

The shadow play that Buffy steps into is amazing. As Dawn reads the story of how in the beginning there was the earth, then demons, then men who caught a girl, chained her up, and forced her to fight, the shadow puppets come to life and we hear the noises from the story. It's a frightening moment that will cause the hairs on the back of your neck to stand on end, but it's well done. Buffy meets with the original men who created the First Slayer and realizes that as a part of the Slayer line, she has been imbued with some of the darkness that she's been trying to fight. By putting demon into the First Slayer, these men forced her into a life that she didn't want. They put evil in her to give her power and help her understand the demons she was fighting against, which would help to explain why Buffy is attracted to darkness and dark men. But when she's given the choice to take more of it into her, Buffy fights back. She's not willing to give up the one thing that makes her strong — her humanity — so that she can fulfill the wishes of a bunch of men. The premise is an interesting one: these Slayers, the kick-ass grrrls who represent feminism in all its strength and glory, were actually created by men and are still controlled by men. Only in "End of Days" will we discover there's a little more to that story than the Shadow Men would have Buffy believe.

The downside to this episode is that Buffy's serious attitude problem has gotten worse, making her come off as an even colder person. It's ironic that she should choose humanity, when to her friends she's becoming more of a monster every day. Kennedy has gone from being the coolest Potential to acting like a bitchy army general toward the other Potentials, and the scene of her shouting at Chloe to do push-ups is disgusting. The viewer wonders why Buffy doesn't say anything, explain to Kennedy that maybe this verbal and mental abuse isn't exactly motivating the troops, but then Buffy begins telling her friends what she thinks of all of them and you realize that she and Kennedy are very much alike. She calls Spike, the person who's stood by her throughout (and who, in the last episode, she told to stay because she "wasn't ready" for him not to be there, even though she still barely gives him the time of day), a wimp who's lost his edge; she asks Anya why she's even there, though it was Buffy herself who asked her to come back to the Scoobies; and she tells the Potentials that Chloe is an idiot and she's sick of carrying them all (not that she's far off with this one, but a little sympathy toward Chloe would be nice considering how Buffy handled her Slayerhood for the first few years). This scene will be the motivator behind the mirror scene in "Empty Places," although it's still not enough to feel comfortable in that episode.

Douglas Petrie has written an excellent episode in terms of language. Great story-line aside, listen to the clever use of language that's reminiscent of the early years, when the Scoobies were always making up their own words. In this episode Anya calls Spike a "wimpire," Andrew says he prefers the term "guestage" to hostage, Buffy refers to Willow as a "Wicca who wonta," and Xander calls the demon that comes out of the portal the "exchange student." This clever attention to language is what sets *Buffy* apart from just about every show on television aside from *Gilmore Girls*, and it's one of the things that's missed the most.

Highlight: Andrew bringing out the Big Board and asking where to put his receipts.
Did You Notice?: When Willow pretends that the Potentials are a cheerleading squad she says, "Bring it on!," a reference to the film of the same name that starred *Buffy* alum Eliza Dushku.
Nitpicks: Buffy considers Andrew the brains of the operation? In what universe? And Wood hands Buffy the Slayer "emergency kit" and says that by right it's hers and was supposed to have been passed down to the next Slayer, but he kept it for sentimental

reasons. It's understandable that he did so as a child who didn't know any better, but why didn't his mother's Watcher, who raised Robin, find the bag and hand it off to the next Slayer? This bag that he kept for "sentimental reasons" didn't have a bunch of photos and trinkets that belonged to his mother; it contained vital information that the next Slayers badly needed. How could he have held on to it for as long as he did, knowing how important his mother's mission was? Finally, Wood is there to give Buffy the kit, but why does he disappear during the ritual?

Willow Wicca Watch: Willow performs a spell to get Buffy back, goes black-eyed, and screams. She sucks the energy out of Kennedy, who is the most powerful person in the room, and despite scaring Kennedy, she manages to open the portal.

Restless Moment: Xander warns Buffy about sitting in the sandbox (which turns out to be the desert she visits in this episode) and tries to protect her (the way he warns her in this episode). In Giles's dream, Willow says that something primal is after them, and they have to learn to understand it or they'll never stand a chance against it. Buffy says to Adam, "We're not demons" and he says, "Is that a fact?" The bag at Buffy's feet in the episode is the bag that Robyn hands her, and it's filled with mud that takes her back to the First Slayer, who reappears in "Get It Done." Finally, Buffy vanquishes the First Slayer by saying, "You're not the source of me."

Going Back to the Beginning: Buffy finds herself back in the same desert she was in in "Restless" and "Intervention."

7.16   Storyteller

Original air date: February 25, 2003
Written by: Jane Espenson
Directed by: Marita Grabiak
Guest cast: Alan Loayza (Stressed Out Boy), Corin Amber Norton (Crying Girl), Sujata DeChoudhury (Shy Girl), ZW Leshner (Feral Teen)

Andrew videotapes Buffy and her friends in action so that people will remember the legacy of Buffy, Slayer of the Vum-pyres.

"Storyteller" is a break from the dark storyline that has been unfolding, and is the funniest episode of the season (Jane Espenson has been a powerhouse this season, co-writing not only "Conversations with Dead People" but this one and four others). It not only reviews this entire season for viewers (which is great, but would make more sense if it had come after a hiatus, rather than before one) but also goes back through many previous episodes and seasons to explain the other characters from Andrew's point of view. Because Andrew tends to emphasize certain things about the characters (Buffy's glamour, Spike's shirtlessness, Xander's perfection) and Mary Sues himself into the story in an idealistic way, the episode almost comes off like fan fiction, as if Andrew were a fan of the show writing the characters into his own little story.

The episode has several highlights: the *Masterpiece Theatre* opening; Andrew's view of himself as supervillain; the retelling of the Dark Willow story with Andrew as a formidable foe; Andrew zooming in on Xander's window handiwork and not noticing the more interesting scene in the foreground; Spike schmoozing for the camera; the pig running by Wood and Buffy in the school basement and Wood hoping it wasn't a student; Andrew's fantasy that he, Warren, and Jonathan will be leaping about in a paradise singing, "We will be as gods!" Jane Espenson has written the funniest episodes of *Buffy*, but this one tops them all.

As the students at Sunnydale High begin to go bonkers because of the hellmouth opening up, Buffy and Wood go to investigate the seal, and Buffy realizes that the one who opened the seal with blood must also close it. The scene with her and Andrew over the seal is a touching one — Buffy comes off as ruthless, but perhaps she's realized that to get things done, she has to suppress all her sympathies (not that she's ever had many for Andrew). Finally, after being a funny character for so long despite having killed Jonathan in cold blood, Andrew shows some remorse for what he's done, and we realize that the death of his best friend has had a serious impact on him.

Highlight: Anya catching Andrew videotaping himself in the bathroom and asking why he doesn't masturbate like the rest of them.

Jane Espenson Says: "This is another episode for which I spent a lot of time on set, so I knew what to expect from the final product, and I loved it. The director, Marita Grabiak, really captured the tone of it, despite having no time to prep the episode. I did particularly like writing for Andrew. One of my favorite things to do is to pick a minor character and try to do whatever I can to give them some complexity. One of the first lines I ever wrote for the show was about Cordelia enjoying standardized tests. . . . I simply liked the idea of giving her a little something expected. With Andrew I was given the chance to do the same thing on a grander scale. With him we had a character who was constantly framing actions in term of narrative, and it was, I'm sure, Joss's idea to make that literal in this episode.

Did You Notice?: The footage of Dark Willow telling Andrew that he has some powerful magick to counter her spells is actually her speaking to Giles, who, unlike Andrew, actually was able to counter her spells. And if you watch Andrew and Jonathan's nightmare in Mexico very closely, you'll spot the Cheese Man from everyone's dreams in "Restless"!

Nitpicks: It's highly unlikely that Andrew could have actually read the language on the knife, but even if we say that he could, why didn't he notice it earlier?

Andrew spins some fantastic tales about his adventures with Warren (Adam Busch) and Jonathan (Danny Strong) in "Storyteller."

Restless Moment: When Spike acts tough for Andrew's camera, it's similar to the scene in Giles's dream when he sees Spike posing for pictures as a tough vampire.

Going Back to the Beginning: When Buffy's at the high school she sees a lonely girl begin to fade, which is a reference to "Invisible Girl." The students all being afraid of things in their lives refers to what Buffy could hear them thinking in "Earshot." The scene of Dark Willow fighting Andrew is a *slightly* altered version of "Two to Go." Andrew mentions swim-team monsters ("Go Fish") and killer prom dogs ("The Prom"), which were care of Andrew's brother, Tucker.

7.17   Lies My Parents Told Me

Original air date: March 25, 2003
Written by: David Fury and Drew Goddard
Directed by: David Fury
Guest cast: Caroline Lagerfelt (William's Mother), K.D. Aubert (Nikki Wood), Juliet Landau (Drusilla), Damani Roberts (Young Robin), Ira Steck (New Vamp)

Through flashbacks, we see what happened between Spike and his mother soon after he became a vampire, and in the present, Robin finally tells Spike why he hates him.

"Lies My Parents Told Me" is at times touching, at times confusing. It asks us to rethink certain characters, shift our sympathies, and see things in a new light. Whether or not it works is another thing.

The "parents" of the title refer to three that we see in this episode. Robin Wood's mother, Nikki, was a vampire Slayer in the 1970s until she came upon Spike one rainy night in 1977. We see how Robin would accompany her on her patrols when he was four and knew how to stay quiet and watch her. Although she tells him (presumably it's a mantra) that "the mission is what matters," he knows that she cares a lot about him and takes care of him. But we see his confusion when he begs her to come home and be a traditional mommy to him and she tells him to go home and stay safe while she finishes off Spike (we know that the opposite will be the case).

William's mother was very ill before he was turned into a vampire. But when he returned home with Drusilla, his first thought was of her. Despite having no soul, he was still a vampire mama's boy, and in a weird twist on the Oedipal myth, he seems to want to kill *and* marry his mother, much to Drusilla's dismay. The monster that he creates in his mother shocks him with her coldness, cruelty, and disturbing eroticism (which is later referenced to hilarious effect in the season-5 *Angel* episode "Lineage"). She tells him how much she hated him clinging to her day after day and forces him to take a drastic measure that will haunt him for eternity.

The final parent is Giles. Since Buffy was 16 years old we've seen him train her, watch over her both professionally and personally, and he has become a bona fide father figure to her. He's been more a father to her than her own father ever was, and ever since the nadir of their relationship in "Helpless," he has kept Buffy's well-being foremost in his priorities, and he left her last season because he believed it was the best thing for her. Now he's back, and as she fights in the cemetery with him by her side we see them as teacher and student for the last time, with him asking her tough questions and her, for once, not making light quips in response. Buffy admits that the choices she would have made at one time have changed; she says that she would no longer make the decision she did at the end of season 5. But the look on her face speaks volumes when she realizes what he is getting at, and with a sinking feeling she races back toward Wood's place. Giles has betrayed her once again, but this time he thought it was for the best. The final scene of her telling Giles that he has taught her all she needs to know is huge, as she once and for all turns her back on the only real parent she has remaining.

The difficulty with this episode is the "Lies" part of the title. Spike and Robin fight tooth and nail in Robin's cross-filled garage area, and when Spike gets the upper hand he tells Robin that Nikki never loved him, but that *his* mother did. It was the monster in her that changed her but she didn't mean any of the words that she said. Therefore, the first two lies are Nikki's declaration of love to her son and Mrs. The Bloody's avowal of hatred to hers. But where is Spike getting his information from? Who's to say that Nikki didn't love Robin? She knew she had a job to do, but she never abandoned Robin. She was trying to make the world safer for him. And as for William's mommy dearest, we've seen several times that vampires contain the essence of the humans within them — vampire Willow was kinda gay and quite powerful, Spike has a soft side to him that comes from William, and Angelus had Liam's lechery and indifference. Angel admits that vampires are a form of the humans they were before, so Spike's suggestion that his mom was really a sweet ol' gal who was being led by the beast within shows he is being blind to reality. What Nikki said to Robin wasn't necessarily a lie, nor was what William's mother said to him. And Giles tells Buffy that she must start being a general and stop acting like one and questions her loyalty to Spike above everyone else, even Dawn. His statements are probably closer to the truth than anyone's.

Highlight: The writers poking fun at Buffy's grandstanding when she says that she gave an inspirational speech to the telephone repairman.

Did You Notice?: In the flashback to Spike's past, when William's mother is singing to him, as he sits at her feet you'll see the scar in his left eyebrow is gone, insinuating that he must have gotten the scar after he became a vampire. The problem is, vampires heal quickly and don't tend to scar, so it should have still been there.

Nitpicks: Giles complains that there isn't a book to be seen in the library, yet in "Help" we saw Cassie in the library, surrounded by far more books than we ever saw in the original Sunnydale High's rather pitiful stacks.

Oops: In "After Life," Spike says that like Buffy, he has also had to claw his way out of a coffin, after he became a vampire. Yet in this episode we see that after Drusilla turned him into one, he disappeared for three weeks on a rampage with her, so there's no way his mother could have buried him. Also, Andrew takes a call from Fred at Angel Investigations in L.A., asking if Willow can come and help them, which Willow does (see *Angel* episode guide, "Orpheus"). However, the episode in which Willow went to L.A. aired on the WB on March 19, a week before this episode. There had been a mix-up in the schedule and originally "Lies My Parents Told Me" had been slotted to appear first.

Restless Moment: Buffy acts like Giles's daughter, begging him to let her play games at the carnival.

Going Back to the Beginning: Giles sees the library for the first time and is infuriated to find that the books seem to have been replaced by computers, an echo of the argument he had with Jenny in "I Robot, You Jane," when she said computers would one day replace books.

7.18   Dirty Girls

Original air date: April 15, 2003
Written by: Drew Goddard
Directed by: Michael Gershman
Guest cast: Eliza Dushku (Faith), Nathan Fillion (Caleb), Mary Wilcher (Shannon), Dania Ramirez (Caridad), Rachel Wilson (Colleen), Carrie Couthworth (Betty), Christie Abbott (Helpless Girl)

When an evil preacher working for the First comes to town and sends Buffy a message that he has something of hers, she decides to go get it back.

"Dirty Girls" is the first episode of what Joss Whedon referred to as the five-part series finale. With the arrival of Caleb, the series ramps up to its final apocalyptic showdown and brings together all the storylines that have been building all season — Buffy as the sometimes reluctant, sometimes overbearing leader; Giles as a Watcher who might have overstayed his welcome; the Potentials as girls who don't quite understand what lies ahead of them; the First as a wily and unbeatable foe; and Spike as someone who is there to watch Buffy's back but might not be able to save her. And this episode ends on a note that is almost unthinkable.

Caleb is a priest who has become a demonic minion to the First. As a human being he preached in churches to women about their sins, telling them they were dirty, and when women responded to his "inspirational" sermons and begged him for help, he murdered them. He has the blood of countless women on his hands, and because he's a misogynist pig and the First needs to wipe out the female population of Slayers, the First saw him as a perfect fit. The First is non-corporeal, so up to this point some of its actions have seemed impossible, but now we discover that it was, in fact, Caleb who put the Bringers together and instructs them, and who blew up the Watcher's Council. Now he's come to Sunnydale to claim his ultimate prize — Buffy.

Faith is back, and with her return comes the unresolved tensions among the Scoobies. Over on *Angel*, Angel has seen Faith's remorse and in it, a bit of himself. He was the one who saw her break down in the alley and beg him to kill her, he saw her turn herself in, and he visits her regularly in prison to help her through her atonement. Buffy, on the other hand, doesn't remember Faith so fondly. Faith tried to kill Buffy and hurt Joyce, and she came on to Spike and had sex with Riley, for which Giles and Dawn both resent her. (For anyone watching and thinking Dawn's memory of Faith and vice versa is an inconsistency, the monks would have altered Faith's memories to make her remember Dawn, and Dawn probably remembers being there when Faith broke into their house.) Buffy hits Faith and asks her accusingly why she's there, but she smartly gives up and accepts that she needs Faith. Besides, it would be rather hypocritical of Buffy to hold a grudge when she'd told Wood a few days earlier that she didn't have time for his vendettas.

In "Lies My Parents Told Me," Giles told Buffy that she had to stop acting like a general and become one, and in this episode she steps up to assume that role. The episode is a difficult one morally, because we've learned on *Buffy* and *Angel* that when you go to war, you have to accept that there will be casualties. Wesley says this very thing in the season-2 *Angel* episode "There's No Place Like Plrtz Glrb" when he recognizes that to be an effective leader he has to make sure there are as few casualties as possible, but if he tries to prevent all casualties, he'll lose. Yet when Buffy makes the same decision in this episode, she'll feel the wrath of the gang (and Giles, the man who has told her for seven years that she has to make tough decisions), even though Xander gives a beautiful speech about why everyone should trust Buffy. As the fight in the winery gears up, Potentials get hurt (one dies), Buffy is thrown around like a rag doll, and one of the "Originals" incurs a wound that will leave him permanently paralyzed. In "Potential," Xander said that he is the one who stands back and sees everything happening around him but feels helpless to do anything. And with the fight in the winery, Caleb makes it so Xander can't even do that. The scene is gory, terrifying, and horrible to watch. It's one thing to see Potentials die, but another thing to see something happen to a character we've grown so close to.

Highlight: Andrew's story of Faith, the other Slayer, who once killed a Vulcan. Amanda: "I thought Faith killed a vulcanologist." Andrew: "Silly, silly Amanda. Why would Faith kill a person who studies Vulcans?"

Interesting Facts: Nathan Fillion played Captain Malcolm Reynolds on *Firefly*. Caleb is the first villain he has played, and he loved doing it. "I think his uniform, being a cleric's robe, you want to look at him and believe that he's nice and apple pie," he said of his character. "You want to believe in his niceness and his charm, but he's an evil kind of crazy man who's righteous. Fear the righteous."

Jane Espenson Says: "Andrew talking about the vulcanologist was a joke that I suggested in the room as we were discussing the episode. I was thrilled that it made it through all the drafts of the script and onto the screen."

Did You Notice?: We all know what Xander was doing at the beginning of the episode in the privacy of his bedroom and what religious types often tell little boys will happen to them if they do it too often. It appears in this case that Xander really *does* go blind.

Nitpicks: Andrew seems to know an awful lot about Faith and tells the Potentials that deep down, she's still a killer. How would he know that? He's never actually met Faith and wasn't around at all during her story arc.

Restless Moment: Xander has a major organ ripped out in "Restless."

Going Back to the Beginning: Faith says she doesn't like hospitals, a reference to the coma she was in in a hospital for almost a year. Andrew's reference to Faith killing a vulcanologist is from "Graduation Day, Part One." Faith tells Spike that she's actually met him before, which was in "Who Are You?" when she was in Buffy's body.

7.19   Empty Places

Original air date: April 29, 2003
Written by: Drew Z. Greenberg
Directed by: James A. Contner
Guest cast: Eliza Dushku (Faith), Nathan Fillion (Caleb), Dorian Missick (Police Officer), Larry Clark (Monk), Mary Wilcher (Shannon), James C. Leary (Clem), Justin Shilton (Munroe), Nathan Burgess (Duncan), David Grammer (Crazy Citizen)

Still reeling from the carnage at the winery, the group is shocked when Buffy announces they have to go back in.

"Empty Places" is the most difficult episode to watch in season 7. All season we've tolerated the whiny Potentials, just as we've put up with Buffy's speeches. But for seven years we've seen Buffy sacrifice so much in her life to save the world again and again, and we've come to respect her for it, whether or not she wants to do a little grand-standing and arrogant speechifying on the side. In "Empty Places," all the nasty comments she's made to people to try to motivate them come back to haunt her.

Willow grapples with the wound that her best friend has sustained and struggles to keep her composure while sitting at his bedside in one of the most tear-jerking moments of the season. Spike and Andrew are sent on a mission from Giles (never a good thing from Spike's perspective), but when they arrive, they make an incredible discovery. Back at home base, the Potentials are complaining about what happened at the winery, and Rona the naysayer continues to whine that she came to Sunnydale for protection and all she has to show for it is a lousy broken arm. The one thing that becomes clear throughout this season is that the nature/nurture argument can certainly come into play even for the Chosen One. Buffy had no choice but to become a Slayer, but Willow, Xander, Dawn, Anya, Spike, and Giles chose to fight the good fight, and they have been by her side for years, helping her when they could have run away screaming. Now they're faced with their biggest foe yet, and they remain optimistic, researching ways to defeat the First, helping Buffy and Giles train the Potentials, and keeping the Bringers at bay. The Potentials, on the other hand, are destined to be fighters, and they can't learn the moves or do the research because they're too busy complaining about how they'd rather have other people protect them and go home to their mommies. These girls are the future Chosen Ones — which doesn't say much for the future.

In the end, though, what happened at the winery has cast a shadow over everything, and after a season of asking Anya why she's there and telling Giles she no longer trusts him and barking orders at the Potentials and refusing to stick up for Wood, Buffy gets hers. It's a scene reminiscent of the party scene in "Dead Man's Party," where Buffy's "friends," and even her own mother, fight with her and completely humiliate her in a room full of people. They all had very good personal reasons for doing so, and were hurting from what they'd interpreted as Buffy's abandoning them. But as viewers we are aligned with Buffy due to the angle of the storylines, so we feel like we are the ones being ganged up on, and this scene is a painful one to watch. Giles, the one person who has always stuck up for Buffy and never come down on her, even when she disappeared between seasons 2 and 3, joins in with everyone else on the Buffy bashing. Willow agrees that Buffy is making the wrong decision. Xander, who just last episode was telling everyone to trust Buffy, agrees that Buffy is no longer to be trusted. Rona tells Buffy that she's sick of hearing about Spike (shut UP, Rona!). Faith tells Buffy that she doesn't know how to follow orders from others. Buffy's army demands a democracy, and when Giles should know better than to stand back and let them have their say, he says nothing. When Dawn finally tells Buffy to leave, the moment leaves us reeling. How could these people turn on her the moment that a few people get hurt? Don't they realize that they've gone this long without losing an eye *because* of Buffy? The end of this episode left a lot of fans absolutely furious and cast a rather unfortunate light on characters we've come to respect and love.

Highlight: Spike telling Andrew how onion blossoms are made: "Tell anyone we had this conversation and I'll bite you."

Did You Notice?: This episode contains one of many references the series has made to the *Harry Potter* book series. Faith refers to the basement, where Anya and Andrew give the seminar, as Hogwarts. In "Bring On the Night," Andrew says that "the First" isn't a very ominous-sounding name, and it should be something like "Lex" or "Voldemort." In "Lessons," Willow confesses to Giles that she thought he was bringing her to England to put her in a mystical prison, and "instead you go all Dumbledore on me." And way back in season 5, not only did Giles open the Magic Box wearing a wizard's outfit, but when Joyce tells Buffy to take Dawn back-to-school shopping at the Magic Box, Dawn retorts, "Mom, I'm not going to Hogwarts." Also, Justin Shilton, who plays Munroe, played Billy in "That Vision-Thing" and "Billy" on *Angel*.

Nitpicks: Dawn tells Buffy it's her house, too, and Buffy needs to leave. Really? Is Dawn paying the bills?

Restless Moment: In Buffy's dream she says she's not really in charge of things. Tara tells her that she's lost her friends, and Buffy says she needs to find them.

Going Back to the Beginning: Giles tells Andrew to bring his pan flute with him on the mission, a reference to "Life Serial," in which Andrew used a pan flute to raise a demon. We first heard of Spike's love of the Bronze's onion blossom in "Triangle," and he complained in "Crush" that the item had been off the menu.

Music/Bands: At the Bronze, Nerf Herder (who performs the *Buffy* theme song in the opening credits) is on-stage playing "Rock City News" and "Mr. Spock" (*American Cheese*).

7.20   Touched

Original air date: May 6, 2003
Written by: Rebecca Rand Kirshner
Directed by: David Solomon
Guest cast: Eliza Dushku (Faith), Fillion, Harry Groener (The Mayor), Dania Ramirez (Caridad), Lisa Ann Cabasa (Injured Girl), Lance E. Nichols (Middle-Aged Man)

With Buffy out of the picture, the Potentials now have Faith as their leader, and Spike tells Buffy what he found at the mission.

For anyone who was angered by the previous episode and the gang's treatment of Buffy, this episode is for you. Rebecca Rand Kirshner's final script of the series is brilliant, and Spike steps in as the voice of us all, returning home to discover what everyone has done. It only takes him a moment to realize that with him out of the way, the gang staged a coup d'état and got rid of Buffy, and as he looks around at them and calls them "sad, sad, ungrateful traitors," we cheer him on from our couches. I couldn't help but think during "Empty Places" that if only Spike were there, this wouldn't be happening. The Potentials, Giles, Wood, and Faith were all smarting because Buffy hadn't been nice to them, and Xander and Willow were upset because of what had happened to Xander. Yet Spike has been abused by Buffy more than anyone, and he still sees the good in her and knows what kind of person she is. It's interesting that the one person among them who is still a demon is also the most human.

When Spike finds Buffy in a nearby house (ah, that sense of vampire smell) it only gets better. All season we've been listening to Buffy deliver one exhausting speech after another, and in the past few episodes the writers have started mocking these soliloquies. But in this scene, Spike tells Buffy what he thinks of her. There are no romantic inclinations in his words, he doesn't pull out a soapbox and talk to her like she's his inferior,

Xander (Nicholas Brendon) and Anya (Emma Caulfield) have broken up, but the spark is still there.

and he doesn't use harshness to motivate her, which is what Buffy has been using on the Potentials. Instead, he tells her why she is the one, and why she deserves to be; why she is the Slayer, and one hell of a woman on top of that. He continues to be the mouthpiece for viewers who have stood by Buffy for seven seasons and watched her become a warrior. His words, and his quiet gesture that follows, motivate her to face Caleb and to use her brain to realize there really is a way to battle him and not lose an eye.

Meanwhile, Faith has taken on Buffy's leadership role and immediately realizes what a difficult and thankless position it is. Kennedy begins griping that Faith isn't listening to her or taking her suggestions into account. All the Potentials begin chattering away at once. Giles mutters to himself in the corner. And Faith, like Buffy, stands up and tells them that they will follow, that she's their leader now, and that this isn't a democracy (ironically, the words she dissed Buffy for using). With that, Faith takes the Potentials on a different mission than the one Buffy had in mind, and the final few seconds of the episode are exhilarating. Buffy discovers what it is that Caleb has been hiding, and Faith finds something much less appealing than she thought she would. Have the Potentials followed the wrong leader? Will Buffy be going into this final battle alone once again? More important, could we have heard the last of Kennedy and Rona's bellyaching?

Highlight: Spike's speech to Buffy, and his response when she says she's doesn't want to be the one: "I don't want to be this good-looking and athletic. We all have crosses to bear."

Interesting Facts: Spike makes a Monty Python reference when he mentions the torturous comfy chair, a nod to the "Spanish Inquisition" sketch from *Monty Python's Flying Circus* (see "Provider" in the *Angel* episode guide). A group of rather inept cardinals attempts to torture an elderly woman by putting her in a "comfy chair" and poking her with soft pillows.

Jane Espenson Says: "If Joss was ever influenced by fan suggestions it would have been in a perverse way, denying them whatever they wanted and expected in order to keep them hooked and surprised. And certainly, I've been faced with negative fan reactions — especially to Buffy sleeping with Parker in my episode "The Harsh Light of Day." I've also had wonderful fan reactions, like the enormous beautiful bunch of roses that arrived at my *Gilmore Girls* office after I announced to a crowd of fans in London that I felt that Buffy did love Spike. The fans take the characters very seriously, which is a wonderful thing."

Did You Notice?: The scythe is the weapon used by futuristic Slayer Melaka Fray in Joss Whedon's comic, *Fray*.

Nitpicks: That jittery reality-show camera movement the director uses at the beginning of the episode is really annoying and distracting. And once the Bringer begins talking about what the First had planned for everyone, Giles gets so angry with him that he slices his throat. Shouldn't Giles have held his rage until he had absolutely everything the gang needed to know from the Bringer? And Xander sustains a major eye wound and his bandages are off less than 48 hours later?

Restless Moment: Riley tells Buffy in her dream that she's on her own, and the First Slayer repeats it to her.

Going Back to the Beginning: In "Graduation Day, Part One," Oz and Willow finally consummated their relationship when Oz told her he was "panicking" and that's what happens when people panic. In this episode, knowing the battle is nigh, a *lot* of people "panic."

Music/Bands: Heather Nova's "It's Only Love" (*South*) plays during the love montage.

7.21   End of Days

Original air date: May 13, 2003
Written by: Doug Petrie and Jane Espenson
Directed by: Marita Grabiak
Guest cast: Eliza Dushku (Faith), Nathan Fillion (Caleb), David Boreanaz (Angel), Christine Healy (Guardian), Lisa Ann Cabasa (Injured Girl)

As Buffy and the gang prepare for the upcoming battle, Buffy receives the last part of the puzzle that tells her where she came from and why she's the Chosen One.

"End of Days" is a sometimes quiet episode in which the characters make their final speeches, talk to one another, and prepare for what's coming. At the time it felt like not much was happening considering there was only one episode left, but there's a definite sense of foreboding, a feeling of the calm before the storm. The fear and discomfort that the characters feel was very real to viewers, who dreaded the end of the show as much as the characters feared the end of the world.

The opening of the episode is a little disappointing, as we discover most of the Potentials walk away from the bomb alive (part of me wanted to see the final fight with Buffy as the lone Slayer, especially after putting up with these whiny girls all season). Of course, Kennedy shows that they have learned nothing when she tells Buffy that they followed Faith and almost got killed as a result. When are they going to take responsibility for their actions? Buffy shows up and saves the day with her amazing new weapon (that sings!) and the scene is exhilarating. But watch how not one person — not the Potentials, Willow, or even Giles — apologizes to Buffy for kicking her out of her house and the game only a few hours earlier. As we've seen with other seasons, Buffy is the one person who has many a grudge to bear and refuses to do so. She could hate Xander for all the things he said about Angel at one time; Giles for tricking her in "Helpless" and almost getting her killed; Willow for humiliating her in "Dead Man's Party," going evil, and trying to kill her; Anya for sleeping with Spike; and Dawn for being, well, Dawn. But she doesn't. She lets things slide off her back because she doesn't have time for vendettas, as she said to Wood in "Lies My Parents Told Me." It's her sense of forgiveness that puts her above all the other characters on the show.

Buffy and Spike talk about what happened the night before, opening up to each other about how special it was (the Spuffies went nuts with happiness). He continues to be a kind, gentle person to her, and for the first time ever, she seems to have had her own "moment" with Spike, telling him that the night meant a lot to her. Until now their relationship has seemed to be something that she does to punish herself, and she is miserable when they are together, but now it seems there might actually be something there, and she's starting to realize what he has done for her. Angel got his soul back because of a curse; Spike got his back for her.

Buffy also tells Xander that his strength has gotten her this far and that she has a mission for him — he needs to get Dawn far away from the battle, because she doesn't want Dawn to get hurt. This action appears to be the fulfillment of the prophetic words Dawn heard in "Conversations with Dead People": "In the end, Buffy won't choose you." Then again, the writers have since stated that the image of Joyce in that episode was the First, not a heavenly vision that was looking out for Dawn's best interests.

In the quest to find out what the scythe is (Is it a special Slayer weapon? Why was it kept from Buffy until now?) Buffy goes to the local cemetery and comes face-to-face with one of the Guardians. After discovering in "Get It Done" that Slayers have some demon in them and were created by men, it's a wonderful relief to discover the important role that women have played as well. This woman — who amusingly retorts, "No, really" when Buffy tells her her name, bringing us back to the original joke of the show's title — explains that in essence, Guardians were Watcher watchers who were guarding the Slayers from an even higher plain than the Watchers were. She describes herself as the "last surprise."

The ensuing battle with Caleb is fun to watch, especially when a familiar voice shouts, "Hey!" just as Buffy's about to give up (the Bangels went nuts with happiness). The reappearance of Angel throws the earlier scene with Spike into confusion. The passionate kiss they share when she sees him isn't just a "Hey, nice to see ya" peck on the cheek; it is the kiss of two long-lost lovers. If the night with Spike had meant so much to Buffy, how could she jump into Angel's arms so willingly?

Highlight: Wheelchair fight!

Interesting Facts: Buffy says that she "King Arthured" the scythe from the stone, which is the obvious reference made when she is able to remove it from the stone with no effort. In the legend of King Arthur, there was a sword in a stone and a decree that whoever could remove the sword from the stone would be the rightful king of all England. Many kings and soldiers came together to joust and fight and earn the chance to remove it from the stone, and young Arthur was passing by and realized he needed a sword for his brother Kay. He walked to where the stone was, saw the sword, removed it from the stone without any effort, and gave it to his brother. Arthur's father took the sword back and had it put back in the stone, where Kay tried to pull it out and couldn't. Once again Arthur took the sword out with no problem and was proclaimed king of England. Interestingly, many people refer to this sword as Excalibur, but it isn't. Later in the King Arthur legend he receives a sword from the Lady of the Lake, called Excalibur, and it becomes his sword for the rest of his battles. Also, "shirty" *is* in fact a word — it's British slang meaning "huffy."

Jane Espenson Says: "The more that *has* to happen in an episode, the less pressure there is, because that's all the fewer decisions that have to happen during the writing process. The hardest scripts to write are the ones in which nothing in particular has to be set up, so the buffet of choices becomes overwhelming."

Did You Notice?: Spike acknowledges the King Arthur legend (and shows he's been watching a lot of Monty Python lately) when he calls the scythe the "holy hand grenade," which is from *Monty Python and the Holy Grail*, Monty Python's brilliant spoof of the King Arthur legend. Also, when the First joins with Caleb, we see the same monster that Willow channeled in "Bring On the Night."

Nitpicks: Maybe I'm missing something, but Buffy tells Giles that the scythe "kills strong bodies three ways." We know it can stake, and the sharp end can slice — what's the third way? And when Dawn says she hasn't left crossbows out since that incident with Miss Kitty Fantastico, is that a sick way of saying that we don't see the cat anymore because she was staked? I hope not. And where did Dawn get a *taser*? Yes, the car is full of weapons, but she's groggy after coming out of a chloroform-induced nap and her head is swirling with confusion. Yet she effortlessly zaps Xander with a taser? Sure. Finally, it seems that Caleb, who is rarely down for longer than a second or two, stays down a conveniently long time while Buffy and Angel kiss, have a little chat, and then get back to work.

Oops: At the end of the previous episode, when Faith opens the box, there are eight seconds left on the bomb. In this episode, which begins with her opening the box again, there are only four seconds left.

Willow Wicca Watch: Buffy asks Willow to do a huge spell that will be bigger than anything she's ever tried before, and Willow is scared she'll turn evil again: "I can hardly do a locator spell without getting dark roots."

Restless Moment: In Buffy's dream, Tara's warning to Buffy — "You think you know what's to come, what you are . . . you haven't even begun" — applies to this entire season, as Buffy finally *does* find out who she is.

Going Back to the Beginning: Anya tells Andrew she did run away once, a reference to her fleeing the impending Ascension in "Graduation Day, Part Two." Xander tells Buffy that if she dies, he'll bring her back to life because "It's what I do." He resuscitated her in "Prophecy Girl" and helped with the spell to bring her back to life in "Bargaining, Part One." Buffy reminding Dawn of her promise to show Dawn the world is from "Grave."

7.22 Chosen

Original air date: May 20, 2003
Written and directed by: Joss Whedon
Guest cast: Eliza Dushku (Faith), Nathan Fillion (Caleb), David Boreanaz (Angel), Mary Wilcher (Shannon), Demetra Raven (Girl at Bat), Katie Gray (Indian Girl), Lisa Ann Cabasa (Injured Girl), Ally Matsumara (Japanese Girl), Kelli Wheeler (School Girl), Jenna Edwards (Trailer Girl), Julia Ling (Potential with Power #2)

The gang stands up to the First's army of Turok-han, with two of them making the ultimate sacrifice, and Willow gloriously fulfills her destiny.

It's all come down to this. In one hour, we watch the fulfillment of the season's hopes while having to say goodbye to the people we've fallen in love with over the last seven years. Some fans adored "Chosen," some hated it, and some weren't sure what they thought of it. Trust me — if you didn't like it, watch it again. It gets better every time.

Buffy and Angel have their final scene together. She does her cookie-dough analogy, which confuses Angel while reminding him why he loves her in the first place. Joss was careful to leave open the possibility that she might end up with Angel one day, and Angel's parting words, "I'm not getting any older," show that he would be interested if that were the case. But Joss *also* leaves open the possibility that Buffy and Spike are destined for one another, as she returns to him and sleeps beside him in his bed after meeting with Angel. (The animosity between the two vampires is always hilarious, with Spike's "portrait" of Angel on his punching bag being the best jab yet.) At the end of the episode, she finally tells Spike that she loves him (fulfilling Cassie's prophecy in "Help"), but he believes she's just saying it — that she admires him but doesn't love him the way she loves Angel. Later that summer, at conventions, James Marsters told fans that Buffy didn't love Spike, but he appreciated her saying so. Joss Whedon, on the other hand, has stated that Buffy really did love Spike. The scene itself, in which Buffy doesn't contradict Spike when he says, "No you don't," would lend credence to Marsters's suggestion, but it's nice that the scene is gray enough to be left up to the fans to decide.

We finally hear what Buffy's plan for Willow has been all along, and it's a doozy. Willow frets about it throughout the episode, but Kennedy finally gives her the strength she needs to go through with it, promising to keep her grounded and not let Willow's power get control over her. Spike's job, on the other hand, is not so clear, and even he doesn't know what will happen when he wears the amulet that Angel has brought from Wolfram & Hart. He agrees to the mission, however, not only to impress Buffy, but because he believes this is his destiny. The First visits Buffy the night before the battle, and it's the only truly disappointing scene in the episode. It would have been nice to bring the season full circle by repeating the scene from "Lessons," where each of the villains from the past six seasons appears (or even had Angel appear as Angelus, which would have been even more heartrending). But instead, it's Caleb, who morphs into Buffy, forcing the real Buffy to face off against herself. But the First's mistake is that by taunting Buffy, it gives her the hint she needs to win the battle.

And what a battle it is. As everyone prepares in the hallway, we can't help but be tense: Will any Scoobies die? Will Willow's spell work? Will Buffy be able to make it through the battle alive or have the words we've heard all season — that she needs to die before one of these girls gets a chance — come true? The scene in the hallway is touching, from Andrew giving his Oscar speech to Anya agreeing to use him as a

Spuffies versus Bangels

One of the most hotly contested topics among *Angel* and *Buffy* fans is whether Buffy is better with Spike or Angel. Those who believe the former call themselves "Spuffies," and the latter are "Bangels." Some of the fiercest debates online or at conventions are between these two groups, and the following is a list of some of the arguments used by each side (there are several more — and there are also numerous fans who believe she shouldn't be with either, as neither Spike nor Angel is good enough for her).

Spuffies:

★ In "First Date," Buffy says she can't figure out why people think she "still" loves Spike, insinuating that she did love him at one time.

★ Spike went to the Cave demon and endured a series of trials to get his soul for Buffy; Angel had a soul foisted upon him. A curse made Angel a better man, whereas Spike became a better man through his love for Buffy.

★ Spike fell in love with Buffy when he was soulless; after Angel had met and fallen in love with her, he lost his soul and felt no love for her whatsoever as a soulless vampire.

★ People too often compare soulless Spike with souled Angel, which is an unfair comparison. Instead, compare season-6 Spike with Angelus and season-7 Spike with souled Angel, and you'll see that Spike is the better person.

★ Angel took advantage of a 16-year-old girl; Spike was sleeping with an adult woman, and therefore the relationship was far more mature.

★ Angel and Buffy had a high school romance, and her "love" for him was nothing more than an infatuation; Spike and Buffy's relationship was a grown-up, more realistic one. What Buffy feels for Angel is nothing more than the idealized romance of a teenager.

★ When Buffy died, Angel went away to a monastery to work through his grief; Spike was devastated (as we saw at the end of "The Gift"), and he watched over Dawn like he promised he would.

★ Spike and Buffy's relationship matured, and by season 7 she was telling him the important things she'd told Angel during their relationship. By the end of the season she was simply lying in bed with Spike, enjoying being next to him rather than needing their connection to be all about the sex.

★ In "Chosen," Buffy chose Spike to be the hero and sent Angel away.

★ At the end of "Chosen," Buffy *did* mean it when she said she loved Spike — she had finally seen that he was a true hero and she loved him for it. We never saw her mourning after the episode, but she undoubtedly did (Jane Espenson said she believed that Buffy did love Spike).

Bangels:
★ In "Selfless," Buffy talks about Angel and says, "I loved him more than I will ever love anything in this life."
★ In "Becoming, Part Two," we flash back to 1996, when Angel first saw Buffy, and we discover that at that moment, he snapped out of his brooding and immediately saw in her a purpose for fighting for the greater good.
★ In "Forever," it's Angel who comes to Buffy's side at her mother's grave, and he doesn't want to do anything but comfort her. When he first shows up, no words pass between them; they simply hold hands and the meaning of why he's there is understood.
★ Angel left at the end of "Graduation Day, Part Two" because he believed his staying would be too hard on her (he did return to her in "The Prom" to give her the special night he thought she deserved). He made her forget everything in "I Will Remember You" because he didn't want to burden her with the knowledge of what they'd had together, and by turning back time, he gave up his own happiness so that Buffy might live.
★ Buffy was shattered at the end of "Becoming, Part Two" when Angel died; at the end of "Chosen," she was smiling moments after seeing Spike die (James Marsters said soon afterward that he believed Buffy didn't love Spike).
★ The only time Buffy ever said she loved Spike was at the end of "Chosen," and she probably meant it as a declaration of admiration rather than romantic love; Buffy has professed her love to Angel on several occasions and shown how much he's meant to her in "Surprise," "Becoming, Part Two," "Amends," "The Prom," and "I Will Remember You," to name a few.
★ Buffy's connection with Spike was only about sex, but she had many long, serious discussions with Angel about her future (or lack thereof), her deepest fears, and her love for him.
★ Spike and Buffy were in an abusive relationship that was mutually destructive. Buffy admitted to Spike that she simply used him, and he said that he didn't care. She was just trying to feel something tangible after being brought back to life.

★ Buffy might have told Spike that their night together in "Touched" was special, but the moment she sees Angel in "End of Days," she's in his arms kissing him passionately, proving it's still Angel who makes her knees go weak.

★ Spike tried to rape Buffy in "Seeing Red," and she says to him, "Ask me again why I could never love you."

★ Buffy might have been young when she was with Angel, but she was mature beyond her years, and their relationship was based on communication and understanding right from the start. Conversely, it took years for her relationship with Spike to develop, despite her being older at the time.

★ Angel and Buffy split up because of external forces (his curse), while Spike and Buffy split up because of internal ones (her never being happy with the relationship and her seeing him as being "beneath" her).

human shield to the gang saying their final words to one another before battle. And then it begins.

The battle against the Orcs — sorry, the Turok-han — happens on three fronts, thus making it a heart-pounding clash as we flip back and forth between Buffy, Faith, Spike, and the Potentials at ground zero; to Anya and Andrew, Xander and Dawn, and Wood and Giles standing as a second front; to Willow in a classroom with Kennedy by her side. The scene of Willow performing the spell is a beautiful one, and we can't help but worry throughout that something terrible is about to happen. But when she's transformed before our eyes into a white witch, it's an amazing moment, made perfect by the very Willow-like remark afterward: "That was nifty!"

The battle scene is wonderfully written, directed, and acted, and it is one of the best scenes of the season. We lose one of our Scoobies, several Potentials, and Spike. In a blaze of glory and maniacal laughter, Spike becomes the hero of the day as he allows everyone else to escape while he disintegrates before our eyes. It's a moment reminiscent of Buffy's final scene in "The Gift," and it brings Spike's arc full circle. It's startling to think that this is the same guy we saw in "School Hard."

"Chosen" is an episode that represents everything that *Buffy the Vampire Slayer* is about: bucking tradition. The principal of Sunnydale High is supposed to be eaten, and in a humorous scene, Wood survives the battle to fight another day. A Slayer is supposed to die young, but Buffy has survived one apocalyptic battle after another intact. She is supposed to fight alone, but after Willow's spell she's surrounded by an army of Slayers. No longer does a young girl have to die to bring forth another one.

ALBERT L. ORTEGA

As *Buffy* draws to a close, we hope the title character (played by Sarah Michelle Gellar) can find some happiness and closure.

Every Slayer from this point on will be born strong and will be able to fight the forces of darkness. Does Willow's spell then doom these girls around the world to a life they maybe don't want? Will they now all die young and alone? Will they have to suffer through the life that Buffy has suffered through for seven years? No, because they won't be doing it alone. Buffy has the strength to fight vampires, but if she doesn't feel like doing it one night, she won't have to. She won't be the lone superhero saving a man in distress; tough women will be everywhere, just waiting for a demon to piss them off so they'll be able to fight. The activation of the Slayers is more than just a nod to grrrl power; it's a metaphorical comment on the show itself. Watching *Buffy* has allowed us to see the potential within each one of us. No one has to put up with high school bullies or unfair university professors or jerkoff boyfriends or untold pain. We'll always have our own personal battles to deal with, but no one can make us less of a person than we are. Now, within the plot line of the show, Willow has made it so these women have the strength to stand up to demons, men, or other women. And they can do it side-by-side with other strong women.

After this episode aired, some fans said that "The Gift" was a more appropriate ending to the series. It wrapped up the current storyline, brought Buffy's life to a close, and showed her destiny a little more clearly than this episode did. But in "The Gift," a serenity came over Buffy's face as she embraced death, and she essentially committed suicide — whether or not she was saving the world — leaving us with the impression that the only way she could truly fight an unbeatable foe was to die and leave the world without a Slayer (since Faith was in a prison somewhere and therefore a new Slayer couldn't be activated). In "Chosen," however, Buffy falls during the battle, making us think that this is the end of her, but while she watches the girls fight around her and listens to the taunts of the First, she realizes she's stronger than this, and she gets up to continue the battle. The final scene of the gang asking Buffy what they'll do now that the world is a very different place is a perfect ending, and once again we see that same look of serenity on her face as we did in "The Gift." Only this time she isn't embracing death — she's embracing life.

The final line of the show is, "What are we gonna do now?" and it prompts the viewer to think, "What will *we* do now?" without *Buffy* on television every Tuesday night. But Joss Whedon took the show out on a high note, an optimistic one, allowing our imaginations to create the next adventures of Buffy and the gang. We can only hope that Xander will find inner peace after what happened to Anya, that Willow will be free of all her inhibitions, that Dawn will remain strong and continue to learn from her sister, that Giles will find a new vocation as the Watcher for many Slayers (and perhaps start a new Watcher's Council that is more forgiving), that Andrew will find a new limited-edition Boba Fett action figure . . . and that Buffy will find happiness.

Highlight: Giles, Andrew, Xander, and Amanda playing *Dungeons & Dragons* and Giles getting badly beaten: "I used to be a highly respected Watcher. Now I'm a wounded dwarf with the mystical strength of a doily."

Interesting Facts: Sadly, the WB issued a press release about a week before this episode aired, letting everyone know that Spike would be going over to *Angel* in the fall, thus watering down the otherwise powerful ending. Fans couldn't mourn Spike's death or see it as the incredibly heroic moment it was because we knew he wasn't gone. It's too bad the network couldn't have waited one week before stealing Joss's thunder.

Did You Notice?: At the end, the Mutant Enemy man looks out at the audience during his "Grr, Argh" march. Also, Spike says, "I'm drowning in footwear!" in response to a nightmare he's having. The comment might be a red herring, but that would be rare in the Whedonverse. Perhaps it's an obscure reference to Spike's calling the Shanshu Prophecy the "sans shoes" prophecy in "The Cautionary Tale of Numero Cinco," a season-5 episode of *Angel*? Finally, when Spike first appeared in Sunnydale in "School Hard," he knocked over the town sign. Then he showed up again in "Lover's Walk" and knocked it down again (because he was driving drunk). Now, in a final gesture, the town sign slowly falls into the crevice made by Spike's amulet, giving him the last laugh.

Nitpicks: That cookie-dough speech. Some people thought it was cute; I thought it was Joss trying too hard to be cute and it just came off as silly. Also, the Turok-han were practically impossible for Buffy to kill earlier, yet the gang wipes them out one by one without much of a problem. And this is just a personal nitpick, but I feel that Anya's death happened so quickly that we weren't given any chance to mourn. That probably makes her death more realistic than any of the others on the show, and it's a necessary evil with a final episode (i.e., we don't see the reactions of the Scoobies in a later episode), but it just seemed like an injustice. Xander's reaction to finding out the news and his subsequent joking about the loss of The Gap might seem like a callous response to the death of a loved one, but it's perfectly in keeping with his character. Xander always wears his love and anger on his sleeve, but he's also learned to cover up his true feelings with a quick joke. We know he'll be mourning Anya on his own later, away from everyone else.

Willow Wicca Watch: Willow performs a spell to turn all the Potentials around the world into Slayers, and in doing so, she turns into a white goddess, with all the power of good magicks running through her.

Going Back to the Beginning: Buffy and Angel first talked about Buffy's future and how they'll never have "little vampires" in "Bad Eggs." In "Welcome to the Hellmouth," Giles repeats the Slayer refrain about how Buffy is the Chosen One who will fight the forces of evil. The First repeats it here. The way Wood talks to Faith is reminiscent of the way Faith treated Xander in "Consequences," after they'd had sex in "The Zeppo," when she tells him they hadn't made a connection with each other and she'd forgotten him when it was over. Kennedy tells Willow, "You're my way," an echo of Willow telling Tara, "You're my always," in "Tough Love." When Andrew's playing *D&D*, he's wearing the Little Red Riding Hood cape that Buffy wore in "Fear, Itself." As the school crumbles around the gang we are reminded of the similar fate that befell it in "Graduation Day, Part Two." But the best return to the beginning of the entire season is the scene of the original four in a circle — Xander, Buffy, Willow, and Giles — with the three younger people talking about going shopping tomorrow while ignoring Giles, a throwback to many similar scenes of the early seasons. As they part from one another, Giles says, "The earth is definitely doomed," an echo of the same statement in "The Harvest," after Buffy had averted her first apocalypse.

"Grr . . . argh"

Angel, Season One

1. 14, not counting Vietnam
2. 1946
3. Allen Francis Doyle
4. 21
5. He taught third grade
6. *The Quintessa*
7. She's auditioning for a commercial
8. A Big Dog
9. The Tulip Room
10. A Hacksaw demon
11. Akron, Miami, and Baton Rouge
12. The groundskeeper at the cemetery
13. May 22
14. Keanu
15. $15,000 plus expenses
16. Blunt, sharp, cold, hot, and loud
17. He was a linen and silk merchant
18. Hastings
19. St. Matthew's Hospital

Angel, Season Two

20. December 16, 1979
21. 1928
22. 68
23. Software that helps blind people surf the Web
24. 24
25. Chow Yun Fat
26. Syphilis
27. A bomb shelter
28. East Hills Teen Center
29. Something by Cat Stevens
30. Highway Robbery Ball
31. Beige
32. Fairfield Clinic
33. May 7, 1996
34. The Stewart Brunell Public Library
35. The scum pits of Ur

Angel, Season Three

36. Senior Associate
37. *Kye-rumption*
38. Grapplar demons
39. Three
40. Julia
41. Daniel
42. Notre Dame
43. Mahta Hari
44. 03
45. 35
46. Steven Franklin Thomas
47. Utah
48. 300 years (ever since the mitosis)
49. Pomegranate
50. Dante's *Inferno*, part one of *The Divine Comedy*
51. He takes a bite from Sunny's chocolate bar
52. Fifty cents or one dollar

Angel, Season Four

53. Mr. Suvarta
54. 14
55. $33 million
56. $300,000 and a car
57. *Relationship*
58. Southern Hampshire
59. *Rhinehardt's Compendium*
60. Murder two; 25 to life
61. North California Women's Facility in Stockton, California
62. Localized Ionic Sensory Activator
63. "Definitely"
64. Helen
65. *Making Mind Control Work for You*

Angel, Season Five

66. Wesley
67. 19
68. Amanda
69. $800,000
70. UC Santa Cruz
71. Death Valley, Nevada
72. Chanel
73. 10
74. *Donkey Kong*
75. "Don't"
76. Feigenbaum
77. The Cotswolds
78. "Why can't I stay?"
79. 11
80. Vahla ha'nesh
81. Zach
82. Stanford
83. Bluebird
84. 10
85. "The Wanton Folly of Me Mum"

Buffy, Season Seven

86. Dance
87. 10 to 4
88. Sjornjost
89. 880
90. October 16, 1980
91. She says she wrote an epic poem about him, comparing him to a daisy, a tower, and a lake
92. Psychology
93. "Man, I hate playing vampire towns"
94. May 2003
95. Mystery
96. Winnie the Pooh
97. Tawarick
98. Knoxville
99. Meg
100. Dawn

Angel Episodes

Angel Writers

Jeffrey Bell

That Vision Thing; Billy (with Tim Minear); Quickening; Couplet (with Tim Minear); Forgiving; A New World; Slouching Toward Bethlehem; Habeas Corpses; Calvary (with Steven S. DeKnight and Mere Smith); Players (with Sarah Fain and Elizabeth Craft); The Magic Bullet; The Cautionary Tale of Numero Cinco; Not Fade Away (with Joss Whedon)

Garry Campbell

War Zone

Elizabeth Craft & Sarah Fain

Supersymmetry; Soulless; Release (with Steven S. DeKnight); Players (with Jeffrey Bell); Shiny Happy People; Unleashed; Harm's Way; Underneath

Steven S. DeKnight

Deep Down; Apocalypse, Nowish; Awakening (with David Fury); Calvary (with Jeffrey Bell and Mere Smith); Release (with Sarah Craft and Elizabeth Fain); Inside Out; Hell Bound; Destiny (with David Fury); Damage (with Drew Goddard); Why We Fight (with Drew Goddard); Shells; The Girl in Question (with Drew Goddard)

Ben Edlund

Sacrifice; Just Rewards (teleplay with David Fury); Life of the Party; Smile Time (teleplay; story with Joss Whedon); Time Bomb

Jane Espenson
Rm w/ a Vu (with David Greenwalt); Guise Will Be Guise

Brent Fletcher
Soul Purpose

David Fury
Lonely Hearts; Parting Gifts (with Jeannine Renshaw); Disharmony; The Price; The House Always Wins; Awakening (with Steven S. DeKnight); Peace Out; Just Rewards (story; teleplay with Ben Edlund); Destiny (with Steven S. DeKnight); You're Welcome; Power Play

Drew Goddard
Lineage; Damage (with Steven S. DeKnight); Why We Fight (with Steven S. DeKnight); Origin; The Girl in Question (with Steven S. DeKnight)

David H. Goodman
Dad; Double or Nothing

Howard Gordon
Hero (with Tim Minear); The Ring; Expecting

David Greenwalt
City Of (with Joss Whedon); I Fall to Pieces (with Joss Whedon); Rm w/ a Vu (with Jane Espenson); I Will Remember You (with Jeannine Renshaw); She (with Marti Noxon); I've Got You Under My Skin (story with Jeannine Renshaw); To Shanshu in L.A.; Judgement (teleplay; story with Joss Whedon); Dear Boy; The Trial (story); Happy Anniversary (teleplay; story with Joss Whedon); Dead End; There's No Place Like Plrtz Glrb; Heartthrob; Offspring; Sleep Tight; Tomorrow

Jim Kouf
Five by Five; The Shroud of Rahmon; The Thin Dead Line (with Shawn Ryan)

Tim Minear
Sense and Sensitivity; Hero (with Howard Gordon); Somnambulist; The Prodigal; Sanctuary (with Joss Whedon); Are You Now or Have You Ever Been?; Darla; The Trial (teleplay with Doug Petrie); Reunion (with Shawn Ryan); Reprise; Epiphany; Through the Looking Glass; That Old Gang of Mine; Billy (with Jeffrey Bell); Lullaby; Couplet (with Jeffrey Bell); Benediction; Home

Scott Murphy
Carpe Noctem; Provider

Marti Noxon
She (with David Greenwalt)

Doug Petrie
In the Dark; The Trial (teleplay with Tim Minear)

Jeannine Renshaw
I Will Remember You (with David Greenwalt); Parting Gifts (with David Fury); I've Got You Under My Skin (teleplay; story with David Greenwalt); Blind Date

Shawn Ryan
First Impressions; Reunion (with Tim Minear); Blood Money (with Mere Smith); The Thin Dead Line (with Jim Kouf); Belonging

Mere Smith
Untouched; Redefinition; Blood Money (with Shawn Ryan); Over the Rainbow; Fredless; Birthday; Loyalty; Ground State; Long Day's Journey; Calvary (with Jeffrey Bell and Steven S. DeKnight); Orpheus

Tracy Stern
The Bachelor Party; Eternity

Joss Whedon
City Of (with David Greenwalt); I Fall to Pieces (with David Greenwalt); Sanctuary (with Tim Minear); Judgement (story with David Greenwalt); Happy Anniversary (story with David Greenwalt); Waiting in the Wings; Spin the Bottle; Conviction; Smile Time (story with Ben Edlund); A Hole in the World; Not Fade Away (with Jeffrey Bell)

Buffy Episodes

Buffy Writers

Steven S. DeKnight
Blood Ties; Spiral; All the Way; Dead Things; Seeing Red

Rob Des Hotel & Dean Batali
Never Kill a Boy on the First Date; The Puppet Show; The Dark Age; Phases; Killed by Death

Carl Ellsworth
Halloween

Jane Espenson
Band Candy; Gingerbread; Earshot; Harsh Light of Day; Pangs; Doomed (with Marti Noxon and David Fury); A New Man; Superstar; The Replacement; Triangle; Checkpoint (with Douglas Petrie); I Was Made to Love You; Intervention; After Life; Flooded (with Doug Petrie); Life Serial (with David Fury); Doublemeat Palace; Same Time, Same Place; Conversations with Dead People (with Drew Goddard); Sleeper (with David Fury); First Date; Storyteller; End of Days (with Douglas Petrie)

Tracey Forbes
Beer Bad; Something Blue; Where the Wild Things Are

David Fury

Go Fish (with Elin Hampton); Helpless; Choices; Fear, Itself; Doomed (with Marti Noxon and Jane Espenson); The I in Team; Primeval; Real Me; Shadow; Crush; Bargaining, Part Two; Life Serial (with Jane Espenson); Gone; Grave; Sleeper (with Jane Espenson); Showtime; Lies My Parents Told Me (with Drew Goddard)

Ashley Gable & Thomas A. Swyden

I Robot, You Jane; Invisible Girl

Drew Goddard

Selfless; Conversations with Dead People (with Jane Espenson); Never Leave Me; Lies My Parents Told Me (with David Fury); Dirty Girls

Howard Gordon

What's My Line? Part One (with Marti Noxon)

Drew Z. Greenberg

Smashed; Older and Far Away; Entropy; Him; The Killer in Me; Empty Places

David Greenwalt

Teacher's Pet; Angel; Nightmares; School Hard (story with Joss Whedon and teleplay); Reptile Boy; Ted (with Joss Whedon); Faith, Hope and Trick; Homecoming

Diego Gutierrez

Normal Again

Elin Hampton

Go Fish (with David Fury)

Matt Kiene & Joe Reinkemeyer

The Pack; Inca Mummy Girl

Ty King

Some Assembly Required; Passion

Rebecca Rand Kirshner

Out of My Mind; Listening to Fear; Tough Love; Tabula Rasa; Hell's Bells; Help; Potential; Touched

Marti Noxon

What's My Line? Part One (with Howard Gordon); What's My Line? Part Two; Bad Eggs; Surprise; Bewitched, Bothered and Bewildered; I Only Have Eyes For You; Dead Man's Party; Beauty and the Beasts; The Wish; Consequences; The Prom; Living Conditions; Wild at Heart; Doomed (with David Fury and Jane Espenson); Goodbye Iowa; New Moon Rising; Buffy vs. Dracula; Into the Woods; Forever; Bargaining; Wrecked; Villains; Bring On the Night (with Douglas Petrie)

Douglas Petrie

Revelations; Bad Girls; Enemies; The Initiative; This Year's Girl; The Yoko Factor; No Place Like Home; Fool For Love; Checkpoint (with Jane Espenson); The Weight of the World; Flooded (with Jane Espenson); As You Were; Two to Go; Beneath You; Bring On the Night (with Marti Noxon); Get It Done; End of Days (with Jane Espenson)

Dana Reston

The Witch

Dan Webber

Lover's Walk; The Zeppo

Joss Whedon

Welcome to the Hellmouth; The Harvest; Prophecy Girl; When She Was Bad; School Hard (story with David Greenwalt); Lie to Me; Ted (with David Greenwalt); Innocence; Becoming, Parts One and Two; Anne; Amends; Doppelgängland; Graduation Day, Parts One and Two; The Freshman; Hush; Who Are You?; Restless; Family; The Body; The Gift; Once More, with Feeling; Lessons; Chosen

Sources

Show Overview

Acker, Amy. Telephone interview with author, 7 May 2004.

Adalian, Josef. "This *Angel* has gone to Heaven." *Variety*, 15 February 2004.

Amatangelo, Amy. "See Charisma act: But not on *Angel*." Bostonherald.com, 19 August 2003.

"*Angel* Celebrates 100th." Sci Fi Wire, 5 December 2003.

"*Angel* Man Stays Put." Sci Fi Wire, 5 September 2001.

Arpe, Marlene. "Father of all vampires mourns show." *Toronto Star*, 16 May 2004.

—-. "Angel fights to the bleak, bitter end." *Toronto Star*, 20 May 2004.

"The Best and Worst of 2001." Zap2It.com, 5 December 2001.

Bianco, Robert. "Be Sure to Catch This *Firefly*." *USA Today*, 20 September 2002.

—-. "*Buffy* Switch Means *Angel* Flies on Its Own." *USA Today*, 22 October 2001.

—-. "The end of *Buffy* feels like a dagger to the heart." *USA Today*, 29 April 2003.

—-. "Show's Creator Takes Stab at 10 Favorite Episodes." *USA Today*, 28 April 2003.

The Bronze VIP Posting Board Archive, www.cise.ufl.edu/~hsiao/media/tv/buffy/bronze.

Dawidziak, Mark. "Biting Stories and Characters Give *Angel* Longevity." *The Plain Dealer*, 4 February 2004.

"*Firefly* to go on Hiatus as Fox Shuffles Midseason." Zap2it.com, 26 November 2002.

Groebner, Simon Peter. "Bye bye 'Buffy': The Slayer bows out after seven seasons of wicked fun." *Star Tribune*, 6 May 2003.

Jensen, Jeff. "The Goodbye Girl." *Entertainment Weekly*, 7 March 2003.

Johnson, Allan. "Baby Gives *Buffy* Spinoff a Fresh Supply of Story Lines." *Chicago Tribune*, 11 April 2002.

Mason, Charlie. "Angel Delivers a Devil of a Time." *TV Guide* (online), 14 August 2001.

Millman, Joyce. "Getting Buffy's Last Rites Right." *New York Times*, 20 April 2003.

"Minear Gets *Angel* Wings." Sci Fi Wire, 3 August 2001.

"No Aliens in *Firefly*." Sci-Fi Wire, 23 July 2002.

"Noxon Confirms Buffy Season 8." Sci Fi Wire, 20 June 2002.

O'Hare, Kate. "*Angel* Adds Cast Member, Wants Pasdar." Zap2It.com, 25 April 2001.

—-. "*Angel's* Minear Discusses Producer Shake-up." Zap2it.com, 13 August 2002.

—-. "Fox's *Firefly* Keeps the Lights On." Zap2it.com, 31 October 2002.

—-. "Sleeping with the Enemy." Zap2it.com, 26 August 2002.

Pierce, Scott D. "*Angel* Was Worth the Wait." *Deseret News*, 15 April 2002.

—-. "Spike Is In; Cordelia Is Out: Renewed *Angel* Revamps Its Cast." *Deseret News*, 27 May 2003.

Richards, J. August. Telephone interview with author, 23 April 2004.

Richardson, David. "Sleeping with the Enemy . . ." *Starburst*, August 2002.

Smith, Christopher Allen, and Michael Tunison. "Saturn Scoop: Whedon Gives on Another Year of *Buffy*." Cinescape.com, 12 June 2002.

"Star Relieved at *Angel's* End." Sci Fi Wire, 5 May 2004.

"A Statement from the WB." Press release at WB.com, 14 February 2004.

Tonkin, Boyd. "Bye bye, Buffy." *The Independent*, 21 May 2003.

"Why is Cordelia off *Angel*?" Sci Fi Wire, 27 May 2003.

Williamson, Kevin. "*Angel's* Slay Ride Ends." *Calgary Sun*, 17 May 2004.

Wrenn, Gregg. "A Touch of Evil." TeeVee.org.

Buffy Goes to College

Adams, Michael. E-mail interview with author, 27 April 2004; 3 June 2004.

Kaveney, Roz. E-mail interview with author, 18 April 2004.

Lavery, David. E-mail interview with author, 16 April 2004; 31 May 2004.

Levy, Sophie. E-mail interview with author, 12 May 2004.

LoCicero, Lisa. E-mail interview with author, 17 May 2004; 1 June 2004.

Ndalianis, Angela. E-mail interview with author, 20 May 2004.

Riess, Jana. E-mail interview with author, 14 May 2004; 2 June 2004.

South, James B. E-mail interview with author, 18 April 2004.

Turnbull, Sue. E-mail interview with author, 19 May 2004.

Wilcox, Rhonda. E-mail interview with author, 29 April 2004; 3 June 2004.

Yeffeth, Glenn. E-mail interview with author, 23 April 2004.

CityofAngel.com

Bratton, Kristy. E-mail interview with author, 26 April 2004.

Holden, Lilian. E-mail interview with author, 26 April 2004.

Obeius, Virginia. E-mail interview with author, 26 April 2004.

Episode Guide

"About Mexican Wrestling Masks." Anymask.com.

Acker, Amy. Telephone interview with author, 7 May 2004.

AMG All-Music Guide, www.allmusic.com.

Brandt, Stacy. "Who Was That Masked Man?" *Daily Aztec*, 5 December 2002.

The Bronze VIP Posting Board Archive, www.cise.ufl.edu/~hsiao/media/tv/buffy/bronze.

Denisof, Alexis. Telephone interview with author, 27 May 2004.

Denman, David. Telephone interview with author, 30 April 2004.

Dream Moods: An Online Guide to Dream Interpretation, www.dreammoods.com.

Espenson, Jane. E-mail interview with author, 2 May 2004.

"Feigenbaum Constant." PlanetMath, www.planetmath.org.

Fury, David. Telephone interview with author, 4 April 2003.

Gordon, Stuart. *The Encyclopedia of Myths and Legends*. London: Headline Book Publishing, 1993.

Grimal, Pierre. *The Dictionary of Classical Mythology*. Oxford: Blackwell, 1996.

The Internet Movie Database, www.imdb.com.

JD. "Cordelia's Psychic Gift is Too Costly on *Angel*." *Soap Opera Weekly*, 2 October 2001.

Kane, Christian. Telephone interview with author, 28 April 2004.

"Lizzie Borden." Crime Library: Criminal Minds and Methods, www.crimelibrary.com.

Lutz, Mark. Telephone interview with author, 21 May 2004.

"The Magic Bullet." The Grand Subversion: JFK Assassination, grandsubversion.com.

"Masked Wrestlers." The Professional Wrestling Online Museum, www.wrestlingmuseum.com.

O'Hare, Kate. "Looking Good While Doing Bad." Zap2It.com, 13 February 2002.

—. "Sean Astin Loves 'Soulless' Angel." Zap2it.com, 2 February 2003.

—. "Skip the Demon to Return to *Angel*." Zap2it.com, 18 October 2001.

Palfrey, Dale Hoyt. "The Day of the Dead." Mexico Connect, www.mexconnect.com, 1995.

"Raiden." *Encyclopedia Mythica*. www.pantheon.org.

Richards, J. August. Telephone interview with author, 23 April 2004.

Romanov, Stephanie. Telephone interview with author, 13 May 2004.

Szarabajka, Keith. Telephone interview with author, 22 April 2004.

Topel, Fred. "Nathan Fillion — Buffy's Last Big Bad." About.com, 1 May 2003.

"Tournament History." Bob Hope Chrysler Classic, www.bhcc.com.

TV Tome, www.tvtome.com.

"What is String Theory?" String Theory Basics, www.superstringtheory.com/basics/
     index.html.

By the same author . . .

Uncovering Alias

An Unofficial Guide
By Nikki Stafford and Robyn Burnett

TV Guide has called it "one of TV's most enjoyable escapist hours ever." But what is the show about? Ask 10 viewers of the show and you'll probably get 10 different answers. *Uncovering Alias* is here to help solve the viewer's questions.

Written as a companion to the show, it features:
- ★ biographies of recurring cast members
- ★ a map of Rambaldi artifacts uncovered by the operatives along with a complete list of what the artifacts are and why each one is significant
- ★ a list of the best *Alias* Web sites
- ★ a history of the series and its accomplishments, including behind-the-scenes information on how each episode is put together
- ★ an extensive episode guide to the first three seasons that helps explain the complexities of the show, including background of the guest stars, music used in each show, an in-depth analysis of the character development, and interesting facts

1-55022-653-3
$17.95 U.S., $19.95 CDN

AVAILABLE IN FINE BOOKSTORES EVERYWHERE

Also by the same author . . .

Bite Me!

An Unofficial Guide to the World of Buffy the Vampire Slayer

Revised Edition
By Nikki Stafford

Released in 2002, *Bite Me!* is the ultimate companion to *Buffy the Vampire Slayer* and is often voted the best guide to the show among fans. It contains:

★ biographies of 14 cast members of *Buffy* and *Angel*
★ a complete episode guide to the end of season six, with tons of interesting facts, highlights, and entertaining analysis
★ a challenging trivia quiz
★ a summary of the posting board parties from 1998 to 2002
★ over 120 all-new photos
★ an in-depth chapter on the history of the show

1-55022-540-5
$17.95 U.S., $19.95 CDN

AVAILABLE IN FINE BOOKSTORES EVERYWHERE